United States–Latin American Relations, 1850–1903

UNITED STATES–LATIN AMERICAN RELATIONS, 1850–1903

Establishing a Relationship

Edited by
Thomas M. Leonard

THE UNIVERSITY OF ALABAMA PRESS

Tuscaloosa and London

Copyright © 1999
The University of Alabama Press
Tuscaloosa, Alabama 35487-0380
All rights reserved
Manufactured in the United States of America

1 2 3 4 5 6 7 8 9 / 07 06 05 04 03 02 01 00 99

∞

The paper on which this book is printed meets the minimum requirements of American National Standard for Information Science-
Permanence of Paper for Printed Library Materials, ANSI Z39.48-1984.

Jacket design by Shari DeGraw

Libary of Congress Cataloging-in-Publication Data

United States-Latin American relations, 1850–1903 : establishing a
relationship / edited by Thomas M. Leonard.
   p. cm.
Includes bibliographical references (p.) and index.

   ISBN 0-8173-0937-3 (alk. paper)
   1. Latin America—Foreign relations—United States. 2. United
States—Foreign relations—Latin America. 3. Latin
America—History—1830–1898. 4. Latin America—History—1898–1948. I.
Leonard, Thomas M., 1937–
   F1418 .U686   1999
   327.7308—dc21   98-58026

British Library Cataloguing-in-Publication data available

For six special Mountaineers:
John Bailey, Jack Campbell, Msgr. Robert Kline,
Jim Phelan, Bob Preston, and Frank Zarnowski

CONTENTS

INTRODUCTION

NINETEENTH-CENTURY RELATIONS between the United States and Latin America can be divided into two distinct periods. The first encompasses the years from 1787 to approximately 1850, during which almost all of the mainland British, Portuguese, and Spanish colonies achieved their independence. In the process of nation-building that followed, each had to adjust to its newfound freedom and had little time for interaction with each other. During the second period, from approximately 1850 to 1903, these nations sought their place in the new world order and in the process markedly increased their contact with each other. By 1903, the basis for a relationship had been established between the United States and Latin America.

From the beginning of the constitutional era in 1787 until the pronouncement of the Monroe Doctrine in 1823, U.S. policy toward Latin America was based upon its own colonial experience, which primarily involved the protection of its border areas from the European powers. In the short run, U.S. policymakers found a need to acquire New Orleans in 1803 and with it accidentally obtained half a continent. This was followed by the acquisition of the Floridas in 1819. With the addition of these territories the United States secured its southern frontier. Throughout the period, the United States maintained that Cuba, then on the periphery, should not fall into the hands of a major European power, specifically the British. As long as the island remained an outpost of a weakened Spain, the U.S. southern frontier remained secure.

As Latin America struggled for its independence after 1816, the United States remained aloof except for statements by government officials and others who drew parallels to the U.S. experience with Great Britain. For example, in 1808 President Thomas Jefferson, in correspondence with Cuban and Mexican independence leaders, noted that their objectives paralleled those of the United States: the exclusion of European influence from the entire hemisphere because the systems of government, economy, and society were vastly different. Subsequently, Congressman Henry Clay became the most visible spokesman for an inter-American connection. He advocated an "American System" that would unite North and South America against European incursion. He also envisioned the southern continent as a vast marketplace for U.S. wares. The culmination of the U.S. affinity with Latin America came with President James Monroe's message to Congress in December 1823, in which he declared the western hemisphere off-limits to European colonization and therefore its political influence. Monroe argued that, free from European intervention, the nations of the western hemisphere would develop true democracies and full commercial intercourse.

Washington's rhetoric proved shallow. The Latin Americans understood that Great Britain, not the United States, had financed its revolutions and kept Spain from attempting to reclaim its colonies in 1823. If this were not enough, the U.S. refusal, between 1824 and 1826, to consider defensive arrangements with Brazil, Chile, Colombia, Mexico, and the United Provinces of Rio de Plata and its lack of enthusiasm for the Panama Congress of 1826 confirmed the emptiness of Washington's commitment to hemispheric affairs.

Furthermore, when the Europeans threatened U.S. hemispheric interests, the United States acted alone, not in concert with its Latin American neighbors. For example, when Washington policymakers understood the extent of British influence on the Central American isthmus in the 1840s, it dealt directly with London. Without consulting the Central American governments, the United States took a path that led to the Clayton-Bulwer Treaty of 1850, by which the United States and Great Britain agreed to end further colonization in the region and not to construct a canal across the isthmus alone. When Spain occupied the Dominican Republic and France occupied Mexico between 1861 and 1867, the United States alone issued words of warning to the governments in Madrid and Paris.

At times the United States seemed to Latin Americans like a foreign interloper. The most notable example is the Mexican War of 1846 to 1848, which resulted in Mexico's loss of more than half of its territory to the United States and contributed to Latin America's postwar fear of further U.S. territorial aggrandizement. That fear increased in the 1850s when the southern slave states desired the acquisition of Cuba and William Walker filibustered in Central America. On two occasions in the mid-1860s the United States flirted with the acquisition of Samaná Bay in the Dominican Republic, but in both instances the U.S. Congress refused to fund the projects. Congress proved equally unwilling to appropriate $7.5 million for the acquisition of the Danish Virgin Islands, despite the fact that the island inhabitants overwhelmingly favored annexation. At the time the United States was too preoccupied with the problems of Reconstruction to be concerned with an overseas empire. Still, to the Latin Americans such flirtations reinforced the notion of U.S. imperial designs in the Caribbean region.

In the four decades following independence Latin Americans also concerned themselves with foreign intervention and convened five conferences to deal with security threats. The first, the Panama Congress of 1826, was convened in response to a call from Simón Bolívar, who wanted the new nations to unite against possible Spanish reoccupation. Delegates from Central America, Colombia, Mexico, and Peru met for nearly a month. The United Provinces of Rio de Plata and Paraguay declined to attend. The Brazilian delegate never left Rio de Janeiro because of an impending conflict with the United Provinces. The Bolivian, Chilean, and U.S. delegates were appointed too late to participate. The delegates signed three treaties and several supplementary conventions, the thrust of which set forth provisions relating to their common defense against the perceived Spanish intention to recapture its colonial empire. The sparse attendance and the failure of the participating governments (except Colombia) to ratify the agreements were harbingers of future meetings.

Representatives from all the newly independent Latin American nations met in 1827 in Tucabaya, Mexico, but the absence of a foreign threat contributed to a failed assembly. The same was true in 1831, when Mexico called for a meeting to discuss a defensive union to prevent a foreign invasion, to mediate international disputes, and to codify public law relating to international debts. Repeated calls in 1838, 1839, and 1840 went unanswered. In each instance, the threat of foreign intervention appeared remote.

In the mid-1840s a foreign threat again appeared on the horizon. A meeting of Bolivian, Chilean, Ecuadorian, Colombian, and Peruvian delegates in Lima, Peru, from December 1847 to March 1848 was instigated by the activities of former Ecuadoran president General Juan José Flores. He had raised an army in Spain and some troops and ships in Great Britain for the purpose of invading Ecuador and establishing a Spanish prince in Quito. Among the resolutions passed at the conference was one reaffirming the non-colonization principle and denying the right of European powers to intervene in hemispheric affairs. With this resolution in mind the conference produced a treaty of confederation calling upon all Latin American states to band together for the military protection of their independence and sovereignty. Neither the treaty nor the two conventions—consular and postal—signed at Lima were ratified by any government, largely because the threat of intervention had passed when the British government forbade the sailing of Flores ships from British harbors. Britain's actions also prompted U.S. president James K. Polk to decline the invitation to send a delegate to the Lima meeting.

A third international meeting in September 1856 at Santiago, Chile, brought together representatives from Chile, Ecuador, and Peru to discuss U.S. territorial expansion. On the heels of its victory in the war against Mexico in 1848 and the Gadsden Purchase in 1853, the United States now appeared poised to take Cuba and Central America. The three delegations initialed the defensive Continental Treaty with provisions similar to that signed at Lima eight years earlier but with the added proviso that no nation permit political émigrés to organize expeditions within their borders for an attack upon their homeland. Also motivated by the actions of U.S. filibusterers, in November 1856 the ministers assigned to Washington, D.C., from Colombia, Costa Rica, El Salvador, Guatemala, Mexico, Peru, and Venezuela initialed an agreement to prevent the organizing of expeditions by political exiles against an allied government; whenever a signatory nation was invaded or threatened by such action, the others would provide military assistance. Such declarations against political émigrés clearly indicated that governments in power stood on unstable grounds. Like their predecessors, neither the Lima nor the Washington agreement was ratified by a Latin American government.

Prompted by the Spanish intervention in the Dominican Republic and the French presence in Mexico, from November 1864 to March 1865 representatives from Bolivia, Chile, Colombia, Ecuador, Guatemala, Peru, and Venezuela gathered in Lima. In May 1861, Spain re-annexed the Dominican Republic at the latter's request, but Spain's harsh rule soon drove the Dominicans to revolt. When the Spanish army arrived to suppress the revolt, it was ravaged by tropical disease, forcing Spain to abandon the island in 1865. In Mexico, what began as a joint British, French, and Spanish effort to force debt repayment soon developed into a colonization scheme by the French emperor Napoleon III. In 1864 he installed Maximilian of Austria in the presidential palace at Mexico City. The foreign presence prompted a Mexican uprising, which cost the French government dearly in men and money. When Napoleon abandoned Mexico in 1865, the isolated Maximilian clung to the vestige of power until he faced a Mexican firing squad in 1867. These foreign incursions generated visions of greater threats and prompted the delegates at Lima to conclude yet another treaty for mutual defense not only against a foreign attack but also against threats from political exiles. And, as in the past, the treaties were never ratified.

The meeting at Lima was the final meeting during the nineteenth century for representatives of Latin American nations who convened to discuss common defense. In addition to poor attendance the five conferences suffered from the declining threat of foreign intervention, nationalistic rivalries and jealousies that prevented cooperation, and insufficient Latin American leadership.

Thus, for several decades following Latin America's independence, the policies of the United States and the various Latin American nations appeared to go in opposite directions despite shared concerns about foreign threats. The initial diplomatic contacts between the two regions only exacerbated the situation. As indicated in the first volume of this series (*United States–Latin American Relations, 1800–1850: The Formative Generations*, 1991), T. Ray Shurbutt and his co-authors indicated that by 1850 the United States had become frustrated with Latin America. Reflecting the nation's general ignorance about Latin America, U.S. diplomatic emissaries found that the newly independent governments were not as democratic as their written and verbal rhetoric implied, that their rigid social structure nowhere matched the dynamism of the United States, and that their underdeveloped economies did not provide much opportunity for the sale of U.S. wares. As a result of their contact with U.S. representatives, the Latin Americans had come to distrust and dislike the United States. The U.S. unwillingness to provide material and diplomatic support for the independence movements from 1810 to 1826, its acquisition of the Floridas in 1819, and its failure to apply the Monroe Doctrine in the years after 1823 contributed to Latin America's distrust of the United States. The attitude and actions of U.S. emissaries to Latin America, most of whom were political appointees with no diplomatic experience and with little or no understanding of the societies they entered, only exacerbated relations between the governments north and south. The diplomats' incessant involvement in local matters and their public criticisms of their hosts' political and social structures prompted Latin America's elite rulers to disdain them. Instead, the positive actions of the British government and its representatives to the New World drove the Latin Americans to Downing Street. Great Britain's financial and material support to the independence movements and its clear indication that it would not permit the restoration of Spanish power in 1823 were enhanced by British loans and favorable trading practices after independence. The combination of international factors added to the domestic political dynamics caused the United States to defer to the British and lose interest in Latin America by 1850.

Although relations between the United States and Latin America drifted further apart between 1850 and 1870, proponents of a more involved policy existed in both regions. In the United States, for example, President James Buchanan (before the outbreak of the Civil War) and Secretary of State William H. Seward (immediately after the war's conclusion) expressed visions of the United States spreading its wings over the hemisphere. In Latin America the Argentine Domingo Sarmiento and the Peruvian Ramón Castilla also called for a more worldly policy. Still, not until several forces in the United States, Latin America, and Europe converged in the 1880s and 1890s was the stage set for the establishment of a more permanent relationship between the United States and Latin America.

Within the United States three divergent groups contributed to the development of the Latin American relationship. First were the advocates of a large navy. Spokespersons like Alfred T. Mahan, Henry Cabot Lodge, Sr., and Theodore Roosevelt pressured Congress to provide funds for an ever-increasing modern fleet and for a worldwide string of naval bases, including in the Caribbean, to provide necessary coal and repair stations. These leaders also envisioned a U.S.-owned canal somewhere on the Central American isthmus to shuttle the navy between the two oceans. Mahan, Lodge, and Roosevelt also argued that a navy and a canal would place the United States among the world's premier powers.

U.S. industrialists formed the second group to advocate a "large policy." Bolstered by a protective tariff that ranged from 40 percent in 1860 to 50 percent in 1890, the Industrial Revolution took hold in the United States. As production saturated the domestic market, the industrialists looked outward. The need for external markets was enhanced by the 1893 depression. Europe already received 80 percent of U.S. exports, and the European presence in South Asia and Africa virtually locked out U.S. goods there. Manufacturers therefore looked to Latin America. In this atmosphere, the U.S. government sent a mission to Central and South America in 1884 and 1885 to examine economic opportunities. In 1889, Secretary of State James G. Blaine hosted an inter-American conference in Washington, and from October 1901 to February 1902 the Mexican government hosted a second conference in its capital. Latin America was fully represented except for the Dominican Republic, which did not send delegates to Washington.

The divergence of interests between the United States and Latin America dominated both meetings. The United States argued for lowering tariff barriers, which the Latin Americans refused to do. Because their primary products, with the exception of sugar, already had easy access to the U.S. market, the lowering of tariffs would actually work against their major European trading partners. Brazil in particular was angered by the U.S. sugar tariff and the privileged entrée that

Cuban sugar had to the U.S. market. Rather than economics, the Latin Americans focused on political issues. Agreements were concluded that made foreign residents subject to host-country laws and that established compulsory arbitration of political disputes. As in the past, neither agreement was ever ratified. The major accomplishment of the these two inter-American conferences was the establishment of the International Bureau of the American Republics (later called the Pan-American Union), which served as a collector and distributor of commercial information.

Allied with the military and commercial interests in the United States were those who argued simply for the uplifting of the backward, undemocratic, and underdeveloped societies of Latin America. Such images had permeated diplomatic reports since the arrival of the first U.S. representatives in the region during the 1820s, and by the 1880s they were popular notions in the United States. According to this perspective, Latin America was a region of backwater republics, where a small elite controlled the political structure and the national wealth. Corruption prevailed; elections, where they existed, were farcical. The masses, uneducated, unskilled, and poverty stricken, had neither political voice nor opportunity for socioeconomic advancement. The brutal Spanish domination of Cuba became the measuring stick for the rest of Latin America. Given these circumstances, altruism was used to justify self-interest. Two events in 1903 illustrate the point. The Platt Amendment, tacked on to the Cuban constitution, and the Hay-Bunau Varilla Treaty, which gave Panama its independence and the United States its canal, contained similar provisions: limitations on foreign policy and foreign debt; permission for the United States to intervene for the maintenance of political order; and U.S. programs for the construction of schools, hospitals, and roads to improve local quality of life. Both treaties laid the groundwork for President Theodore Roosevelt's corollary to the Monroe Doctrine in 1904, by which the country reserved the right to interfere in the internal affairs of misbehaving Latin American nations.

The aloofness of the United States from hemispheric affairs in the generation after 1823, the arrogance of its territorial expansion in the 1840s and 1850s, and the overconfidence in its industrial development in the 1880s and 1890s, all contributed to Latin America's distrust of its northern neighbor. At the same time, however, Latin American liberals, proponents of economic growth and modernization in the 1880s and 1890s, also envied the material progress of the United States.

Latin American liberals such as Porfirio Díaz in Mexico, Justo Rufino Barrios in Guatemala, and José Balmaceda in Chile came to their presidential palaces in the latter part of the nineteenth century espousing the positivist philosophy. They also understood that the absence of investment capital in their countries was a legacy of the Spanish colonial experience. In application this meant that the liberal leaders willingly made generous concessions to foreign investors in order to aid the development of export-based economies.

These liberals came to power at a propitious time. Europe, in the midst of the industrial revolution, was looking for markets, raw materials, and investment opportunities. Led by Britain and followed by Germany and France, with the United States a distant fourth, trade and investment inundated Latin America. Only in Cuba did the United States dominate the economy. The Europeans engaged in trade for foodstuffs such as sugar, beef, and grain; primary products including guano, nitrate, and wool; and industrial metals. The British and Americans were the primary investors in transportation: roads, railroads, docks, and ports. Unfortunately, the economic boom brought little development beyond Latin America's capital cities. Politics remained in the elitists' hands, workers were poorly paid, and tariff and tax policies permitted the importation of technology and the export of goods almost duty free. This stagnation reinforced the prevailing view in the United States that Latin America was backward.

Finally, events in Europe also contributed to the establishment of the U.S. relationship with Latin America in 1903. When the German Kaiser Wilhelm II dismissed Chancellor Otto von Bismarck in 1890, he directly challenged Great Britain in announcing that Germany would have a navy and a global empire second to none. The German expansion program forced the British to search for new friends. To gain U.S. confidence, the British government gave recognition to U.S. preeminence in Latin America. Britain accepted the Monroe Doctrine in 1895 by permitting the United States to settle its Orinoco River Valley dispute with Venezuela; ensured the U.S. position among the European nations during the Spanish-American War in 1898; and with the second Hay-Pauncefote Treaty in 1901 permitted the United States to build its own trans-Isthmian canal.

By the end of 1903, the United States was poised to implement a relationship with Latin America on its own terms. As a new naval power with bases in the Caribbean, the United States was prepared to defend the canal it was about to construct across the isthmus of Panama. As a member of the world's industrial elite it needed the markets and raw materials that Latin America offered. And as the Progressive reformers were preparing to address economic, political, and social ills at home, they were also preparing to take their mission abroad. The responses of the individual Latin American countries to all of this were predicated upon the century-long experiences they had with the United States. While each country shared a mistrust of the United States, some were more susceptible to U.S. overtures than others.

Until Robert Beisner published *From Old Diplomacy to The New* in 1975, the historiography of late-nineteenth-century U.S. foreign policy could be organized into three schools of thought: (1) the traditionalists, who argued that the United States served as a beacon of liberal-democratic progress for the world to imitate; (2) the progressives and their new left and "world systems" descendants, who placed emphasis on economic expansion as the motivating factor for global involvement; and (3) the realists, whose amoral power-political view placed international status at the forefront of foreign policy decision making. In contrast, Beisner demonstrated that a combination of environmental changes in the United States and in the structure of international politics and the shifting perceptions of the material world by policymakers transformed the paradigm that had defined U.S. foreign policy prior to 1900. Beisner's approach demonstrates the interrelation of domestic and geopolitical influences on the formulation of foreign policy. This volume reflects Beisner's analysis regarding the United States and adds to the mix the domestic and geopolitical factors that influenced the foreign policies of Latin American nations in the late nineteenth century.

Starting where Shurbutt and his colleagues left off, this volume examines the relationships between the United States and selected Latin American countries within the environment of change between 1850 and 1903. The chapters are arranged in a pattern that demonstrates the varying degrees of importance attached to the diplomatic relationship. Mexico and Cuba, where U.S. interests predated 1850, were affected by expanding economic and security interests concerning the immediate border areas of the United States. Relations with Colombia are considered the next priority because of the U.S. determination to construct a canal at the isthmus of Panama, which in turn would bring relations with Central America and Venezuela into consideration. The Caribbean region has often been described as the U.S. backyard or the American Mediterranean. Throughout the nineteenth century Peru seemed farthest from the United States in terms of distance and culture, yet it became a focal point of private U.S. entrepreneurs and a point of conflict in regional affairs. Argentina and Chile, even farther distant, envisioned themselves as the dominant force on the Southern Cone and a major player in international affairs. This combination of factors brought Peru, Argentina, and Chile into conflict with each other and at times with the United States. Finally, the chapters on Brazil and Paraguay and Uruguay illustrate U.S. relations with countries on the periphery of its national interests.

Rather than constraining the contributors to this volume to a single consistent theme, the individual country relationships are examined within the context of the most relevant theme or themes. Such an approach provides the reader with a more realistic understanding of the complexity of the relationship that the United States had with each Latin American country and its place in the larger conceptual framework of the nineteenth century. For example, a major characteristic of this period was the entrance of U.S. entrepreneurs into Latin America, where they received generous concessions from the liberal political leaders, especially in Mexico, Central America, and Peru. In Cuba, Spanish authorities permitted the expansion of U.S. interests, largely in sugar, but economic policies made in Madrid often conflicted with the easy exportation of sugar to the United States. The Brazilian monarch Dom Pedro II was anxious to reach a trade agreement with the United States, but the U.S. tariff system mitigated against Brazil's exports. Both restrictive U.S. tariffs and the British economic presence worked against trade expansion in Colombia and to a lesser extent in Venezuela, Paraguay, and Uruguay. In stark contrast stood Argentina and Chile, where a global vision and the exportation of primary products directly competed with the United States. Orientated toward Europe, the Argentines and Chileans preferred its manufactures to those from the United States. The British remained Latin America's dominant trading partner throughout the nineteenth century, a fact reflected in Latin America's disinterest in the Pan-American Conference of 1889.

Closely associated with the businessmen's adventures were Washington's efforts to press their claims whenever a Latin American government interfered with the entrepreneurs' operations. Diplomats across the region spent much time protecting the interests of private businessmen against government encroachment. Also, the 1853 Gadsden Purchase, for the construction of a railroad line to California, and the U.S. involvement in Panama in 1885 raised Latin American fears that the United States would seek territory on the southern continent.

Regarding hemispheric political relations, the United States acted independently in pursuing its own interests. Washington begged off from interfering in the Uruguayan independence movement in 1828 and did little more than protest the French imposition of Maximilian on Mexico. Nor did it use the Monroe Doctrine in Latin American interstate disputes. On other occasions the United States offered or was invited to serve as the arbiter of international conflicts between various Latin American nations. Among the more notable were the War of the Triple Alliance, which pitted Paraguay against Argentina, Brazil, and Uruguay; the War of the Pacific, in which Peru and Bolivia confronted Chile; and the Orinoco River Valley territorial dispute between Great Britain and Venezuela. At other times the United States interfered in regional matters or internal affairs for its own purposes. For example, Washington encouraged a union of the Central American states to offset British influence on the isthmus. Beginning with the Ten Years' War in Cuba from 1868 to 1878, the United States interfered in Cuban political matters to protect its own interests and eventually gained Cuba's independence from Spain. From the time of the Bidlack-Mallinaro Treaty in 1846, the United States became entangled in Colombia's internal affairs, culminating in the decision to encourage Panama's independence movement in 1903. Much of this interference was justified on moral grounds, namely that the Latin Americans were incapable of bringing rational settlements to disputes or to resist European encroachment. Over the course of this half-century, U.S. policymakers did not hold a high opinion of the Latin Americans. They continued to see governments steeped in Spanish tradition that neither represented the people in form or function and that kept the masses entrapped in poverty.

Clearly, throughout the period from 1850 to 1903 the United States did not have a consistent policy for each of the Latin American nations, save the goal of protecting private entrepreneurs threatened by local political crises. What became apparent by the century's end, however, was that the United States had increased its presence throughout Latin America, whether via individual entrepreneurs or Washington's political actions. To the Latin American countries, the United States appeared as the dominant partner in their individual relationships, a perception that often earned the United States the "imperialist" label.

I would like to thank T. Ray Shurbutt and Malcolm MacDonald for the opportunity to undertake this project and Nicole Mitchell, director of The University of

Alabama Press, for guiding the project to its completion. Credit for the historical value of the volume belongs to each of the contributors and the peer reviewers provided by the Press. The editorial guidance given by Suzette Griffith and Carol Davis enhanced the volume's readability. And again I thank my wife, Yvonne, for her enduring patience with me, for I spend what must seem like an endless amount of time in archives and libraries and in front of a computer.

1

MEXICO

Conflicting Self-Interests

Don M. Coerver

ALTHOUGH THE UNITED STATES AND MEXICO emerged from the Mexican-American War in much different conditions, they would follow similar paths in domestic affairs during the 1850s: growing domestic discord leading to civil war. The war had been a great success for U.S. expansionism but would greatly complicate future efforts at expansion. The United States was now a Pacific power in need of improved transportation and communication to link its different regions. This interest in new transit routes drew U.S. attention to both northern Mexico and the isthmus of Tehuantepec as possible locations for U.S.-owned railroads. Any effort at expansion was immediately drawn into the larger national controversy over extending the area of slavery. Supporters of expansionism believed that the Compromise of 1850 and its doctrine of popular sovereignty would break the linkage between territorial extension and the spread of slavery, permitting continued expansion into the 1850s. This optimistic assessment soon unraveled in the face of growing national disunity during the decade, much of it sparked by disagreement over continued expansion.[1]

While the United States dealt with the problems of absorbing its newly acquired territory, an even more desperate situation confronted Mexico. Mexico had paid dearly for its defeat, but its substantial sacrifice had not relieved it of any of its fundamental problems: militarism, political factionalism, financial instability, and the risk of further foreign intervention and territorial loss. Regional revolts and separatist movements threatened further national disintegration. The U.S. payment of $15 million brought only brief relief to the endemic crisis in public finances, as the fundamental fiscal problems of the Mexican government remained uncorrected. Mexico would be given little time to adjust to the loss of half of its national territory before confronting new expansionist pressures.[2]

Continued U.S. Expansion: The Gadsden Purchase and Filibusters

The most immediate problem in U.S.-Mexican relations was the implementation of the Treaty of Guadalupe Hidalgo, in particular the determination of the new boundary line between the two countries. Article V of the treaty required that each nation appoint a boundary commission headed by a commissioner and a surveyor to establish jointly the boundary, with the results being considered part of the treaty. The commissions were to meet at San Diego, California, no later than 30 May 1849 and mark the boundary through its course to the mouth of the Rio Grande.[3]

The boundary commissions encountered difficulties from the beginning. The U.S. commissioner, Ambrose B. Sevier, died before the survey team left for California. The team took the Panama route to California, only to be delayed by the hordes of gold seekers rushing to the coast. The Mexican boundary commission was encountering similar difficulties. Its commissioner, General Pedro García Conde, was involved in a coach accident on his way to the Pacific Coast; the Mexican team also had trouble getting transportation because of competition from the forty-niners. The net result of these misadventures was that the survey was not begun by the treaty deadline of 30 May 1849.[4]

The two commissions initiated their work on 6 July 1849, with a major dispute over the starting point on the Pacific, south of San Diego. As the survey proceeded eastward, disagreements developed within the U.S. commission and between the two survey teams. A joint survey of the boundary between the two Californias was completed despite various distractions, including the shooting of the new U.S. commissioner, John B. Weller, by his chief surveyor, Andrew Gray. The two commissions then agreed to interrupt their work and renew the survey by working west from El Paso. When the two commissions reconvened, there was a new U.S. commissioner, John Russell Bartlett, and there was also an unanticipated problem: El Paso had been misplaced. The treaty provided that the boundary would run westward from a point on the Rio Grande eight miles above El Paso; the map that provided the basis for the treaty, however, placed El Paso 34 miles north and 100 miles east of its actual location. Bartlett and García Conde agreed on a compromise starting point that corrected the eastward mistake but recognized the incorrect—more northerly—location on the Rio Grande, some 42 miles above El Paso. The compromise boundary that resulted provoked criticism in Washington and the removal of Bartlett as boundary commissioner.[5]

The dispute over the boundary west of El Paso was one of several factors influencing new efforts at expansion by the United States. The territory "lost" by the United States in the boundary compromise, the Mesilla Valley, was considered an essential part of a projected route for a transcontinental railroad; U.S. settlers were also moving into the area, provoking conflicting claims by local officials to jurisdiction in the region. The new administration of Democrat Franklin Pierce, who took office in March 1853, was determined to rekindle expansionism despite the growing sectional crisis. The continuing financial instability of Mexico and the return of Santa Anna to power in 1853 spurred U.S. hopes for another transfer of territory.

President Pierce appointed as his minister to Mexico James Gadsden, a southerner and a railroad executive. Gadsden received detailed instructions regarding various proposals to purchase Mexican territory. The minimum U.S. demand was for the Mesilla Valley and sufficient land south of the Gila River to permit construction of a transcontinental railroad; for this minimum area the United States was willing to pay $15 million. The maximum U.S. offer was $50 million to acquire what the Pierce administration described as the "most natural boundary" between the two countries; this would involve the transfer of Baja California as well as major portions of all of the Mexican border states. When negotiations began with Santa Anna's government in late November 1853, Gadsden presented the maximum U.S. position but quickly retreated to the minimum area necessary for construction of a transcontinental railroad. The treaty signed by Gadsden on 30 December 1853 encountered major opposition when it was presented to the U.S. Senate, which reduced the amount of territory involved as well as the payment from $15 million $10 million. Pierce accepted this minimal version, fearing that a further delay in settling the boundary might lead to war. Santa Anna was disappointed in the modified treaty but quickly approved it because he needed the funds to suppress the growing opposition to his government. The treaty provided that the Mexican government would be paid $7 million upon the exchange of ratifications, which took place in Washington on 30 June 1854; the remaining $3 million would not be paid until the boundary had been "surveyed, marked, and fixed."[6]

Conditions in the U.S.-Mexican border region had encouraged filibustering activities since the early 1800s. Mexico's liberal immigration policy in regard to Texas basically preempted the need for filibustering in the 1820s.[7] When Texas revolted and achieved independence in 1836, the Mexicans viewed it as the culmination of a slow-motion filibustering action that had lasted over a decade. The annexation of Texas in 1845 and the acquisition of the Mexican Cession in 1848 failed to dampen the enthusiasm for filibustering; instead, the 1850s were to be a "golden age" for U.S. filibusters, with Mexico again the principal target.

Filibusters from the United States made repeated incursions into northern Mexico in the 1850s. While Texas continued to be a popular launching point for filibustering, California also figured prominently in such activities. California offered a ready recruiting ground for filibusters where the gold-rush arrivals were typically young, male, eager for adventure, and interested in quick wealth. Expedition leaders often tried to disguise their activities as "colonization" schemes to deceive both U.S. and Mexican officials; the supposed riches of Baja California and Sonora soon attracted the attention of disappointed forty-niners. Several expeditions set out from California during the decade, the most famous incursions being led by William Walker, who would gain even greater notoriety for his filibustering in Central America.[8]

Although filibustering expeditions such as Walker's were uniformly unsuccessful, they embittered and complicated U.S.-Mexican relations during the 1850s.

Mexican authorities were convinced that U.S. officials were lax in enforcing the neutrality laws or were actively assisting the filibusters; either view could be correct depending on the individual operation involved. Indeed, U.S. neutrality legislation made it illegal to organize a military expedition on U.S. soil against any nation with which the United States was at peace. Enforcement of the restriction was always difficult and often unpopular. Typically there was strong support for expansionism in the areas where filibustering expeditions were organized. When U.S. officials adopted a hard line against filibustering, it was often because they believed that such unofficial efforts at expansion were interfering with official attempts to acquire additional territory.[9]

Reforma Mexico and the United States

An important factor in Mexico's attraction as a target for filibusters was the chaotic political situation in the country during the 1850s. Santa Anna's willingness to part with national territory both reflected and contributed to the mounting liberal opposition to his government. The need for funds to suppress revolts was a major motive behind the sale whereas the alienation of additional territory added to the ranks of Santa Anna's opponents. Santa Anna's claim that he had sold a small piece of worthless territory to avoid the forced loss of a much larger area did not satisfy his critics. The liberal revolution of Ayutla began in March 1854 under the leadership of Juan Álvarez. The U.S. government had become increasingly disenchanted with Santa Anna over his efforts to develop closer ties with European countries and continuing disputes over provisions of the Gadsden Treaty. Minister Gadsden was an enthusiastic supporter of the liberal cause and was highly critical of Santa Anna's administration.[10]

The overthrow of Santa Anna in August 1855 ushered in the "reform" period (*La reforma*) in Mexican history. The liberals were dedicated to introducing major reforms in Mexican society but were hindered by conservative opposition and divisions within their own ranks over the extent and pace of reform. The liberals had mixed emotions about the United States. Much of the liberal program drew its inspiration from the U.S. model, and many liberal leaders, such as Benito Juárez, had been in exile in the United States. The liberals, however, were concerned about continuing expansionist pressures by the United States and fears that the United States might be able to exploit Mexico's chronic internal disorder.

Relations between the United States and reforma Mexico got off to an early and promising start when Gadsden recognized the government of provisional president Juan Álvarez on 10 October 1855. Álvarez had been in the presidency for less than a week at the time of recognition, and Gadsden defied the European representatives who had earlier supported a conservative replacement for Santa Anna. Gadsden's relations with the new liberal government declined immediately amid continuing problems with the treaty of 1853. The United States had already paid seven of the ten million dollars due Mexico under the treaty to the government of Santa Anna but was withholding the remaining three million until the boundary had been finalized. The resignation of Álvarez in December 1855 put Ignacio Comonfort in the presidency. Gadsden did not have a high opinion of Comonfort, and relations between the two deteriorated rapidly. In May 1856 Comonfort's government asked that Gadsden be recalled, a request granted by the State Department in June. Gadsden remained until October 1856 when his replacement, John Forsyth, arrived in Mexico City.[11]

Although some of the difficulties in U.S.-Mexican relations were due to Gadsden's personality and personal agenda, more fundamental problems were also at work. The proceeds from the Gadsden Purchase had no long-term effect on Mexico's financial problems, and the liberals were unable to develop a fiscal system that would support their political and economic goals. The liberal reform program culminated in the promulgation of a new constitution in February 1857. The moderate Comonfort easily won election to the presidency in the first elections under the new constitution, but his short, stormy tenure would soon end in civil war.

At the same time the constitutional convention was meeting, the new U.S. ambassador, John Forsyth, arrived. Like Gadsden, Forsyth was a southerner with important political connections. He had served in Mexico during the war and spoke Spanish. The instructions given the new minister reflected the shopping list of problems affecting U.S.-Mexican relations. Priority should be given to allaying any Mexican fears about the United States having "sinister views" (territorial ambitions) in regard to Mexico. Forsyth should pursue tariff concessions and seek a settlement of the longstanding claims issue arising out of the Treaty of Guadalupe Hidalgo. He should also impress on the Mexican government the continuing interest of the United States in the right of transit across the Isthmus of Tehuantepec.[12]

Forsyth's early contacts with the liberal government encouraged him to believe that it was giving serious thought to agreeing to a U.S. protectorate over the country in response to Mexico's worsening relations with Britain, France, and Spain. As Mexico's principal trading partner and creditor, Britain was increasingly disenchanted with the liberal government's inability to establish financial and political order. France was convinced that Comonfort was pursuing policies that were playing into the hands of U.S. expansionists while the Spanish government was threatening military intervention over Mexico's debt problems. Rumors of a U.S. protectorate had surfaced soon after the fall of Santa Anna; although liberal leaders were vigorous in their public denunciation of the idea, privately some cautious interest in the project was present.[13]

Only three weeks after his arrival in Mexico City, Forsyth outlined his plan for a protectorate to Secretary of State Marcy. Forsyth saw the protectorate as being composed of an offensive-defensive military alliance, a claims settlement, a commercial treaty, a postal convention, and an extradition treaty. The United States would have to make a substantial loan to the liberal government to promote political and financial stability. There would also be a reorganization of the Mexican army, with Mexicans providing the enlisted personnel while U.S. officers filled the leadership positions. Consequently, U.S. immigrants would be needed to "develop the great natural resources of this superb country." Whereas Forsyth acknowledged that such a scheme might be "visionary speculation," he concluded his proposal with a provocative question: "If they could be transmuted into realities, should we not enjoy all the fruits of annexation without its responsibilities and evils"?[14] Forsyth soon tried to translate his "visionary speculation" into reality. The U.S. minister presented his plan in a limited way to the Mexican minister of foreign relations, Ezequiel Montes, a supposed opponent of any protectorate arrangement. Forsyth, however, believed that Mexico's domestic and diplomatic problems were "gradually working to a general solution of all questions" between the United States and Mexico.[15]

Forsyth's confidence proved justified when Montes indicated an interest in "arriving at a total arrangement." This total arrangement took the form of a series of agreements drafted and approved in less than five weeks with the stipulation that the agreements be considered as a package, not separately. One agreement provided for a $15 million loan by the United States to Mexico, with the United States retaining seven of the fifteen million to pay U.S. claims and the English debt; the remaining $8 million would be made available immediately to the Mexican government upon ratification of the agreement. A postal treaty provided for the establishment of a weekly steamship service between Veracruz and New Orleans with each government providing an annual subsidy of $120,000. A frontier reciprocity agreement provided for the free flow of a limited list of products across the land frontier in either direction. A final agreement established a joint claims commission to evaluate claims against both governments with a provision for arbitration by the French emperor if needed.[16]

The Mexican government was optimistic that the Forsyth-Montes agreements would be ratified by the United States. Timing, however, was working against the agreements, which arrived in Washington in late February 1857. The U.S. Congress was nearing the end of its session; more important, a new president, James Buchanan, would take office in early March. Buchanan had defeated Pierce for the Democratic nomination, and his election to the presidency would also mean a new secretary of state, Lewis Cass. When the agreements were presented to outgoing secretary of state William Marcy, Marcy refused to submit them to Congress, citing the short time remaining in both the congressional session and Pierce's term in office. It would be up to the new administration to take action on the agreements. Buchanan and Cass quickly rejected the agreements on the grounds that the United States would effectively be purchasing commercial privileges, which was contrary to the country's support for the "most liberal competition and the freest trade."[17] The Buchanan administration was more interested in territorial expansion than in economic expansion, as Mexico would soon discover.

Buchanan's previous foreign policy experience provided a good indication of the direction his Mexican policy would take. Buchanan had served as Polk's secretary of state from 1845 to 1849, overseeing the Treaty of Guadalupe Hidalgo and unsuccessfully trying to purchase Cuba. As minister to Great Britain from 1853 to 1856, Buchanan was one of the authors of the controversial "Ostend Manifesto" of 1854, which advocated the purchase or forcible acquisition of Cuba. Buchanan's secretary of state, Lewis Cass, was also a long-time supporter of expansion. Although Buchanan retained John Forsyth as minister to Mexico, the president provided the ambassador a new—and much different—set of instructions in July 1857. Buchanan directed Forsyth to conclude a treaty "providing for the arrangement of a new boundary and the adjustment of mutual claims." The new boundary would involve the purchase of all of Baja California, most of Sonora, and all of Chihuahua north of the 30th parallel. Forsyth was to offer $12 million for the territory and was authorized to go as high as $15 million. The United States would retain $2 million of the purchase price to pay claims by U.S. citizens against Mexico. The instructions also emphasized the need to settle the issue of transit rights across the Isthmus of Tehuantepec. Forsyth was to press the Mexican government for a free port on each side of the isthmus and for permission for the United States to employ military force to protect the security of transit should the Mexican government be unable to do so. The instructions included drafts for a boundary\claims treaty and a Tehuantepec transit treaty.[18]

Buchanan's instructions brought a very undiplomatic response from Forsyth, who said that the instructions placed him in an "untenable position" and went against the "uniform tenor of my despatches to the Department." His earlier communications to Washington had made it explicit that the current Mexican government was unwilling to alienate "one foot of the national territory." From a more practical standpoint, Forsyth pointed out the financial inadequacies of the proposed treaties. The United States was now offering a maximum of $15 million for approximately the same territory it had been willing to pay up to $30 million for in in 1853. The United States was now seeking transit rights in the Isthmus of Tehuantepec without any compensation to Mexico when ten years earlier Buchanan as secretary of state had offered $15 million for similar rights.[19] Despite his misgivings, Forsyth presented the two draft treaties to the liberal government. The Comonfort administration rejected the proposed treaty for the new boundary, considering "inadmissible any plan based upon a cession of any portion of the national territory." Mexico could not accept the Isthmus transit treaty because it "depreciated her rights of sovereignty over that territory."[20]

The rapidly deteriorating political situation in Mexico provided some hope for Buchanan that the United States could exploit the circumstances for territorial gain. Comonfort's actions as both provisional and constitutional president had provoked increasing political as well as armed opposition. By mid-November Forsyth was reporting that Comonfort's situation was so desperate that he was willing to "dispose of a part of the National Territory." On 11 January 1858 conservative general Félix Zuloaga revolted against Comonfort, designating himself as president. Forsyth quickly recognized the new conservative government, believing that efforts to acquire territory would produce an "auspicious result" if Zuloaga held on to power.[21]

Instead of Zuloaga establishing a dominant position, Mexico entered into a three-year civil war with Benito Juárez leading the liberals while the conservatives went through a series of leaders. The liberals established their capital at Veracruz,

Mexico's principal port and an important source of revenue and supplies. The conservatives controlled Mexico City and most major urban areas. Forsyth's rapid recognition of the conservative regime avoided, at least temporarily, the dilemma of which government to recognize. There was little reason for the Buchanan administration to take exception to Forsyth's action since the United States usually recognized whichever government controlled Mexico City and Forsyth was optimistic that conservative financial problems could be converted into sale of territory. On 1 March 1858 Forsyth reported that Zuloaga and his cabinet had unanimously agreed on the necessity to sell territory but were awaiting a military victory against the liberals before taking action.[22]

After a conservative military victory in early March, Forsyth made a formal proposal on 22 March 1858 to Zuloaga's minister of foreign relations, José Luis Cuevas. Forsyth's proposal included Buchanan's earlier offer for territory and transit rights in Tehuantepec as well as portions of the earlier Montes-Forsyth agreements in the form of a reciprocity agreement and a postal treaty. Forsyth received a quick but unfavorable response to his propositions. Cuevas reported that President Zuloaga had rejected all of Forsyth's points, including the territorial transfer, which was described as harmful to Mexico's "true interests and good name." In his response to the rejection on 8 April 1858, Forsyth immediately adopted a hard line on the claims issue, observing that the rejection of the territorial sale must mean that the Mexican government "has other views and plans to propose for the settlement of these claims in full."[23] Forsyth's exchanges with the conservative government became increasingly acrimonious. He informed the Zuloaga government on 21 June that he was breaking relations until further instructions were received from Washington. The further instructions turned out to be an order for Forsyth to withdraw the legation and return to the United States.[24]

Forsyth's withdrawal gave Buchanan a chance to reassess his methods, if not his goals, in regard to Mexico. Buchanan continued his pursuit of territory and transit rights but was willing to explore possibilities other than outright purchase. The president spoke of acquiring territory through a process of immigration and annexation as had taken place in Texas or through establishment of a military protectorate over certain areas that would ultimately lead to their acquisition. Buchanan took up the call for a protectorate in his annual message to Congress in December 1858. Citing the "anarchy and violence" prevailing along the U.S.-Mexican border, Buchanan requested congressional authorization to create a military protectorate over parts of Sonora and Chihuahua, including the establishment of military posts in the area. Caught up in the sectional crisis, Congress refused to grant the authorization.[25]

In his message proposing a protectorate, Buchanan indicated that the only hope for a peaceful settlement of differences with Mexico lay with the liberal government. He then dispatched a secret agent, William Churchwell, to Mexico to evaluate the conservative and liberal positions and make a recommendation on recognition. In early February 1859, Churchwell recommended immediate recognition of the liberal government, claiming that it controlled sixteen of the twenty-two Mexican states and enjoyed the support of an estimated 70 percent of the population.[26]

Churchwell's mission added to the gathering momentum to recognize the liberal government but provided only limited hope of realizing Buchanan's project for territorial acquisition. Rather than immediately recognize the liberal government with no real estate in return, Buchanan dispatched the new U.S. minister to Mexico, Robert M. McLane, with instructions to use his discretion in determining which government, if any, to recognize. As soon as a government was recognized, McLane was to begin negotiations on a treaty for transit rights and the cession of Baja California. McLane arrived in Veracruz on 1 April and immediately entered into talks with the Juárez government; the basis for these talks was a series of points upon which the liberal government had earlier indicated to Churchwell a willingness to "negotiate affirmatively," including the cession of Baja California, transit rights, claims adjustments, and reciprocal trade. When McLane extended official recognition to the liberal government on 6 April 1859, however, the Juárez government did not acknowledge Churchwell's specific points but instead made a vague promise to "adjust in an honorable and satisfactory manner" all questions pending when relations had been suspended. The conservative government in Mexico City responded to the recognition of Juárez by accusing the United States of suspending relations with the conservative government because it would not sell a "considerable part of national territory."[27]

Recognition proved disappointing to both the Buchanan administration and the Juárez government. The United States had conceded its principal source of leverage without any cession of territory by Mexico. The liberal government had expected that recognition would lead to loans by both the U.S. government as well as private U.S. financial sources. The Buchanan administration had little enthusiasm for a loan to the liberals unless real estate was involved; the military situation of the liberals and the possibility of foreign intervention discouraged private lending to the liberals.[28]

By late 1859 financial and military pressures pushed the Juárez regime to sign two agreements with the United States. Their latest financial gambit—using nationalized church property as collateral for loans—had proved to be unsuccessful. Their lack of military success against the conservatives was only part of a broader picture of military problems. Fears of European intervention had been growing throughout 1859, and there were indications that the Buchanan administration was preparing to use military force. In the first two weeks of December, Minister McLane and Mexican minister of foreign relations Melchor Ocampo conducted negotiations and drafted two agreements, signing them on 14 December. The two agreements were made up of a "Treaty of Transit and Commerce" and a convention to enforce the treaty and to "maintain order and security" in Mexico and the United States. The treaty granted the United States three transit routes: one southern route through the Isthmus of Tehuantepec and two northern routes, one from "any suitable point on the Rio Grande" to the port of Mazatlán and the second from the Arizona-Sonora border to the port of Guaymas. Free ports would be established at the end of each transit route. Mexico had sovereignty in the transit areas and primary responsibility for security of the transit routes, although it could request U.S. military assistance if needed. In the event that U.S. lives or property were in "imminent danger," the United States could intervene on its own initiative. As compensation the United States agreed to pay $4 million, with $2 million to be retained by the U.S. government to pay claims by U.S. citizens against the Mexican government. The convention accompanying the treaty was designed to promote military cooperation along the border and to maintain "order and security in the territory of either Republic." If either country was unable to provide for the safety and security of part of its territory, it was obliged to call on the other republic for military assistance and to pay the expenses of the requested intervention. Any disorder along the common frontier would be dealt with in a cooperative manner by the authorities of both countries.[29]

Both McLane and Ocampo believed that the agreements would quickly be ratified and would benefit both parties. McLane returned to Washington in February 1860 to help influence Senate ratification. The treaties, however, encountered immediate and stiff opposition. When the McLane-Ocampo agreements came to a vote on 31 May, the Senate rejected them by a vote of 18 to 27. The split was on clearly sectional lines; southerners cast 14 of the 18 affirmative votes while northerners cast 23 of 27 negative votes.[30]

The rejection of the McLane-Ocampo agreements meant that Mexican liberals would not be able to count on an official military relationship with or financial assistance from the U.S. government. While the U.S. Senate was debating the agreements, conservative forces under General Miguel Miramón began an attack on the liberal capital of Veracruz. Miramón planned to coordinate his land attack with a seaborne attack by two steamers purchased and outfitted in Havana, Cuba. He launched this attack in early March 1860, but the seaborne phase of the operation never took place. The liberal government had warned U.S. officials of the two steamers, classifying them as "pirate vessels"; this gave the U.S. naval force at Veracruz an excuse to seize the vessels and take them to New Orleans, where a U.S. court later ruled that the two steamers had been illegally seized. His plans disrupted, Miramón broke off the assault.[31] After the failure of Miramón's attack on Veracruz, conservative military fortunes went into a rapid decline. The liberals then went on the offensive, which culminated in the capture of Mexico City on 25 December 1860. The arrival of Juárez in the Mexican capital on 11 January 1861 marked the end of a bitter three-year civil war in which Mexico had avoided national disintegration, the sale of more territory, and the establishment of a U.S. protectorate. As the civil war in Mexico was coming to a conclusion, an even deadlier and more destructive civil war was about to begin in the United States, with important results for U.S.-Mexican relations.

The United States, the Confederate States, and Mexico

On the same day that Juárez triumphantly entered Mexico City, Alabama became the fourth state to secede from the Union. The outbreak of fighting in April

1861 reversed the situation that had existed during the War of the Reform; now it would be the Mexican government under Juárez that would have two different U.S. governments with which to contend. Both the United States and the Confederate States of America followed foreign policies emphasizing the importance of European relations, especially with Britain and France; both were to be disappointed by the results. The North had expected a favorable response from Europe, especially from Britain, with its strong abolitionist sentiment. Britain, however, declared its neutrality and recognized the belligerent status of the Confederacy, a move imitated by France. The southerners flattered themselves that the textile industries of Britain and France were so dependent on southern cotton that both countries would have to support the Confederacy; this "king cotton diplomacy" would dictate a policy of European support, ranging from recognition to possible armed intervention against the United States. The South, however, had miscalculated the degree of economic dependency as well as the flexibility of textile producers. The economic dislocation of the war did not place significant pressure on Britain to intervene on behalf of the Confederacy; France—more sympathetic to the southern cause—was more interested in taking advantage of the U.S. Civil War than in getting involved in it.[32]

After Europe, Mexico figured prominently in the diplomatic activities of the Confederacy and the United States. Texas, a Confederate state, shared about half of Mexico's northern boundary. The Confederacy was also counting heavily on the Texas-Mexico border as the most promising way to circumvent the Union naval blockade of southern ports instituted in late April 1861. The Union concerned itself primarily with trying to thwart Confederate plans for Mexico as well as preventing European intervention in Mexico, prompted by the liberal government's continuing financial difficulties. Of necessity the North had to focus most of its attention and resources on activities east of the Mississippi River, giving sporadic attention to Texas and the Mexican connection.

The Confederacy sent as its representative to the Juárez government John T. Pickett, who had served as a filibuster in the 1850s and as U.S. consul at Veracruz while it was the liberal capital. The Confederacy was not interested in winning official recognition from the Mexican government, only treatment as a belligerent. Pickett realized that the Mexican government attributed earlier U.S. expansionism to southern influence and hastened to assure liberal officials that the South had no expansionist designs on Mexico. He even talked about the "retrocession of a portion of the territory" taken earlier from Mexico by "the late United States." Although disclaiming any southern interest in expansion, Pickett on several occasions threatened Mexican officials with invasion and annexation. When Pickett attempted to develop contacts with conservative elements, he was expelled in late 1861, having done nothing to promote Confederate interests.[33]

While Pickett was blundering toward expulsion in Mexico City, Confederate diplomacy in the crucial Texas-Mexico border area was in much more capable hands. The principal Confederate agent in northern Mexico was José Agustín Quintero, a Cuban by birth but a Confederate citizen. Quintero early grasped the key role that cross-border trade could play and developed close ties with the dominant figure along the Rio Grande, Santiago Vidaurri. Although nominally a liberal, Vidaurri had taken advantage of his location and the distractions of the War of the Reform to establish a nearly independent position in the key states of Coahuila and Nuevo León. Vidaurri saw in an expanding trade with the Confederacy a major source of revenue with which to finance his continued defiance of the central government. As Vidaurri's control spread to the neighboring state of Tamaulipas with its key port of Matamoros, opportunities for trade expanded considerably. Vidaurri even suggested a possible political union between some of the northern Mexican states and the Confederacy.[34]

In the Mexican capital U.S. diplomacy was in the capable hands of Thomas Corwin. Appointed minister to Mexico in April 1861, Corwin had no prior diplomatic experience but did have an extensive political résumé upon which he could trade. He had served as governor of Ohio, in the U.S. House and Senate, and also as secretary of the treasury; more important to the Mexicans, Corwin had a lengthy history of opposing expansionism and had been a bitter critic of the Mexican-American War. Corwin had the threefold responsibility of promoting U.S. interests, blocking Confederate activities, and propping up the Juárez government. In pursuit of these goals, Corwin negotiated a series of agreements with the Juárez administration in late 1861 and early 1862.

In December 1861 Corwin concluded postal and extradition treaties with the Juárez government that were ratified and went into effect in June 1862. With Mexico's European creditors mobilizing for intervention, Corwin negotiated two loan treaties aimed at saving the Juárez regime. The first treaty, signed in November 1861, provided that the United States would lend Mexico $9 million, with the loan to be secured by a lien on all public lands, mineral rights, and nationalized church property in Baja California, Chihuahua, Sonora, and Sinaloa. The loan would be made only if Britain and France would agree to abandon their decision, made the previous month in London, to intervene to collect debts. In February 1862 the U.S. Senate overwhelmingly rejected the treaty, citing a general opposition to U.S. involvement in Mexico's chronic financial problems. Even before the Senate rejected the first treaty, Corwin had started negotiations on a second loan treaty, signed in April 1862. The second treaty provided for an $11 million loan secured by the public lands and nationalized church property in all of Mexico. Corwin hoped that the changed international situation would lead to ratification. The anticipated tripartite intervention by England, France, and Spain had become a reality in January 1862; of more importance, in April 1862 the tripartite intervention became a unilateral French intervention when England and Spain withdrew their forces. Despite the French threat to Mexico, the Senate once again rejected the loan treaty.[35]

The French Intervention

The United States had been worried about the possibility of foreign intervention in Mexico for some time. The major restraint on intervention had been fear of the U.S. response, which had basically been eliminated by the outbreak of civil war. The excuse for intervention came when the Mexican government formally announced in July 1861 that Mexico was suspending payment on the foreign and domestic debt for two years. The response of the major European powers came in October, when England, France, and Spain agreed to intervene in Mexico for the sole purpose of debt collection. When it became evident that France was implementing a broader imperialist scheme, England and Spain abandoned the intervention in April 1862.[36]

The Confederates saw new diplomatic opportunities in the French intervention. The Juárez government had refused to recognize the Confederacy, openly favored the Union cause, and was having difficulty maintaining order along the northern border. A French-controlled government held out the possibility of recognition, of increased trade across the Rio Grande, and of some kind of political linkage between Mexico and the Confederacy. Any U.S. opposition to the French intervention might lead France to adopt a more pro-Confederate policy. The Confederacy optimistically dispatched an "envoy extraordinary and minister plenipotentiary" to the new imperial Mexican government to discuss a military alliance and commercial relations, but Maximilian declined even to meet with the Confederate representative. Whereas some Confederate officials thought the French intervention improved the prospects for southern expansion into Mexico, Napoleon III of France actually intended to acquire part of the Confederacy.[37]

The United States made a major effort diplomatically to prevent the tripartite intervention and increased its opposition to intervention when it turned into an effort to transform Mexico into a French-controlled empire with an imported European monarch, Archduke Maximilian of Austria. Even before Napoleon's plans for Mexico became fully known, Secretary of State Seward in early 1862 had indicated that he would not recognize a European monarchy in Mexico. This refusal to recognize Maximilian did not mean an active policy of supporting the Juárez administration. Liberal efforts to get financial and military support from the United States proved unsuccessful in the early phase of intervention. The financial demands imposed by the U.S. Civil War helped to defeat the Corwin loan proposals in 1861 and 1862. The liberals were especially in need of military supplies across the northern border from the United States because Mexico had no military production capacity of its own and the French navy controlled the Mexican coasts. The United States, however, in November 1862 imposed a ban on the exportation of military supplies because the supplies were needed by U.S. forces and out of fear that the arms might end up in Confederate hands.[38]

The Juárez government—often operating through its minister to the United States, Matías Romero—had to resort to nonofficial channels to acquire aid from the United States. While Romero worked diplomatically for the removal of the export ban, he also worked covertly to ship arms across the border to the liberal government. The Juárez government also appointed three special commissioners to deal in arms and seek loans: Generals Plácido Vega, Gaspar Sánchez Ochoa, and José Maria Carvajal. Vega and Sánchez Ochoa operated primarily in California, whereas Carvajal was active in New York City and Washington. The activities of the commissioners produced mixed results. Efforts to float loans or sell bonds generally failed. The smuggling of arms, however, enjoyed greater success. General Vega in particular kept a steady stream of assorted military goods flowing from California to Mexico.[39]

The wanderings of the Juárez government greatly complicated the conduct of relations between the United States and Mexico. Advancing French troops had forced Juárez to abandon Mexico City on 31 May 1863, creating a vagabond liberal government that would not return to the capital for more than four years. Juárez moved north, setting up his nomadic capital in more than a dozen different locations and placing himself at the end of a long and tenuous communication line; reports from Romero in Washington often took more than a month to reach Juárez. The location of the U.S. minister, Thomas Corwin, also contributed to the confusion and delay. Corwin remained in Mexico City after the flight of Juárez, making it easy to communicate with Maximilian's government, which the United States did not recognize, but hard to communicate with the Juárez government, which the United States did recognize. Corwin's location may have contributed to an increasing partiality toward the empire that he found difficult to conceal. The minister's pro-imperial views finally led to his resignation in September 1864.[40]

Relations between Mexico and the United States changed rapidly after the end of the U.S. Civil War in April 1865. On 3 May 1865 President Andrew Johnson revoked the ban on the exportation of arms that had been in effect since November 1862. Arms manufacturers in the United States had large inventories on hand at war's end and were looking for new markets for their surpluses. Another postwar surplus also came into play: large numbers of trained soldiers with limited economic prospects and a taste for adventure. Various plans developed to organize volunteer U.S. forces to serve in Mexico with the liberals. In addition to purchasing arms, the major liberal agents in the United States were all involved in recruiting efforts as well. Most of these volunteer activities produced little in the way of positive results for the liberal cause, but a small group of U.S volunteers raised by General Gaspar Sánchez Ochoa fought with distinction as the "American Legion of Honor" until the liberal victory at Querétaro in May 1867.[41]

The end of the U.S. Civil War also provided a new problem for U.S.-Mexico relations: the movement of Confederate exiles into Mexico. Confronted with the political and economic uncertainties of defeat, many southerners looked to Mexico for a new life or a new opportunity to fight. Maximilian adopted a policy of admitting Confederate exiles as long as they entered Mexico unarmed, promised to obey the imperial government, swore not to attack neighboring countries, and pledged to settle outside of the frontier areas or the Isthmus of Tehuantepec. Maximilian officially declined to let Confederate exiles join the imperial army, but a limited number did serve in the Foreign Legion under French command. The liberal government permitted Confederate exiles to enter Mexico as long as they were unarmed and conducted themselves in a peaceful manner. The liberals did not recruit volunteers in former Confederate areas, and the original recruits for the American Legion of Honor were all Union veterans. Regardless of which government admitted them and where they settled, most Confederate exiles soon grew disenchanted with their adopted country and returned to the United States.[42]

The most important result of the end of the U.S. Civil War was the ability of the United States to threaten military action if the French did not withdraw. Thus U.S. policy reflected a struggle between high-ranking army officers favoring immediate military action and Secretary of State Seward, who believed that steadily mounting diplomatic pressure could force a French withdrawal and produce the collapse of Maximilian's empire. Victorious Union generals such as Ulysses Grant and Philip Sheridan considered the French presence in Mexico as unfinished business of the U.S. Civil War. French control of northern Mexico was tenuous, and Grant had dispatched Sheridan with 50,000 veteran troops to the Rio Grande. Sheridan encouraged rumors that his force was preparing to invade Mexico, sent scouts into northern Mexico, and provided extensive supplies to liberal forces, including 30,000 muskets. Seward intervened to curb the provocative activities of Sheridan along the border, believing that other factors were operating that—along with U.S. pressure—could help produce the withdrawal of the French.[43]

By late 1865 an accumulation of problems was pressuring Napoleon III to remove his forces. The French military position in Mexico was going from stalemate to decline as it became obvious that a decisive defeat could not be inflicted on the liberals. The intervention had also been a financial failure; Maximilian was not furnishing financial support for the French troops as promised and was not paying the debts owed French creditors. There was growing uneasiness with the situation in Europe, especially the expansionist intentions of Prussia. Domestic opposition in France to the intervention was also on the rise. The United States added to Napoleon's discomfort with a steady escalation in diplomatic pressure. In November 1865 Seward announced the appointment of a new minister to "republican Mexico": former Union general John A. Logan, who had publicly supported the Juárez government and had called for war with France. In his annual message to Congress on 4 December 1865, President Johnson made no specific reference to the French intervention in Mexico but pointedly indicated that it would be a "great calamity" if any European power challenged the U.S. "defense of republicanism against foreign interference." Two days later Seward rejected a French offer to withdraw its forces in exchange for U.S. recognition of Maximilian's empire, requesting instead that the French set a specific date for withdrawal. By February 1866 Seward had stopped requesting and started demanding that the French set a specific date for terminating the intervention.[44]

In January 1866 Napoleon III informed Maximilian that French forces would be withdrawn from Mexico, citing the financial problems of the intervention. On 6 April Seward received official word from the French that they would be withdrawing from Mexico in three stages: November 1866, March 1867, and November 1867. Seward kept the pressure on the French, urging them to speed up the withdrawal. In November 1866 Seward dispatched General William T. Sherman and the new U.S. minister to Mexico, Lewis D. Campbell, to Mexico to ensure that the French withdrawal was going forward as promised and to make contact with Juárez.

The two representatives never contacted Juárez and refused to land at French-controlled Veracruz; the mission did indicate that the United States was not assuming that the French would withdraw as promised.[45]

Instead of delaying their departure, the French were actually moving out ahead of schedule. Seward assumed all along that the withdrawal of the French would lead to the rapid collapse of Maximilian's empire and issued instructions that nothing be done to hamper or embarrass the French departure. After Maximilian decided to cast his lot with the Mexican conservatives, French troops pulled out of Mexico City on 5 February 1867; the last of the French forces left Mexico on 12 March. Maximilian left Mexico City shortly after the French to make what proved to be a last stand at Querétaro, which fell to liberal forces on 15 May 1867. There were well-justified fears about the physical safety of the deposed emperor, who was captured along with some of his leading generals. Seward directed U.S. minister Campbell to intervene on Maximilian's behalf, but the dawdling Campbell had returned to the United States without ever presenting his credentials to the liberal government. After a one-day trial, a military tribunal ordered Maximilian executed, and the order was carried out on 19 June 1867.[46]

Following the civil wars in both countries, the United States and Mexico were in need of both political reconstruction and economic development. Enthusiasm for expansion in the United States had not died out altogether, but there was growing interest in the commercial and investment opportunities offered by Mexico rather than in acquisition of more Mexican territory. Many in the United States believed that northern Mexico would one day become part of the United States, but this annexation would be a peaceful process resulting from U.S. economic penetration and immigration. Mexican leaders were worried about the situation in the northern border states, but philosophically their views on Mexico's future economic development emphasized the importance of attracting U.S. capital and technology. The liberals were alienated from the major European powers as a result of the intervention and had no significant relationship with any Latin American country. History and geography had bequeathed Mexico an intimate—if often stormy—relationship with the United States. Liberal emphasis was shifting from political reform to economic development. Liberals, as well as U.S. investors, embraced the traditional wisdom that Mexico was a country of vast potential wealth waiting to be developed. The failed efforts to establish a protectorate indicated the liberal willingness to have U.S. investors participate in Mexico's economic "regeneration."[47]

Two civil wars, tripartite foreign intervention, French occupation, and an imposed monarch failed to diminish the interest of U.S. investors in Mexico. In fact, U.S. diplomats in Mexico such as Minister Thomas Corwin and Consul at Mexico City Marcus Otterbourg collected information and made suggestions useful to potential U.S. investors or traders. Secretary of State Seward enthusiastically supported this approach, anticipating that economic penetration would lead to peaceful annexation. Many of the liberal efforts to float loans or purchase arms in the United States were connected to business concessions to U.S. agents. Although most of these projects produced little in the way of tangible results, they indicated the path of cooperation that would be taken in the future by the successors of Juárez and other U.S. investors.[48]

Problems on the Border

The border had been a leading source of friction between the United States and Mexico throughout the nineteenth century. The Treaty of Guadalupe Hidalgo in 1848 and the Gadsden Treaty of 1853 redefined the border as an international boundary but did little to resolve the substantive problems connected with a lengthy common border stretching almost 2,000 miles. The boundary was poorly marked west of El Paso; even the Rio Grande was of limited value as a natural boundary due to periodic changes in the channel of the river. The border was a frontier region as well as a boundary; the six Mexican states bordering on the United States constituted almost half of Mexico's geographical area but contained less than 10 percent of the national population. The composition of the border population was also a problem. A large percentage of the border population on the U.S. side was of Mexican origin; this group maintained a variety of ties with Mexico and was accustomed to moving freely across the boundary.[49]

The political situation in the border region added to the area's varied problems. The border zone was at a great distance from the central authorities in both countries, making it easy for national officials to ignore the area during moments of calm but difficult to exert control in the area when difficulties arose. Both nations had positioned a large percentage of their military forces in the border zone, but the troops available could still not adequately maintain security. On the U.S. side, Texas was suffering from the dislocations of "reconstruction" whereas Arizona and New Mexico would maintain territorial status until 1912. Regional leaders in the northern Mexican states such as Santiago Vidaurri and Juan Cortina often enjoyed a degree of independence from central authority that complicated border relations.[50]

The border area posed a number of economic problems for U.S.-Mexican relations. Because the area could not support an agricultural economy at the time, settlers turned to pastoral pursuits; with large herds of wild and semi-wild cattle roaming the region, cattle rustling became a well-organized business. Rustlers from both sides of the border used the international boundary as a shield, stealing cattle in the other country and returning home to dispose of them. Rustling became such a problem that both countries appointed commissions to investigate the situation in the early 1870s. The U.S. commission concluded that the rustling was being conducted by Mexican bandits who operated freely due to the "effete and corrupt" inaction of Mexican border authorities. The Mexican commission noted that the U.S. settlers most implicated in the rustling were those who made the most exaggerated claims about Mexican responsibility.[51]

Often connected with the rustling problem was the existence of the *zona libre,* a duty-free zone established in 1858 by the governor of Tamaulipas, Ramón Guerra.

The zone created a 20-kilometer-wide strip along the northern boundary of Tamaulipas, which bordered on the United States and into which European goods could be imported duty free for consumption in the zone. One of the goals of the zone was to discourage smuggling from the United States by making it cheaper to purchase European goods, but instead of discouraging smuggling, the zone actually encouraged it. Imported goods that were supposed to be consumed in the zone were often smuggled into the United States or other parts of Mexico. Instead of abolishing the zone as U.S. officials requested, the Mexican congress in 1870 extended it to the other states on the Rio Grande.[52]

Mexican officials also complained about revolutionary activities launched from U.S. soil against the Mexican government. Both Santiago Vidaurri and Juan Cortina used their Texas connections to defy the central Mexican government. The hotly contested presidential election of 1871 resulted in yet another term for Juárez but also led to revolts, most prominently the Plan of La Noria, championed by General Porfirio Díaz. Some of the strongest support for the revolt was in the north, and officials of the Juárez administration complained that Díaz supporters were using Texas as a base to organize reinforcements and to ship arms to revolutionaries in Mexico. Complaints that U.S. officials along the border were not enforcing the neutrality laws became a staple of border diplomacy.[53]

Indian raids along and across the border produced an endless series of diplomatic complaints and financial claims against both governments. As with banditry and smuggling, each party claimed that the perpetrators came from the other side, committed their illegal actions, and then re-crossed the border where they found a safe haven. Mexican officials were highly critical of the U.S. policy of concentrating Indians on reservations that the Mexicans viewed as little more than bases from which the Indians could raid into Mexico.[54]

Amid the litany of border problems, one positive note emerged: the signing of a treaty on 4 July 1868 establishing a joint claims commission. Claims by citizens of both countries against both governments had been accumulating since 1848; many of these claims had their origins in problems related to the border, especially Indian raids. Under the provisions of the treaty, each country would appoint one commissioner to evaluate claims; if the two commissioners could not agree, an umpire selected in advance would decide the claim. The claims commission convened in August 1869 and encountered so many cases that the deadline for completing its activities had to be extended on four different occasions. The commission worked almost a decade, evaluating 1,017 cases submitted by the United States totaling over $470 million and 998 cases submitted by Mexico for over $86 million. The commission dismissed the vast majority of claims on both sides; it approved 186 U.S. claims worth $4,125,622.20 and 167 Mexican claims for $150,498.51. The commission instructed the Mexican government to pay the balance owed the United States—$3,975,123.79—in annual installments of $300,000 beginning in January 1877. The commission ended its evaluations in November 1877, although legal actions arising out of its decisions continued until 1899.[55]

The Rise of Porfirio Díaz

While the United States worried about the situation on the international frontier, Mexico's domestic politics showed signs of growing instability. The reelection of Juárez in 1871 had split the liberal party into factions supporting Juárez, Sebastian Lerdo de Tejada, and Porfirio Díaz. Díaz revolted but attracted little popular support. The sudden death of Juárez in July 1872 put in as interim president Sebastian Lerdo de Tejada, who the following October easily won election to a full term. Díaz did not challenge Lerdo in 1872 and even accepted a political amnesty from him for his earlier revolt. When Lerdo announced that he would seek reelection in 1876, Díaz supporters issued the Plan of Tuxtepec in January 1876, calling for effective suffrage and no reelection of the president or state governors. Díaz—fearing arrest—went to Brownsville, Texas, where he raised a small force and attacked Matamoros in March. The contest for power became a three-way struggle when José María Iglesias, president of the Mexican supreme court, declared that the elections for president were fraudulent and that the presidency had devolved upon him as constitutional successor to Lerdo. Díaz defeated Lerdo and then Iglesias, both of them going into exile in the United States.[56]

When Díaz assumed the "executive power" on 28 November 1876, he also assumed responsibility for dealing with Mexico's border problems and for the payment of the first installment on the claims debt due in January 1877. The most immediate diplomatic problem, however, was the question of recognition. The fact that Díaz had come to power by revolution and that doubts were present about his hold on power dictated a cautious policy on the part of the United States. Many U.S. officials were also hopeful that they could extract various concessions from the Díaz administration in exchange for recognition. Díaz had also unnerved U.S. business interests by announcing during the course of his revolution that all contracts issued by the Lerdo government would be considered null and void. The U.S. government was uncertain about whether Díaz could pay the claims installment and equally uncertain about whether the United States should accept it, perhaps implying recognition.[57]

When the United States did not grant early recognition, the first payment on the claims debt assumed even greater importance. Díaz levied a special tax and floated a loan to acquire the needed funds, which were sent on a Mexican warship to meet the deadline of 31 January 1877 for payment in Washington. Upon receiving the payment, U.S. Secretary of State Hamilton Fish emphasized that receipt did not involve recognition of Díaz. Fish had originally given Foster discretionary authority to recognize Díaz but had revoked it when the Díaz administration accepted the U.S. view that receipt of payment did not imply recognition. Recognition then became linked to Díaz's constitutional election to the presidency; when Díaz won elections held in February 1877, the United States did not extend recognition and shifted the emphasis to a settlement of border problems as a prerequisite for recognition. When Díaz assumed power constitutionally in May, other nations began to extend recognition; by July 1877 the United States was the only nation with representation in Mexico City that had not extended recognition.[58]

With the recognition issue unresolved, the United States moved toward a unilateral resolution of border violence. The United States for some time had followed an unofficial policy of permitting its troops to cross the international boundary when in hot pursuit of bandits or Indians. This unofficial policy became an official policy on 1 June 1877 when General Edward Ord, commander of the military Department of Texas, received authorization to order border crossings at his own discretion. The Díaz administration responded by directing General Geronimo Treviño, commander of the Division of the North, to cooperate with U.S. officers but to use force to block any crossing of the boundary. Both Ord and Treviño favored cooperation rather than confrontation. Ord directed his forces to cross the boundary only when there were no Mexican troops in the area, and Treviño worked actively to coordinate his troop movements with those of Ord.[59]

Shortly after the issuance of the Ord Order, Minister Foster approached the Díaz administration with a shopping list of items to negotiate, which could easily be interpreted as a list of demands for the granting of recognition: a new commercial treaty, a general postal convention, abolition of the frontier free zone, protection for U.S. investments, the return of Indians who had fled reservations in the United States, an agreement on forced loans from U.S. citizens, the confirmation of concessions made by the Lerdo government, and an agreement on reciprocal crossing of the boundary. Minister of Foreign Relations Ignacio Vallarta gave a blunt response: the Díaz government would not seek renewed relations based on "degrading concessions."[60] Foster continued to press Vallarta for concessions with minimal results. Vallarta indicated that he was willing to link recognition to a border agreement but that recognition must precede the agreement. President Díaz dispatched more troops to the border but indicated that there would be no negotiations until after recognition. Pressure from the U.S. Congress finally led on 9 April 1878 to the extension of recognition.[61]

The settlement of the recognition issue did not bring the improvement in relations anticipated by both nations. Although there had been substantial movement toward a reciprocal crossing treaty, Díaz refused to sign such an agreement until after the Ord Order was revoked. The United States wanted to reverse the sequence: a treaty first, then revocation of the order. There were renewed signs of progress late in the Díaz administration; in February 1880 the United States announced that it was revoking the order, removing a major obstacle to negotiations. A new U.S. minister, P. H. Morgan, arrived in April 1880, replacing Foster, who was closely linked with the struggle over recognition. Díaz himself would not be able to benefit immediately from these improved relations. Honoring his no-reelection promise, Díaz turned over the presidency on 1 December 1880 to his chosen successor, General Manuel González.[62]

González was able to build on the negotiations that had taken place during the first Díaz administration. As a native of one of the northern border states, Tamaulipas, he had firsthand experience with the problems plaguing the U.S.-Mexico border. Officials in both the United States and Mexico considered the border situation to be the most pressing issue between them and believed that a reciprocal crossing agreement was crucial to controlling the border region. Once the United States had accepted the principle that crossing would be reciprocal and not unilateral, negotiations then centered on what conditions would be applied to crossings. On 29 July 1882 a reciprocal crossing agreement was signed incorporating what were basically the limitations proposed by the Mexican government. Crossings would apply only to Indian raids and would take place only if in hot pursuit. Crossings could occur only in deserted areas and were completely prohibited along the lower Rio Grande. The pursuing force was to notify local officials of its actions and break off pursuit if it lost the trail. The agreement did not bring a rapid end to Indian raids across the border, but it did promote greater military cooperation along the border and did create a positive environment for the negotiation of additional agreements. At a minimum, it spared the Mexican government the embarrassment of having U.S. forces engaging in unilateral crossings.[63]

Mexican and U.S. officials attributed part of the border difficulties to the inadequate marking of the international boundary in many areas. On the same day that the reciprocal crossing agreement was signed, Mexico and the United States signed a treaty calling for the surveying and marking of the boundary from the Pacific Ocean to the Rio Grande. Each nation would appoint a commission composed of a survey group and a group to repair old markers or place new ones.[64]

The two countries also dealt with problems arising from the portion of the boundary formed by the Rio Grande. According to the Treaty of Guadalupe Hidalgo, the boundary followed the center of the Rio Grande; in those areas with more than one channel, the boundary followed the deepest channel. The channel of the Rio Grande, however, was subject to constant change, and the existence of islands in the river further complicated jurisdiction. In 1884 a dispute arose over jurisdiction of the island of Morteritos near Roma, Texas. The settlement of the Morteritos dispute was based on the principle that would be at the heart of a treaty signed on 12 November 1884. The treaty established as the official boundary the dividing line set down by the survey made in accordance with the Treaty of Guadalupe Hidalgo; subsequent changes in the river channel were not to affect the location of the boundary. Although the treaty only made official what was already unofficially in practice, it served as a starting point for settling future disputes arising from changes in the Rio Grande into the 1960s.[65]

The U.S. Role in the Porfirian Economic Development

The return of Díaz to the presidency in 1884 marked the beginning of a tenure that would last until May 1911. For both Díaz and his successor Manuel González, the restoration of political order was a means to an end: economic development. Once peace was established, development would follow, aided by large inputs of foreign capital and technology. The United States as an economic model exerted considerable influence on Díaz, who had visited the neighboring country while

González was president. Díaz and González were also the heirs of earlier—often unsuccessful—development efforts by Benito Juárez and Sebastian Lerdo.

⊂ A number of factors made the United States the principal country in terms of foreign penetration of Mexico's economy. Geographical proximity provided the United States with a major advantage in trade and investment. The peaceful transfers of presidential power in 1880 and 1884 did much to calm fears about Mexican political stability. The U.S. rise to international industrial preeminence took place during the Díaz years. While the United States was on the rise, its two principal competitors—Britain and France—were both involved in diplomatic difficulties with Mexico going back to the intervention in the 1860s. France did not renew relations with Mexico until 1880, followed by Britain in 1884. With official relations broken, nationals of both countries were reluctant to increase their investments in Mexico.[66]

With U.S. investors confident of Mexico's material potential, more U.S. direct investment went to Mexico between 1876 and 1911 than to any other country. Although this investment made its way into all sectors of the economy, most of it went into railways and mining. Railroad entrepreneurs pressured the U.S. government to recognize Díaz and during his first administration received five concessions for over 2,500 miles of track and subsidies amounting to $32 million. Despite growing financial problems, the González administration in fiscal 1883–84 provided over a million pesos in subsidies to the Mexican Central Railway and the Mexican National Railway, the two U.S.-owned lines that were to link Mexico City with the Texas border. Many U.S. mining entrepreneurs active in the southwestern part of the United States moved into northern Mexico. Ores from U.S.-owned mines in northern Mexico were often shipped over the border to smelters in the United States. The Guggenheim interests led the way in smelting and later purchased mining properties as well, consolidating their operations in the giant American Smelting and Refining Company (ASARCO), which engaged in extensive activities on both sides of the border. Edward L. Doheny and other U.S. investors pioneered Mexican oil development in the last decade of Díaz's rule. Developers from the United States were big purchasers of land in Mexico for purposes ranging from livestock raising to rubber plantations. Although a new commercial treaty signed in 1883 never went into effect, the United States by the mid-1880s had replaced Britain as Mexico's principal trading partner.[67]

The influx of technology, capital, and people from the United States was bound to produce a response in Mexico and affect relations between the two countries. Mexicans of every political persuasion and social standing found their lives changed—or threatened with change—by U.S. penetration of the Mexican economy. The U.S. presence seemed even greater than it was because of the high-profile nature of investments (railroads, mining, oil) and the geographic concentration of investments in the central plateau and northern border states. Railroads furnished a good example of the ambivalent response that U.S. investment produced. Despite the enthusiasm for railroad construction, there was strong opposition to railroad lines running north-south. When a close political and military ally of President González sought a concession to build a railway in Sonora running to the Arizona border, he was informed that the "President has shown little disposition to grant concessions to construct railroads which touch the American frontier." Lower-class opposition took a more overt form; there were constant reports of stones being thrown or even shots being fired at trains on U.S.-owned lines.[68] More U.S. citizens were in Mexico than in any other Latin American country, and Mexico City had the largest U.S. colony—10,000 by 1910—in Latin America. Wherever they lived in Mexico, U.S. émigrés tended to live apart and tried to bring their culture with them. Fears were already expressed that U.S. culture might overwhelm Mexican culture. In U.S.-owned firms, immigrants from the United States dominated the managerial and technical positions, leaving the less-skilled, lower-paying jobs for Mexicans. Both Díaz and González made efforts to counterbalance U.S. influence by attracting European capital but enjoyed only modest success. When Mexicans felt the negative aspects of being part of the world economy, they often blamed the dominant role played by U.S. immigrants for their problems.[69]

Porfirian Decline and the Prelude to Revolution

Perhaps, the most striking feature of U.S.-Mexican relations in the last two decades of the Porfirian system was the virtual absence of major issues between the two countries until exile revolutionary activities in the United States began to trouble relations. By the early twentieth century, however, the limits of Porfirian development and the problems of U.S. economic penetration were becoming apparent. Supporters of the Díaz regime could point to major economic advances, especially in the fields of transportation and communication. For most Mexicans, however, Porfirian prosperity was a myth; Díaz's development policies led to a decline in the standard of living for the rural workers who constituted most of the workforce and population. The hazards of dependency development were driven home by the decline in demand for Mexican products in the early 1900s, followed by the spread of the Panic of 1907 from the United States to Mexico, injuring even the elite who had been benefiting most directly from Porfirian policies. The rate of U.S. investment actually increased after 1900, further highlighting the dominant role of foreign capital in the economy. The Porfirian system was suffering from political hardening of the arteries, with Díaz himself approaching eighty. While some found it impossible to imagine a Mexico without Díaz as leader, others found it hard to believe that a veteran of the Mexican-American War of 1846–48 was still leading Mexico well into the twentieth century. The reigning political elite proved incapable or unwilling to make the political adjustments demanded by its own modernization program.[70]

Díaz had started his lengthy rule in the 1870s amid major border problems and disagreements with the United States; he would leave office in similar circumstances. The southwestern United States, especially Texas, had long served as a breeding ground for revolutionary activities, as Díaz knew from personal experience in 1876. These revolutionary activities never completely stopped but ceased to be important diplomatic issues in the 1880s and 1890s. Beginning with the revolutionary activities of Ricardo and Enrique Flores Magón in 1906, exile activities along the border took a more militant turn. The Díaz administration became increasingly disenchanted with what it saw as the failure of U.S. officials to deal with the cross-border arms trade and to enforce neutrality laws. There were few restrictions on the sale of arms, and implementation of the neutrality laws had always been uneven and unpredictable. Local, state, and federal officials on the U.S. side often operated with a vague understanding of the laws involved and their various spheres of jurisdiction. As Mexico moved toward the centennial celebration of its independence in 1910, it was on the verge of its greatest social upheaval in history and the most violent phase in its relations with the United States since 1848.[71]

Relations between the two countries followed an unpredictable trajectory for much of the half century following the Mexican-American War. Expansionism by the United States remained at the center of relations during the 1850s and 1860s. Although the Gadsden Purchase of 1853 would be the last transfer of territory, Mexicans of both liberal and conservative views harbored suspicions about U.S. territorial ambitions even when the U.S. Civil War interrupted and deflated expansionist plans. Whereas Mexican liberals of the 1850s viewed various protectorate schemes as alternatives to annexation, many on the U.S. side saw them as preludes to annexation. If any of the protectorate schemes had gone into effect, the financially pressed liberals would have mortgaged important parts of Mexico, with many on the U.S. side eager to foreclose on the mortgage. From the late 1860s on, liberal governments in Mexico were in a position to pursue policies that would lead to closer economic relations with the United States; at the same time, the U.S. approach to Mexico was switching from territorial acquisition to economic penetration. U.S. involvement in the Mexican economy during the Díaz years vaguely approximated the earlier liberal view of an economic protectorate but with more volatile results; the dominant role of U.S. investors in the Mexican economy ultimately destabilized the Porfirian system, made U.S. investments a target for revolutionaries, and disturbed U.S.-Mexican relations well into the twentieth century. The dreams of desperate liberals in the 1850s had helped to lead the way to the Revolution of 1910.

2

CUBA

Sugar and Independence

Louis A. Pérez, Jr.

CUBA CROSSED THE MIDPOINT of the nineteenth century in the throes of insurrection and invasion, during a time of recurring conspiracies and of rumors of many more that never came to fruition. These were extraordinary times in the United States and Cuba: William Walker in Nicaragua, Narciso López in Cuba, and the annexationist plots and filibustering expeditions in Cuba all served to give dramatic expression to some of the most militant expansionist impulses associated with Manifest Destiny.

These were years of uncertainty and change in Cuba. Creole discontent with Spanish rule was deepening and expanding. Economic difficulties always tended to induce political dissatisfaction, and the midcentury point was no different. Spain's imposition of arbitrary taxes, discriminatory tariffs, and other measures seen to hamper Cuban trade with the United States became principal points of contention between creole producers and *peninsular* authorities. By midcentury, the United States had overtaken Spain as Cuba's principal trading partner, and Spanish interference with these expanding commercial relations was a source of continuing concern.

Annexationist stirrings peaked and subsided in both countries during the 1840s and 1850s. In the United States, expansionist elements were in political ascendancy and pursued the acquisition of Cuba with new vigor. In 1848, President James K. Polk offered Spain $100 million for Cuba, without success. Six years later President Franklin Pierce raised the offer to $130 million, also without effect. In 1854, the U.S. ministers to Spain, France, and England met in Ostend, Belgium, and publicly urged the United States to renew its offer to purchase Cuba. The Ostend Manifesto warned that if Spain refused to sell, "then, by every law, human and divine, we shall be justified in wresting it from Spain if we possess the power."[1]

These were also years of rising annexationist activity in Cuba—in part a response to the increase in expansionist rhetoric and activity in the United States. Efforts by the United States to purchase the island raised Cuban expectations, as did the Ostend Manifesto, and all served to encourage hope in Cuba that annexation was imminent. Similarly, Cubans must have been heartened by the Texas experience, when slaveowning settlers seceded from Mexico in defense of slavery and subsequently joined the Union.[2]

Annexationist activity waned on both sides of the Florida Straits at about the same time. The United States became increasingly absorbed with complicated domestic issues, many of which had direct implications for Cuba. Eventually the debate over slavery in the United States all but foreclosed any possibility that new slave territories would be admitted into the Union. All through midcentury the Cuba issue intruded into U.S. domestic politics in ways that dimmed Cuban prospects for annexation.

Conditions were changing in Cuba as well. Annexationist sentiment in Cuba was on the wane—for some it was an idea whose time would never come, and for others it was an idea whose time had passed. Many had earlier supported union with enthusiasm, and others had given their resigned support, but by the late 1850s and early 1860s nearly everyone in Cuba was having second thoughts. The Emancipation Proclamation in the United States in 1863 had a chilling effect among sugar planters, many of whom had earlier looked to annexation to the north as the way to save slavery in Cuba. They now derived some solace from their failed efforts. Those who previously advocated annexation as the best defense for slavery now opposed it—for the same reason.

In the 1860s Cuba also became absorbed in its internal problems. The rise of a new conservative ministry in Spain brought a wave of reaction on the island. The opposition press was silenced, critics were exiled, political meetings were banned, and opponents were imprisoned. Spain chose this moment to raise old taxes and introduce new ones. In March 1867, colonial authorities imposed a new series of protectionist duties on foreign products that amounted to four times the amount charged for Spanish goods—a particularly severe burden on a population now so utterly dependent on foreign imports. The United States immediately responded in kind, raising tariffs on Cuban products by 10 percent.

A new round of tax increases would have been ill conceived at any time. On this occasion it was also ill timed. Tax increases coincided with and contributed to economic dislocation. The economy plunged into a deep recession. Sugar production declined. So did prices, which by 1866 had fallen to their lowest point in almost fifteen years. In December 1866, the principal banks on the island suspended payments and brought sugar transactions to a temporary halt, adding further to the general climate of uncertainty.

Discontent spread anew, and now, without prospects of obtaining relief through reform, creoles in growing numbers were inclined to seek remedy through revolution. By 1868, ranking representatives of the eastern creole bourgeoisie, cattle barons from Camagüey and sugar planters from Oriente—Carlos Manuel de Céspedes, Salvador Cisneros Betancourt, Francisco Vicente Aguilera, Bartolomé Masó, Pedro Figueredo, and Ignacio Agramonte—were deep in conspiracy against Spain.

The First War for Independence

On 10 October 1868, the *Grito de Yara* (Ten Years War) began the revolutionary period in Cuba and brought quick calls for independence from Spain. The rebellion expanded quickly across the eastern provinces—first throughout Oriente province, then westward into neighboring Camagüey, and eventually if only briefly into the eastern regions of Las Villas province. By the early 1870s, the uprising had attracted more than 40,000 supporters.[3]

Almost from the outset, the United States took a dim view of Cuba's efforts to free itself from Spain and pursued two elements of its long-standing Cuba policy: opposition to Cuban independence and support for Spanish sovereignty. Unable to acquire Cuba from Spain, the United States adopted an alternative approach to annexation: Cuba could remain outside the United States as long as it remained within the Spanish empire. The principle of "no transfer," as it became known, occupied a position of central importance in U.S. thinking about Cuba for much of the nineteenth century. The proposition rested on a number of corollary tenets, central to which was a U.S. commitment to the defense of Spanish sovereignty against all challenges, external as well as internal. Annexation would come eventually, even inevitably, U.S. opinion was certain, as long as sovereignty over Cuba did not pass to a third party. Continued Spanish sovereignty in Cuba served U.S. interests, and it was considered a necessary if perhaps only temporary condition until such time as circumstances permitted the anticipated transfer of the island to U.S. control.

For many in the United States the withering of Spanish sovereignty in Cuba represented the last act in a drama destined to culminate in annexation of Cuba. All through the nineteenth century the United States upheld the status quo and defended the Spanish claim to rule from both internal challenge and outside threat. In 1823 Thomas Jefferson counseled President James Monroe to "oppose, with all our means, the forcible interposition of any power, either as auxiliary, stipendiary, or under any other form or pretext, and most especially [Cuba's] transfer to any power, by conquest, cession or in any other way."[4] Twenty years later, Secretary of State John Forsyth authorized the U.S. minister in Madrid to reassure Spanish authorities "that in case of any attempt, from whatever quarter, to wrest from her this portion of her territory, she may securely depend upon the military and naval resources of the United States to aid her in preserving or recovering it."[5] Secretary of State John M. Clayton stated this policy succinctly in 1849: "The news of the cession of Cuba to any foreign power would, in the United States, be the instant signal for war."[6]

This notion of colonial succession, whereby the United States would replace Spain in Cuba, was predicated on the defense of the status quo and the maintenance of Spanish rule. Until such time as Spain proved incapable of maintaining its authority over Cuba, Spanish sovereignty over the island would be supported as the most efficacious alternative to annexation. Guaranteeing Cuba's "independence against all the world *except* Spain," Thomas Jefferson reasoned, "would be nearly as valuable to us as if it were our own." The U.S. minister in Spain, John Forsyth, assured Spanish authorities in 1822 that U.S. "interests required, as there was no prospect of [Cuba] passing into our hands, that it should belong to Spain."[7]

During the Ten Years War (1868–78), the Cuban insurgent appeal for recognition of belligerency status was steadfastly denied. Recognition of the Cuban provisional government, President Ulysses S. Grant explained, was "impracticable and indefensible" and belligerent status was "unwise and premature."[8] Secretary of State Hamilton Fish was contemptuous of the intellectual and moral quality of Cubans, believing that a population consisting of Indians, Africans, and Spaniards was incapable of successful self-government. Cuban independence from Spain was undoubtedly inevitable, Fish understood, but the proposition that separation from Spain signified sovereignty for Cuba was a matter of quite another kind, and an eventuality to be resisted in Washington.[9]

Hence, through the better part of the Ten Years War, the United States sustained its commitment to Spanish sovereignty. The United States urged Spain to introduce reforms as a way to appease disgruntled Cubans and also to end the war with Spanish rule intact. At one point Grant offered to broker an agreement between Spain and the insurgents in order to guarantee colonial rule in exchange for colonial reform.

The United States may have been unwilling to negotiate annexation with the Cubans, but it was not unwilling to discuss with the Spaniards acquisition of the island for itself. Indeed, many in Washington were hopeful that the war would disrupt conditions sufficiently enough to encourage Spain to sell the island. Secretary of State Fish was optimistic that a prolonged, destructive, and costly war in Cuba would force Spain to part with the island. The Cuban insurrection, Fish commented at a cabinet meeting in April 1869, promised to expose the "madness and fatuity" of Spain's continued sovereignty; ultimately, the war would produce "a condition of affairs, a state of feeling that would compel all the civilized nations to regard the Spanish rule as an international nuisance, which must be abated, when they would all be glad that we should interpose and regulate the control of the Island."[10] At several points during the war, the Grant administration explored the possibility of purchasing the island from Spain.

By the late 1870s, however, Spanish authorities were bringing the war to a successful end. Spain had established its military superiority and was now prepared to discuss with Cubans the terms of political reconciliation. In the end Spain promised reform, and this pledge served as the basis of the peace settlement with the rebellious Cubans. By the terms of the Pact of Zanjón in February 1878, Spain committed itself to a wide range of political reforms and economic concessions. Cuban insurgents received amnesty and most laid down their arms.[11]

Linking to the U.S. Economy

The Ten Years War was something of a watershed, the great divide of Cuba's nineteenth century. After 1878, Spain remedied some of the structural sources of

Cuban discontent, with varying degrees of success. Slavery was abolished within a decade. Trade policies were modified. In 1884 and again in 1886, Spain negotiated limited reciprocal trade agreements with the United States, eliminating the differential flag system and abolishing some of the more onerous import duties and taxes. Political concessions began auspiciously enough, and early indications suggested that this time Spain would make good on its commitment to colonial reforms.

But it was also true that after 1878 some of the more pronounced contradictions of the colonial political economy became more noticeable and gave both new form and new direction to the Cuban pursuit of a separate nationality. The effects of the Ten Years War continued to influence the course of Cuban internal development and the character of Cuban international relations. The disruption of Cuban sugar production during the war had encouraged the expansion of sugar elsewhere in the world. Cane production increased in Latin America and Asia and beet sugar production expanded in Europe, together effectively challenging Cuban primacy in world markets.[12]

Crisis was not far behind. The collapse of sugar prices affected every sector of the local economy and announced calamity for Cuba. By the mid-1880s, the island was in the throes of depression. Seven of Cuba's largest trading companies failed, business houses closed, and banks collapsed. In the first three months of 1884, business failures amounted to more than $7 million.

The postwar economic crisis set the stage for a new round of U.S. expansion into the colonial economy. For nearly a century, the Cuban economy had organized around commercial relations with the United States, depending increasingly on U.S. markets, U.S. capital, and U.S. imports. This connection determined Cuban production strategies, influenced local consumption patterns, and, inevitably, shaped the character of Cuban political discourse. After 1878, U.S. participation in the Cuban economy assumed new forms and functions. Cuban producers were in desperate need of new capital and fresh sources of credit, neither of which was readily available within the existing Spanish framework. Increasingly they turned to the United States, with far-reaching and permanent consequences. Credit transactions increased in value and volume through the 1880s, and for many credit staved off bankruptcy.

But redemption was short-lived, and costly. For many, economic conditions did not improve, and increasing numbers of Cuban planters lost their property to U.S. creditors. During the last decades of the nineteenth century, U.S. ownership of property in Cuba expanded, initially through foreclosure and subsequently through additional sales by planters in distress. Many planters survived the crisis of the 1880s, but only at the cost of their traditional supremacy over production. The price of solvency was increasing displacement and eventual dependency. Across the island the Cuban grip over production slipped, announcing the demise of the creole planter class.

Developments in Cienfuegos gave the dramatic expression of the transformation overtaking colonial sugar production. "For the last ten or fifteen years," reported U.S. consul William P. Pierce in 1883, "every sugar estate in the jurisdiction of Cienfuegos has either changed ownership by reason of debt or is now encumbered with debts to an amount approximating the value of the estate." Planters had borrowed heavily, Pierce indicated, to "obtain more capital to preserve that which he had," and even usurious rates of interests had not deterred planters, for "it was the only plank on which he could hope to float through his troubles." Pierce concluded tersely and prophetically: the "planter . . . has so far failed in his calculations, and he may loose the title to his estate."[13]

The end was not long in coming. As early as 1884 Edwin Atkins and Company from Boston foreclosed on the Soledad estate owned by Juan Sarria. Atkins subsequently acquired the Carlota plantation from the Ramón de la Torriente family, the Caledonia estate from the heirs of Diego Julián Sánchez, the Guábairo property from Manuel Blanco, the Limones farm from the Vilá family, and the Brazo estate from the Torre family. From the impoverished Carlos Iznaga family Atkins purchased Vega Vieja and Manaca and obtained long-term leases on Algoba. The Santa Teresa plantation was purchased from Juan Pérez Galdos, and Veguitas was secured from José Porrúa. From the Barrallaza family Atkins bought the Vaquería property. Hard times obliged Tomás Terry to sell the San Agustín estate to Atkins. The Rosario farm, owned by Juan Sarria, was later attached to Soledad. The Atkins interests also secured long-term leases on San José, Viamones, and San Esteban.[14] Outside investors expanded all through the region. The New York banking firm Eaton Stafford and Company acquired a number of sugar estates between Cienfuegos and Trinidad. Merchant William Stewart acquired the 4,500-acre La Carolina estate. In 1892, the American Refining Company acquired the Trinidad Sugar Company. The E. & L. Ponvert brothers of Boston expanded their holdings around the 4,000-acre Hormiguero estate in Palmira, buying out or foreclosing on the smaller properties of local insolvent Cuban planters.

Through all of the nineteenth century the U.S. presence in Cuba expanded in all directions, in Havana and in the provinces, and into all sectors of the economy. Citizens from the United States took up residence in Cuba, and as their numbers increased and their roles expanded, so too did their importance. They arrived to operate the sugar mills, build the railroads, work the mines, and farm the land. In addition, U.S. capital expanded early into the local economy, including sugar plantations, mines, commerce, cattle ranches, and coffee estates. Furthermore, U.S. citizens organized trading companies and established boarding houses. They were money lenders and shippers, buyers and sellers, engineers and machinists. They arrived in growing numbers to operate and service the industrial equipment imported from the United States, especially modern steam-powered mill machinery, the steamships, and the railroads. Their control over Cuban mineral resources expanded.

Increasingly through the latter decades of the nineteenth century the Cuban economy became more integrated into the U.S. system. The economic crisis of the 1880s facilitated the process. The decline in the world price of sugar, the rise of new competitors, and the loss of old markets motivated the Cubans to seek a secure and stable place in the U.S. market on as favorable terms as possible.

Cuban dependence on U.S. markets increased markedly during the 1870s and 1880s, as beet sugar growers in France, Austria, and Germany expanded production and displaced Cuban exports from European markets. Beet sugar, accounting in 1853 for only 14 percent of total world production of sugar, had by 1884 come to represent 53 percent of the international supply. By the end of the 1880s the United States offered the only market with the capacity to absorb Cuba's expanding production. These circumstances underscored the urgency of promoting close commercial ties between the countries, with Cubans especially mindful of the heightened importance of the U.S. market.

These were also years when the Cuban economy underwent structural changes as a result of the U.S. connection. Cuba soon relied on the U.S. market to sustain its economic growth. Commercial ties with the United States loomed large over Cuban production strategies, consumption patterns, and, inevitably, political alignments. The logic of this relationship seemed at once self-evident and incontrovertible, central to almost everything else in Cuban society.

Change also assumed new forms, many of which implied discontent and disaffection. The reorientation of Cuban trade away from Spain and toward the United States released powerful forces inside Cuba. Change exposed the contradictions of colonialism and demonstrated in many and varied ways that Cuban development could no longer be contained within existing colonial structures. The Spanish strained to accommodate the changes transforming Cuba but increasingly revealed itself incapable of coping with the situation. Spain could not furnish enough shipping to handle Cuba's growing foreign trade or ensure markets for Cuba's expanding production. Nor could it provide the capital to finance the expansion or furnish the technology to support it.

The implications were not ambiguous. The importance of Spanish participation in the Cuban economy was diminishing. Spain simply lacked the material resources and technological knowledge required to continue as a major force in Cuba. Cuban development had been swift, in some sectors spectacular, and production advances and industrial innovation had transformed key sectors of the colonial economy.

Meanwhile capital from U.S. investors expanded into other sectors of the Cuban economy. In the principal Cuban cities U.S. companies operated the utilities. Control over Cuban mineral resources by U.S. companies expanded. The Bethlehem Steel Corporation organized the Juraguá Iron Company Ltd. and the Ponupo Manganese Company, both near Santiago de Cuba. The Spanish American Iron Company (Pennsylvania Steel Company) operated manganese and nickel mines near Daiquirí. The Sigua Iron Company established control over mining activities near El Caney. In one year, 1892, more than $875,000 worth of iron ore was shipped to the United States from the port of Santiago de Cuba.

These developments were themselves at once products and portents of shifting colonial relationships. In the space of one decade, the Cuban economy, revived with U.S. capital and relying on U.S. imports, reorganized itself around U.S. markets. By the early 1890s, investment in Cuba by U.S. companies was accounted at $50 million and in fact was probably far greater. By the early 1880s nearly 94 percent of Cuba's total sugar production was exported to the United States. "De facto, Cuba is already inside the commercial union of the United States," commented U.S. Consul Ramón O. Williams in 1882, and added:

> The Island is now entirely dependent upon the market of the United States, in which to sell its sugar cane products; also that the existence of the sugar plantations, the railroads used in transporting the products of the plantations in the shipping ports of the island, the export and import trades of Cuba based thereon, each including hundreds of minor industries, such as the agricultural and mechanical trades, store houses, wharves, lighters, stevedores, brokers, clerks and bankers, real estate owners, and shopkeepers of all kinds, and holders of the public debt, are now all directly related to the market of the United States to the extent of 94 percent for their employment.[15]

Growing reliance on U.S. markets had two immediate consequences. First, it intensified Cuban demands for greater local control over trade regulations and commerce. Second, it created new pressure on Madrid to negotiate a commercial treaty with the United States on terms as favorable as possible to Cuban producers and consumers.

Trade relations were in fact strengthened in 1891, when Spain and the United States negotiated the Foster-Cánovas agreement whereby Cuba received preferential access to U.S. markets in exchange for Spanish tariff concessions on U.S. imports. The effects were as dramatic as they were far-reaching. Sugar production expanded in spectacular fashion. From some 632,000 tons in 1890, output approached 976,000 tons in 1892, reaching for the first time the historic one-million-ton mark in 1894.

Not unexpectedly, the 1891 agreement further stimulated investment by U.S. companies in Cuban sugar production. In 1892, the American Refining Company obtained the Trinidad Sugar Company. A year later, a group of New York sugar merchants organized the Tuinucú Cane Sugar Company and established operations in Sancti-Spíritus. Also in 1893 and in Sancti-Spíritus, a group of New Jersey investors acquired control of the 3,000-acre Mapos estate. By far the most spectacular acquisition during these years was registered in 1893, when a New York firm headed by Benjamin Perkins and Osgood Walsh obtained control of the Constancia estate in Cienfuegos. At 60,000 acres in size, the Constancia plantation was the largest single sugar property in the world.

The long-range effects of reciprocal trade after 1891 went far beyond sugar, however. By 1893, Cuban imports from the United States accounted for almost half of total U.S. exports to Central and South America ($24 million out of $62 million). Cuban exports to the United States increased from $54 million in 1890 to $79 million in 1893—a figure approximately twelve times larger than Cuban exports to Spain. Spain on the other hand accounted only for some $10 million of Cuban exports while providing the island with $34 million of its imports.[16]

The Road to Independence

By the 1890s, dissatisfaction with colonialism had evolved into a dispute as much between Cubans as between Cubans and Spaniards. Inequity in Cuba by the 1890s had a peculiarly homegrown quality. That the sources of oppression in Cuba were more internal than external and more social than political was the premise around which armed separatism took shape. Cubans continued to speak of independence, but now they also spoke of war, as a method of redemption and a means of social change. Around the idea of *Cuba Libre* a new constituency had come together: the politically displaced, the socially dispossessed, the economically destitute—Cubans for whom armed struggle seemingly offered the only means to redress historic grievances against the colonial regime and its local defenders. Consequently, at least two obstacles stood in the way of independence: *peninsulares* and planters.

In fact, there was a third obstacle: the United States. So profoundly did *Cuba Libre* challenge the system of colonialism and so unyieldingly did it proclaim the primacy of Cuban interests that it placed separatists squarely on a collision course with the United States. The *independentista* formula was simple: Cuba for Cubans—but nearly a hundred years of U.S. policy had been dedicated to preventing that goal.

In sum, *Cuba Libre*, in its final formulation in the 1890s, could not proceed far without profoundly affecting Cuban political relations with Spain, class relations in Cuba, and Cuban economic relations with the United States. So interrelated were those elements that one could not be changed without the others being affected. The end of the colonial regime threatened nothing less than the overthrow of the structures that had at once underwritten *peninsular* rule, sustained the property and privilege of creole elites, and sanctioned participation by U.S. interests in the local economy.

Political discontent was only one aspect of colonial disaffection. In 1894, the Wilson-Gorman Tariff Act rescinded the U.S. tariff concession on Cuban exports, imposing a new duty of 40 percent ad valorem on all sugar entering the United States and thereby dismantling the cornerstone of the Foster-Cánovas reciprocal trade arrangements between Washington and Madrid. Spanish authorities responded swiftly and in kind by canceling duty concessions to U.S. imports. A full-fledged trade war seemed inevitable.

The sudden disengagement of Cuba from its prosperous but brief and privileged participation in the U.S. market had jolting consequences. Cuba lost preferential access to the only market with the capacity to absorb its expanding sugar production and insulate it from the uncertainties of world competition. The restoration of Spanish tariffs also raised the threat that the United States would retaliate by banning Cuban sugar altogether.

Profits declined immediately and production dropped. Sugar exports valued at $64 million in 1893 plummeted to $45 million in 1895 and $13 million a year later. The one-million-ton sugar harvest of 1894 collapsed to 225,000 tons in 1896.

Table 1. Select Trade Prices, 1891–1894

	1891–1893	1894
Iron bridge material	free	$48.00 per ton
Iron or steel rails	free	10.00 per ton
Iron or steel tools	free	25.00 per ton
Machinery	free	15.00–60.00 per ton

Source: Pulaski F. Hyatt to Secretary of State, 12 October 1894, Despatches from United States Consuls in Santiago de Cuba, 1799–1906, General Records of the Department of State, Record Group 59, National Archives, Washington, D.C.

The situation was no less daunting after 1894, and the sugar producers faced the grim prospect of losing preferential access to the equipment, machines, and spare parts around which the industry had organized after midcentury. In Santiago de Cuba, new duties on materials from the United States after mid-1894 raised prices on all imports (table 1). Moreover, the loss of preferential access to the U.S. market occurred simultaneously with a sudden drop in world sugar prices. For the first time in the history of Cuban sugar production, the price of sugar dropped below two cents a pound.

The impact of the crisis of 1894 went far beyond the sugar system, however. No facet of Cuban society was unaffected. Merchants, traders, and retailers who had replaced their traditional commercial ties with suppliers in Spain for dealers in the United States now faced ruin. Unemployment rose, commodity goods decreased, and prices increased. The price of imported foodstuffs soared. Government duties passed directly onto consumers, and prices reached unprecedented heights. The restoration of colonial customs duties meant that all Cubans would henceforth pay higher prices for vital food imports (table 2). As costs increased, the availability of higher-priced goods decreased. The U.S. imports dropped and shipping declined. By October 1894 half of the U.S. steamers serving Santiago de Cuba had been withdrawn from service.[17]

The Cuban sense of economic deprivation served to underscore a growing cognizance of political powerlessness. As Cuban producers and consumers grew increasingly dependent on trade with the United States, they were more and more affected by U.S. market vagaries. The well-being of the island depended more and more on forces over which Cubans had little direct control. Throughout the crisis of the 1890s, Cuban producers and consumers found themselves reduced to passive onlookers in a momentous economic drama involving the very solvency of the Cuban economy and powerless to control the vital forces governing their lives.

There was an element of familiarity to these events, and Cubans were growing weary of them. "Here we are tired of protesting against the exorbitant levies used to keep Yankee goods out of Cuba," *La Lucha* lamented in Havana. "In vain, too,

Table 2. Select Foodstuff Prices, 1893–1895

	1893–1894	1894–1895
Wheat	$ .30 per 100 kilos	$3.95 per 100 kilos
Flour	1.00 per 100 kilos	4.75 per 100 kilos
Corn	.25 per 100 kilos	3.95 per 100 kilos
Meal	.25 per 100 kilos	4.75 per 100 kilos

Source: Ramon O. Williams to Edwin F. Uhl, 5 January 1895, Despatches from U.S. Consuls in Havana, 1783–1906, General Records of the Department of State, Record Group 59, National Archives, Washington, D.C.

have been our efforts against the imposition of prohibitive duties on American goods. We have not been heard in Madrid; because we are miserable and long suffering colonists, our clamors are undeserving of the attention of those who govern and misgovern."[18]

Once again the question of Cuba's status and the nature of its relationship with Spain resurfaced as topics of political debate and public discussion. An enormous sense of uncertainty and uneasiness settled over the island. "The residents and commercial interests here," the U.S. consul in Santiago de Cuba reported in late 1894, "are protesting loud and strong against being thus summarily cut off from their natural commercial allies, and this action on the part of the home government adds greatly to the feeling of unrest that pervades all classes."[19] Prosperity required the expansion of trade, and that in turn required the reduction of Spanish control. The brief cycle of prosperity resulting from close economic ties with the United States made the prospect of returning to the regimen of Spanish exclusivity as inconceivable as it was inadmissible.

The new separatist war, the "Grito de Baire," began on 24 February 1895, in much the same fashion as others before it had: localized skirmishes, mostly in the remote mountains of eastern Cuba, seemed too distant to cause planters and politicians in western Cuba undue concern. But in early summer matters assumed a sudden gravity. What began as an affair of local proportions soon assumed a national scope. Insurgent armies marched out of the eastern mountains into the rich cattle-grazing ranges of Camagüey in the summer, through the fertile sugar lands of Matanzas and Havana in the autumn, and into the lush tobacco fields of Pinar del Río by winter. In the course of ten months, the insurrection reached regions of Cuba never before disturbed by the armed stirrings of nationality.

The creole elite held few illusions after 1896. For decades local property owners had clung to the colonial regime for protection, and by the final years of the nineteenth century, Spain was on the verge of defaulting on its sole raison d'être for Cuba. Members of the beleaguered colonial bourgeoisie contemplated their impending extinction with deepening despair. Growing more certain that Spain's hold over Cuba was slipping, they were now prepared to sacrifice traditional colonial relationships for an alternative source of protection and patronage. They were finally confronted by what they had most feared through the nineteenth century—a successful populist uprising—and they needed assistance quickly.

Only U.S. intervention, many concluded, could end the insurrectionary challenge and redeem the beleaguered social order. In June 1896, nearly a hundred planters, lawyers, merchants, and manufacturers petitioned President Grover Cleveland for U.S. intervention in the conflict. "We cannot," the petitioners wrote, "express our opinion openly and formally, for he who should dare, whilst living in Cuba, to protest against Spain, would, undoubtedly, be made a victim, both in his person and his property, to the most ferocious persecution at the hands of the government." Spain, the petition continued, could offer Cuba nothing for the future except continued destruction and ruin. Nor did property owners find comfort at the thought of independence. If continued Spanish rule threatened to result in ruin, independence promised to lead to havoc. "Can there be no intermediate solution?" the petitioners asked. Without confidence in Spain, and uncertain about the future under Cuban rule, property owners asked Washington to intercede in their behalf: "We would ask that the party responsible to us should be the United States. In them we have confidence, and in them only."[20] "The worst thing that could happen to Cuba," wrote another planter, "would be independence." Cubans, he added, "cannot bring a firm and stable government to the island."[21] In early 1897, a U.S. correspondent in Havana reported that planters, merchants, and businessmen had concluded that Cuba was lost to Spain and that they hoped for U.S. intervention and, ultimately, U.S. annexation of the island.[22] Later that year, William H. Calhoun, a special agent dispatched to Cuba by the State Department to report on local conditions, commented that "Cuban planters and Spanish property holders are now satisfied that the island must soon slip from Spain's grasp, and would welcome immediate American intervention."[23]

From the outset of the war, the Cleveland administration upheld longstanding U.S. policy approaches to Cuba: opposition to Cuban independence and support of Spanish sovereignty. Its reasoning was familiar. Cuban independence, the administration feared, would result in political instability, social conflict, and economic chaos. The participation of large numbers of people of color in the insurrection, in positions of political prominence, and in possession of arms generated further reasons to fear the sudden end of Spanish rule. Even the "most devoted friend of Cuba" and the "most enthusiastic advocate of popular government," Secretary of State Richard B. Olney insisted, could not look at developments in Cuba "except with the gravest apprehension." Olney continued:

> There are only too strong reasons to fear that, once Spain were withdrawn
> from the island, the sole bond of union between the different factions of
> the insurgents would disappear; that a war of races would be precipitated,
> all the more sanguinary for the discipline and experience acquired during
> the insurrection, and that, even if there were to be temporary peace, it

could only be through the establishment of a white and black republic, which, even if agreeing at the outset upon a division of the island between them, would be enemies from the start, and would never rest until the one had been completely vanquished and subdued by the other.[24]

The United States affirmed its support for Spanish sovereignty. As early as 1895 Cleveland demanded adherence to U.S. neutrality laws and vigorously pursued their enforcement. Washington also cooperated with Spain to combat Cuban filibustering expeditions organized from the United States. Between 1895 and 1896, U.S. authorities successfully intercepted more than half the Cuban expeditions fitted in the United States and vigorously prosecuted offenders. Of the seventy expeditions organized in the United States during the entire war, only a third reached Cuba.[25]

But the United States also concluded early that Spain was doomed to failure. "While the insurrectionary forces to be dealt with are more formidable than ever before," Secretary of State Olney wrote in September 1895, "the ability of Spain to cope with them has visibly and greatly decreased. She is straining every nerve to stamp out the insurrection within the next few months. For what obvious reason? Because she is almost at the end of her resources." Olney concluded: "Spain cannot possibly succeed."[26]

The inability of Spain to subdue the insurrection convinced the Cleveland administration that only sweeping reforms in Cuba, including autonomy, could bring the rebellion to an end while preserving Spanish sovereignty. Only a political solution could preserve the colonial status quo, albeit in modified form.

In the United States, support of Spanish sovereignty was based on the expectation that Spain would establish its authority over the rebellious colony—if not immediately through military success, then eventually by way of political concessions. Washington was convinced that autonomy would serve both to placate dissident Cubans and discredit the separatist leaders who spurned the Spanish offer. In either case the insurrection would come with Spanish sovereignty restored and preserved.

An American War

The passage of a year changed everything. In 1897 the Republican administration of William McKinley pressed colonial reforms with new vigor, and a new Liberal ministry in Madrid under Praxedes Mateo Sagasta ceased to oppose reforms—both for the same reasons. The war had stalled into a campaign of attrition—one that Spain could not possibly win. The Spanish army was on the defensive and confined to the principal cities; the Cuban army was on the offensive and controlled the countryside. The economies of both Cuba and Spain were approaching collapse.

In the autumn of 1897, in part due to U.S. pressure, in part as a response to deteriorating conditions, the Spanish Liberal ministry undertook a series of far-reaching reforms. In October, Madrid appointed moderate governor general Ramón Blanco. Amnesty was issued and political prisoners were released. In December, Spain announced a new autonomist constitution, and then it installed a liberal creole government on 1 January 1898.

Colonial reforms doomed Spanish rule in Cuba. For the defenders of *Cuba Española* the liberal reforms assumed fully the proportions of treason. The loyalists denounced the creole autonomist government, insisting that it was only opening a back door to power for subversives. Radicals would quickly overrun moderates, revolution would overtake reform, and autonomy would become independence. "All classes of the Spanish citizens," U.S. Consul Fitzhugh Lee reported in late 1897, "are violently opposed to real or genuine autonomy because it would throw the control of the island into the hands of the Cubans and rather than that, they would prefer annexation to the United States or some form of an American protectorate."[27]

The establishment of a liberal government convinced loyalists, *peninsulares* and creoles alike, that Spain had lost the will to defend its sovereignty in Cuba. Many detected in these developments evidence that Spain was preparing to abandon the island. The more thoughtful among peninsulares and creoles understood, too, that the new autonomist government lacked the means to wage war and was without authority to make peace. The establishment of a government of creole moderates dealt the final body blows to conservative resolve in Cuba. Developments in late 1897 and early 1898 undermined the morale of the only forces in Cuba who, apart from the insurgents, still retained the loyalty and will to win.

Rallies and mass meetings across the island denounced the new autonomist government. Appeals for U.S. intervention increased. In November 1897, the U.S. vice consul in Matanzas reported that "nearly all Spaniards, businessmen, and property holders in this province wish and pray for annexation to the United States."[28] Fitzhugh Lee reported similarly from Havana. "A large majority of the Spanish subjects," he wrote in November 1897, "who have commercial and business interests and own property here will not accept Autonomy, but prefer annexation to the United States, rather than an independent republic or genuine autonomy under the Spanish flag."[29]

By the end of the year sentiment for U.S. intervention had become public. In December 1897, a statement published in Havana and signed by business people and property owners claiming to represent 80 percent of the island's wealth denounced the autonomist regime.[30] During that same month, a meeting of property owners in Cienfuegos concluded with a resolution urging President McKinley to establish a protectorate over Cuba. In February 1898, leading *peninsulares* established a formal commission for the purpose of securing U.S. assistance. "The Mother country cannot protect us," one spokesman insisted. "Blanco will not protect us. If left to the insurgents our property is lost. Therefore, we want the United States to save us."[31]

Reforms that were too much for loyalists were too little for separatists. Insurgent Cubans denounced autonomy and rejected outright accommodation with

Spain based on anything less than complete independence. "It is the firm resolution of the army and people of Cuba," vowed General Máximo Gómez, "who have shed so much blood in order to conquer their independence, not to falter in their just cause until triumph or death crowns their efforts."[32] Two weeks later, Gómez reiterated the Cuban position: "We no longer ask concessions. . . . Even were Spain's proposals bona fide, nothing could tempt us to treat with her. We are for liberty, not for Spanish reforms."[33]

Rather than conciliating Cubans, the reforms actually made them more intransigent. Separatist morale soared. "Spain's offer of autonomy is a sign of her weakening," Provisional President Bartolomé Masó proclaimed.[34] General Calixto García agreed: "I regard autonomy only as a sign of Spain's weakening power and an indication that the end is not far off."[35]

Reforms had failed. Spain had made as a last resort the ultimate concession to preserve its empire, but its sovereignty was coming to an end. New optimism lifted insurgent morale to an all-time high. Never before had separatists been so certain of triumph as they were in early 1898. Preparations for the last desperate battles began. In eastern Cuba General Calixto García prepared to lay siege to Santiago de Cuba. In the western zones, insurgent commanders began to encircle the larger inland provincial cities. Máximo Gómez now wrote confidently about preparations for the final assault against Spanish strongholds. With "cannons and a great deal of dynamite," Gómez predicted that "we can expel them by fire and steel from the towns."[36]

The United States also understood that the failure of reforms ended hopes that Madrid would reestablish sovereignty over the island. "Spain will lose Cuba," Secretary of State John Sherman concluded ruefully. "That seems to me to be certain. She cannot continue the struggle."[37] Assistant Secretary of State William R. Day concurred. "The Spanish Government," he wrote in March, "seems unable to conquer the insurgents."[38] In a confidential memorandum, Day went further:

> Today the strength of the Cubans [is] nearly double . . . and [they] occupy
> and control virtually all the territory outside the heavily garrisoned coast
> cities and a few interior towns. There are no active operations by the Span-
> iards. . . . The eastern provinces are admittedly "Free Cuba." In view of
> these statements alone, it is now evident that Spain's struggle in Cuba has
> become absolutely hopeless. . . . Spain is exhausted financially and physi-
> cally, while the Cubans are stronger.[39]

Against the landscape created by the receding tide of Spanish sovereignty, Washington confronted in Cuba that which had been anathema to all U.S. policymakers since Jefferson—the specter of Cuban independence. The implications of the "no transfer" policy were now carried to their logical conclusion. Because the United States could not permit Spain to transfer sovereignty over Cuba to another power, it also could not permit Spain to cede sovereignty to Cubans.

A new urgency characterized U.S. diplomacy. The United States increased pressure on Spain. On 27 March, Washington delivered a three-part ultimatum to Madrid: an armistice until 5 October, an end to resettlement programs and permission to distribute U.S. relief supplies, and the participation of President McKinley as mediator to negotiate an end to the rebellion. In return, the United States promised to use its "friendly offices to get insurgents to accept the plan."[40]

After another ten days of equivocation and frantic negotiations, Spain capitulated. On 5 April, the Queen Regent proclaimed a unilateral cease-fire in Cuba, effective immediately and to last through October. On 10 April, Washington received Spain's formal acceptance of the essential provisions of McKinley's 27 March ultimatum.[41] That same day in Havana, Governor General Blanco ordered all Spanish forces to halt operations.[42]

McKinley had scored a victory on all fronts except one; he had failed to make good on the U.S. part of the 27 March ultimatum: to use his "friendly offices to get insurgents to accept the plan." Indeed, the collapse of the U.S. proposal was due less to Spanish equivocation than to the U.S. inability to obtain Cuban acquiescence to the cease-fire. Such an arrangement, the insurgent leaders insisted, could only benefit Spain and have calamitous consequences on the Cuban war effort. Separatist army chieftains denounced the cease-fire and ordered the insurgent forces to continue operations. "They have to be hit hard and at the head, day and night," General Calixto García exhorted his troops. "In order to suspend hostilities, an agreement is necessary with our Government and this will have to be based on independence." "More than ever before," Máximo Gómez proclaimed, "the war must continue in full force."[43]

The Cuban rejection of the Spanish cease-fire offer ended all U.S. hopes that a dreaded summer campaign in 1898 could be averted. Spain had attached only one condition to its agreement: that Cubans observe the cease-fire. Spain now had no choice but to resume field operations and face inevitable military defeat.

In the early spring, events were being shaped by forces beyond the control of the United States and Spain: Cubans were determining the course. Once Spain refused to transfer sovereignty over Cuba to the United States, and once Cubans rejected the continuation of Spanish sovereignty in any form, U.S. politicians faced two prospects: independence or intervention.

The Cuban revolution threatened more than the propriety of colonial rule or property relations in the colonial regime. It also challenged the expectation of colonial succession, for in ending Spanish sovereignty in 1898, Cubans also endangered the U.S. claim of sovereignty. Aquisition of Cuba by the United States was always envisaged as an act of colonial continuity, formally transferred and legitimately ceded by Spain to the United States—an assumption of sovereignty over a territory presumed incapable of a separate nationhood.

The success of the Cuban rebellion changed all this. The United States was as alarmed at the prospect of a Cuban victory as it was exasperated at Spain's inability to end the war. Neither repression nor concession had worked. Spanish sovereignty had slipped beyond recovery. If Washington did not act, that sovereignty would be lost also to the United States.

So it was that in April 1898 President William McKinley requested from Congress the authority to intervene militarily in Cuba: to declare war against Spain, but in fact also against Cubans. The president's war message provided portents of policy: no mention of Cuban independence, nothing about recognition of the Cuban provisional government, not a hint of sympathy for *Cuba Libre,* nowhere even an allusion to the renunciation of territorial aggrandizement. The U.S. purpose in Cuba, McKinley emphasized in his war message, consisted of a "forcible intervention . . . as a neutral to stop the war." McKinley explained: "The forcible intervention of the United States . . . involves . . . hostile constraint upon both the parties to the contest."[44] The United States intended to neutralize both Spaniards and Cubans and establish its own superiority over the island. Administration opponents in Congress made repeated attempts to recognize the provisional Cuban republic, and by mid-April McKinley yielded to compromise. Congress agreed to forego recognition in exchange for the president's acceptance of a disclaimer. Article IV of the congressional resolution, the Teller Amendment, specified that the United States "hereby disclaims any disposition of intention to exercise sovereignty, jurisdiction, or control over said island except for pacification thereof, and asserts its determination, when that is accomplished, to leave the government and control of the island to its people."[45]

Restricted Independence

The U.S. intervention in 1898 changed everything. It was meant to do so. A Cuban war of liberation was transformed into a U.S. war of conquest. And it was the victory to which the United States first laid claim, and from which much else would flow. The Cuban war for national liberation was transfigured into the "Spanish-American War," nomenclature that in more than symbolic terms served to ignore Cuban participation and announced the next series of developments. The U.S. forces had not arrived as allies of Cubans or as agents of Cuban independence. They had gone to war, as they always said they would, to prevent the transfer of sovereignty to a third party.

The exclusion of the Cubans began as soon as the U.S. troops arrived. The U.S. commanders moved insurgent forces behind front lines to play support roles. Cuban commanders were routinely ignored. Negotiations for the surrender of Santiago de Cuba in July were conducted without Cuban participation, and by the terms of the surrender Cubans were barred from entering the city. Astonished Cuban commander Calixto García asked U.S. army chieftain William R. Shafter for clarification of the agreement. He learned that Santiago de Cuba was now considered a territory conquered by the United States and "part of the Union." The decision to deny Cubans access to the city, General Shafter explained publicly, was based on the fear that insurgents could not be restrained from attacking unarmed Spanish soldiers, abusing women, and plundering the city.[46]

Indignation swept across Cuban camps. General García denounced the proposition that Santiago de Cuba was "part of the Union." "I will never accept," the

Cuban commander vowed, "that our country be considered as conquered territory."[47] García bristled at the charge that the Cuban army could not be trusted to enter Santiago de Cuba. "Allow me to protest against even a shadow of such an idea," García stated to Shafter; "we are not savages who ignore the principles of civilized warfare. We respect too much our cause to stain it with barbarity and cowardice."[48]

These developments gave early form to the fundamental cross purposes in which Cuban and U.S. leaders found themselves in 1898. By war's end the estrangement was all but complete. Insurgent commanders became sullen and noncooperative. Some withdrew from joint operations and broke off relations with U.S. forces. Calixto García resigned, proclaiming that he was "no longer disposed to continue obeying the orders and cooperating with the plans of the American Army" and warning his comrades against relinquishing any authority to the "army of the intervention."[49]

Not only the surrender negotiations for Santiago de Cuba in July but also the terms of the peace protocol in August were negotiated without Cuban participation. So too was the peace treaty concluded in Paris later that autumn.

That treaty, the Treaty of Paris, formally passed sovereignty to the United States in 1898. The U.S. military occupation began January 1899 and ended in May 1902. For three and a half years, Cuba was administered as an occupied territory by a military government. These were years of reconstruction and revival, during which a moribund economy began to emerge from the paralysis of more than three years of war. Production resumed, plantations revived, and employment increased. Sanitary programs improved living conditions. Public-works programs aided in this process, as highway construction, building projects, and transportation facilities stimulated further Cuban revival.

The U.S. occupation also attended to the matter of Cuba's future relations with the United States. In January 1901, Secretary of State Elihu Root outlined four provisions he deemed essential to U.S. interests. First, "in transferring the control of Cuba to the Government established under the new constitution the United States reserved and retains the right to intervention for the preservation of Cuban independence and the maintenance of a stable Government adequately protecting life, property and individual liberty." Second, "no Government organized under the constitution shall be deemed to have authority to enter into any treaty or engagement with any foreign power which may tend to impair or interfere with the independence of Cuba." Root also insisted that to perform "such duties as may devolve upon her under the foregoing provisions and for her own defense," the United States "may acquire and hold the title to land, and maintain naval stations at certain specified points." Last, he stated that "all the acts of the Military Government, and all rights acquired thereunder, shall be valid and be maintained and protected."[50]

These were the essential features of the Platt Amendment, enacted into law by the U.S. Congress in February 1901. An adequate if imperfect substitute for annexation, it transformed Cuban sovereignty into an extension of the U.S. national system. Restrictions imposed upon the conduct of foreign relations, specifically the denial of treaty authority and debt restrictions, as well as the prohibition against the cession of national territory, were designed to minimize Cuban international entanglement.[51]

News of the Platt Amendment provoked widespread protest in Cuba. Anti-U.S. demonstrations were held across the island. Former insurgent chieftains alluded menacingly to the necessity of returning to the field of armed struggle to vindicate the *independentista* ideal. Municipal councils, civic and community organizations, and veterans associations cabled protests to U.S. authorities in Havana and Washington. Indeed, apprehensions increased sufficiently to prompt U.S. authorities to arrange for the Key West naval squadron to pay a courtesy call to the island.

In April 1901 Cuban misgivings were somewhat calmed when a Cuban commission visited Washington to receive personal assurances from President McKinley that the Platt Amendment would never be used to limit or in any other way restrict Cuban sovereignty. In June 1901 a still bitterly divided Cuban commission voted to accept the Platt Amendment.

The Platt Amendment met all traditional U.S. demands. It reconciled longstanding U.S. security and commercial interests in the region with the Teller Amendment. Something of a substitute for direct and formal annexation, it served to transform the substance of Cuban sovereignty into an extension of the U.S. national system. The restrictions imposed on the Cuban conduct of foreign relations, specifically the denial of treaty authority and debt restrictions, as well as the prohibition against the cession of national territory to foreign powers, were designed to minimize Cuban international entanglement.

Cuba had indeed obtained its independence, in a manner of speaking, or at least it had obtained the appearance of independence. In fact, Cuba obtained self-government without self-determination and independence without sovereignty. This was not what Cuban independentistas set out to achieve when they launched the redemptive revolution of 1895. Also, the fact that the U.S. intervention thwarted the independence project carried forward to another time when Cubans would confront the United States in pursuit of self-determination and national sovereignty.

The extensive destruction of property during the war and U.S. occupation after the war inaugurated a new and decisive phase in U.S. economic penetration of the island. Cuban property owners emerged from the war in debt, with neither capital nor credit. The total urban indebtedness of some $100 million represented more than three-quarters of Cuba's declared urban property value of $139 million. A similar situation existed for rural real estate, the total value of which was set at some $185 million with a mortgage indebtedness of $107 million.

Entrepreneurs from the United States swarmed to Cuba after the war in search of defunct plantations, ruined farms, and abandoned estates. Opportunities were manifest. "Nowhere else in the world," exulted one U.S. investor, "are there such chances for success for the man of moderate means, as well as for the capitalist, as Cuba offers today. . . . I advise the capitalist to invest in Cuba, and seriously suggest to the young and ambitious man to go to Cuba and cast his fortune with those of the island." "It is simply a poor man's paradise and the rich man's mecca," proclaimed the *Commercial and Financial World*.[52] "Land, at this writing," two former U.S. consular agents reported in 1898, "can be bought in unlimited quantities at from one-half to one-twentieth of its value before the insurrection. For the ordinarily prudent man with some capital, who is willing to work, the island has opportunities for success and wealth through safe and profitable investments, the equal of which can be found in no other place."[53]

Opportunists from the United States looked upon Cuba as a place of new possibilities. The vision was irresistible, and the timing was propitious: Cuba offered a new frontier at about the time Frederick Jackson Turner was lamenting the passing of the old one. It was described variously as "virgin land" and a "new California."[54] "Americans . . . have on their southern seaboard another California," observed traveler Isaac N. Ford as early as 1892. "Indeed," exulted Leonard Wood in 1901, "the island may be called a brand new country."[55] Cuba offered opportunity in the form of cheap land and new hope to farmers, miners, ranchers, and small investors, precisely the kind of people who had settled the last U.S. frontier.

The expulsion of Spain in 1899 opened the island to new forms of contact with U.S. interests and deepened the impact of the old forms. Gradually the United States became reconciled to control as a substitute for possession, and it was thus arranged in the Cuban constitution of 1901 and later by formal treaty.

Arriving by the thousands, the U.S. opportunists formed a new generation of self-styled pioneers who were consciously reenacting the drama of taming the wilderness, only this time in the tropics. They arrived as carpetbaggers and gamblers, brokers and vendors, homesteaders and settlers. Mostly they were small farmers and colonists, drawn to Cuba by the availability of land and the hope that tariff concessions on Cuban agricultural exports would create new business opportunities for industrious and enterprising settlers. They would grow citrus fruits, pineapples, and vegetables for export to U.S. markets.

In the years immediately following the end of the war, U.S. citizens of all social types swept across Cuba with projects and schemes of all kinds. They looked upon Cuba as a place to make their fortunes. The island filled with U.S. agricultural colonists as thousands of homesteaders from the United States established new communities, and across the island appeared new Cuban towns with such improbable names as McKinley, Ocean Beach, Riverside, Garden City, Palm City, Omaja (Ohaha), and Bartle.

To no lesser degree than the powerful capitalists and large corporations, they displaced Cubans and quickly claimed possession of countless tens of thousands of acres of farmland and sugar estates that were either defunct or in default. They were preceded by land speculators and real estate agents, who overran war-torn Cuba looking for bargains and cheap public land and resold tracts in subdivisions to U.S. colonists.

Control by U.S. companies over sugar production expanded during and immediately after the occupation. As early as 1899, R. B. Hawley organized the Cuban-American Sugar Company and acquired possession of the 7,000-acre Tinguaro estate in Matanzas and the Merceditas mill in Pinar del Río. The same year, Cuban-American organized the Chaparra sugar mill around 70,000 acres of land in Puerto Padre. In 1899 a group of U.S. investors acquired the 80,000-acre Francisco estate in southern Camagüey province. The American Sugar Company acquired damaged estates in Matanzas. In 1901 the Nipe Bay Company, a subsidiary of the United Fruit Company, acquired title to 40,000 acres of land also in the region of Puerto Padre. Later that year, United Fruit purchased 200,000 acres near Banes, a vast tract of land that included scores of partially destroyed and defunct estates. Within a decade of independence, almost the entire Oriente north coast, from Baracoa on the east to Manatí on the west, had passed into control by U.S. companies.

Also during these years the Cuba Company completed the construction of the Cuba Railway through the eastern end of the island, acquiring in the process some 50,000 acres of land for rail stations, construction sites, towns, and depots and a right of way some 350 miles long. The Cuban Central Railway purchased the Caracas estate in Cienfuegos from Tomás Terry. The Cape Cruz Company acquired the estates of Aguda Grande, Limoncito, and San Celestino, a total of 16,000 acres near Manzanillo. Joseph Rigney, an investment partner with United Fruit, acquired the San Juan and San Joaquín estates and the damaged Teresa Mill, all in the region around Manzanillo.[56]

Control by U.S. companies over mining also expanded. The principal mineral deposits were located in Oriente and included iron, manganese, copper, and lead, distributed in two principal regions in the north and south. Mines in the south, located in the districts of El Caney, Firmeza, Daiquirí, Ponupo, El Cristo, and Bayamo, were controlled by the Juraguá Iron Company (Pennsylvania Steel Company and Bethlehem Iron Company), the Spanish-American Iron Company, the Sigua Iron Company, the Eastern Steel Company, the Cuban Steel Ore Company, and the Ponupo Manganese Company. The principal mining zone in the north was located in Mayarí and was owned almost entirely by the Spanish-American Iron Company. Copper deposits around El Cobre were worked by the San José Copper Mining Company. Other copper deposits in Puerto Príncipe, Santa Clara, and Matanzas were owned by the Cuban Copper Company. Between 1899 and 1902, the military government issued a total of 218 concessions, 134 of which were located in Oriente province. The 21 claims of the Juraguá Iron Company in El Caney totaled as estimated 1,140 acres of land. In 1905 the Spanish-American Iron Company acquired 28,000 acres in Mayarí. Spanish American Iron, the largest holder of iron property, owned a total of 134,569 acres of surface options and an additional 150,986 acres of mining rights. In all, nearly 500,000 acres were distributed among approximately 2,000 mine operations.[57]

Capital from U.S. investors also moved into transportation. The Santiago Railroad Company, the Cuba Railway, the Cuban Eastern Railway, and the Guantánamo Railroad were only the most prominent rail lines owned by U.S. investors.

Electric transportation on the island was also dominated by capital from U.S. companies. The Havana Electric Railway Company, a New Jersey corporation, established control of the capital's transportation system during the occupation. The Havana Central linked the capital to Marianao and Mariel.[58]

Foreign capital also controlled the utilities. The Spanish American Light and Power Company of New York provided gas service to major Cuban cities. Electricity was controlled by two U.S. corporations, Havana Central and Havana Electric. In Caibarién, electrical power was provided by the Caibarién Electrical Company, owned by P. B. Anderson. Contracting companies from the United States established branch offices in Havana and competed for government projects. The Havana Subway Company acquired monopoly rights to install underground cables and electrical wires. In addition, U.S. capital controlled telephone service through Red *Telefónica de La Habana*, which ultimately was absorbed by the Cuba Telegraph and Telephone Company. Various U.S. investors controlled the Cárdenas City Water Works as well as the Cárdenas Railway and Terminal Company. The Havana Electric Railway Company provided trolley service in the capital.

Employing mostly U.S. builders, contractors from the United States constructed the public buildings, roads, and bridges of the early republic. Engineering firms from the United States constructed the major port works in Havana and other large coastal cities. The T. L. Huston Contracting Company secured the government contract for dredging the principal ports and constructing concrete and pile wharves in Havana and Santiago de Cuba. The Huston Company also received the concession to build the highway network from Havana west to Pinar del Río. A subsidiary firm, the Huston Concrete Company, obtained the contract for constructing a new sewer system in Havana. The Snare and Triest Company of New York constructed steel bridges, drawbridges, and a fixed bridge for several railroad lines, several lighthouses along the south coast, and a power plant outside Havana. The Tropical Engineering and Construction Company constructed the water supply system of Havana and several power plants in Matanzas.

Some three-quarters of the cattle ranches with an estimated value of $30 million were owned by U.S. investors, principally the Lykes brothers. Sisal farms were owned by International Harvester and banana lands by United Fruit, Standard Fruit, and DeGeorgio Fruit. The Harris Brothers Company provided the government with its principal source of stationery, office supplies, and paper products. The Havana Advertising Company controlled the key advertising contracts and billboards.

In 1903, Cuba and the United States signed three treaties that consummated more than fifty years of relations and inaugurated a new era in Cuba-U.S. ties. The Permanent Treaty of 1903 gave the Platt Amendment formal and binding form. What had been originally an appendix to the Cuban Constitution of 1901 was given legality in the context of international law. The Permanent Treaty guaranteed the United States an institutional presence in Cuban internal affairs, and until its abrogation in 1934 it served as the basis of Cuba-U.S. relations.

The two countries also signed a Reciprocity Treaty. Reciprocity revived economic ties through a tariff schedule that conceded to Cuban agricultural exports a 20 percent reduction in duties. In return, Cuba granted the United States a 20 percent concession on most items, increased to 24, 30, and 40 percent for selected categories. Most imports in the 20 percent category were products that had previously dominated the Cuban market, and hence a tariff reduction was not expected to affect trade. The higher reductions were for goods for which U.S. officials anticipated competition either from other Western Hemisphere nations or from European producers, and these included glassware, earthenware and stoneware, cotton and linen goods, boots and shoes, chemicals, paper, dyes, soap, rice, butter, preserved fish and fruits, canned vegetables, and perfumes.

Reciprocity accelerated the integration of the Cuban economy into the U.S. system. The elimination of Spanish colonial trade restrictions, most notably the abolition of discriminatory tariffs and differential flag duties, immediately opened the Cuban economy to penetration by U.S. companies. In the end, reciprocity discouraged Cuban diversification and perpetuated local reliance on imported foodstuffs. Preferential access to U.S. markets deepened Cuban dependency on sugar production and increased control by U.S. firms over this strategic sector of the economy. As early as 1902, 55 of a total of 223 mills were owned by U.S. entrepreneurs, accounting for 40 percent of Cuban sugar production. By the mid-1920s, of the total 184 mills, U.S. companies owned 41, producing 63 percent of the total crop.[59]

The reduction of Cuban duties opened the island to U.S. imports on highly favorable terms. The privileged access granted to U.S. products created a wholly inauspicious climate for Cuban investment. Even before 1903, the dearth of capital and depressed economic conditions combined to thwart the development of local industry. After reciprocity, prospects for local enterprise diminished further. The U.S. manufacturers saturated the Cuban market and hindered the development of local competition. Reciprocity not only deterred new industry, it also had a deleterious effect on existing enterprises. Many could not compete with U.S. manufactures. Some cut production, other reduced operations, and still others failed.

Finally, in 1903 Cuba and the United States also signed a treaty establishing a naval station at Guantánamo Bay. This treaty executed the clause in the Platt Amendment whereby Cuba leased to the United States land in Bahía Honda and Guantánamo for coaling and naval stations. The United States later exchanged the leasing rights in Bahia Honda for an enlarged territory in Guantánamo.

The three treaties of 1903 consolidated the political, economic, and strategic position of the United States not only in Cuba but also in the Caribbean region in general. Washington had closed off the principal points of entry into and out of the Caribbean. By 1903, the Caribbean had become the American Mediterranean.

3

COLOMBIA

Troubled Friendship

Helen Delpar

RELATIONS BETWEEN COLOMBIA AND the United States from 1850 to 1903 are marked by contradictions. Despite Colombia's closeness to the United States, commerce between the two countries remained limited during the period, and Colombia's political turmoil and slow economic growth made it an uninviting field for foreign investment. At the same time, however, the United States was intensely concerned with developments on the isthmus of Panama, then a Colombian province, for several reasons. The Bidlack-Mallarino Treaty (1846) imposed on the United States unique rights and responsibilities with respect to Panama, including a pledge to keep open any transit route that might be constructed across the isthmus. Capitalists from the United States built the Panama Railroad, which after its inauguration in 1855 served as the principal mode of transporting freight and passengers across the isthmus, and there was always a sizable contingent of U.S. citizens living there as transients or permanent residents. As the century progressed, the United States increasingly viewed Panama as its preserve, possibly as a site for an inter-oceanic canal, but at all events as a place where the intrusion of other nations—even that of Colombia, whose sovereignty the United States was bound by the Bidlack-Mallarino Treaty to uphold—was resisted. Colombian nationalism was outraged by U.S. pretensions in Panama, yet the isthmus was marginal to the political and economic life of the country. As a result, when U.S. officials aided Panamanian secessionists in detaching the isthmus from Colombia in 1903 to hasten construction of a canal, Colombia protested vehemently but did not sever diplomatic relations and soon adopted a policy of accommodation.

The contemporary emphasis on the Panamanian dimension of U.S.-Colombian relations from 1850 to 1903 is reflected in modern historiographical treatment of the subject. There is an extensive literature in both Spanish and English relating to U.S. policy in Panama, especially the role of the United States in isthmian independence. However, only two English-language works address other aspects of the U.S.-Colombian relationship, and only as part of general surveys: E. Taylor Parks,

Colombia and the United States, 1765–1934 (1935) and Stephen J. Randall, *Colombia and the United States: Hegemony and Independence* (1992). Colombians have explored their country's relations with the United States only in general histories of Colombian diplomacy. Despite the merits of all these works, they are not sufficiently complete or analytical to establish a historiographical tradition, except on the issue of Panama's secession from Colombia.

Liberal Colombia

The modern republic of Colombia obtained its independence from Spain under the leadership of Simón Bolívar in 1819 and initially formed, along with Ecuador and Venezuela, part of the nation known as Gran Colombia.[1] In 1822 the United States became the first non-Hispanic nation to recognize Gran Colombia; Great Britain followed in 1825 and France in 1830. The dissolution of Gran Colombia in 1830 brought no interruption in relations between the United States and Colombia, but they were hindered by discriminatory Colombian duties that adversely affected U.S. exports and shippers.[2] Although the volume of trade may have been disappointing, both Colombians and Americans expressed keen interest in promoting transportation, whether by highway, railroad, or canal across the isthmus of Panama.

The issues of tariff discrimination and U.S. access to transisthmian transportation were addressed in the Bidlack-Mallarino Treaty of 1846. The treaty marked the beginning of a "transcendental change" in Colombian foreign policy, which had been hitherto oriented toward Europe.[3] Although the treaty was to form the basis of U.S. hegemony in Panama, at the time Colombia saw it as a bulwark against European arrogance and ambition. In the 1830s France and Great Britain had subjected Colombia to humiliating claims because of alleged injuries to two of their consuls. Now British encroachments in Central America threatened Colombian sovereignty on the isthmus. Several incidents in the early 1840s suggested that the British intended to extend the borders of their Mosquito Coast protectorate to embrace territory claimed by Colombia, especially at Bocas del Toro in Panama. As a result, President Tomás Cipriano de Mosquera—along with Secretary of Foreign Relations Manuel María Mallarino and his undersecretary, Manuel Ancízar—became convinced of the desirability of looking to the United States as guarantor of Colombian interests in Panama. According to Colombian historian Germán Cavelier, England's "aggressive imperialism thrust [Colombia] into the arms of the United States, for the usurpations of the English in [Mosquitia] and their clear ambitions in Panama convinced the government that it was impossible to obtain security for the isthmus in England," making necessary a "quasi-alliance" with the United States.[4]

After Benjamin A. Bidlack arrived in Bogotá on 1 December 1845 to serve as U.S. chargé d'affaires, President Mosquera proposed negotiations to eliminate discriminatory duties and guarantee Colombian control of the isthmus. The resulting treaty, which was signed on 12 December 1846, provided for the adoption of the most-favored-nation principle and for the end of discriminatory duties on U.S. vessels. The treaty also granted religious freedom to U.S. citizens resident in Colombia and permitted them to establish burial places for those who died in Colombia. Article 35 guaranteed that the right of way across the isthmus would be "open and free" to U.S. citizens and merchandise upon any mode of communication that already existed or might be constructed. In the same article, the United States guaranteed "the perfect neutrality" of the isthmus in order to prevent interruption of free transit as well as Colombia's "rights of sovereignty and property" over the isthmus.

The Colombian Congress quickly approved the treaty the following May. In the U.S. Senate it faced opposition from those who thought that article 35 involved the United States in an "entangling" foreign alliance. To dissipate these fears President Mosquera dispatched General Pedro A. Herrán, his son-in-law and predecessor as president, to Washington as Colombian minister. Herrán proved to be an effective lobbyist, and the senate ratified the treaty on 3 June 1848 by a vote of 29 to 7. Colombian fears of British expansionism were further assuaged by the signing of the Clayton-Bulwer Treaty (1850), in which the United States and Great Britain disavowed territorial ambitions in Central America; in addition, the two nations agreed that neither would seek exclusive control of a canal in Nicaragua and by extension any other site in Central America.

As the Bidlack-Mallarino Treaty was being debated in Washington, three New York entrepreneurs—William H. Aspinwall, John Lloyd Stephens, and Henry Chauncey—were seeking a concession to build a transisthmian railroad in Panama. Initially granted by Herrán and confirmed in 1850 by the Colombian Congress, the concession gave the Panama Railroad Company a monopoly of railway transportation for forty-nine years. The forty-seven-mile line was completed in 1855, making it the first railroad in Colombia.[5]

The construction of the Panama Railroad coincided with a new era in Colombia as economic and political liberalism gained ascendancy and dominated public policy for a generation. After 1886 the resurgence of the Conservative party brought changes in the formal structure of the government and in political economy. Most elites, however, regardless of philosophical orientation and party affiliation, remained committed to the expansion of trade and investment and to the further integration of Colombia into the North Atlantic economy. Despite these ambitions, at the start of the twentieth century Colombia probably had a lower degree of integration into the world economy than any other Latin American country.[6]

Colombia's development lagged behind that of its neighbors for several reasons, notably the country's difficult topography and chronic political turmoil. In 1851 the population totaled nearly 2.5 million, most of whom lived on the slopes and basins of the three Andean cordilleras that traverse the country from south to north. The capital, Bogotá, had a population of approximately 30,000 in 1851. Located in the Eastern Cordillera at an elevation of 8,600 feet above sea level, the city was isolated from both the rest of Colombia and the outside world. Bogotá's access to the principal Caribbean ports—Cartagena, Barranquilla, and Santa Marta—was by way of the Magdalena River, a journey that required at least a week even after the introduction of steam navigation in the 1840s. Communications with other important cities, such as Medellín and Cali, was equally difficult.

Despite the break with Spain, little changed in Colombia until the late 1840s when the administrations of President Mosquera (1845-49) and José Hilario López (1849-53) undertook to abandon colonial policies and institutions that were believed to hinder national development. Under Mosquera, who was at that time affiliated with the embryonic Conservative party, tariffs on most goods were reduced by more than 25 percent, and steps were taken to end state control over the production and sale of tobacco. The administration of López, a Liberal, continued the reformist tendency by abolishing slavery and dividing communal Indian landholdings. In 1850 the Jesuits were expelled, and later Liberal administrations adopted other measures aimed at reducing the power of the Catholic Church.

Another policy favored by nineteenth-century Liberals—federalism—was introduced in the 1850s with the creation of nine states: Antioquia, Bolívar, Boyacá, Cauca, Cundinamarca, Magdalena, Panama, Santander, and Tolima. Under the constitution of 1863, the states were defined as sovereign entities while the federal government, headed by a president who served a two-year term, had only limited powers. Elections were regularly held throughout the period, but neither party was willing to surrender power easily, and disgruntled losers frequently resorted to force to dislodge incumbents. Nationwide revolts occurred in 1851, 1854, 1859-61, 1876-77, 1884-85, 1895, and 1899-1902, but only one of these revolutions—that of 1859-61—was successful in permanently driving a government from power.[7]

The Liberal regime was destroyed by Rafael Núñez, who served as titular president almost continuously from 1880 to 1894. An ardent Liberal in his youth, Núñez became convinced during a long stay abroad that a more highly centralized and interventionist government would be better able to quell the disorder that characterized Colombian politics and impeded economic growth. He also shed his youthful anticlericalism. After returning to Colombia in 1874, he broke with the dominant Liberal faction, known as the Radicals, became the leader of the dissident Independent Liberals, and in 1885 allied himself with the Conservatives. A new constitution (1886) strengthened the presidency and the central government while reducing the nine states to the status of departments. In addition, Catholicism regained its traditional position as the official religion of the state. Despite the greater power exercised by the central government in the new regime, which was known as the Regeneration, political turmoil did not disappear. In fact, Colombia's most devastating revolution—the War of the Thousand Days (1899-1902)—occurred during this period.

The Liberal ascendancy of the mid-nineteenth century coincided with the emergence of tobacco as a major export product. The tobacco boom proved short-lived as the Colombian product failed to match its competitors in quality and packaging. After 1880 coffee became the leading export, accounting for 55 percent of the value of all exports by the mid-1890s. Manufacturing remained negligible despite the restoration of protective tariffs in the 1880s.

While tobacco, coffee, and other exports stimulated economic growth after 1850, Colombian gains remained modest in comparison with those of other Latin American countries. Short periods of expansion (1850–57, 1870–73, 1878–82, 1883–92) alternated with longer eras of falling export prices and unfavorable terms of trade (1858–69, 1874–77, 1888–93, 1899–1910). Although the high cost of transportation inhibited both foreign and domestic trade, little progress was made in railroad or highway construction. As late as 1904, there were only about 350 miles of railroad track in Colombia. The introduction of the first telegraph line (outside of Panama) in 1865 improved communications somewhat. By 1892 the telegraphic network totaled approximately 6,000 miles.[8]

Colombian trade statistics for the nineteenth century are incomplete, but it is clear that commerce with the United States rose significantly after 1850 despite occasional periods of decline. Moreover, Colombia's trade with the United States increased relative to that with other countries, and by 1910 the United States had become the principal market for Colombian products, especially coffee. In 1905–9 the United States took more than 70 percent of Colombian coffee exports.

During the same period Colombian imports from the United States rose from approximately 400,000 gold pesos annually in 1854–59, or 15.8 percent of the total, to nearly 5 million gold pesos annually in 1910–11, or 28.6 percent of the total. Although its relative importance declined, Great Britain remained the leading source of Colombian imports, providing nearly 6 million gold pesos annually in 1910–11, or 34.1 percent of the total.[9]

The U.S. investment in Colombia between 1850 and 1903 remained modest and was concentrated mainly in transportation. J. Fred Rippy estimated that in 1881 total U.S. investment in Colombia amounted to $14 million, with $8 million of this figure represented by the Panama Railroad. Total U.S., British, and French investment has been estimated at $37 million in 1913–14. On a per capita basis only the Dominican Republic among the Latin American nations had less investment from these countries than Colombia.[10]

Besides the Panama Railroad, the major transportation enterprise built with U.S. capital was a railroad linking the port of Cartagena and Calamar on the Magdalena River. The railroad, sixty miles in length, was built in 1891–94 by Boston capitalists headed by Samuel B. McConnico. McConnico and his associates also built a warehouse, a covered pier, and other port facilities in Cartagena. In 1897 they founded the Compañia Fluvial de Cartagena to provide steamer service on the Magdalena. In 1906 these enterprises came under British control.[11]

Except for diplomats and a handful of engineers, businessmen, and Protestant missionaries few Americans resided in Colombia outside of Panama. One of the most popular U.S. citizens to live in Colombia over a long period was Henry R. Lemly, a native of North Carolina and graduate of West Point (1872). Lemly was a first lieutenant in an artillery regiment when he and another officer came to Colombia in 1880 to organize the School of Civil and Military Engineers, which had been recently founded to provide professional military training to Colombian officers. Washington turned down a request for an extension of Lemly's leave, but in 1886 Minister Dabney H. Maury reported that many Colombians, including President Núñez, wanted him to return. This request was apparently granted, and Lemly was still in Colombia in 1895 when the U.S. chargé, Jacob Sleeper, conveyed a request for still another extension of his leave. Sleeper declared: "Lemly's presence here, has oftentimes turned the thoughts of this people toward their natural protector, viz: the United States, when otherwise, they would have thought only of Europe." After the extension was denied and no other U.S. officer was offered, Colombia secured the services of two French officers.[12]

Colombian elites often availed themselves of the opportunity to travel to North America as well as Europe, and very few prominent political leaders had not visited the United States. As early as the 1850s schoolboys and young men were being sent to U.S. preparatory schools and colleges, especially for technical training. Other Colombians also established commercial firms in the United States or sought employment in mercantile houses. Still others were given diplomatic assignments in the United States, including several men who served as president: Herrán, Manuel Murillo Toro, Eustorgio Salgar, and Santiago Pérez. Rafael Núñez lived in the United States from 1863 to 1865. Important exceptions to this pattern of travel to the United States were two Conservative chief executives of the late nineteenth century: Miguel Antonio Caro, who never left the environs of Bogotá, and José Manuel Marroquín, who ventured as far as a neighboring province only once.[13]

In general Colombians articulated very positive views about the United States, which was always perceived as a model providing a variety of lessons for Latin America. Numerous aspects of U.S. society provoked admiration. Among the most prominent was the astounding economic abundance of the United States. In an 1887 newspaper article Rafael Núñez noted the "prodigious" material growth of the United States, adding: "if the prosperity of a people is measured by the development of its population, of its commerce, of its factories, farms and mines, of public revenues, of its banks and railroads, etc., the prosperity of the United States has no equal in history."[14] Other aspects of the U.S. society that drew favorable notice included its religious toleration, its educational system, and the generosity of its philanthropists.

Liberals often posited a causal connection between U.S. prosperity and its political institutions, arguing that the establishment of federalism and political liberty would set Colombia on a similar path. By contrast, having become a proponent of strong, highly centralized government in his later years, Rafael Núñez maintained that the U.S. constitution conferred great powers on the presidency and that they had been expanded under Andrew Jackson and Abraham Lincoln. Strong executive power was needed in the Latin American countries too, he asserted. A convert to tariff protectionism while many Liberals adhered to free-trade concepts, Núñez also pointed out that U.S. growth had occurred behind a barrier of high tariffs.[15]

In short, Colombian writers, regardless of political orientation, tended to point to the U.S. example to help make their case when arguing a particular position. Of course, certain aspects of U.S. society produced criticism or concern. Mistreatment of Indians and blacks was often censured. The great wealth of the United States was seen to have some harmful consequences, such as the influence of money on politics. While admiring U.S. material prosperity, Núñez also expressed alarm over the concentration of so much wealth in so few hands, a condition that might even engender "the poisonous plant of socialism."[16]

Although the United States attracted many prominent Colombians, few Americans of distinction traveled to Colombia or resided there. The men appointed to the position of U.S. minister were of middling rank, and none went on to hold a major political or diplomatic post. The most prominent was perhaps George W. Jones (1859–61), who had been one of the first two men elected to the U.S. Senate from Iowa. A Democrat with southern sympathies, he converted to Catholicism before leaving for Colombia.

One of the longest serving U.S. diplomats was William L. Scruggs, a Republican from Georgia whose political services brought him appointment as minister in 1873.[17] He served until 1876 when the failure of Congress to appropriate funds for the legation led to its temporary closure. Scruggs was reappointed in 1882, serving until the accession of a Democratic administration brought about his recall in 1885. Another long-serving diplomat was Charles B. Hart, editor of the Wheeling, West Virginia, *Intelligencer,* who was minister from 1897 to 1903.

The few U.S. observers who had firsthand experience in Colombia did not consider it a model worthy of emulation. Instead, U.S. travelers and diplomats who left written accounts of their impressions rarely found anything commendable about Colombian society and government. Their attitude is not surprising in view of the fact that Colombian society was shaped by two influences that most people from the United States found distasteful if not abhorrent: Spanish culture and Roman Catholicism. For example, Isaac Holton, a New England botanist who wrote an account of his travels in Colombia in 1852–54, was offended by nonobservance of the Sabbath and by the failure of priests to observe their vows of chastity and suggested that Catholicism was responsible for what he perceived to be the general laxity of morals in Colombia. Allan A. Burton, who was minister from 1862 to 1867, concluded that Colombian whites were typical of Spaniards in general; among their qualities he listed cruelty, improvidence, indolence, and passionate addiction to gambling, lying, and fraud.[18]

Diplomats from the United States were frequently critical of the political culture and institutions of Colombia. Stephen A. Hurlburt, who served as minister from 1869 to 1872, believed that "the best of the Spanish American race are unfit to exercise intelligently the functions of free citizens." Hurlburt's verdict on the regime established by the constitution of 1863 was often quoted by its critics: "an organized anarchy, most skillfully directed to the perpetuation of revolution and the consecration of secession." Ernest Dichman, who was appointed minister in 1878, articulated views similar to Hurlburt's, advising Secretary of State William

H. Evarts: "it should be borne in mind, as a charitable consideration, and without wishing to deny the possibilities of development which this republic presents, that as a nation the people of this country may be described as grown up children playing at government."[19]

Commerce and Claims

Besides issues related to isthmian transit and U.S. rights under the 1846 treaty, diplomacy between Colombia and the United States most frequently revolved around differences over commercial regulations and the claims of U.S. citizens who sought compensation for injuries—physical and financial—suffered at the hands of Colombians. The position adopted by each government on specific issues depended in part on the merits of the case as well as the linkage between a given issue and other matters pending between the two countries. The U.S. secretaries of state and ministers in Bogotá sometimes assumed a hectoring, even belligerent tone in their communications with Colombia. The latter's diplomats, on the other hand, were quick to defend the prerogatives of national sovereignty and to resist U.S. pressures for compliance, often by delaying a final outcome as long as possible.

An example of such conflict occurred in the late 1880s after the Colombian government began to reserve for itself the right to award exclusive privileges for the manufacture or sale of certain products, such as ice and matches. In 1888 the government awarded the exclusive right to produce and sell ice in Panama to a Colombian group headed by Eduardo Uribe & Company. The monopoly was a blow to a U.S. firm, the Boston Ice Company, which had been doing business in Panama since 1865. The latter company won some concessions, such as an extension of the deadline set forwarding the contract, but it refused to bid for the contract itself.

The company's complaints gained a sympathetic hearing in Washington. Secretary of State Thomas F. Bayard claimed that the creation of the monopoly violated the 1846 treaty, which he asserted provided for "unlimited liberty of trade" and warned that the monopoly would be "a serious blow" to friendly relations between the United States and Colombia. Bayard expected that Colombia would compensate the Boston Ice Company for losses it might suffer. His successor, James G. Blaine, went further, insisting that the company be reinstated in its business. In response, Colombian officials maintained that the establishment of the monopoly was a purely internal matter that in no way violated the 1846 treaty.[20] After the Colombian government banned the importation of matches in the late 1890s, the United States again complained to no avail.

A more serious instance of Colombian refusal to accede to U.S. demands occurred over the issue of tariff reciprocity. Although mutual reductions of tariffs were discussed without success in the 1870s and 1880s, reciprocity became a source of conflict between the two nations in the early 1890s. The McKinley Tariff Act of 1890 contained a reciprocity clause authorizing the president to remove from the free list exports of coffee, hides, sugar, and other products from countries that imposed "reciprocally unjust and unequal duties" on U.S. goods. Since these and other Colombian exports entered the United States duty free, the clause could be used to pressure Colombia into lowering tariffs on U.S. goods. While many U.S. products already entered Colombia duty free, the United States frequently had an unfavorable balance of trade with Colombia, as was the case in 1889, 1890, and 1891.

Several Latin American countries signed reciprocity treaties with the United States, but Colombia balked, though characteristically it did not categorically reject the concept of reciprocity. Nevertheless, public officials and journalists, including the titular president, Rafael Núñez, then living in retirement in Cartagena, pointed out that reciprocity would be harmful to Colombia. Since it had signed treaties containing most-favored-nation clauses with several European states, it would be compelled to grant them similar concessions. The result, Colombians feared, would be a drastic fall in tariff collections, the government's main source of revenue.

When no satisfactory resolution was reached, President Benjamin Harrison issued a proclamation (15 March 1892) placing duties on Colombian coffee, sugar, and hides. The Colombians complained that this action violated the most-favored-nation clauses of the 1846 treaty, but their protests were ignored. However, the controversy ended after the Democratic victory of 1892 and the passage of the Wilson Tariff Act of 1894, which ended reciprocity agreements negotiated under the McKinley Tariff. Colombian coffee and hides were soon restored to the free list. Although U.S. imports declined in 1893 and 1894, they soon began to rise and surpass former levels.[21]

A perennial source of conflict between the two governments stemmed from claims brought by U.S. citizens for injuries or financial losses suffered at the hands of Colombians, usually during periods of civil unrest. The U.S. diplomats in Bogotá were assiduous in pressing claims upon the attention of the Colombian government, which normally sought to force claimants to seek satisfaction in Colombian venues before appealing to their governments. If this course proved unsatisfactory either to the claimant or to the U.S. government, negotiations might become so protracted as to delay resolution of the claim for years. Colombian penury also contributed to the delay in settling claims.

The most serious dispute between Colombia and the United States over injuries suffered by U.S. citizens arose as a result of the Watermelon Riot of 15 April 1856 in the city of Panama. The riot, which began after a U.S. visitor refused to pay a Panamanian vendor for a slice of watermelon, led to the deaths of about twenty persons, nearly all of them from the United States. In addition, the Panama Railroad station and other U.S.-owned businesses were destroyed.[22]

The Pierce administration promptly dispatched naval forces to Panama and appointed Amos B. Corwine to investigate the riot. Confirming early reports by U.S. observers, Corwine not only blamed the violence entirely on the Panamanian populace but also alleged that the governor and other officials had premeditated and participated in the attacks on U.S. citizens and property. Corwine also suggested that the United States seize the isthmus. Lino de Pombo, secretary of foreign relations in the administration of Manuel María Mallarino, disputed these conclusions and attributed the disturbances to the fact that the discovery of gold in California and the construction of the Panama Railroad had introduced hordes of unruly and arrogant Americans into the peaceful Panamanian milieu.

Unimpressed by Pombo's rebuttals, Secretary of State William L. Marcy sent Isaac E. Morse to Bogotá to join the U.S. minister, James B. Bowlin. On 3 December 1856 they were instructed to press upon Colombia a draft treaty that not only would have required it to compensate the victims of the riot but also would have severely compromised its sovereignty in the cities of Panama and Colón and within a strip twenty miles wide along the railroad route.

Pombo rejected the draft treaty as well as an ultimatum demanding immediate payment of $400,000 to settle claims growing out of the riot. The resulting impasse had not been resolved when Morse left Bogotá on 17 March 1857. Bowlin departed in frustration soon afterward, leaving Colombia without a U.S. minister until 1859. Negotiations were then transferred to Washington, where Pedro A. Herrán was again sent as minister. Realizing that some accommodation of the U.S. position was necessary, he signed a treaty with the new secretary of state, Lewis Cass, on 10 September 1857. Although it fell far short of the draft treaty of 1856, it contained an admission of Colombian liability for the Watermelon Riot and provided for the settlement of all claims filed by U.S. citizens against Colombia by 1 September 1859. This treaty, ratified with modifications by both governments, led to the payment by Colombia of a total of $412,393.95 in principal and interest. All the claims were cleared by 1874.[23]

Meanwhile, the U.S. Civil War had raised the possibility of European claims against the federal government and led Secretary of State William Seward to adopt a more moderate position on this matter than his Democratic predecessors. In 1866 he advised Minister Burton to suspend pursuit of a claim that was to be presented to the Colombian courts, however slow South American tribunals might be:

> The people who go to these regions and encounter great risks in the hope of great rewards must be regarded as taking all the circumstances into consideration, and cannot with reason ask their government to complain that they stand on a common footing with native subjects in respect to the alleged wants of an able, prompt and conscientious judiciary. We cannot undertake to supervise the arrangements of the whole world for litigation, because American citizens voluntarily expose themselves to be concerned in their deficiencies.

Despite Seward's admonition, later that year Burton professed such exasperation at delays in settling claims that he halted his mission, an action for which he was reprimanded by the secretary.[24]

An issue that complicated many discussions of claims was the fact that foreign residents of Colombia frequently took part in the country's turbulent political life. The Colombian government maintained that foreigners who suffered injuries or damages to their property as a result of their participation in Colombia's internal political disputes could not legitimately seek protection from their own governments. One such case arose when two U.S. expatriates were killed and another severely wounded during a riot in Cartagena in 1867. The three men had entered the service of Colombia by becoming officers of the *Rayo*, formerly the *R. R. Cuyler*, which had recently been engaged in blockade duty off the Florida coast. After being purchased by the Colombian government, the *Rayo* sailed for Cartagena.[25] Unhappy because their pay was overdue, the U.S. members of the crew of the vessel became active participants in a political conflict between the states of Magdalena and Bolívar, of which Cartagena was the capital.

On 1 September 1867 the U.S. crewmen were attacked by a mob that included officers and men of the Colombian army. Secretary Seward asked for an investigation into the matter and "condign punishment" for the guilty parties as well as payment of indemnities to the victims and their families. In 1869, however, Seward instructed the U.S. minister to discontinue efforts on behalf of the U.S. sailors on the grounds that they had entered the service of another country and "brought down upon themselves, whether rightly or wrongly, the lawless revenge of opposing belligerents." Seward noted that Colombia had disbanded the battalion to which the rioting soldiers had belonged and had promised compensation to the families of the murdered men. The fact that the three victims had left the U.S. Navy to serve the Confederacy and had not submitted to U.S. authority after the Civil War also made Seward reluctant to pursue the case further. In addition, the secretary was unwilling to lay down "a principle by which foreigners who engaged during our civil war in the service of either of the contending parties would be justified in invoking the intervention of their native sovereign to secure indemnity for the injuries and losses they received in that service."[26]

The United States was merely an interested bystander in the claim that has been called "the longest, the most complex, and the most costly in Colombian history."[27] In this dispute, which involved an Italian national, President Grover Cleveland served as an arbitrator, and the United States later tendered its good offices. What is perhaps most significant is that Colombia looked to the United States as its protector during the controversy, especially in 1898 when an Italian squadron appeared off the coast of Cartagena to press the claim.

The case involved one Ernesto Cerruti, a native of Turin who had served under Giuseppe Garibaldi in the fight for Italian unification and who settled in the Colombian state of Cauca in 1869. He married a granddaughter of former president Mosquera and became a businessman in Cali, counting among his associates several prominent Liberal politicians. These connections did not endear him to the Conservatives or to the dissident Liberals known as Independents, who were also offended by his outspoken anticlericalism. After the revolution of 1884–85, when the Conservatives and Independents triumphed over their Liberal adversaries, the new authorities of Cauca declared that Cerruti had forfeited his status as a neutral and seized his property and that of his firm, Ernesto Cerruti & Company, in which several Colombians were partners. When it appeared that he might be jailed for rebellion, he was rescued by a contingent of Italian troops that had been landed at the Pacific port of Buenaventura.

Thus began the Cerruti claim, which dragged on until 1910 and indeed became more complex as time passed. Initially, Cerruti sought restitution of his property and compensation for damages, a position in which he was supported by the Italian government. Colombia conceded that the Cauca proceedings against Cerruti had been irregular but maintained that by his notorious involvement in Colombian politics he had lost all right to protection by the Italian government.

As the conflict began, the U.S. minister reported to Washington that it was widely believed in Colombia that it would receive U.S. support in its conflict with Italy. This belief proved to be unfounded, but Secretary Bayard was pleased when Spanish mediation was proposed. This would be a mode of settlement, he said, that would not "excite the serious concern the United States could not but feel, were a European power to resort to force against a Sister Republic of this Hemisphere as to the sovereign and uninterrupted use of a part of whose territory we are guarantors."[28]

After the Spanish mediator's ruling in 1888, Colombia returned Cerruti's personal property to him. Steps were also taken to pay him an indemnity, but no agreement could be reached on the amount due. Moreover, although the mediator had ruled that Cerruti's firm could not be the subject of an international claim, the Italian government refused to exclude such a claim from future negotiations.

The next step was arbitration by President Cleveland, whose award of 2 March 1897 gave little satisfaction to Colombia and in fact complicated the affair even more. He not only ruled that Colombia should pay £60,000 to Cerruti for damages to his property and that of his firm but also stated in article 5 that Colombia should protect him against the claims of the firm's creditors. Colombia paid the £60,000, but it immediately sought modification of article 5. However, the State Department made it clear that neither Cleveland, nor his successor, William McKinley, would reopen the arbitration.[29]

Colombia's reluctance to comply with article 5 led the Italian government to resort to stronger measures. In mid-July 1898, as Colombians were about to celebrate their national holiday, four Italian warships appeared in the Bay of Cartagena. Local officials assumed that the squadron was on a friendly visit, but it soon became evident that its commander, Admiral Candiani, had come to present an ultimatum. He demanded that Colombia accept Cleveland's award in full and reach an agreement with Cerruti's creditors within three months, paying £20,000 immediately as a token of good faith.[30]

The Italian ultimatum was presented weeks before President Miguel Antonio Caro was due to leave office. According to Minister Hart, Caro considered the Italian action a case of "moral aggression," in which a comparatively strong power was determined to humiliate a weaker one. In Caro's opinion, Hart reported, "ampler scope should be given to the Monroe doctrine, so that it may include aggressions of this . . . character."[31] Despite Caro's hopeful reference to the Monroe Doctrine, the U.S. government, though concerned, took a dispassionate view of the affair, probably because it was preoccupied with the war against Spain and because the Italians were seeking to execute an award made by a U.S. president.

Although the United States would not go as far as the Colombians had hoped, it informed the Italian foreign minister, Admiral Felice Canevaro, that it "greatly deplored" the hostile measures being taken against Colombia. Canevaro denied that Italy's intentions were hostile and declared that it would accept the good offices of the United States only to obtain Colombia's acquiescence in the award. The U.S. chargé in Rome suspected that the Italian government was "anxious to make political capital for itself by causing it to appear that it has maintained a rather unyielding attitude toward the United States."[32]

The crisis was defused when Colombia paid the £20,000 demanded and agreed to compensate Cerruti's creditors, whose claims were to be evaluated by a commission in Bogotá. The deadline was extended to eight months, however, through the efforts of the United States. Angered over what it considered Italy's duplicity in dispatching the squadron, Colombia severed diplomatic relations with Italy a short time later. The United States again used its good offices to bring about the resumption of relations in 1899, a task made easier by Italy's annoyance over the excessive demands of some of the creditors.[33]

The Cerruti case was not completely resolved until 1910, but the events of the years 1885–98 illustrate the Colombian tendency to look to the United States for assistance in a crisis. This attitude had been seen earlier in the events leading to the signing of the Bidlack-Mallarino Treaty. It is ironic that it reappeared in 1898, just as the United States was emerging from the Spanish-American War as an ambitious world power. Colombia's perhaps shortsighted eagerness for U.S. help was a counterpoise to its defense of its sovereignty in the conflict over reciprocity and other issues, especially in matters relating to Panamanian affairs. Even here, however, Colombian administrations of the late nineteenth century saw no contradiction in appealing to the United States for assistance in suppressing domestic insurrection.

Panama: The Focal Point

Throughout the second half of the nineteenth century Panama remained the focal point of U.S. diplomacy with Colombia. As already noted, it was the only region of the country with substantial U.S. investment and the only region that attracted large numbers of U.S. citizens. The Bidlack-Mallarino Treaty gave the United States special responsibilities in Panama. Finally, Panama's suitability as a site for a transisthmian canal also fixed U.S. interest in that region. This interest became even stronger in the late nineteenth century as a result of the abortive French effort to build a canal in Panama in the 1880s and the growing U.S. belief in the military and economic necessity of a U.S.-controlled waterway in Central America.

According to the Colombian census of 1870, Panama had a population of approximately 205,000 in that year. Although stock raising and agriculture were carried in the interior of the state, Panama's economy since the colonial period had been based largely on the transport of goods across the isthmus. The city of Panama, located on the Pacific side of the transisthmian route, had been founded in 1680 after an earlier city had been destroyed by Henry Morgan; it had a population estimated at 25,000 in 1881. Colón was a newer city, having been built as the Caribbean terminus of the Panama Railroad. Both cities were dominated by a largely white elite of merchants, businessmen, and public officials whereas the majority of the population was of African origin. With the construction of the railroad and the French canal project, the native population was augmented by an influx of West Indians, Asians, and Europeans, as well as Americans and Colombians from other sections of the country.[34]

Panama's unique geographical situation and economic interests, coupled with the difficulty of communication with Bogotá, contributed to a desire for local autonomy. As a result, when federalism gained support in the 1850s, Panama became the first of the Colombian regions to be established as a self-governing state (1855). Under the constitution of 1863, Panamanians elected their own chief executive and enjoyed considerable autonomy. In addition, no duties were collected in Panamanian ports, in accordance with an 1835 decree. Panama yielded a direct financial benefit to the federal government, however, as a result of a new contract signed with the Panama Railroad Company in 1867. Its provisions included an extension of the company's concession for a period of ninety-nine years starting in 1875. In return the company was to pay $1 million to Colombia upon approval of the contract and an additional $250,000 annually.[35] Of the latter sum, $25,000 was turned over to Panama each year.

During the federal era Panamanian politics proved to be extremely unstable, even by the turbulent standards of nineteenth-century Colombia. State presidents, most of them Liberals, were frequently ousted by irregular means as a result of factional disputes. These upheavals were usually linked to national politics, for Panama cast one of the five state votes required to elect the federal president. To supporters of one candidate or another, therefore, a sympathetic state president could mean an additional vote. With the restoration of centralism in 1886, Panama, like the eight other states, became a department whose governor was appointed by the president.

After 1846 the Bidlack-Mallarino Treaty frequently gave rise to disputes between the U.S. and Colombian governments. The United States generally interpreted the treaty as giving it authority to veto Panamanian or Colombian initiatives regarding isthmian fiscal and commercial policy. For example, the United States vigorously opposed a tonnage tax on vessels entering Panamanian harbors that was enacted by the state of Panama in 1855 and subsequently authorized by the Colombian Congress. The United States held that the tax violated, in the words of Secretary Marcy, "the spirit and policy" of the 1846 treaty and the contract of the Panama Railroad and threatened to use force to block collection of the tax. Rejecting these claims, Herrán asserted that additional revenue was needed if Co-

lombia was to provide adequate security on the transit route and avoid disturbances like the Watermelon Riot. His arguments proved unavailing, however, and
the tax was never enforced. The United States also opposed a short-lived Colombian decree in 1885 that levied duties on goods entering Panamanian ports.[36]

Pretensions by the United States to hegemony in Panama can also be seen in
the periodic deployment of U.S. troops on the isthmus. Historian Michael Conniff
has identified fourteen instances of such intervention between 1856 and 1903.[37] It
should be noted that U.S. intervention usually occurred during periods of armed
conflict in Panama or in Colombia as a whole and occasionally was requested by
the Colombian government. The position of the U.S. government, as stated by Seward in 1865, was that the 1846 treaty authorized U.S. intervention only to protect
the isthmus from foreign invaders, not domestic insurgents. If freedom of transit
across Panama was endangered, however, intervention might be considered.

The most significant episode of U.S. intervention in the nineteenth century
occurred in 1885 during a major revolution aimed at overthrowing the second administration of Rafael Núñez. This intervention is noteworthy partly because of
the number of troops involved. More important is the fact that the intervention
had the effect of assisting the Colombian government in suppressing local insurgents, thereby undermining Seward's definition of U.S. responsibilities under the
1846 treaty. As historian Daniel H. Wicks has observed, U.S. actions in 1885 also
served as a "dress rehearsal" for intervention in Panama in 1903.[38]

The revolution of 1884–85 began soon after Núñez assumed the national
presidency for the second time. The leader of the Independent Liberals, he was dis-
trusted by the Radical Liberal faction because of his recent overtures to the Conservative party and his calls for constitutional reform to strengthen the national
government. An uprising of Radicals in the eastern state of Santander produced a
nationwide revolt that ultimately proved unsuccessful in toppling Núñez. The crucial event occurred when Núñez appealed to the Conservatives for armed assistance in crushing the insurgents. The triumph of Núñez meant, in effect, the end
of Liberal ascendancy in Colombia. The new regime with its centralist constitution was ostensibly supported by Independent Liberals as well as Conservatives,
but many of the former rejoined the Radicals or were pushed aside by the Conservatives, who became increasingly dominant.

Events in Panama during the revolution followed a tortuous course as local
Radical and Independent leaders jockeyed for control. Contributing to the unrest
was the fact that early in 1885 many of the Colombian troops stationed on the isthmus were moved to the northern coast to reinforce government forces there. Their
commander was Ramón Santodomingo Vila, chief executive of Panama, who was
temporarily succeeded first by Pablo Arosemena and, after his resignation, by
Carlos A. Gónima. These events produced a rebellion by Radical chieftains Rafael
Aizpuru in Panama City and by Pedro Prestán in Colón. During the revolution
communications by telegraph and by mail were suspended or disrupted throughout the country; as a result, officials in Bogotá remained ignorant of events in
Panama and elsewhere for long periods.

As the rebellion began, Minister Scruggs advised Washington to send a naval vessel to Panama. Replying on 20 January 1885, Frederick T. Frelinghuysen, secretary of state in the outgoing Arthur administration, informed Scruggs that naval vessels would be stationed in isthmian waters to protect U.S. interests. On 17 March the *Wachusetts,* under Commander Alfred T. Mahan, arrived in the port of Panama and, at the request of Arosemena, landed forty men to occupy the railroad buildings; they returned to their ships on 27 March in the mistaken belief that Aizpuru and Gónima, who had replaced Arosemena, had reached an accommodation.[39]

Meanwhile, across the isthmus the *Galena* had also landed a force to protect U.S. property, but the railroad route remained blocked as the city fell into the hands of Prestán. On 31 March the *Colón,* a vessel owned by the Pacific Mail Steamship Company, arrived with a cargo of arms. Prestán demanded the weapons, but company officials refused to comply, supported by the U.S. consul, R. K. Wright. Prestán's response was to arrest Wright and several company employees. At this the commander of the *Galena,* Theodore Kane, seized the *Colón* with its cargo still aboard and ordered his entire contingent of 114 sailors and marines ashore. Colombian troops now arrived in Colón, and Prestán, facing defeat, allegedly ordered the burning of the city, which was virtually destroyed. Prestán fled, and Kane took control of the city.[40]

At this point the newly installed Cleveland administration decided to send substantial reinforcements to Panama. On 2 April, Rear Admiral James J. Jouett, commander of the North Atlantic Squadron, was ordered to sail to Colón with the *Tennessee.* On 5 April, Commander Bowman H. McCalla was sent to Colón aboard a Pacific Mail steamer carrying 250 marines and 150 sailors. Another Pacific Mail steamer had already sailed with 200 marines.[41]

Upon arriving in Colón, Admiral Jouett debarked his men after obtaining provisional approval from the Colombian commander, Ramón Ulloa. McCalla, who arrived on 15 April, had ambitious goals for U.S. efforts in Panama, possibly including a lengthy stay. On 24 April he briefly occupied the city of Panama to prevent a battle between Aizpuru's forces and a large detachment of Colombian forces that was expected shortly. McCalla and Jouett also contemplated barring the landing of the Colombian forces, but Secretary Bayard wired that such interference was "wholly unauthorized." The Colombian troops, under the command of Rafael Reyes, arrived on 28 April. At a meeting that day Admiral Jouett brokered an agreement providing for the surrender of Aizpuru, thus ensuring the government's control of the isthmus.[42]

Meanwhile, in Bogotá Minister Scruggs and presumably the Colombian government were unaware of events in Panama. On 14 April, however, Scruggs sent a telegram relaying a Colombian request for U.S. intervention in Panama. As late as 20 April there was no authoritative information about Panama; on that day he wrote that "beyond the fact of very serious disturbances on the Isthmus, nothing is definitely known here." Additional information was undoubtedly forthcoming, for on 21 April he reported in a telegram that the Colombian government considered Aizpuru and Prestán responsible for the burning of Colón and asked U.S. forces to capture them pending the arrival of Colombian troops. Bayard replied that the U.S. guarantee embraced only international neutrality, not intervention in local strife. Scruggs explained in response that he had sent his telegram of 21 April regarding the capture of Aizpuru and Prestán only at the "urgent and repeated request" of the Colombian government, for he knew that the United States could not comply with the Colombian request. However, when informed that the United States had moved to guarantee neutrality of the isthmus and to keep the transit open, Núñez had expressed appreciation for its "prompt and efficient action."[43]

Thus, the government in Bogotá solicited U.S. intervention in conformity with the 1846 treaty even as a large naval contingent was already on the scene. Regardless of the information about events in Panama available to the Núñez administration, it is clear that it considered U.S. intervention a weapon in quelling the revolution. Although the Cleveland administration viewed intervention only as a means of keeping the transit route open, the actions of the naval officers on the scene had the effect of hindering the insurgents and helping the government, just as Núñez had hoped. Similar consequences would follow U.S. interventions in 1901 and 1902 during the War of the Thousand Days. In addition, as some naval officers intended, the intervention helped fix the perception among Americans that Panama was a U.S. dependency.

The Canal Crisis

Since the 1850s Americans had increasingly treated Panama as a U.S. dependency in which Colombian sovereignty could be abridged under certain circumstances. By acquiescing in, or inviting, the landing of U.S. forces, the Colombian government had contributed to that perception. This trend reached its climax at the turn of the century after the failure of the Colombian Senate to ratify an isthmian canal treaty and the secession of Panama with U.S. support in 1903.

These events have generated a large body of scholarly writing, often aimed as much at condemning or exculpating the leading actors as at clarifying motives and issues. A recent study by Richard Collin stresses a cultural clash between the Catholic provincialism of Bogotá and "Protestant American tenacity." The leading Colombian historian of the crisis, Eduardo Lemaitre, contrasts the "aggressive and warlike" Theodore Roosevelt with the passive and melancholy Colombian chief executive, José Manuel Marroquín. In addition, he belittles the legitimacy of Panama's secessionist movement. Despite its age, Dwight C. Minor's 1940 volume remains the best and most detailed study of U.S.-Colombian relations in 1902-3.[44]

In the United States, interest in constructing an isthmian canal revived after the Civil War. There was support for such a venture in Colombia as well, though its support was qualified by concern over its sovereignty in any canal zone that might be created. Treaties authorizing U.S. construction of a canal in Panama were signed in 1869 and in 1870, but neither secured ratification. The Colombian Senate voted against ratification of the 1869 treaty; it ratified the 1870 treaty with amendments, but the U.S. Senate failed to bring the latter document to a vote. These failures fanned support for other prospective canal sites, especially Nicaragua, which was the unanimous choice of an interoceanic canal commission in 1876.

The situation was soon transformed by the formation of a private French company to construct a sea-level canal in Panama under the leadership of Ferdinand de Lesseps, renowned as the builder of the Suez Canal. The French firm acquired a concession that had been granted by Colombia to Lucien Wyse in 1878. This concession gave the company the right to build and operate a canal in Panama for ninety-nine years, after which it was to revert to Colombia. The company also purchased control of the Panama Railroad, over whose route the projected canal was to be built.

Leaders in the United States became alarmed over the strategic and commercial implications of a French canal. The State Department dispatched Ernest Dichman to reopen the Bogotá legation soon after the granting of the Wyse concession and instructed him to investigate every detail of the contract. President Rutherford B. Hayes affirmed the prevailing view in 1880 when he announced: "The policy of this country is a canal under American control. The United States cannot consent to the surrender of this control to any European power or to any combination of European efforts." The French project also encouraged backers of the Nicaraguan route who organized the Maritime Canal Company in 1889. Even after the French suspended operations in Panama the same year, Nicaragua remained the preferred route for a U.S.-constructed canal, and its supporters sought official financial support for the Maritime Company. During this period the United States also acted to remove a major obstacle to a solely U.S.-owned canal—the Clayton-Bulwer Treaty, which barred exclusive U.S. control of any canal built in Central America. The second Hay-Pauncefote Treaty (1902) superseded the Clayton-Bulwer Treaty and allowed the United States to build and operate a canal open to the ships of all nations.[45]

Meanwhile, in 1893 the successor to the French firm, the New Panama Canal Company, obtained from Colombia an extension of the Wyse concession obliging it to open a canal by 31 October 1904; an agreement in 1900 extended the deadline until 1910. The new company was unlikely to complete a canal; its shareholders could profit only if its assets—the concession from Colombia, the railroad, and the partially excavated canal—were purchased by the United States. As Minor has shown, William Nelson Cromwell, counsel for the company, waged an effective "fight for the Panama route" in the United States.[46]

In January 1902, after the company offered to sell its property to the United States for $40 million, a second canal commission agreed unanimously that Panama was "the most practicable and feasible" site for an isthmian canal. Proponents of the Panama route triumphed again in June 1902 when Congress passed the Spooner Act. The act committed the United States to build a canal in Panama after acquiring the property of the company and negotiating an agreement with Colombia. If these conditions were not met within a "reasonable time," the United States could turn to Nicaragua.

Negotiations between Colombia and the United States were already underway in Washington when the Spooner Act was passed. The economic and military power of the United States, coupled with its self-confidence after the Spanish-American War, would have placed Colombia at a disadvantage in the best of circumstances. However, its weakness was exacerbated by chaotic political conditions at home.[47] By the late 1890s the dominant Conservative party had fractured into two factions, the Nationalists and Historical Conservatives. The factions briefly coalesced in 1898 to elect Manuel A. Sanclemente as president and José Manuel Marroquín as vice president, but differences over economic and political issues persisted. Meanwhile, the Liberals, resentful over their near total exclusion from power since 1885, rose in revolt against the Sanclemente administration in 1899. Although the Liberals proved unable to defeat the government, they represented a serious threat for the next three years. The conflict, known as the War of the Thousand Days, cost thousands of lives and proved devastating to an economy already reeling from a drop in world coffee prices. On 31 July 1900, members of the Historical faction removed Sanclemente in favor of Vice President Marroquín, who they believed would end the war quickly. This belief proved unfounded as Marroquín refused to make any concessions to the Liberals and turned on the Historical Conservatives who had brought him to power.

Panama, where the revolutionaries enjoyed much popular support, became the scene of heavy fighting in 1901 and 1902. The war in Panama again occasioned the landing of U.S. forces and in one case produced tension between the two governments. The first significant instance of intervention came in November 1901 at the urging of Acting Governor Aristides Arjona while the Liberals briefly occupied Colón. Two hundred fifty men from the battleship *Iowa* were landed to occupy and guard railroad facilities. In the opinion of Tomás Herrán, secretary of the Colombian legation in Washington, the deployment of these forces was "extremely obstructive" to the revolutionaries and allowed the government to mount an effective campaign against them.[48]

The arrival of a large Liberal force under Benjamín Herrera on 24 December 1901 again threatened government control of the isthmus over the following months. In September 1902 U.S. naval forces not only took control of the railroad without waiting for a Colombian request (though one was soon forthcoming), but for a time they also refused to transport government troops across the isthmus. Colombian protests brought a reversal of this policy, but not before it had stirred ill will toward the United States in Bogotá. Moreover, despite the assurances of the State Department that no infringement of Colombian sovereignty had been intended, it is clear that the United States had now assumed the right to interpret the 1846 treaty unilaterally.[49] Although they controlled most of the isthmus except for the cities of Panama and Colón, the Liberals also found themselves restricted by the U.S. Navy. Partly for this reason, Herrera signed a peace treaty with government representatives aboard the U.S.S. *Wisconsin* on 21 November 1902, thereby ending the war.

Three estimable Colombians took part in the discussions leading to a canal treaty. Carlos Martínez Silva, who was named minister to Washington in December 1900, was a former cabinet minister who had played a key role in the installation of Marroquín the previous July. His retirement early in 1902 was due largely to his disapproval of Marroquín's policy toward the insurgents. His successor, José Vicente Concha, had also served in Marroquín's cabinet but had never traveled abroad. He left his post in November 1902 because of his criticism of the recent U.S. intervention in Panama and reluctance to sign a draft canal treaty. His place was taken by Tomás Herrán, who had accompanied Martínez Silva as legation secretary. The son of Pedro A. Herrán, he was well acquainted with the United States; he was a graduate of Georgetown University and had been U.S. consul in Medellín for approximately eight years.

Regardless of their respective virtues and defects, all three had to negotiate from a position of weakness. Until the passage of the Spooner Act, there was a strong possibility that the United States would reject the Panama route in favor of Nicaragua. Even with the passage of the act, Nicaragua remained an alternative if an agreement satisfactory to the United States could not be reached. The Colombians also realized that if a treaty was not forthcoming, Panama might secede from Colombia with U.S. help. Moreover, the signing of the second Hay-Pauncefote Treaty made it clear that Great Britain could no longer be considered a counterweight to U.S. ambitions in Central America. Another problem for the negotiators was that instructions from Colombia were late, ambiguous, or contradictory. As a result, they often acted independently of their superiors in Bogotá.

By contrast, Secretary of State John Hay merely had to produce a treaty that would fulfill the provisions of the Spooner Act. Holding the upper hand, he became increasingly impatient with Colombian vacillation. A major source of conflict during and after the negotiations was compensation for Colombia from the New Panama Canal Company for the right to sell its assets to the United States. According to the Wyse concession, Colombian consent was required before they could be transferred to another nation, yet the Colombian negotiators failed to seek a financial agreement with the company or to incorporate a clause providing for such an agreement into the draft treaty. When Concha formally raised the subject on 11 November 1902, Hay replied that the proposed amendment was "wholly inadmissible." Hay was willing to increase the annuity to be paid to Colombia by the United States, but he declared on 21 January 1903 that he would not consider or discuss any other changes in the treaty draft.[50]

The Hay-Herrán Treaty was signed on 22 January 1903. In the first article Colombia authorized the sale of the assets of the New Panama Canal Company to the United States. The United States received the exclusive right to build, operate, control, and protect an interoceanic canal on Colombian territory for one hundred years, renewable for similar periods at the option of the United States. Colombia also granted to the United States for one hundred years a zone five kilometers (about three miles) wide on either side of the canal route. In this zone the United States was to establish judicial tribunals that were to have exclusive jurisdiction over all controversies between U.S. citizens and between them and citizens of countries other than Colombia. As compensation the United States was to pay Colombia $10 million upon ratification of the treaty and $250,000 per year.

The U.S. Senate ratified the treaty on 17 March 1903 by a vote of 73 to 5. In Colombia the end of the war permitted the election of a new Congress, all but two of whose members were Conservatives. It passed several important measures of political and fiscal reform before the Senate began to consider the treaty in July 1903.[51]

Having ended the war to the government's advantage, Marroquín was ostensibly in a strong position to secure ratification of the treaty by a legislative body made up entirely of fellow Conservatives. In reality, as Thomas R. Favell and others have shown, he was a discredited chief executive completely lacking in organized political support.[52] To many of his foes, embarrassment of the vice president was of greater urgency than passage of the treaty. Moreover, Marroquín transmitted the treaty without a recommendation, in effect abdicating his administration's responsibility for the document.

Marroquín's conduct underscored the fact that the treaty had few friends and many opponents, especially in the press. On 15 April 1903, A. M. Beaupré, the legation secretary who had just been named minister, reported that public attitudes toward the treaty were uniformly hostile. "This fact is clear," he wrote, "that if the proposed convention were to be submitted to the free opinion of the people, it would not pass."[53]

Critics in the Senate and in the press objected primarily to two features of the treaty. First, they argued that several provisions, especially the article authorizing the establishment of U.S. tribunals in the canal zone, weakened Colombian sovereignty in Panama. Second, they were unhappy over the treaty's financial arrangements and contended that Colombia should receive a share of the $40 million to be paid to the New Panama Canal Company.

These concerns were reflected in the report of a Senate committee appointed to study the treaty. In its report of 4 August the committee recommended approval of the treaty with several amendments. Colombian sovereignty was to be affirmed more clearly. In addition, the New Panama Canal Company was to be required to reach an understanding with Colombia before the latter would agree to the transfer of the concession. Minor calls the proposed amendments "reasonable and statesmanlike" on the whole; they were apparently aimed at winning the support of Senate moderates.[54]

Hay, however, was adamantly opposed to changes in the treaty and communicated his views to Beaupré on several occasions, warning on 9 June that any modification might disrupt friendly relations between the two countries. On 31 July he informed Beaupré: "The Colombian Government and Congress should realize the grave risk of ruining the negotiation by improvident amendment." Beaupré communicated these messages to the government, which in turn shared them with the Senate. He admitted that his notes were undiplomatic but believed that strong language was necessary to secure ratification of the treaty. However, when his notes were read to the Senate, they produced great indignation, further damaging prospects for the treaty.

When the decisive vote took place on 12 August, the outcome was not unexpected. The treaty was rejected by a vote of 24 to 0, with two abstentions. The motion also stated that no antagonism toward the United States or its canal project was intended, and many, including Beaupré, expected negotiations to continue.[55] Instead, the treaty rejection led directly to the secession of Panama on 3 November 1903. The new republic received U.S. recognition on 6 November. The Hay-Bunau-Varilla Treaty, which authorized the United States to build, operate, and defend a canal in Panama, was quickly drafted and approved in both countries.

Despite the fact that many had predicted the secession of Panama if a canal treaty was not approved, the events of 3 November surprised Colombians. Perhaps most shocking was the role of the United States in the planning and execution of the independence movement and its determination to block with force any Colombian effort to reconquer the isthmus. The United States, which was pledged to preserve Colombian sovereignty over Panama by the treaty, had acted instead to subvert it.

Some Colombians spoke of invading Panama, and the government appointed a commission to travel to the isthmus and to the United States to seek redress. The head of the commission, Rafael Reyes, a treaty supporter who would succeed Marroquín in 1904, soon became convinced of the futility of such efforts for several reasons. In the United States, the action of the Roosevelt administration to ensure construction of a canal in Panama won applause even from Democrats and would not be reversed. A military campaign against Panama would mean a hopeless war against the United States, and there was no evidence of Panamanian desire for reunion with Colombia. The major European powers as well as all the other countries of Latin America recognized Panamanian independence within a few months.[56]

A further consideration was an awareness that Colombia's own failings—not only the blunders of the Marroquín administration but also the country's incessant political turmoil—had contributed to the outcome. Thus, Tomás Herrán condemned the "imbecilic government" of Colombia as well as the "vile and treacherous" behavior of the United States. Also persuasive is Joseph L. Arbena's suggestion that, despite Colombian condemnation of the United States, Panama was of limited importance: "The Isthmus had always seemed distant from the mainland, its inhabitants of a different breed, its ties to national institutions very weak; to some Colombians the Isthmus had been a source of more harm than good."[57]

In view of these realities Colombia embarked on a policy of accommodation with the United States. This was the goal of Reyes, who committed his administration to political reconciliation and economic modernization at home and the improvement of Colombia's standing abroad. Treaties providing for a modest financial indemnity for Colombia and Colombian recognition of Panama were negotiated but were never ratified by Colombia. Indeed, they provided an opportunity for Reyes's critics to assail his administration and led to his resignation in 1909.[58]

The departure of Reyes did not alter the policy of seeking accommodation with the United States, despite periodic eruptions of popular anti-Americanism. This policy reached fruition with the approval of the Thomson-Urrutia Treaty (1914), which awarded Colombia the sum of $25 million. Ratification of the treaty in the U.S. Senate was delayed by opposition to a section containing a statement of "sincere regret" that the relations of the two countries had been marred. It was only after Roosevelt had died and the offending passage removed that the treaty was ratified in the United States (1921).[59]

By now commerce between the two countries had expanded significantly, and U.S. capitalists were poised to make large investments in Colombia. Moreover, as Reyes had expected, Colombia had benefited from the opening of the Panama Canal in 1914. With the shift of coffee cultivation to western Colombia after 1900, coffee could now be shipped from the Pacific port of Buenaventura instead of the traditional Caribbean ports. "Because coffee was a fairly bulky commodity relative to its value, the benefits of the canal enjoyed by Colombia were great—whatever the cost in hurt pride, national territory lost, and the infringement of sovereignty."[60]

Thus, the secession of Panama can be considered an uncharacteristically acrimonious interval in the pattern of generally cordial U.S.-Colombian relations that had developed after 1850. During the nineteenth century such intervals had occurred most frequently as a result of conflicts over Panama. Now that this irritant was removed, the growing economic ties between the two countries and the continuing favorable image of the United States among Colombian elites combined to foster relatively cordial relations during most of the twentieth century as well.

4

CENTRAL AMERICA

The Search for Economic Development

Thomas M. Leonard

T HE FIRST EDITION OF John Lloyd Stephens's *Incidents of Travel in Central America: Chiapas and Yucatán* (1841)[1] gave U.S. readers their initial glimpse of Central American geography, its people, and the Indian ruins that graced the isthmus, but it did little to generate interest in the region. Enthralled with Manifest Destiny and always in search of opportunities to acquire additional lands, most U.S. entrepreneurs looked westward, to Texas, California, and Oregon. Others, like the New England merchants, sought large markets in Asia. Only a few politicians, such as Senator Thomas Hart Benton of Missouri, proposed that the United States expand south to the isthmus at Panama, and they did it more for humanitarian than economic or security reasons. At the time, U.S. entrepreneurs saw Mexico and Central America as areas in need of political and social development.[2]

With U.S. attention focused elsewhere, during the 1840s Great Britain expanded its interests in the isthmus, thanks largely to the efforts of its chargé d'affaires, Frederick Chatfield. He pressed for settlement of claims made by British citizens against the governments of the five Central American republics, negotiated special trade treaties with the republics, and defended British claims to the logging region in what is now Belize, to the Bay Islands off the Honduran coast, and to its self-proclaimed protectorate over the ill-defined Miskito kingdom on Nicaragua's Caribbean coast, which stretched as far south as San Juan River bordering Costa Rica and which was the perceived Caribbean terminus for a projected transisthmian canal. Although many of Chatfield's actions exceeded his assigned duties and official British policy, his endeavors left the distinct impression on Central Americans that Britain had territorial designs upon the isthmus. So frightened were the Central Americans that on several occasions during the decade they unsuccessfully appealed to the United States to countervail the British gains.[3]

The situation changed in 1848, with the end of the Mexican War and the discovery of gold in California. Together these incidents heightened U.S. interest in a transit route across the isthmus. They found the British anxious not to be left out of any such project. Thus began a half-century in which the U.S. government grew increasingly concerned with Central American political dynamics, and private businessmen sought greater economic opportunity. Both desired a transisthmian canal route. By 1903 Central America had become a focal point in U.S. foreign policy.

Removing the British Presence

Anxious to check the British presence in Central America in the 1840s, President James K. Polk dispatched two emissaries to the region: Elijah Hise in 1848 and Ephraim G. Squier in 1849. They completed treaties with Nicaragua that granted the United States canal rights on the San Juan River with the obligation to guarantee its security. Squier went on to Honduras, where he arranged the cession to the United States of Tigre Island in the Gulf of Fonseca, considered the terminus for a canal. These actions were clear violations of their instructions and of the traditional U.S. policy of avoiding entangling alliances. Furthermore, by setting his sights on Tigre Island, Squier had infuriated the British minister to the region, Frederick Chatfield, who ordered British gunboats to the island. Because cooler heads prevailed in Washington and London, a crisis was avoided. Without consulting any of the Central American governments, the United States and Great Britain completed the Clayton-Bulwer Treaty in 1850.

The treaty stipulated that neither signatory alone could undertake the construction of a transisthmian transportation route or construct fortifications in its vicinity, nor could they "occupy, or fortify, or colonize, or assume or exercise any dominion over . . . any part of Central America." For the moment, the treaty cooled tempers and alleviated possible war between the United States and Great Britain. But it left unresolved the question of British claims in Belize, the Bay Islands, and the Miskito lands in Nicaragua as far south as the San Juan River, which bordered Costa Rica and was the perceived Caribbean terminus for the projected transisthmian canal. These became contentious issues in the decade following the signing of the treaty.[4]

The tension caused by the treaty's vagueness intensified as a result of the events on the isthmus that followed the California Gold Rush of 1849. For many persons seeking fortunes in California the route across the isthmus of Panama and Nicaragua became their link between the east and west coasts of the United States. Greytown, a British enclave at the mouth of the San Juan River, was not prepared for the onslaught because it lacked hotels and amusement places for travelers to pass idle time awaiting their "bongos" to take them up the San Juan to Lake Nicaragua. Into this vacuum stepped New York entrepreneur Commodore Cornelius Vanderbilt. His Accessory Transit Company used steamboats instead of "bongos" for the trip up the San Juan. From Lake Nicaragua they would travel by macadam road to San Juan del Sur on the Pacific coast, where they would connect with other vessels for the trip to California. By 1852, some 10,000 passengers per month traveled the route. Travelers' needs transformed Greytown into a delightful place, with amusements, gambling houses, and the opulent St. Charles Hotel. The increased traffic also resulted in confrontation between the British and the Americans.[5]

The Clayton-Bulwer Treaty made Greytown a free port, denying the British badly needed revenue to meet the requirements of port municipal services. To circumvent the problem, the British charged harbor fees in order to free local revenues. Of all the merchants who operated in the waters off Greytown, only Vanderbilt refused to pay the British harbor fees because his community across the bay at Punta Arenas did not utilize any of Greytown's facilities. The confrontation came to a climax on 21 November 1851 as Vanderbilt's *Prometheus* prepared to leave Punta Arenas for New York after refusing to pay the British port charges. When the British brig o' war *Express* fired three shots across the bow of the *Prometheus,* Vanderbilt, who happened to be on board, agreed to ante up, but after the ship arrived in New York he immediately took his case to the U.S. government. The Fillmore administration accepted Vanderbilt's argument and successfully pressured the British to make restitution and to instruct its naval commanders in Greytown not to enforce the payment of harbor fees until the issue was resolved by diplomatic agreement. Demonstrating renewed interest in the isthmian region, the United States now claimed that Great Britain lacked the legal authority to exercise police jurisdiction over U.S. merchant vessels not only in Greytown but everywhere else in Central America. Policymakers in Washington also asserted that the Clayton-Bulwer Treaty required the British to withdraw from the Miskito Coast. Although London was willing to negotiate the issue of harbor fees, it refused to vacate any territory on the grounds that the Clayton-Bulwer Treaty only prevented future colonization on the isthmus.[6]

Events in Great Britain, however, proffered an opportunity for a reasonable settlement of the issues arising out of the 1850 treaty. In 1851 Lord Palmerston resigned as British foreign secretary, and the irascible Frederick Chatfield was recalled from Central America. Confronted with more serious problems on the European continent, successive British administrations sought a face-saving solution to the Central American crisis. But the United States was not in an accommodating mood. Despite a growing sectional crisis that would eventually lead to civil war, policymakers in Washington remained determined to force the British withdrawal from Central America and its adjacent islands.[7]

The first opportunity for an agreement came in early 1852 when the Nicaraguan government sought to assert its authority over the Miskito kingdom. The issue became entwined in U.S.-British relations and led to a proposed settlement initialed in Washington by Secretary of State Daniel Webster and British minister John Crampton on 30 April 1852. The proposal provided that Greytown become a free city, that the rights of the Miskito Indians be protected, and that the Costa Rican–Nicaraguan boundary along the San Juan River be firmly established. As with the 1850 Clayton-Bulwer Treaty, neither the Costa Ricans nor the Nicaraguans were consulted during the negotiations; when they were informed of the agreement one month after it had been concluded, they refused to go along. Control of the of the San Juan River was important to the Costa Ricans and Nicaraguans, and it remained a contentious issue until 1903, when the United States abandoned the San Juan River site to construct its canal in Panama. In addition to the boundary problem, the Nicaraguans also claimed that the continued British presence at Greytown was an unacceptable violation of the Monroe Doctrine.[8]

If Britain appeared willing to abandon Central America, it also acted to secure its future commercial and political interests in the region when, in March 1852, it proclaimed the "Colony of the Bay Islands," which included Roatán, Bonacca, and four neighboring islands off the Caribbean coast of Honduras. London acted on the mistaken premise that the United States was solely concerned with an isthmian canal project. When the British quickly dismissed the Honduran protests, the U.S. attitude stiffened. In Washington, the Senate Foreign Relations committee concluded that the Bay Islands were an integral part of Honduras and that the British seizure of them violated not only the Clayton-Bulwer Treaty but also the Monroe Doctrine. Britain was warned not to construct any permanent establishments on the islands. The committee also concluded that Britain should withdraw from Belize because that region legally belonged to Guatemala. When James Buchanan arrived in London in September 1853 as the new U.S. minister, his objective was clear: removal of all pretexts of British interference within isthmian and insular Central America. The British appeared equally determined. Foreign Secretary Lord Clarendon sharply noted that "British honor required . . . a paper regard for the interest and well being of the Misquitos because of the old connection with them" and that there could be no discussion of the Bay Islands.[9]

Amid the diplomatic impasse between the United States and British governments, tension increased between their citizens at the mouth of the San Juan. Greytown had fallen upon hard times, failing to keep pace with the needs of travelers transiting the isthmus. Meanwhile, Vanderbilt's enclave at Punta Arenas prospered and came to dominate both cargo and passenger traffic. Vanderbilt also continued to refuse to pay the British harbor fees. In 1853, when Vanderbilt failed to honor a financial requisition, frustrated local British officials, acting on their own, set ablaze some buildings in Punta Arenas. The incident set the stage for another confrontation in 1854, when new U.S. minister to Nicaragua, Solon Borland, arrived with the predetermined notion that the British authorities in Greytown were nothing more than "pirates and outlaws" from Jamaica. Borland demanded reparations for the damage done to the American Transit Company's buildings a year earlier and also declared diplomatic immunity for Captain T. T. Smith, the commander of an American river steamer who was being sought by the British on murder charges. After British officials rejected Borland's declarations, he stood by as Captain George N. Hollins of the U.S. Navy ordered his warship, the *Cyane*, to bombard Greytown. When news of the razing reached London, Minister Buchanan correctly asserted that Hollins had acted on his own. In Washington, Lord Clarendon thought the same. But President Franklin Pierce and Secretary of State William Marcy were not conciliatory. In his annual message to Congress on 4 December 1854, Pierce accused the British of making "groundless claims" and having "mischievous designs" on Punta Arenas. These were last words about the Greytown incident. The United States never paid for the pillage and the city never recovered.[10]

Rather than discuss their claim to the Bay Islands with the United States, the British tightened their grip. In 1856 the Honduran minister to London, Pedro A. Herrán, concluded an agreement that made the Bay Islands a free state under Honduran sovereignty. This arrangement was meant to provide protection to the British subjects residing there. The Honduran government, sharing its neighbors' desire for the removal of all foreign influence from the region, rejected the proposal. The British remained on the Bay Islands.

British mistrust of U.S. intentions concerning the isthmus soon increased. Many of the British were convinced that the United States supported William Walker's filibustering in Nicaragua. The atmosphere intensified when President Buchanan asserted that the British were illegally holding their possessions in Central America and that Washington's interpretation of the Clayton-Bulwer Treaty was the only correct one. The U.S. Senate resolved that Britain should live up to its obligations under the treaty or abrogate, further inflaming the relationship. In this ambience, Britain's First Lord of the Admiralty declared: "We are fast drifting into war with the U[nited] States." But the British were not to be bullied. Although Britain had been drained by the costs of the Crimean War and was anxious to withdraw from Central America, and although Lord Clarendon told the U.S. minister to London, George Dallas, that His Majesty's government "would not give three coppers to retain any post on the Central American territory or coast from which she could not honorably retire," at the same time Clarendon emphasized that the British would not succumb to U.S. jingoism.[11]

In the face of U.S. obstinacy, the British determined to find their way out of Central America. In 1859 Lord John Russell sent Charles Wycke to Central America to negotiate settlements with Guatemala, Honduras, and Nicaragua. The British secured their position in Belize when Guatemalan dictator Rafael Carerra accepted Wycke's proposal for the British construction of a railroad connecting Guatemala's interior to the Caribbean coast. Wycke's treaty with Honduras recognized the latter's sovereignty over the Bay Islands, but with the proviso that Honduras not transfer them to a third party or interfere with the British residents of the islands. The Honduran government also agreed not to interfere with the Miskito Indians within their boundaries. In the final agreement, the 1860 Treaty of Managua, the British agreed to relinquish their protectorate over Nicaragua's Miskito Coast, including Greytown, which became a free port under Nicaraguan control.[12]

Although the British did not extricate themselves from Central America following the treaties of 1859 and 1860, their presence on the isthmus did not create diplomatic problems with the United States until the 1890s. Instead of withdrawing, the British confirmed their control of Belize in 1861 by incorporating it into the colonial administrative system and naming the colony British Honduras. The failure to construct a road from Guatemala's interior to the Caribbean coast continued to cause problems between those two nations that remained even after Belize's independence in 1981.[13]

Nicaragua's Miskito Coast proved to be more troublesome. Charging that the Nicaraguan government failed to grant the Miskito Indians self-government, the British refused to surrender their protectorate over the Indian territory. In an 1879 arbitration case, Emperor Franz Josef of Austria affirmed British control over the Miskito Territory, and this decision provided the region with a sense of security and opened the door to foreign investment, particularly by U.S. Confederate expatriates who poured into the Miskito Territory. By 1885, these foreign entrepreneurs produced enough bananas on their plantations along the Escondido River to compete favorably in many U.S. cities from New Orleans to New York. By 1890, more than 90 percent of the region's wealth was under the control of private U.S. citizens. Investments were valued at $2 million, and in 1893 trade with the United States reached $4 million. American southern lifestyles prevailed, particularly at Bluefields, where private clubs, restaurants, and hotels served high quality wines, liquors, cigars, and "fancy eatables." Schools patterned on U.S. models thrived, and an English-language newspaper reported stateside news. A bottling plant produced ginger ale, ginger beer, champagne, lemonade, and "sasperilla." A German club boasted of its spacious lounging, reading, and smoking rooms and its gymnasium. All of this was threatened in 1894 when Nicaraguan president José Santo Zelaya viewed the Miskito Reserve as an economic asset.

In February 1894, under the pretext of a Honduran invasion, Zelaya ordered his troops to Bluefields and imposed martial law over the entire Miskito Territory. The U.S. businesses fared poorly under martial law. Their concessions and contracts were voided, and export taxes were levied on bananas. Initially the U.S. government appealed directly to Zelaya, but otherwise it took no action on behalf of the U.S. enclave. Washington reasoned that, since they were residents of a foreign country, the Americans were subject to local laws.

The British thought otherwise and decided to act on behalf of its residents in the region and assert its right to protect the Miskito Indians from Nicaraguan abuse. In March 1894, British troops arrived at Bluefields; this was a direct violation of the Clayton-Bulwer Treaty according to the *New York Tribune*. But the editors of the *Tribune*, like the policymakers in Washington, understood that a forced removal of the British would cause permanent damage to U.S. economic interests in the region, to say nothing of the rights of U.S. citizens living there. Despite this reality, Secretary of State Walter Q. Gresham chose to chastise the British rather than cooperate with them. Gresham charged the British with violating the Monroe Doctrine, the Clayton-Bulwer Treaty, and the 1860 Treaty of Managua, but he also informed the Americans residing in the Miskito Territory that the United States would not intervene there.

Although Gresham claimed credit for what followed, he ignored the fact that, as in the 1850s, Great Britain faced more serious problems on the European continent. Also, by 1894 Britain had wearied of its commitment to the Miskito Indians.

In the summer, the British withdrew their ships from Bluefields and stood by when the Nicaraguans expelled some 600 Jamaican administrators from the Miskito Territory. British protests to Managua clearly indicated an abatement of commitment. The Nicaraguans also became more tactful in their dealings with the Miskito. With the United States standing aside, the three groups recognized that the time had come to implement the terms of the 1860 treaty, which provided for the incorporation of the Miskito Reserve into the country of Nicaragua. Following the approval of the delegates representing all the tribes within the reserve, Nicaragua took control of the territory in November 1894. The act of incorporation was generous. It exempted the Miskitos from Nicaraguan military service and from personal taxes. Only Miskito Indians were to hold municipal offices in the Reserve.

Because the Miskito representatives were unable to write, S. C. Braida, U.S. consul at Bluefields, signed the document for them. With the stroke of a pen an estimated 6,000 Miskito Indians and 1,500 other residents were placed under Nicaraguan authority. The British withdrew quietly, to the satisfaction of Managua and Washington, but the entrepreneurs and Indians remained at the mercy of the mercurial Zelaya.[14]

The British withdrawal from the Bay Islands and the Miskito Coast, but not from Belize or the Clayton-Bulwer Treaty, owed more to the dynamics of British policy than to U.S. diplomacy. Confronted with political changes on the European continent and weary of commitments to distant and unprofitable colonies, the British were prepared to abandon the latter. As for the United States, its willingness to deal directly with Great Britain before and after the Clayton-Bulwer Treaty did little to enhance its image in Central America. Washington's failure to invoke the Monroe Doctrine against British territorial claims and against British actions in Nicaragua reaffirmed the Central American perception that the Monroe Doctrine was a self-serving piece of rhetoric.

Colonies, Commerce, and Investments

The experience at Bluefields typified the effects of ever-increasing numbers of U.S. citizens in Central America during the last half of the nineteenth century. From 1854 to 1864, three U.S. colonization schemes in Central America met with failure but left a bitter legacy that contributed to growing Central American mistrust of U.S. intentions on the isthmus.

On 15 December 1854, the *New York Times* reported on the visit of "Colonel" Henry L. Kinney to Washington to apprise government officials about the anticipated development of Nicaragua's Miskito Coast by Kinney's Central America's Land and Mining Company. The *Times* predicted that Central America would someday occupy an influential position in the family of nations, particularly "if her advantages of location, climate and soil are availed of by a race of 'Northmen' who shall supplant the tainted, mongrel and decaying race which now curses" the region.

Kinney, a self-made Texas real estate and livestock tycoon, acquired questionable title to 22.5 million acres in Nicaragua, 70 percent of country, including the Miskito Territory. In an effort to legitimize the title, Kinney sold 225,000 shares of stock, each convertible to 100 acres of land in Nicaragua. Although Kinney attracted few colonists, he still managed to earn the wrath of Nicaraguan officials. Claiming that the Kinney grant was illegal, the Nicaraguan and Costa Rican governments implored the United States to put a stop to Kinney's escapade. Secretary of State William L. Marcy rejected the appeal on the grounds that the U.S. government had no authority to prohibit a private company from the peaceful pursuit of its objective. Without U.S. government support and confronted with Nicaraguan opposition, Kinney's stay in Greytown was short, and he returned home bankrupt in 1856. When Kinney again attempted to establish a colony in Nicaragua in 1858, only a U.S. Navy rescue effort saved him from a dark fate at the hands of local officials.[15]

If the apparent indifference of the U.S. government toward the Kinney expedition fueled Central America's belief that Washington had territorial designs on the isthmus, the escapades of William Walker solidified that perception. The origins of Walker's arrival on the isthmus are found in the political rivalry between Liberals and Conservatives that had dominated Central America's political landscape since independence. This was a conflict that often traversed national borders. Since the late 1840s violence between the two factions had taken a heavy toll on the economic and social development of the region. In 1854 it appeared that the Nicaraguan government would come under Conservative control and that the Conservatives would spread their influence to Honduras, where a U.S. entrepreneur, Byron Cole, was part owner of the Honduran Mining and Trading Company, which was ready to exploit a large tract of land. Cole feared that a Conservative administration in Honduras would result in the cancellation of his company's contract. To protect his investment, Cole concluded that in order to maintain the political status quo in both countries the Nicaraguan Liberals needed to be retained in power. To achieve that objective Cole convinced the Liberals in León that William Walker and his private army could save their cause and, in effect, keep the violence from spreading to Honduras.

Walker, whose checkered career included stints as a journalist, lawyer, and doctor, made his way to California in 1853. There he met Byron Cole, who offered him a contract to engage 300 men into the Nicaragua's Liberal army. To circumvent an 1818 neutrality law that forbade U.S. citizens from serving foreign armies, the two men altered the contract to make it read like a colonization grant.

With his "56 immortals," Walker arrived in Nicaragua in May 1854 to a warm reception. After forcing the Conservatives to sue for peace eighteen months later, Walker set out to dominate local politics, modernize the Nicaraguan economy, and eventually construct a transisthmian canal. To solidify the venture he sought to engineer a Central American union with Nicaragua as its hub. He first created a puppet government headed by the aging Patricio Rivas, who in turn appointed Walker commander in chief of the Nicaraguan army. Then, in a farcical election on 29 June 1856 Walker became president of the country despite the fact that the Nicaraguan constitution forbade foreign-born persons from holding office.

To accomplish the modernization of Nicaragua, Walker needed to eliminate the privileged position of local elites and the vestiges of Spanish authority. The elites were to be replaced by immigrants from the United States, and a new legal system was planned. By presidential decree Walker rescinded the prohibition of slavery that had dated from independence in 1821 and established a system of indentured servitude and forced labor. He also instituted a complex system of landownership that deprived many of the local elite of their wealth, issued scrip as legal tender, and made the English language coequal with Spanish. Infuriated, displaced Nicaraguan elites soon found allies outside the country's borders.[16]

Among the Nicaraguans' newfound friends was Cornelius Vanderbilt. Local managers of his Accessory Transit Company manipulated company stock at Vanderbilt's expense, advanced "President" Walker $20 million in gold bullion against the company's debt to the government, and agreed to transport emigrants from the United States to Nicaragua at $20 per head. In February 1856, during the ensuing intracompany struggle, Walker canceled the Transit Company's concession. The U.S. State Department refused to intercede on Vanderbilt's behalf, on the grounds that the company had been incorporated in Nicaragua and it was there that the crime had been committed. The frustrated Vanderbilt had reason to become a willing partner with Walker's opponents.

The Pierce administration's failure fully to apply neutrality laws designed to prevent the private shipment of arms and mercenaries abroad only enhanced the argument that the United States had larger designs on the isthmus. Federal authorities in New York and San Francisco did little to prevent ships from sailing to Nicaragua filled with arms and colonists.[17]

Equally damning of U.S. policy were the activities of Minister John K. Wheeler, a well-connected North Carolina plantation owner who was initially accredited to Nicaragua's Conservative government in 1854. Wheeler took it upon himself to extend recognition to the new Rivas government in 1856. Wheeler also shared Walker's view that the Central Americans were incapable of self-government and that the only road to Nicaragua's modernization was through slavery. In late 1856, Secretary of State William Marcy finally recalled the minister, but the recall did little to dampen the perception that the United States had quietly sanctioned the Walker escapade.[18]

The Central American fear of an eventual U.S. takeover was reinforced by their growing cognizance of a substantial U.S. southern interest that hoped for an empire beyond U.S. borders. In the 1850s they began to look toward the Caribbean. While Cuba drew the most attention, many notable southerners, particularly in coastal cities on the Gulf of Mexico, supported Walker. Among these "imperialists" were Pierre Soulé, Jefferson Davis, J. D. B. DeBow, and John A. Quitman. The most active was Soulé, who reportedly raised $500,000 for Walker and purchased a confiscated Nicaraguan plantation for well under market value. Soulé also was responsible for the expansionist plank of the 1856 Democratic platform.[19]

In London, Foreign Secretary Lord Clarendon suspected that Walker was trying to create conditions in which the United States could eventually take direct
control of the isthmian transit route. In the mid-1850s, however, European events,
notably the Crimean War, took precedence and forced London to adopt a cautious
policy. In late 1855 London sent mixed signals. For example, its West Indian squadron was increased by three large ships, but a Costa Rican and Guatemalan request
that British naval ships visit their waters to demonstrate London's disapproval of
Walker's presence on the isthmus was turned down.[20]

Walker faced an array of potential opponents, and when the tide turned
against him in 1856 these forces coalesced, each for its own reason. Led by the
presidents of Costa Rica and Guatemala, the other isthmian statesmen joined the
Nicaraguans in battle against the foreign intruder. Vanderbilt, anxious to recover
his concession, happily supplied money for arms that the British willingly sold
to the Central American forces. Following a year-long siege at his last holdout in
Rivas, Nicaragua, Walker surrendered under terms favorable to himself but damaging to the long-term interests of the United States. Rather than turn Walker over
to the Central Americans, the commander of the U.S. warship *St. Mary's,* Charles
E. Davis, provided safe conduct out of Nicaragua for Walker and the filibusterers.
Walker returned to Greytown in 1858, only to be arrested and deported to the
United States. Undaunted, he returned again in 1860 to the Honduran coast, where
he was captured in Trujillo by a regiment of British troops. Refusing their protection, Walker was turned over to the Hondurans, who quickly tried him and then
executed him on 12 September 1860. Whereas U.S. southern newspapers carried
stories of his execution without comment, President James Buchanan subsequently
noted that it was his country's destiny to spread its culture throughout the entire
Americas and "should events be permitted to take their natural course . . . Central
America will contain an American population which will confer blessings and
benefits upon the natives."[21]

As a result of U.S. filibustering in the 1850s, Central Americans anticipated
future U.S. incursions and could only hope that the Europeans would come to their
rescue. Unfortunately for the Central Americans, Europe was much too preoccupied with its own political turmoil to be interested in the affairs of the isthmus.

Central American fear became reality on 3 December 1861, nine months after
the start of the U.S. Civil War. President Abraham Lincoln asked that Congress
take steps to colonize free blacks abroad, an idea that had surfaced as early as 1815.
This time Secretary of State William H. Seward suggested Central America as a
destination for the slaves because its agricultural society paralleled that of the
southern plantations. He even suggested that a colony be established at Livingston,
Guatemala, because blacks already resided there. At the same time, Seward ration-
alized that a U.S. extension into the region would blunt European interests concerning the isthmus.[22]

In July 1862, the Central Americans rejected the suggestion that a black colony
be established in their midst and in so doing demonstrated their own sense of ra-
cism, which Washington's policymakers had not anticipated and did not under-

stand. In rejecting the proposal, Antonio J. Irisarri, minister to the United States for Guatemala and El Salvador, expressed dismay at the president's referral to blacks as equals, and this attitude was reconfirmed by the U.S. representatives on the isthmus. In Nicaragua, A. B. Dickinson described the Central American mood when he wrote that the locals "feel indignant at the idea of being ranked with the North American Negro." Guatemalan dictator Rafael Carerra suggested that the United States establish a black colony in the territory it "stole" from Mexico in 1848. Such remonstrances demonstrated how little the U.S. political leaders knew about Central America's social history. Nothing came of the proposal, but the incident exacerbated Central American mistrust of U.S. intentions.[23]

Whereas the three colonization schemes of the 1850s and 1860s demonstrated U.S. lack of sensitivity toward Central American social dynamics, Minister Charles Riotte in 1861 demonstrated the low esteem that U.S. observers held for Central American politics:

> The family feuds become affairs of state, and the ascendancy to political preponderance is often sullied with acts of unwarrantable cruelty, practiced not so much against the political adversary as upon the enemy of the tribe. It is seldom the greediness of gain which causes the outbreak of hostilities, but rather the desire for influence and power.[24]

Since 1821, political power in Central America rested with the socioeconomic elites whose families predated independence. During the early nineteenth century, these elites were divided into two groups. The Conservatives clung to preferences rooted in the Spanish past, favoring a strong central government and a privileged church, eschewing economic expansion beyond their historic contacts. In contrast, the Liberals, usually merchants, preferred a decentralized government, a less-privileged church, and the extension of contacts and markets to the wider world. But neither the Conservatives nor the Liberals anticipated sharing political power with members of the nonwhite racial groups: *mestizos,* Indians, and blacks.[25] Another century would pass before those groups gained political power. Through the 1850s this Conservative-Liberal conflict prompted U.S. diplomats to describe local politics in most unflattering terms. When the bitter rivals Guatemalan President Rafael Carerra and Salvadoran President Gerardo Barrios died in 1865, Riotte penned, "Humanity . . . it seems to me has on the whole gained in losing both of them."[26]

The loss of Carerra and Barrios, however, did not end the interstate rivalry for dominance of the region. From the time of their deaths until the end of the nineteenth century, several attempts were made to form a union of all or some of the states. Given the region's history of intra- and interstate rivalries, which had condemned it to economic backwardness, Washington's policymakers came to believe that union provided the best means for advancing the region's economic development and efficiently managing its foreign affairs. In 1874, Secretary of State Hamilton Fish instructed newly appointed minister George Williamson to work for regional unification, but after visiting all five republics Williamson reported that without leadership and popular support, the prospects for union remained remote.[27]

Obviously Williamson had misjudged the capabilities of Justo Rufino Barrios, a Liberal who served as Guatemalan president from 1871 to 1885. In 1871, Barrios fashioned an alliance with his Liberal counterparts in El Salvador and Honduras to combat their Conservative enemies. Nothing materialized until 1885, when Barrios proclaimed the unification of all Central America, to be achieved by force if necessary. Political leaders in the other four countries resented Barrios's interference in their internal affairs. The Mexicans, fearful that Barrios intended to use the union to regain control forcefully of Chiapas, offered assistance to the four and assembled troops along the Mexican-Guatemalan border at Chiapas.

With the threat of war on the horizon, Secretary of State Thomas Bayard announced that the United States would use its influence to avert a conflict and promote peace. Bayard instructed the U.S. minister in Guatemala, Henry C. Hall, to mediate the dispute. Washington also dispatched five warships to the region, ostensibly to protect U.S. lives and property but actually to impress the Central Americans. The U.S. effort failed, and war broke out in March 1885. The two-day conflict ended with Barrios's death in battle at Chalchuapa, El Salvador. With his death the drive for union ended.

Two years later, in January 1887, representatives of the five nations gathered in Guatemala City for a month-long conference that produced several agreements. The nations recognized each other's territorial integrity, agreed not to interfere in each other's internal affairs, set up a procedure for the arbitration of mutual disputes, and agreed to establish a mutual free-trade union by 1890. To policymakers in Washington, the political agreements held out the promise for tranquility, and a trade union presented greater economic opportunity. Journalist Robert Ogden was more realistic. Writing in the *Nation* on 27 July 1887, Ogden correctly predicted that the region's historic record, marked by "jealous officials, unscrupulous rulers, and [an] ignorant population," would prevent the best of intentions from reaching fruition.

Secretary of State James G. Blaine revived Washington's interest in a regional union in 1889 when he instructed the newly appointed minister to Central America, Lansing B. Mizner, to encourage unification efforts. Blaine also discussed potential unification with the Central American delegates to the first Pan-American Conference, which convened in Washington in October 1889. The goal of union supported Blaine's vision of a continental system in which conflicts between the states of the western hemisphere would be reduced and commercial relations between the United States and all of Latin America improved. Blaine, however, failed to persuade anyone.

Before the century came to an end the Central Americans twice more attempted to bring about a union among themselves. The first effort came in November 1889 in Managua, but the plan died within seven months when a power struggle in El Salvador resulted in a change of governments. The final attempt in the nineteenth century came in 1895, when the presidents of Honduras, Nicaragua, and El Salvador met in Ampala, Honduras, and created a loose confederation in which no one would surrender autonomy to the central government. The United States extended recognition to this Greater Republic of Central America, but nothing of substance materialized before its demise in 1898 when El Salvador withdrew.[28]

In favoring a Central American union, Washington policymakers paralleled the historical experiences of the five republics to those of the United States in the years preceding the constitution, when interstate rivalries hampered efforts to achieve political stability and economic prosperity. This parallel prompted U.S. policymakers to believe that a constitutional union imposed on the five Central American republics would bring success similar to that in the United States. They were mistaken.

The restrictive philosophy of the Central American Conservative political leadership had contributed to the region's failure to develop economically in the years following independence. That began to change with the emergence of Liberal leaders across the isthmus beginning in the 1870s. Men like Justo Rufino Barrios in Guatemala, José Santos Zelaya in Nicaragua, Tomás Guardia in Costa Rica, Luis Bográn in Honduras, and Tomás Regalado in El Salvador were impressed by the economic growth of Western Europe and the United States, and they pursued policies that encouraged similar export-orientated economies in hopes of modernizing their own societies. Like their counterparts elsewhere in Latin America, they accepted Auguste Comte's idea of "sociocracy" and Herbert Spencer's evolutionary theory of society, which held that economic growth and prosperity needed to take hold before political democracy could be introduced. Well into the twentieth century, Central America's Liberal leaders remained obsessed with economic development, placing their faith in scientific and technical education and "western" values.[29]

Although in the beginning the Liberals were idealistic, they soon lost sight of their goals. They continually postponed political reforms and remained insensitive to the needs of workers. Their legacies were the modernized capitals of Guatemala City, Managua, San José, San Salvador, and Tegucigalpa, but the rural areas in each country were virtual backwaters of society.[30]

Even from the start of the era of independence in the 1820s, many in the United States hoped for increased trade with Central America. The leading proponent of this hope was Congressman Henry Clay of Kentucky, who envisioned the wares of the Old Northwest being transported down the Mississippi River to the Caribbean. Thereafter, each U.S. minister appointed to the isthmus was instructed to report on potential markets. Furthermore, with the loss of its guaranteed markets in Spain, Central Americans were looking for new opportunities. The mutual desire for increased trade resulted in the 1825 Treaty of Amity and Commerce between the United States and the Central American Federation, but the treaty lapsed in the 1840s after doing little to improve the situation. Great Britain became the region's largest trading partner and foreign investor.

In the 1870s the reunified United States began looking abroad for markets for its manufactured goods. At the same time the Central American Liberals were offering generous conditions for trade and investment. Although the United States remained a distant second to Great Britain in both exports and total trade with Central America, exchanges between the two revealed the underdevelopment of the isthmian economies. Exports from the United States to the region included unprocessed agricultural products; semi-manufactured goods such as tools, arms and munitions, and hardware; petroleum and kerosene; flour; and cheap cotton cloth. Imports to the United States from Central America included food products of relatively high bulk and low unit value, such as sugar, hides, wool, cacao, fruits, rubber, quinine bark, and other tropical products.[31]

The reasons for poor trade relations were numerous. Higher shipping and insurance costs and unfavorable exchange rates contributed to the increased cost of U.S. products, which in some instances were 70 percent higher than the original sale price. Whereas Central American governments relied on tariffs as their chief source of income, the high import duties on U.S. goods also resulted from the long-standing presence of British emissaries, who secured favorable terms for their merchants. Over the years, U.S. representatives and travelers did little to improve relations. Seldom were they fluent in Spanish, and they also permitted personal prejudices to interfere with business relations. Trade with the United States was further complicated by the lack of Caribbean ports along the isthmus, except for the San Juan River basin used by Nicaragua. The major Central American ports were on the Pacific coast. The Panama Railroad, completed in 1855, offered some prospect for improvement, but its primary user, the U.S. Mail and Steamship Company, was more interested in U.S. intercoastal trade, Latin America's west coast, and the Far East than it was in Central America.[32]

In 1877, Secretary of State William Evarts instructed U.S. consuls throughout Latin America to inform the department on a regular basis about local market demands, prices, and the potential for U.S. exports. In the early 1880s, the State Department began issuing a monthly volume of consular reports. In 1884 and 1885 the U.S. government sent a special commission to Central and South America to search out new markets. Before its departure, the commission visited several U.S. manufacturing centers for advice on possible exports to the western hemispheric countries. Despite this renewed interest in Central America there was little change in trade balance. While the dollar value increased for both imports and exports, the percentage value of total trade remained about the same.

Although the British, Germans, and French remained Central America's leading trade partners until the end of the century, the United States earned the reputation as the most aggressive marketeer in the region. Much of the trade increase may be credited to the development of export-based economies and the agriculture, mining, transportation, communication, and manufacturing sectors by the Liberals in the latter part of the nineteenth century. Each nation sent lavish exhibits to the 1884 and 1885 Cotton Centennial Expositions in New Orleans, evidence of the Crescent City's concentrated effort to become the preeminent U.S. trading partner with the isthmian republics. Central American Liberals attracted foreign investment capital by granting generous tax concessions and passing lax labor laws. The foreigners quickly identified and melded with the local elites, further securing their investments.[33]

Concessions granted to mining companies by President Marco Aurelio Soto of Honduras mirrored those granted to other entrepreneurs throughout the region. The mining companies were permitted to import all machinery, equipment, and materials necessary for the day-to-day operation of a mining camp duty free. Ores were also exempted from export duties and all municipal and national taxes. Because of the lack of local industry, imports included shoes, canvas tents, blankets, clothing, soap, canned fish, sugar, flour, and beer, all considered essential to daily operation. The companies also received water and timber requisition rights. Subsequently, President Luis Bográn instituted the *mandiento* press-gang labor system to meet the labor demands of the mining companies. Bográn also utilized government funds to advertise the availability of ores on the world market through traveling exhibits. Among the earliest U.S. investors was Thomas Lombard, through his Yuseman Mining Company and Chicago Honduran Mining Company. The most successful mining concern was the New York and Honduran Rosario Mining Company, headed by Washington S. Valentine. Valentine expanded the company's operations into many ancillary fields and capitalized on the timber rights received with the land grants. His influence was so pervasive that he was dubbed "the King of Honduras."

The generosity of the concessions, however, brought little prosperity to Honduras. The mining companies ancillary operations—hotels, transportation of charcoal (for fuel), and salt manufacture—were profitable to the parent companies but brought little to the country because they were considered essential to the mining industry and thus were exempt from taxation. As the older mines petered out and civil war plagued the country in the 1890s, foreign investment drastically declined and the country gained the reputation as an investment "rat hole."[34]

Both foreign investors and the Central American governments themselves recognized the need for good roads and ports. Unfamiliar with steep terrain, dense vegetation, and torrential rains, foreign entrepreneurs often underestimated the cost and time extent of projects.

Although much was accomplished, railroad concessions were repeatedly given to foreign companies that failed to raise sufficient capital to see the projects to their completion. The environment opened the door to corruption. Honduras suffered the most. By 1909 the country had a mere sixty miles of track to show for its $120 million debt obligation.

Among the more successful U.S. railroaders was Minor C. Keith, who built Costa Rica's first steam rail line. Completed in 1911, it connected the Caribbean port of Limón to San José. In Guatemala two U.S. consortiums received lucrative contracts to build railroads between the Pacific port of San José and the coffee center at Esquintla and from Champerico to Retalhuleu. British investors owned and operated the El Salvador Railroad Company, connecting the country's interior with the coastal ports. Although these ventures were highly successful, the foreign investors, not the Central American governments, received the bulk of the profits.[35]

At the same time new deep-water ports were opened on the isthmian Pacific coast at Champerico in Guatemala and at La Union and La Libertad in El Salvador, but none provided regular service to the United States and Europe. The Caribbean ports—Livingston, La Ceiba, Puerto Cortéz, Bluefields, and Limón—remained dreary clutters of wooden shacks and warehouses. During the late nineteenth century only Guatemala made significant progress, developing a Caribbean outlet at Puerto Barrios. Along with other opportunities presented foreign capitalists, the Guatemalans offered generous concessions for port improvements.

The Central Americans were equally anxious to develop public utilities and services. In Costa Rica, Minor Keith oversaw the completion of the nation's first telegraph and telephone systems and financed the installation of streetcars in San José. George Ross held the exclusive contract in Limón for street maintenance and garbage collection.[36] Entrepreneurs from the United States pursued similar projects elsewhere on the isthmus.

In addition to the more visible projects, U.S. entrepreneurs found profit in lesser-known businesses. For example, in Guatemala V. S. Storm held a monopoly on the importation of barbed wire and had special licenses to import machinery for the sugar, rice, and coffee industries. Despite a limited local demand, Robert Cleaves controlled the market for imported gang plows, cultivators, reapers, threshers, and the Jersey cow! John W. Protheerve held a concession for an ostrich farm, and William J. Forsyth held one for quinine trees.[37]

Nevertheless, few U.S. entrepreneurs came to the region. In 1895 Lewis Baker, the minister to Nicaragua from the United States, observed that U.S. investors had the capacity to develop the "foundations of control of this rich little country," but apparently only a few took advantage of the opportunity. That same year consul Thomas O'Hara reported more than 1,400 inquiries about possible investment opportunities in Nicaragua, but only a handful appeared seriously interested in seizing the opportunities available.[38] The Central American Liberal political leaders may have hoped that their policies would spark an industrial revolution and build a more sophisticated society, but it did not happen. Capital was still in short supply, and skilled labor and technology were equally absent.

The British remained the dominant investors in the region, particularly in railroads, which did not produce a high return. Investments in other areas also performed poorly. For example, mining brought almost no returns, and public utilities yielded income only on debentures. The aggregate British investment in Central America seldom yielded more than 3 percent. Such evidence suggests that Minister Baker and Consul O'Hara misjudged the benefits of investing in Central America. Minor Keith was more the exception than the rule.[39]

Despite their encouragement of mining, transportation, merchandising, and other commercial pursuits in the late nineteenth century, Central America's Liberal leaders emphasized the development of agro-export economies to provide the income for the modernization of their societies. With the exception of Honduras, climate and soil conditions were conducive to the cultivation of coffee. The Guatemalan model also illustrates what happened in Costa Rica, El Salvador, and Nicaragua. Shortly before 1880, President Barrios stimulated coffee output by exempting the product from export taxes and establishing government nurseries to distribute coffee plants free of charge to farmers who could not afford to buy them. These measures were concurrent with a worldwide increase in the consumption of coffee. As a result, the number of acres devoted to coffee production doubled between 1880 and 1889 to 760,000 acres. Foreign investors came into the field. By 1913, the first year that statistics on ownership by nationality appeared in Guatemala, 170 coffee *fincas* were owned by Germans and 1,657 by Guatemalans. But the German *fincas* were larger and more efficiently managed, producing 358,000 quintals of coffee compared to 525,000 quintals produced by Guatemalans. To meet the need for labor, the government passed vagrancy laws that forced Indians to enter into contractual relations with the *finca* owners. Overreliance on coffee, however, resulted in the importation of basic foodstuffs.

Other countries encouraged the production of sugar, cacao, rubber, and timber to avoid the pitfalls of monoculture. Generous concessions were granted to foreign entrepreneurs. For example, in 1894 the H. C. Emery Company of Boston received an exclusive five-year contract to cut mahogany, cedar, and rosewood in eastern Nicaragua at the cost of one gold peso for each log exported and the planting of two seedlings for every tree cut. In its first six months of operation, the company cut 3,349 trees without touching the bulk of those available. Still, by World War I, coffee remained the primary agricultural product and major export commodity, accounting for 85.2 percent of Guatemala's exports, 80.4 percent of El Salvador's; 63.3 percent of Nicaragua's, and 35.2 percent of Costa Rica's.[40]

Few foresaw that the banana industry—the "empire in green and gold"—would succeed because it had such inauspicious beginnings. First introduced to the United States in 1866, bananas wrapped in tinfoil sold for ten cents each at the Philadelphia Centennial Exposition ten years later. By the 1890s, bananas were no longer a curiosity and found a limited market in large cities. By then, two business groups dominated the banana trade from the tropics. The first was Boston Fruit Company, founded by Lorenzo Baker and Andrew Preston, which established subsidiaries throughout the Caribbean and marketed bananas in the mid-Atlantic and northeastern regions of the United States. The second group was a consortium of small companies owned by Minor Keith, which shipped fruit from Colombia, Costa Rica, Panama, and Nicaragua to New Orleans and Mobile, Alabama.

The crucial year for the banana industry was 1899, when the three men created a business alliance of necessity (Baker, Preston, and Keith). With their operations hampered by the vicissitudes of weather and Central American politics, they realized that they could achieve a more constant and reliable flow of fruit if they spread their production to several areas so that a disaster in one area could be counterbalanced by production in another. Thus the United Fruit Company was born. Within a few years, United Fruit became the world's largest banana pro-

ducer, owning land in Central America and the Caribbean, operating the Great
White Fleet consisting of nearly forty ships it owned or chartered, and holding
title to 112 miles of Central American railroads linking the banana plantations to
the sea. Early in the twentieth century, United Fruit controlled 80 to 90 percent of
the banana market in the United States.[41]

By 1900 commerce in Central America had increased substantially, but favorable trade balances did not bring prosperity. Foreigners dominated not only trade
and shipping but also banking, making capital available only at high interest rates.
Concessionaires controlled local markets for consumer goods to the exclusion of
native residents. Only those at the apex of Central America's political and economic structures realized some benefit from the foreign investors, while those at
the bottom remained at the subsistence level. Thus, despite Liberal publicizing, Central America still had the characteristics of a premodern society. In 1898, William
E. Curtis told his *Forum* readers that, with the exception of limited advantages in
Costa Rica, modernity had not yet reached Central America. Misgovernment remained the greatest obstacle to the region's development. Revolutions were a game
among the elite, Curtis observed, and the masses, "if left alone may never rebel."
Locals invested their money abroad to avoid the risks of political turmoil at home.
A constitution such as El Salvador's was meaningless because the country was
ruled by a "small group of politicians who maintain their power by military force
and are overthrown as often as the opposition can form an army to carry out a
conspiracy."[42]

Despite their jaundiced view of Central America, U.S. businessmen and policymakers saw the isthmus as a site for a transisthmian canal.

A Canal under U.S. Control

In 1513, the Spanish conquistador Vasco Núñez de Balboa marched across the
isthmus of Panama and discovered that only a narrow strip of land separated the
Atlantic and Pacific Oceans. Although fellow conquistador Hernán Cortés envisioned a transisthmian canal, and although in 1524 King Charles V of Spain ordered the first official survey of the region for the location of a possible canal,
nearly 400 years would elapse before a canal linked the two oceans.[43]

From the time of Thomas Jefferson's presidency until the end of the Mexican-
American War in 1848, the U.S. government, preoccupied by domestic considerations and with Asian and Latin American commercial relations minimal at best,
did not consider a canal constructed on its own initiative feasible. The government
assumed that such a project would be undertaken by private investors. Should foreigners complete the task, the United States insisted that the canal be subject to
"equal rights" and "free and open transit" for all nations and not "exclusive control" by any single nation. Great Britain shared the opinion that private entrepreneurs rather than government should undertake the canal project and that the canal should be open to world commerce on an equitable basis. Thus, despite the

heated rivalry on the isthmus in 1848 and 1849, and preoccupied with events on the European continent, London was willing to accept the 1850 Clayton-Bulwer Treaty.

With the British commitment in hand, the United States made it clear that it did not want another nation to construct a canal. In 1857, Washington warned Costa Rica and Nicaragua that it would not tolerate the granting of preferential canal rights to Felix Belly of France, who had extracted a joint concession to construct a canal along the San Juan River. Belly's project died for lack of funding.[44]

The U.S. government's commitment to the private construction of a transisthmian route also was expressed in 1847 congressional legislation that provided for the subsidization of a steamship line to link the east coast with the California and Oregon territories. Then, William Aspinwall and Cornelius Vanderbilt constructed transportation routes across the Central American isthmus. Aspinwall and his associates constructed a railroad across the isthmus at Panama and, as indicated above, Vanderbilt developed a transit system across the San Juan River linking two of his shipping companies to provide for U.S. intercoastal trade. Once the Panama Railroad opened in 1855, it quickly replaced the more inconvenient sea-land passage provided by Vanderbilt, which went out of business in 1868. Only after the completion of the U.S. transcontinental railroad in 1869 did the Panama Railroad fall on hard times.[45]

Many Central Americans also envisioned a privately constructed canal. In the 1820s Juan José Cañas and José Aycinena visualized a transisthmian canal that would draw world shipping to Central America, spur local agriculture and industry, and make the region a maritime power. The canal would foster road-building, which in turn would bring local wares to market and attract Europeans, who through intermarriage with locals would engender a more ambitious and educated populace. Such was the vision of the "new" Central America that persisted throughout the nineteenth century. As a result, the Central American governments became willing partners to many private but poorly financed schemes for a canal. Before the official canal project was codified in the 1903 Hay-Bunau-Varilla Treaty, the governments entered into some forty-five agreements, all with generous concessions, with individuals whose projects never materialized.[46] They failed to realize, however, that Panama itself did not achieve economic prosperity when it served as the transit root in the Spanish mercantile system, nor did the Panama Railroad Company flourish in the mid-nineteenth century.

After the U.S. Civil War, as Central Americans anxiously sought construction projects, opinion in the United States increasingly took on a "go it alone attitude." The first step in that direction came with the 1867 Dickinson-Ayón Treaty between the United States and Nicaragua. While the treaty guaranteed Nicaragua's sovereignty over all transit routes through its territory, it also obligated the United States to protect any canal through the country and guaranteed U.S. canal privileges in any project that Nicaragua might undertake with a third party. For the first time, the United States took on the defense obligation of a proposed transisthmian transportation route.[47] The treaty provided the basis for a number of abortive attempts at canal building in Nicaragua until 1902, when the Nicaraguan government abrogated it.

In 1869, Ulysses S. Grant entered the White House determined to have the United States build a canal itself. His interest dated back to 1852, when 150 men in his army unit lost their lives to cholera while crossing Panama. As president he directed Navy Secretary Adolf E. Borie to conduct a route survey, noting that it should be a U.S. canal.[48]

Grant's willingness to forego the canal provisions of the Clayton-Bulwer Treaty and to apply only the colonization principles marked an important shift in U.S. policy. Cognizant of Grant's attitude, outgoing secretary of state William H. Seward announced in early 1869 that henceforth the United States would be "unwilling to enter into an entangling alliance with other nations for the construction and maintenance of a passage" across the isthmus. The U.S. minister to Colombia, Stephen A. Hurlburt, unsuccessfully sought to replace the Bidlack treaty with Colombia without the provisions for joint protection.[49]

Nothing further occurred until January 1876, when after four years of study President Grant's Interoceanic Canal Commission recommended that a canal be built across Nicaragua, using the San Juan River. This route shortened the distance between Atlantic and Pacific coastal ports and was considered to be less threatened by landslides and floods. Considering a projected cost of $100 million, the commission estimated that it would save $50 million over the Panama route. The commission was unequivocal: "the route known as the 'Nicaraguan route' . . . possesses, both for the construction and maintenance of a canal, greater advantage, and offers fewer difficulties from engineering, commercial, and economic points of view, than any one of the other [proposed] routes."[50]

As a result of the commission's report Nicaragua remained the chosen site until 1902. Faced by the projected cost, Grant momentarily backed away from his position that the United States be the sole constructor and controller. He now suggested that the canal be built by several countries and placed under international supervision. British, French, German, and Dutch bankers were not receptive to the idea, nor were the British willing to abrogate the Clayton-Bulwer Treaty. Meanwhile, the Nicaraguans refused to surrender territorial sovereignty to an international control commission, viewing such a commission as a violation of the Clayton-Bulwer Treaty. The Costa Ricans also rejected an international canal along the San Juan River. In contrast, President Barrios of Guatemala, sensing the arrival of the Americans and being anxious to exert his influence over the isthmus, attempted to broker U.S. acquisition of the Honduran Bay Islands, long considered strategically important to a canal's Atlantic terminus. Although Secretary of State William Evarts rejected the Barrios offer, he encouraged the formation of a federation consisting of Guatemala, Honduras, El Salvador, and Nicaragua in order to secure a canal treaty with Nicaragua.[51] Nothing came of Evarts's suggestion.

Unnoticed in 1876 was the Canal Commission's observation that the Clayton-Bulwer Treaty covered only Central America, leaving both the isthmus at Tehuantepec, Mexico, and at Panama, then part of Colombia, open to foreign speculation.

Only after a French company headed by Ferdinand de Lesseps, who had built the Suez Canal, concluded an agreement with Colombia in 1879 to construct a canal through Panama, did the U.S. public begin to demand that any canal constructed across the isthmus be a U.S. project.[52]

The efforts of a French company to build a canal across Panama, with an international guarantee of neutrality, prompted the United States increasingly to demand controlling influence over the route. U.S. politicians argued that the Monroe Doctrine provided the protective shield against such an action. As early as 1872, when Nicaraguan President Anselmo Rivas discussed the financing of a canal with London bankers, the U.S. minister to Costa Rica, Charles N. Riotte, warned that any large European investment in the isthmus violated the Monroe Doctrine.[53] In 1881, in response to the French project, the U.S. House of Foreign Affairs Committee resolved that "the construction of any public work, connecting the waters of the Atlantic and Pacific, by any European government or power . . . would be in violation of the spirit and letter of the Monroe Doctrine, and could not be sanctioned by the Government of the United States."[54]

President Rutherford B. Hayes was most emphatic: "the policy of this country is a canal under American control." The United States, he continued, "cannot consent to the surrender of this to any European power or to any combination of European powers." In addition to citing the Monroe Doctrine, secretaries of state James G. Blaine and Frederick T. Frelinghuysen called for the abrogation of the Clayton-Bulwer Treaty and the exclusive control of any transisthmian canal by the United States. Frelinghuysen described the Clayton-Bulwer Treaty "as a thing of the past [and] should no longer be considered as forbidding the United States to acquire control of the canal."[55]

Secretary Blaine also used national security as a justification for a U.S.-controlled canal. He explained that "for the protection of the distant shores of her own domain, for the drawing together of the extremes of Union," the United States should control any waterway linking the Atlantic and Pacific oceans. Journalist John Kasson added that "no chance should be left to convert a weak Central American state into another Egypt by means of foreign possessory rights in another isthmian canal." Such a presence in Central America, Kasson argued, not only threatened the United States economically and militarily but also threatened to drag the United States into the intrigues of European politics.[56]

In 1880, amid the jingoism, Aniceto G. Menocal, a navy engineer and surveyor and a member of Grant's Interoceanic Canal Commission, received a canal concession from Nicaragua. With a group of other investors, Menocal formed the Maritime Canal Company. The Menocal contract ignited political intrigue on the isthmus. Acting on his own, the U.S. minister to Central America, Cornelius A. Logan, suggested to President Barrios of Guatemala that he approach the United States with the suggestion that it assume a protectorate over a Central American union headed by Barrios. Logan concluded that such a protectorate upheld the Monroe Doctrine and cleared the path for the construction of a canal solely under U.S. auspices. Barrios seized the moment and in August 1880 dispatched Arturo Ubico to Washington, where he found President Hayes unwilling to pledge support to Barrios's regional unity plan in return for a canal concession. The same was true four years later, when Barrios told Secretary Frelinghuysen that he would personally take "your final canal proposal" to Nicaragua and see that it was accepted.

Although the U.S. government refused to become involved in Central American political dynamics to achieve its canal treaty objective, the increased diplomatic activities intimidated Nicaragua. Fearing that Barrios might force it to participate in a Central American union that in turn would impose a most unfavorable agreement upon it, Nicaragua's minister to Washington Joaquín Zavala concluded a treaty with Frelinghuysen. The treaty provided for a U.S.-constructed canal, administered by a joint board of directors controlled by the United States. Although there was no fortification provision, the Frelinghuysen-Zavala Treaty established a perpetual alliance under which the United States agreed to protect Nicaraguan integrity.[57]

The *New York Times* exemplified the U.S. enthusiasm for the Frelinghuysen-Zavala Treaty: "It is unquestionably true that the Nicaraguan Government did not desire to make this present treaty . . . [but] the will of a mighty nation of 55,000,000 of homogeneous, progressive, and patriotic people is of course irresistible when it runs counter to the wishes of feeble and unstable Governments like those of Central and South America." The *New Orleans Daily Picayune* was equally adamant when it declared that the United States must adopt a policy of southward territorial aggrandizement and that the Nicaraguan treaty was only an opening wedge. "American enterprise will soon annex the whole of Central America," the paper concluded.[58]

As expected, the Nicaraguan Senate ratified the 1884 Frelinghuysen-Zavala Treaty. President Chester A. Arthur submitted the treaty to the U.S. Senate before leaving office, but President-elect Grover Cleveland withdrew it from consideration in 1885 because the provisions for a perpetual union with Nicaragua and protection of its territory were contrary to the long-standing principle of no entangling alliances.[59] Thus, while the United States demanded that European powers not construct a canal and proclaimed the right to do so itself, Washington officials, if not diplomats in the field, were unwilling to become directly involved in Central American affairs.

Amid the diplomatic maneuvering, Menocal's Maritime Canal Company went bankrupt in 1884. Reconstituted in March 1887, the company reached a new agreement with the government at Managua that granted it control of the canal for ninety-nine years, after which control would revert back to Nicaragua. All goods and materials necessary for the canal's construction received duty-free status. The agreement also placed Menocal's company under a tight time schedule. It required the company to complete its survey within a year, to commence construction within two and a half years, and to complete construction in ten years. Consistent with their long-standing belief that a canal would benefit all isthmian nations, the governments of El Salvador, Guatemala, and Honduras expressed pleasure with the project.[60]

Only Costa Rica demurred, because of its disputed boundary with Nicaragua along the San Juan River. The issue was submitted for arbitration to President Cleveland, who ruled in 1888 that Costa Rica had a right to advise in the canal's construction but that the 1858 Jerez-Cañaz Treaty did not give it the right to make interoceanic canal grants; only Nicaragua had that authority. Cleveland also determined that Costa Rica was entitled to compensation for such favors and privileges conceded by Nicaragua but that it could not share in any profits the canal generated. Although Costa Rica was not satisfied with the rulings, the construction roadblocks apparently were cleared.[61]

In 1889, the U.S. Congress approved legislation that incorporated the Maritime Canal Company, with the proviso that the government assume none of the company's financial responsibilities. The company began its work in Greytown a year later, the first ever actual construction efforts on the Nicaraguan canal route. By 1893, the company had spent approximately $4 million on dredging the Greytown harbor, clearing the jungle, and other preliminary work, but the project collapsed because of a lack of funds. Only U.S. government intervention prevented cancellation of the contract by President José Santos Zelaya of Nicaragua at the expiration of the treaty in 1898 on the grounds that the canal had not been completed within the required ten years.[62]

During the final decades of the nineteenth century new pressure groups, more powerful than individual construction companies, came forward in favor of a U.S. government transisthmian canal. These groups viewed Central America as a stepping stone to the more important areas of trade, specifically Asia and the west coast of South America.

When William McKinley took the presidential oath in March 1897, he found himself surrounded by a group of imperialists: Navy Secretary Theodore Roosevelt, Admiral Alfred T. Mahan, and Senators Henry Cabot Lodge Sr. and Cushman Davis. Their "large policy" was described as a program to make the United States "indisputably dominant over the western hemisphere, possessed of a great navy, owning and controlling an Isthmian canal, holding naval bases in the Caribbean and Pacific, and contesting, on at least even terms, with the great powers, the naval and commercial supremacy of the Pacific Ocean and the Far East."[63] The two major prizes—Asia and the west coast of Latin America—were not to be colonized but rather economically exploited while given the benefits of western culture. To reach these strategic areas, an interoceanic canal was needed.[64]

Although Mahan and his colleagues recognized the economic potential of the new markets that would result from a canal, the litany of support from the business community made the point more clearly. Chambers of commerce, boards of trade, and in some cases state legislatures, from California to New York to South Carolina and Louisiana, approved resolutions endorsing a transisthmian canal. A common theme to their rhetoric emphasized that a canal would enhance the capabilities of the United States to market its wares in Asia and along the west coast of South America. Nothing was said about potential markets or business opportunities in Central America.[65]

In addition to the economic benefits, ideological rationalizations were also offered. Social Darwinism explained the magnificence of U.S. agricultural and industrial abundance, and expansionist advocates used the rhetoric to justify taking western culture to the so-called backward areas of the world. There developed a sense of obligation to uplift the world's backward and inferior peoples.[66] The Central Americans fell within this purview.

By the century's end, these forces converged to create a national demand for the U.S. government to undertake an isthmian canal project. What began as a desire to prevent Europeans from building a canal had become a national obsession for security, markets, and morals. President McKinley clearly expressed this attitude when he told Congress in 1898 that "our national policy now more imperatively than ever calls for its [transisthmian canal] control by this government."[67]

At the time, the chief obstacle to building a canal was diplomatic rather than physical. Still bound by the Clayton-Bulwer Treaty, the United States could not by itself construct a transisthmian waterway. If the U.S. interests appeared anxiously aggressive, the British were prepared to acquiesce. Engaged in the Boar War in South Africa, confronted with a fluid political situation on the European continent, and challenged for naval supremacy and colonial dominance by Germany, London sought friendship with the United States. The resultant second Hay-Pauncefote Treaty in 1900 superseded the Clayton-Bulwer pact and gave the United States a free hand to build, control, and fortify a canal.[68] With the British removed, where the canal would be located remained the only question.

Given the history of previous canal schemes, the Nicaraguan route remained most favored. In December 1899 Senator John T. Morgan of Alabama called up from the Senate Foreign Relations Committee his perennial Nicaraguan Canal Bill and for the first time received serious opposition from the so-called Panama Lobby, headed by William Nelson Cromwell of the New York law firm Sullivan and Cromwell. The firm represented the New Panama Canal Company and pushed for the more southern route. Morgan nevertheless steered legislation through the Senate authorizing a U.S. government canal in Nicaragua. Morgan's opponents derailed the bill in the House of Representatives and secured legislation calling for the Walker Commission to return to Central America in March 1899 for a comparative study of the Nicaragua and Panama routes.

In November 1901 the Walker Commission issued its report. As expected, it recommended the Nicaraguan route at an estimated cost of $189 million compared to $149 million for the Panama route, in addition to the $109 million the New Panama Canal Company wanted for its properties there. In response, the House of Representatives approved a measure proposed by Rep. William P. Hepburn of Iowa calling for the purchase of Nicaraguan and Costa Rican territory and the construction of a canal thereon for no more than $140 million. Despite Morgan's efforts, the Senate refused to do more than continue discussion of the proposed project.[69]

Throughout the debate Congress gave little attention to either the dynamics of Central American politics in general or the attitude of President Zelaya of Nicaragua in particular. After all, the Central Americans had always expressed their interest in a canal and had offered generous concessions to get one. Zelaya and President Rafael Iglesias of Costa Rica, like many of their predecessors, believed that a canal would bring economic prosperity to their countries. Zelaya in particular favored a U.S. government–sponsored project, confident that it would come to fruition unlike previous private undertakings.

As Congress debated, Secretary of State John Hay, who favored the Nicaraguan route, and William L. Merry, the U.S. minister assigned to Costa Rica and Nicaragua, conducted negotiations in both Washington and Central America for a canal along the assumed route on the San Juan River. In Washington on 1 December 1900, Secretary Hay signed a protocol with Nicaragua's minister Louis Corea and its foreign minister Fernando Sánchez whereby the two governments agreed to enter into canal negotiations once the U.S. Congress approved the appropriate legislation. Hay concluded a similar protocol with Costa Rican minister Tomás Calvo four days later. Although without details, the protocols stipulated that in return for the exclusive right to build a canal along their common border and then through Nicaragua, the United States would pay Nicaragua $5 million and Costa Rica $2.5 million.

In Central America, Merry shuttled between Managua and San José promoting the advantages of a canal and suggesting possible canal provisions, even showing copies of the Hepburn Bill to both governments. Merry continuously labored for concessions and treaty details, despite unclear instructions from Hay and lack of congressional action. Sounding like the expansionists of the 1850s, the confident Merry wrote Hay in February 1902 that it would not be long before U.S. citizens would dominate the commercial and political interests of Nicaragua. "It will be the commencement of the *Americanization* of Central America," Merry concluded. Unfortunately, Merry failed to gauge accurately Zelaya's and Iglesias's dissatisfaction with the snail's pace of the U.S. decision-making process.

Amid all of these maneuvers from 1900 until 1902 and despite Morgan's intense efforts, the Senate still had not taken up the canal issue. As the Senate prepared for its debate on the canal issue from January to June 1902, the forces favoring Panama crystallized.

In January, the New Panama Canal Company dropped its asking price to $40 million, making the price of the Panama and Nicaraguan routes competitive. In response, the Walker Commission issued a supplemental report favoring Panama. In March, the Senate Committee on Inter-Oceanic Canals approved the Hepburn Bill by a vote of 7 to 4, an indication of growing opposition to the Nicaraguan site.

The increased interest in Panama prompted Hay and Merry to step up the pressure on Calvo and Corea and the governments in San José and Managua. Iglesias and Zelaya refused to make any definite commitments. The Costa Ricans appeared headed for debate on a constitutional amendment relative to the canal, and Zelaya was reluctant to surrender civil jurisdiction in the proposed canal zone area. In the meantime Hay received a proposal from Colombia regarding the Panama route. All materials became available to the Senate when it began its debate of the canal issue on 4 June 1902. On the Senate floor Mark Hanna of Ohio led the cause for Panama, while Morgan appeared to stand alone in favor of the Nicaraguan route. The debate focused on the physical advantages and cost of each route and the cost of acquiring the French properties. Only occasionally did Central American politics enter the debate.

In the end the Spooner amendment, given little attention four years earlier, was narrowly approved. It authorized the president to pursue the Panama route first and only if that plan were unsuccessful to turn to Nicaragua. The fight for the Panama route had ended. Seventeen months later, Panama achieved independence from Colombia and the United States got its canal.[70] Both the Costa Ricans and the Nicaraguans registered their displeasure with the course of events. Spurned again by the United States and mistrustful of its immediate northern neighbor, Costa Rica quickly returned to its traditional isolation from regional affairs. The jilted Zelaya directed his efforts toward a Central American union.

The period from 1850 to 1903 ended where it had begun—on the transisthmian canal issue. During these years the United States had become a self-confident nation by gaining British recognition of the Monroe Doctrine and by becoming an industrial nation with global aspirations and a belief that its society far surpassed others, particularly in the underdeveloped world.

During the same period, the Central American Liberals came to power with vision for modernizing their nations through the encouragement of foreign investment and the development of export-based economies. They also believed that a transisthmian canal would bring unmeasured benefits to the region. But, lacking self-confidence, the Central Americans fell victim to foreign interlopers, particularly European and then U.S. private entrepreneurs.

Until the United States decided to build its own canal, Central America remained on the fringes of policy, but the U.S. perception that Central America was a backward and underdeveloped region would serve as the basis for much U.S. policy after 1903.

5

VENEZUELA

Wars, Claims, and the Cry for a Stronger Monroe Doctrine

William L. Harris

THE FOUNDATIONS OF U.S.-Venezuelan relations from 1850 to the beginning of the twentieth century were established during the thirty-year period that preceded the midcentury. Well before 1850 diplomacy between the two nations was clearly preoccupied with debt payments and suzerainty. The United States pressed for compensation for losses its citizens suffered in Venezuela during the wars of independence, whereas Venezuela in turn attempted to get its fiscal house in order and fight fraudulent claims. The United States began the development of a hemispheric policy that ultimately would lead, though hesitantly, to the Monroe Doctrine, including both the Olney and the Roosevelt Corollaries. Although complaining of the encroaching presence from the north, Venezuela actually pressed for a stronger interpretation of the Monroe Doctrine. In essence Venezuela helped the United States develop the Monroe Doctrine as a guideline both for debt settlement and for boundary considerations.

Between 1810 and 1830, the young United States watched as revolutions transformed Latin America. Led by the great Simón Bolívar, Venezuela achieved its independence as part of Gran Colombia and then went its own way in 1830. In Washington, policymaking began as early as 1811 with the establishment of the "no transfer" principle. A few years later, in 1819, having acquired Florida from Spain, the United States began a policy of contiguous, transcontinental expansion. In 1823, the Monroe Doctrine established, in principle at least, that no European power should form colonies or attempt to oppress or control any of the nations of the Western Hemisphere. But the British seizure of the Malvinas (Falkland) Islands in 1833 and European incursions in Mexico and La Plata in 1838 prompted no outcry from Washington. A Caracas journalist, however, referred to U.S. adventures in Texas as those of "bandito texanos."[2]

Meanwhile, the United States and Venezuela had begun their formal diplomatic relations. The United States officially received a diplomat from Venezuela in 1822 (when Venezuela was still part of Gran Colombia), and Venezuela received its first chargé from the United States in 1835. In 1836, despite internal stress and the presence of British and French forces off the coast, the two nations executed a treaty of peace, friendship, navigation, and commerce in Caracas. Meanwhile, the first U.S. chargé spent most of his time pursuing various U.S. claims against Venezuela.[3]

Turbulence characterized relations in the 1840s. In the United States, Manifest Destiny contributed to the Oregon Fever, the annexation of Texas, and war with Mexico. President James K. Polk's war message of 11 May 1846 seemed to restrict the Monroe Doctrine to the Northern Hemisphere, but that same year the Bidlack Treaty with Colombia gave the United States a stake in the isthmus of Panama. Two years later, when Polk offered to buy Cuba, Manifest Destiny appeared rampant and ever more threatening to Venezuela.[4]

In Venezuela the outcries of journalists, both liberal and conservative, and rural violence, at once social and political, added to the confusion. British settlers in the east and U.S. bankers in Caracas added outside pressures, which became of greater concern to the Venezuelans. In 1848 legislative violence prompted the dissolution of Congress, and many prominent Venezuelans retired permanently from politics. To stoke both foreign and domestic fires even more, explorers found major gold deposits in Guyana in 1849.[5]

Confusion continued to characterize Venezuelan-U.S. relations. One U.S. diplomat would have settled claims against Venezuela through an ultimatum and naval blockade if necessary. For this and other actions crowds molested the man and his wife in Caracas. His successor called for warships to protect U.S. citizens and genuinely feared revolution and a takeover by the British through the growth of Guyana to the east. While claiming that 4,000 mulattos and blacks controlled Caracas, he overrode his concern and executed three claims conventions with his host government. The Venezuelan minister of foreign affairs, however, complained directly to his counterpart in Washington that the representative in Caracas was not neutral and denied the supposed influence of the British from Guyana. Secretary of State James Buchanan thus issued a letter of reprimand. In 1849, Venezuela, hard-pressed both within and without, passed the Espera law, declaring a moratorium on governmental debts.[6]

In sum, by 1850 the United States had expanded contiguously and expressed interest in even more expansion, but it had not yet given the Monroe Doctrine much definition. The United States wanted Venezuela to pay its debts but, questioning the capability of the government in Caracas to govern itself, had difficulty requiring its representatives in Caracas to maintain their neutrality. For its part, Venezuela was strapped by political and military turmoil and could not pay its debts to Washington or anywhere else. In the years that followed the Venezuelans would seek a new beginning, a new kind of diplomacy in their relations with Washington.

Wars and Claims: 1850–1889

Incredible events colored the decade of the 1850s in both the United States and Venezuela. Understandably, these domestic happenings affected the foreign policies of each country, as reflected in their relations. Later both countries suffered serious civil wars. After its war the United States continued its domestic growth and groped toward becoming a major world power. This is reflected in increased U.S. pressure on Venezuela to pay its debts and in the refusal of the United States to give full diplomatic recognition to Venezuela. In addition, Venezuela continued to have extensive political problems, even after its great war, but ultimately the country reached a period of relative stability under the leadership of the great liberal *caudillo*, Antonio Guzmán Blanco. Furthermore, Venezuela successfully resisted the fraud prevalent in many of the claims lodged by the United States and sought to give definition to the Monroe Doctrine itself.

In the 1850s the northern republic progressed toward civil war, the Compromise of 1850 with its slavery issue merely delaying the inevitable. That same year, the Clayton-Bulwer Treaty put the United States on an equal footing with Great Britain in the event an isthmian canal were constructed. The Kansas-Nebraska Act and the Dred Scott Decision of the Supreme court added fuel to the sectional fire between the North and the slaveholding South.[7]

Simultaneously, in Venezuela anarchic caudillism prevailed. The Monagas brothers, José Tadeo and José Gregorio, controlled the presidency. They sat atop a turbulent situation punctuated by pressures from the British through Guyana and the movements of the old *llanero*, José Antonio Páez. Perhaps the most notable domestic event of the decade was the abolition of slavery in 1854. By the end of the decade Venezuela had shifted to the right under the presidency of Julian Castro, and José Tadeo Monagas had fallen *cobardemente!* While cowardly, the fall set the stage for the Federal War, which lasted over a decade.[8]

Diplomatically, relations between the two countries remained turbulent. While Venezuela encouraged U.S. investment in the eastern gold fields but backed off after a status quo agreement with the British, U.S. entrepreneurs invested in a proposed railway from the port of La Guaira to Caracas. And Benjamin Shields, the diplomat reprimanded for lack of neutrality, received an appointment as a special claims agent, hardly a good omen for the Venezuelan hope to negotiate a more favorable treaty, particularly as Secretary of State John M. Clayton viewed claims settlements as a prerequisite. However, Shields and his successor executed a convention in 1852 for various damages suffered by U.S. interests in 1818–19 and 1827.[9]

There is no question that activities elsewhere fueled the love-hate perspective Venezuela had toward the United States. The comings and goings of the *llanero*, Páez, often with activity in New York, and the growing incursions of such filibusters as Narciso López in Cuba and William Walker in Nicaragua, plus the Gadsden Purchase in 1853, doubtless colored the view in Caracas.[10]

Despite the difficult setting, entrepreneurs from the north continued their activities in Venezuela, and some turned their attention to guano. Ship captains found deposits of this rich natural fertilizer (bird droppings built up over centuries in nesting areas) in the Caribbean. Actions and diplomacy surrounding the deposits on tiny Aves Island, in the northeastern quadrant of the Caribbean, pushed all other U.S. claims against Venezuela to the background for several years. In 1853 Philadelphia entrepreneurs began operations on Aves Island only to be displaced the next year by a group from Boston. Venezuelan naval forces, at the behest of the

Philadelphians, expelled everyone from the island. A classic example of power claims technique then ensued.[11]

The dominant claimants, the Boston business firm of Shelton, Sampson, and Tappan, vigorously pursued their claims in both Washington and Caracas. By early 1855 they had persuaded Secretary of State William L. Marcy to claim Aves Island by right of discovery and to pursue reparations for damages and losses inflicted, a claim of both sovereignty and damages. In the next few months arbitrators settled a Dutch claim of sovereignty for the same island while the U.S. Congress passed the Derelict Guano Islands Law. Applications of this law gave the United States small pieces of real estate over a rather wide geographical basis. Meanwhile, Venezuelan authorities sent a special agent to Washington in an unsuccessful attempt to preempt the claim.[12]

Henry Shelton Sanford, the aggressive lawyer for the Boston group, enjoyed more success. In addition to his vigorous work in Washington, Sanford made two trips to Caracas. There he cajoled the U.S. minister, Charles Eames, and retained influential Venezuelans, the most notable being a well-placed young attorney, José María Rojas. In 1859 a new government, a coalition of liberals and conservatives, executed a claims convention on the Aves Island issue. Although final payments stretched out for several years, the Aves Island claims were handled with great dispatch and success, much above the average.[13]

In other matters before the outbreak of civil war in both countries, perhaps the most notable was a series of attempts to negotiate a new treaty between Venezuela and the United States. Whereas Venezuela had canceled the original treaty of 1836 in 1848, of necessity the Caracas authorities felt constrained to continue negotiations in Washington due to the presence of the *llanero* leader Páez in the United States. But in 1858 Páez returned home, and the two countries achieved a new treaty of friendship, commerce, and navigation two years later, just on the brink of civil war in both nations.[14]

The wars now came. In Venezuela a pronouncement in Coro in 1859 signaled the beginning. While it is remembered as the Federal War, more or less terminated by the Treaty of Coche four years later, it was fought along ideological lines, between the old *patriciates* (conservatives) and the new oligarchs (liberals). Perhaps the new, true aristocracy would be one of talent. However, the power vacuum continued until 1870 and the actual rise to power of Antonio Guzmán Blanco.[15]

In the United States, South Carolina seceded from the union in late 1860, after the election of Abraham Lincoln. The war raged in many areas of the nation, from Louisiana to Pennsylvania, with the definite shift in favor of the Union coming in July 1863, with Union victories simultaneously at Vicksburg and Gettysburg. Thereafter, other actions led to the final surrender at Appomattox Courthouse and the assassination of Lincoln, both in April 1865.[16]

During the wars, the two countries continued diplomatic functions. Just before the secession of South Carolina, for example, President James Buchanan pled strict neutrality in the case of the war already raging in Venezuela. Venezuela, however, chose the side of the Union as the North was fighting against slavery, which

Venezuela already had eliminated. Reflecting this position, Venezuelan authorities did not allow a Confederate raider to leave a prize in Puerto Cabello. During the short-lived dictatorship of Páez from 1861 to 1863, U.S. ministers in Caracas were uncertain in their recognition of that government. However, Secretary of State William H. Seward did not sanction recognition.[17]

The year 1863 was a crucial year for both nations, and opportunities and problems presented themselves in both directions. For example, a U.S. plan to develop cotton plantations in Venezuela failed because of disturbances there. Union ships called at Venezuelan ports to speed up the lagging Aves Island claims payments. And Henry Sanford, the Aves attorney, assisted in the acquisition of a Venezuelan loan in London and thus received more claims money. Venezuela offered to send a cavalry unit to help the Union, the price being a pact of confederation with the United States against European intervention. In effect, the southern republic would broaden and strengthen the Monroe Doctrine. Such was not to be the case, however, as the French intervened in Mexico and civil war still raged to the north.[18]

It was business as usual, however, regarding claims and other matters. As foreign claims increased, the Venezuelan government limited them to the value of any property taken for public use and wrestled with such problems as local taxes. Claims issues generally were such a serious matter that Pascual Casanova, the minister of foreign relations, published a booklet on the matter. Interestingly, he frequently cited the U.S. minister, E. D. Culver. And when Guzmán Blanco lifted the privileges of a U.S. consul who failed to attend a *Te Deum* celebrating a particular defeat of rebels, Secretary of State Seward responded in kind. As the civil war to the north ended in 1865, Minister Culver continued pushing vigorously for a claims settlement, and it seemed that warships came more frequently. That same year the huge Price grant conceded to U.S. business interests all vacant and unused land in Guyana and Amazonas to the south. However, though this concession would have helped develop the east, check British encroachments from Guyana, and provide an outlet for Confederate refugees, it came to naught in five years and became yet another claim to be handled, along with, for example, U.S. losses in an insurrection in Apure.[19]

But events appeared promising in 1866, when Minister Culver signed a claims convention with Rafael Seijas, the minister of foreign relations. The convention called for a mixed commission with a U.S. commissioner and a Venezuelan commissioner. An arbitrator would make the final decision in the case of disagreement. Culver's replacement, James Wilson, kept the pressure on Seijas with tough correspondence and naval shows of force. Wilson, however, apparently suffering from an "acute illness," died of delirium tremens in a gaming house in Caracas run by a chronic claimant, Seth Driggs. Driggs, no one else being available, closed the legation himself, perhaps after examining various documents germane to his interests.[20]

Despite this tragicomic interlude, the commission began its work while political struggles raged in Venezuela and the conservatives returned to power. By August 1868, the commission had completed its work and issued 360 certificates with a total value of $1,253,310. The question of payment, however, was another matter, as rebellions drew heavily on the limited monies available. Not only were the means of tax collection affected, notably in the ports with problems caused by a French blockade, also, rural unrest circumscribed the potential amount of revenue to be taxed.[21]

More important, the Venezuelan government questioned the validity of the claims certificates issued by the mixed commission. However, continued turbulence delayed formal complaints. To the north former minister Culver advised the Venezuelan consul in New York that he hoped Venezuela would not submit to the work of the mixed commission. And by the end of 1869, James Partridge, the minister-resident in Caracas, was convinced that there had been fraud.[22]

The fraud perpetrated by the mixed commission in 1868 was an incredible operation. Thomas N. Stillwell had been appointed as minister to replace Wilson, the drunkard. William P. Murray, his brother-in-law and a man with prior claims experience against Venezuela, accompanied him to Caracas. David Talmadge, a New York coal merchant with business operations in Caracas, became the commission member appointed by the United States. The original Venezuelan commission member, Guzmán Blanco, had been replaced by Francisco Conde. The arbitrator, the tie breaker, was Juan Machado, a former business associate of Talmadge in Caracas. This loaded mixed commission had examined the claims and issued certificates of payment, which at the insistence of Talmadge were made payable to the bearer. All three of the U.S. appointees left Caracas immediately after the commission completed its work and took with them the major part of the certificates issued.[23]

Meanwhile, though Guzmán Blanco definitively triumphed in 1870, he ruefully had the opinion that all actions in the Ministry of Foreign Relations concerned indemnities. When President Grant observed that Venezuela was the only South American government with which the United States had bad relations, Guzmán Blanco responded in a lengthy letter in which he referred to "a scandalous fraud, a monstrous coalition against the truth, against the law, against the interest and honor of both countries." He also claimed that former minister Culver had inflated U.S. claims.[24]

Hit and miss diplomacy now became the order. The U.S. minister, W. B. Pile, suggested that the northern republic handle all Venezuelan debts and that cutters might be present to insure tariff collections. Pile, however, was years ahead of the Roosevelt Corollary as applied to the Dominican Republic. For his part, Guzmán Blanco sent Juan Bautista Dalla Costa to Washington to pursue the claims question.[25]

Pile's replacement, Thomas Russell, did not improve matters when his criticism of Venezuela and Guzmán Blanco became public in 1876. The secretary of state recalled him from an untenable position in Caracas and simultaneously lifted the diplomatic status of Dalla Costa in Washington. In an interesting turn of events, a young Venezuelan general resigned his commission and pursued Russell's daughter, Nelly, when the family returned to the United States. Former minister Pile, meanwhile, became a special Venezuelan commissioner in Washington, where he worked with Dalla Costa on the claims issue.[26]

In the midst of these confusing actions, Guzmán Blanco took time out to address problems with Holland, the issue being Curaçao. Earlier, in 1869, Guzmán Blanco had launched his successful revolution against the Venezuelan conservatives from that island. Later, in 1874, an unsuccessful revolt against him originated there. The next year, having failed to get the good offices of the United States in this matter, he broke relations with Holland. Subsequently, he wanted either to stop all commerce with the island or to buy it from the Dutch.[27]

Meanwhile, in Washington Pile and Dalla Costa pursued the issue of the fraudulent mixed commission. They reported directly to Guzmán Blanco and soon were joined by another lobbyist, W. B. Matchett. Matchett worked vigorously in the halls of Congress to achieve a new ruling. Finally, in June 1878, the U.S. Congress repealed the original claims convention of 1866, while Dalla Costa pursued the establishment of a new one.[28]

The confusion continued, however, because from 1877 to 1879 Guzmán Blanco was in Europe following the completion of his seven-year presidency, remembered as the *Septenio*. On the death of his ally, President Francisco Linares Alcántara, in November 1878, Guzmán Blanco's enemies came out into the open. They dramatically tore down the statues honoring Guzmán Blanco, but he prevailed and regained the presidency in 1879. The northern republic, simultaneously, passed through the early years of President Rutherford B. Hayes and Secretary of State William M. Evarts. Despite early confusion regarding the recognition of the new government in Caracas, both parties now returned to the claims issue.[29]

Work continued apace in both Washington and Caracas. Pile, Dalla Costa, and Matchett worked vigorously in Washington to supply Secretary of State Evarts with the evidence he wanted. In July 1882, the U.S. House Foreign Affairs Committee decided to go point by point with the various claims as determined on the basis of the original convention of 1866 but based on a new mixed commission. Rather bluntly, Congress felt "The [earlier] Commission was a conspiracy whose results are full of fraud." The lobbying in Washington had borne dividends.[30]

In Caracas, simultaneously, efforts centered on solving the problems of all claims due. These efforts came about in part because France broke relations with Venezuela in 1880 over the issue of debt payments. When this happened, the Venezuelan minister in Paris, as per instructions, had turned his country's interest over to the U.S. embassy there, perhaps an indication of the desire of his government to be close to the United States in all regards. That same year, Secretary of State Evarts had agreed for the United States to administer the Venezuelan customhouses and pay the exterior debt provided other creditor nations would accept the agreement and provided such action would not compromise his government's claims. Unfortunately, France claimed priority settlement. Though not implemented, this planned procedure can be seen as a precursor to the Roosevelt Corollary.[31]

Meanwhile, progress continued on the fraudulent claims issue. In March 1883, President Chester A. Arthur approved a joint congressional resolution calling for the president to pursue the issue of the old claims convention of 1866. Arthur should seek a new commission to meet in Washington. Subsequently, on 5 December 1885, A. M. Soteldo of Venezuela and Secretary of State Thomas F. Bayard signed a treaty for revising the grants made under the convention of 1866. A similar mixed commission would meet in Washington, and the selection process would be the same. The certificates of payment issued would be payable to the respective claimants. It is interesting that Guzmán Blanco, between presidencies, did not want a new mixed commission. However, being in Europe at the time, he was not directing the action from Caracas. Finally, after two clarifying conventions in 1888, the two countries prepared to solve the great claims problems. Doubtless the successful executions of these conventions was based, at least in part, on the gradual development by the northern republic of a more conciliatory and workable policy toward the republics to the south.[32]

The new mixed commission, organized in September 1889, completed its work within a year. Claimants presented a total of 254 of the old certificates, all declared null and void and then considered anew, as a total of fifty petitions plus thirteen new ones. The commissioners finally arrived at the total claim of $982,572, somewhat less than the original figure of $1,253,310. Interestingly, Henry Sanford, the attorney for the Aves Island claimants of 1859, received $20,000 through this second commission as he had lost funds due to selling Venezuelan bonds as part payment of the earlier debt acknowledged. And Seth Driggs, the great chronic claimant and operator of the Caracas gaming house, received nothing for his multiple claims. There was no known fraud associated with the work of this second commission, perhaps because of the simultaneous activities in Washington of the First Pan-American Congress, the precursor to the Pan-American Union, now known as the Organization of American States.[33]

Whereas wars and claims extended beyond the date of the claims convention of 1888, these two subjects were the focal points of relations between the United States and Venezuela from 1850 to 1889. The civil war to the north and the federal wars to the south complicated attempts to resolve the nagging claims issue, which finally was solved, at least on paper, in 1889. Before then, however, serious problems in eastern Venezuela had already arisen.

Guyana: 1880–1899

The extreme eastern and southern parts of Venezuela are relatively uninhabited and isolated. Striking geographical characteristics include the *llanos* in the Orinoco River valley and the great towering mesas to the south and east. The discovery of gold, diamonds, asphalt, and more recently iron ore has given great value to the area, especially since the middle of the nineteenth century. People from the settlements scattered along the Essequibo River in what was British Guiana clashed with Venezuelans who explored what they called Guyana. This pitted the great British Empire against the tiny young republic of Venezuela. As the problems grew and the United States became larger and stronger, Venezuela sought U.S. help against Great Britain more and more.

The Guyana problem is clearly the major theme in relations between Venezuela and the United States late in the nineteenth century. Other themes and incidents during this time colored the diplomatic relations between the two countries, which finally led to the independence of Panama in 1903 and the U.S. intervention in the Dominican Republic the following year.

The Guyana problem had early roots. Great Britain received the area from Holland in 1814, and as early as 1822 Gran Colombia complained about British intrusions. Perhaps Robert H. Schomburgk planted the major seed of discord in 1840 with the publication of *A Description of British Guiana, Geographical and Statistical.* A German naturalist in the service of Great Britain, Schomburgk traveled extensively in the Orinoco Delta and to the south. He noted that the "boundary which separates the British settlements from Venezuela and Brazil has never been determined." With the problem clearly in the public realm, Alejo Fortique, the Venezuelan minister in London, addressed the issue. Lord Aberdeen responded to Fortique that the frontier markers were merely "provisional, not an act of possession." Aberdeen also advised Fortique that even though the governor of British Guiana would be instructed to remove the posts placed by Schomburgk, this would not affect any British claims. Nothing came of these early negotiations, however, as Fortique died in 1845 and an agreement signed in Caracas in 1850 maintained the status quo.[34]

In the interim the U.S. minister in Caracas feared as early as 1846 the British might take over Venezuela through actions in Guyana. And major gold strikes came in Guyana at midcentury, just as Venezuela executed the status quo agreement and encouraged U.S. investment in gold and other operations as a means to check the British. In the following years, the action continued erratically, with Venezuela advising the United States formally of continuing incidents then finally directly soliciting aid.[35]

Attempts at settlement, investments, loans, and occasional seizures characterized the next few years. Turmoil in Caracas in 1857, for example, precluded any action on the part of a special British agent sent to address the issue. Still, English bankers continued their activities, as Guzmán Blanco, the rising liberal star, negotiated a large loan in 1863 in London. The gold craze in Caracas can be seen in the petition in 1867 of José María Rojas, the Aves Island attorney, to secure a particular Guyana claim. U.S. entrepreneurs began operation of the Venezuelan Steam Transport Company on the Orinoco but subsequently lost two ships to rebels. The South American Company, another U.S. operation, lost its Guyana concessions through a forced sale. In 1874, Pile, the erstwhile minister, received an Orinoco monopoly and later bought the vessels of the Venezuelan Steam Transport Company. Two years later, the president of Venezuelan Guyana confiscated eight hundred U.S. mining operations. Apparently the rewards, both to U.S. and British entrepreneurs, were worth the risk.[36]

These troubles notwithstanding, Venezuela set the stage for negotiating the Guyana frontier with Great Britain when Guzmán Blanco claimed title eastward to the Essequibo River in an address to Congress in 1877. The minister of foreign relations in Caracas included the United States in the action by sharing a copy of appropriate correspondence to Lord Derby. But fitful negotiations in London over the next few years yielded no progress.[37]

Action improved, however, with the appointment of Simón Camacho to replace Dalla Costa as the Venezuelan representative in Washington. An excellent selection and formerly the Venezuelan consul in New York, Camacho had been in the United States for some time, had married a U.S. citizen, and had written about and traveled extensively in the United States. Best remembered for his *Cosas de los Estados Unidos,* Camacho also had written graphically of the exit of the old *llanero,* Páez, from New York in 1858. Present at the assassination of President James S. Garfield in July 1881, he rendered direct assistance to those affected. Doubtless his assistance during this tragic interlude contributed to the encouraging words for Venezuela when President Arthur made his first annual speech later that year. The appointment of Camacho was at once wise and fortuitous.[38]

A frontier incident in late 1882 provided the opening Camacho needed. British warships cruised in the mouth of the Orinoco, and the British installed a telegraph line in Punta Barima at the southern tip of the Orinoco Delta. Camacho quickly wrote Secretary of State F. T. Frelinghuysen and noted the need for arbitration to end the growing controversy. He noted, further, that only the United States could propose arbitration with true force and decide the question of the Guyana border to the satisfaction of Venezuela.[39]

Simultaneously, in Caracas the government of Guzmán Blanco advised the U.S. minister there, Jehu Baker, of the bellicose British actions. Baker, in turn, advised Frelinghuysen of these actions and the Venezuelan desire for arbitration. The secretary of state responded that if Venezuela formally solicited arbitration, then the United States would propose to Great Britain that the question be submitted to the arbitration of a third power. Guzmán Blanco, however, confidentially advised Baker that he wanted the United States to be the arbitrator. Then the English proposed that tariff differentials, claims, and the Guyana frontier all be settled by treaty. Venezuela responded that all territory west of the Essequibo be arbitrated, which proposal the British, in turn, rejected.[40]

This stalemate notwithstanding, the actions of entrepreneurs from the northern republic continued unabated in troubled eastern Venezuela. For example, Horace R. Hamilton signed a contract for the exploitation of all unused lands in the state of Bermudez in the east. This concession passed on to the New York and Bermudez Company, which ultimately became a major asphalt producer. Also, Cyrenius C. Fitzgerald, former manager of the large Callao gold mining operation in Guyana, received a huge grant in 1883. Fitzgerald sold this concession to the Manoa Company, which operated in Guyana and numbered Guzmán Blanco and other notable Venezuelans as stockholders. Clearly, more and more businessmen from the northern republic had vested interests in Guyana, and doubtless this helped with the diplomacy. To help the cause even more, Guzmán Blanco created the special Delta Territory as another means to attract U.S. investment in Guyana.[41]

Guzmán Blanco then relinquished the presidency and went abroad in a diplomatic status. First stopping in New York to attend the dedication of an equestrian statue of Simón Bolívar, he then visited Secretary of State Frelinghuysen. Although the latter would not accept the proposal of a treaty of alliance, he felt a treaty of reciprocity might be possible.[42]

Moving on to London, the liberal *caudillo* discussed Guyana and other issues with the British. Unfortunately, a rebellion in eastern Venezuela preempted any substantial progress. This rebellion, supported and supplied in part by the same Rojas of the Aves Island claims, created problems in British Guiana, Trinidad, and various locations in eastern Venezuela. While the British authorities in London and elsewhere helped Guzmán Blanco and other Venezuelan authorities to root out the rebellion, there was a delay in the negotiations.[43]

Returning home in 1886 for a final two-year term as president, Guzmán Blanco now directed the Guyana issue from Caracas. The representative in Washington, A. M. Soteldo, worked concurrently on both the renewed mixed claims accounts and the frontier problem. He enjoyed success to the point that the new Secretary of State Thomas F. Bayard directed the U.S. minister to Great Britain to proffer his country's good offices in the settlement and made clear reference to the Monroe Doctrine. "The doctrines we announced two generations ago . . . have lost none of their force . . . in the progress of time." But, the time had not yet come for serious negotiations, while in British Guiana the governor publicly questioned the validity of a Venezuelan railroad concession linking Ciudad Bolívar to Guasipati.[44]

Early the next year Soteldo solicited Bayard's opinion regarding breaking diplomatic relations between Venezuela and Great Britain. Although Bayard felt it would be unwise, Venezuela broke relations on 20 February 1887. Intrusions, overall claims to the Orinoco, and the presence of British "constables" to control trade on the southern tip of the Orinoco Delta precipitated the break.[45]

That same year, Venezuela sought public support with the publication of *Correspondence Between the Venezuelan Government and Her British Majesty's Government about the Question of the Frontier*. This book contained the pertinent letters between the two governments from late 1883 through the note that broke relations. Considering this publicity in English, perhaps it is not surprising that the U.S. Senate the next year asked the president to submit the correspondence "concerning the boundaries between British Guiana and Venezuela." Secretary Bayard remained cautious, however, noting that British intrusions in Guyana were by individuals and not the government, and he would not authorize the U.S. minister in London to assist in the matter. The flow of pro-Venezuelan material in English continued with *Venezuelan International Law: British Boundaries of Guyana*. This six-hundred-page compendium, prepared by Rafael Seijas, a noted Venezuelan jurist, contained "every document relating to the British boundaries of Guyana, and in it are included and assembled all the political, administrative, geographical, scientific and historical antecedents."[46]

In Washington, meanwhile, the new administration of President Benjamin Harrison and Secretary of State James G. Blaine offered little help. Not to be discouraged, however, Chargé Francisco Antonio Silva noted to Blaine in early 1889 that the continued British intrusions in Guyana were "a true acquisition of territory in America to which the Monroe Doctrine is opposed." And to draw the northern republic in even more, he noted the many U.S. interests working contracts in the area and specifically mentioned the Manoa Company and its problems with British authorities. British actions at the end of the year tended to support Silva, when a decree from British Guiana proclaimed British sovereignty over the mouth of the Orinoco and declared Barima, at the southern part of the wide delta, a British port.[47]

The pressure continued in early 1890 with the appointment of Nicanor Bolet Péraza to Washington. The year before he had been the Venezuelan representative to the Pan-American Conference in Washington. Now, he reminded Blaine that only the United States could help Venezuela, for the European nations, irritated at the present closeness of the several American states, would be of no help. Apparently this approach succeeded, for Blaine wrote William L. Scruggs, the new minister in Caracas, that the northern republic should "take an advanced and decisive step in support of the claims of Venezuela." Pending this step, the southern republic established police stations near Barima, the port claimed by the British.[48]

Scruggs now came to the fore in Caracas. In a meeting with Minister of Foreign Relations Rafael Acevedo, Scruggs, acting beyond his instructions, implied that the so-called Aberdeen line, one of several Guyana frontier lines, might be a means of arbitration. For a proposal too "advanced and decisive," however, Blaine censured Scruggs. Although the United States wanted a settlement, there was not yet a specific program at hand. Having lost his effectiveness, at least for the present, Scruggs busied himself on such minor issues as arranging for the son of a former Venezuelan president to attend West Point.[49]

After he left Caracas in 1894, Scruggs entered into the service of Venezuela in a setting that appeared unfavorable at first glance. Grover Cleveland had replaced Harrison as president and former secretary of state Bayard had become the minister to Great Britain. The new secretary of state, W. Q. Gresham, merely advised Bayard that Cleveland wished a pacific arrangement to the problem.[50]

Events and value systems of the time, however, made the setting for the work of Scruggs more favorable. For example, the British landed marines on the Mosquito coast of Nicaragua in the spring of 1894. This action disturbed many people in the United States because of canal interests, and even though the marines left the next year there was much publicity and general criticism of British policy in the Western Hemisphere. However, during the national debate, John Bach McMaster, a leading historian of the time, noted that the Monroe Doctrine did not commit the United States to take part in wars such as this and did not apply if the British held Nicaraguan ports only as long as necessary to obtain payments. The Monroe Doctrine continued in a state of flux.[51]

In a broader sense, circumstances beyond Mosquito and the general setting of U.S. values at the time helped the case of Venezuela and agent Scruggs. Many leaders wanted a hemispheric railway, and the Cubans were rebelling again. Though Alfred Thayer Mahan and others solicited Anglo-Saxon unity, Theodore Roosevelt denounced "Anglomaniacs." This was the period of the "New Manifest Destiny," and the United States had reached the stage of the major world powers. No British marines would run over this vigorous nation. More directly, young Senator Henry Cabot Lodge noted that Great Britain continuously extended the Guyana lines it might submit to arbitration. To Lodge this violated the Monroe Doctrine, and the United States should take a stand. Scruggs had a very favorable atmosphere, indeed, in which to persuade the United States to commit fully to the assistance of Venezuela.[52]

Scruggs first acted by publishing in late 1894 a tract titled "British Aggressions in Venezuela, or the Monroe Doctrine on Trial." This geopolitical study of the controversy viewed British actions as a menace to Venezuelan autonomy. Scruggs noted the "vital principles involved" and questioned whether they should be abandoned or maintained. Given the atmosphere of the time, this tract went through four editions and even sold on newsstands. Perhaps not surprisingly, early the next year a congressional resolution "most earnestly" recommended arbitration between Venezuela and Great Britain. The resolution passed both houses, Cleveland quickly signed it, and the death of Secretary of State Gresham actually might have helped the Venezuelan cause.[53]

Gresham's successor, Richard Olney, now came to the fore. This aggressive man, formerly the attorney general, crafted a note to Ambassador Bayard in Great Britain with the instruction that it be shared with the British. In this note, dated 20 July 1895, Olney reviewed the historical perspective of the Guyana controversy and took great license with political, geographical, and social concepts. It was "not a historical tract, but a diplomatic communication for the instruction of Great Britain, and . . . for the edification of the American people." This famous communication, known as the Olney Corollary to the Monroe Doctrine, stated that the United States was "practically sovereign" in the Western Hemisphere. British pressure on Venezuela would be regarded as a violation of the doctrine, and peaceful arbitration with U.S. help was the only solution. Despite the bluster, Olney actually was merely asking the British to agree to arbitration, but doubtless there were cheers in Venezuelan circles.[54]

In his annual message on 2 December, President Cleveland noted that he still had not received a British response to the Olney note and insisted on arbitration. Shortly thereafter the response arrived, and Lord Salisbury, clearly stating there was no sanction in international law for the Monroe Doctrine, claimed British title west to the Schomburgk line in Guyana. Cleveland, assisted by Olney, quickly prepared a special message to Congress in which he stated that it was incumbent on the United States to determine the true boundary. While noting the friendship of the two English-speaking nations, he observed that the United States could not submit to "wrong and injustice, and the consequent loss of national self-respect and honor." Congress quickly passed a bill to fund the expenses of a commission he would appoint to report on the Guyana issue.[55]

The next year, 1896, began with Great Britain on the defensive on all fronts. The failed Jameson Raid in the Transvaal, German sympathy for the Boers in South Africa, and the Franco-Russian alliance in the Far East all compromised

British diplomacy. These problems, coupled with the fact that the Monroe Doctrine was "rapidly becoming an American fetish," strengthened the Venezuelan position. Cleveland, meanwhile, quickly appointed the commission to "Investigate and Report upon the True Divisional Line between the Republic of Venezuela and British Guiana."[56]

The commission worked rapidly and benefited from an array of publications. Scruggs led the way with numerous missives concerning English geographers and the mistakes of Lord Salisbury. The "Blue Book," Great Britain's published position, prompted a Scruggs rejoinder pointing out its fallacies. Venezuela published an updated *Historia oficial de la discusión entre Venezuela y la Gran Bretaña sobre sus límites en la Guyana.* A study of Venezuela by William L. Curtis contained a segment on Guyana and reproduced the 1895 exchanges between Washington and London. The commission also received information about the visit of Joseph Chamberlain, the British colonial secretary, to the United States in September. Chamberlain met privately with Olney and the latter agreed that arbitrators would only consider Guyana areas settled for less than fifty years. This prescription, not surprisingly, precipitated riots in Caracas.[57]

On 2 February 1897, Venezuelan and British representatives signed the arbitration treaty in Washington. The treaty called for a tribunal of five jurists to meet in Paris. Of the two jurists representing Venezuela, the Supreme Court of the United States chose one and the president of Venezuela the other, while the Judicial Commission of the Privy Council chose the two British jurists. A fifth jurist, the chief arbitrator, would be chosen by the first four or, without agreement, by the King of Sweden and Norway. No territory occupied effectively for fifty years would be subject to negotiation.[58]

The tribunal met in Paris the summer and early fall of 1899, with the proceedings delayed as the chief arbitrator often attended instead the First Hague Peace Conference. Lawyers and specialists made lengthy arguments. The agent for Venezuela, the same Rojas of the Aves Island claims and the rebellion of 1884, felt Venezuela had the better arguments. However, the unanimous decision generally favored the British, as it closely approximated the original Schomburgk line, which awarded much of the originally contested territory between the Orinoco and the Essequibo Rivers. The major exception guaranteed Venezuela the entire Orinoco Delta and placed the lower end of the arbitral line south of Barima.[59]

How the five jurists rendered a unanimous decision gives cause to pause and reflect. The chief arbitrator, Federico de Martens, a distinguished Russian international lawyer, counseled with the two U.S. jurists representing Venezuela and advised the British jurists to hold to the Schomburgk line. Wanting a unanimous decision, he prevailed on the two U.S. jurists to accept the Schomburgk line except farther south of Barima, thus guaranteeing the Orinoco Delta to Venezuela. The furious U.S. jurists considered it a fraud in view of the arguments. However, they capitulated to guarantee the Orinoco Delta and to preclude further British intrusions.[60]

In retrospect, it was a decision based on hard politics perhaps more than on legal-historical arguments. An attorney for the Venezuelan side, Severo Mallet-Prevost, quickly summed it up in this manner: "The decision was forced upon our arbitrators, and in strict confidence, I have no hesitation in saying to you that the British arbitrators were not swayed by any consideration of right or justice and that the Russian arbitrator was probably induced to take the stand which he took by considerations entirely foreign to the question." Although Venezuela gained the mouth of the Orinoco, the circumstances of the rest of the arbitration have left a bad taste, even at this writing, in the mouths of many Venezuelans.[61]

A Claims Postscript Leading to the Roosevelt Corollary

In the years immediately following the Guyana decision, Venezuela had continued claims problems while the United States grappled with the interpretation of the Monroe Doctrine. Both countries operated in complicated settings.

The "New Manifest Destiny" remained rampant in the northern republic. While Cleveland had refused to act on it in 1893, Hawaii was annexed before the turn of the century. The activities of Valeriano Weyler and others in Cuba led to war with Spain. Whereas the war began in 1898 on rather idealistic grounds to help the Cubans, before the end of the century expansionist sentiments definitely were in the majority. After the war, perhaps the greatest challenge the United States faced was the issue of an isthmian canal.[62]

Venezuela's complications had a more domestic setting. After the permanent ouster of Guzmán Blanco in 1889, five different caudillos held executive power for the next twelve years, a true "Reversion to Anarchy." Strong men from the Andes dominated national politics at a costly price as over 10,000 people lost their lives in the power struggles. Despite this tragic domestic turmoil, the southern republic pursued the Guyana issue to a final decision and also settled its outstanding problems with Holland. Still, the old problem of how to pay foreign debts remained large, for the southern republic had not yet become a petroleum giant.[63]

From a broader perspective an isthmian canal loomed large in the foreign affairs of the United States. When the French began construction in 1881 of a canal in Panama, then part of Colombia, President Hayes observed that "the policy of this country is a canal under American control." Congress then chartered the Maritime Canal Company of Nicaragua to pursue a rival route. In 1902 the Hay-Pauncefote Treaty replaced the Clayton-Bulwer Treaty of 1850. This second arrangement with Great Britain cleared the way for the northern republic to construct its own canal. Debate in Washington next centered on the location. Would it be Nicaragua or Panama, where French efforts had floundered? The pendulum swung to the Panama route and the proposed Hay-Herrán Treaty with Colombia. Colombian refusal to approve the treaty led to successful revolution in Panama in 1903 and the Hay-Bunau-Varilla Treaty. The United States now could construct its own canal.[64]

The resultant Panama Canal Zone, coupled with the acquisition of Guantánamo Bay on the southern coast of Cuba and also Puerto Rico, the latter two as a result of the Spanish-American War, gave the United States outposts on the western and northern rims of the Caribbean basin. Venezuela, with its coastline on the southern rim, now loomed even larger to the northern republic, especially as Theodore Roosevelt became president after the assassination of William McKinley in 1901. In his first annual message, even before the acquisition of the Canal Zone, Roosevelt noted, regarding the Monroe Doctrine, that while there should be no non-American acquisition of territory, it did "not guarantee any state against punishment if it misconducts itself." Misconduct—that is, failure to pay foreign claims—precipitated the final set of diplomatic circumstances between the northern and southern republics in the three years leading to the acquisition of the Canal Zone.[65]

In Venezuela, Cipriano Castro had consolidated his power. But extensive turmoil, including continued high casualty rates, doubtless made it very difficult to pay foreign debts. Therefore, gunboat diplomacy might be in order. And there was nothing wrong with it from the perspective of the United States, provided no territory was taken. Germany, fearing losses on a loan, led the way, with Great Britain and Italy joining in. The French, working directly with Venezuela on pending claims, did not join.[66]

The naval blockade of Venezuela occurred in late 1902. President Castro asked U.S. Minister Herbert W. Bowen to act as arbitrator for Venezuela. Bowen, having earlier protected the British and German legations in Caracas from mob action, quickly agreed. Interestingly, the presence of numerous U.S. ships in Trinidad at the time resulted in gunboat diplomacy on both sides, as it were.[67]

Bowen signed the protocols for Venezuela with the three aggrieved nations and others that had claims. He remanded the final settlement to the International Court of Justice at The Hague, which appointed Federico de Martens, the chief Guyana arbitrator of 1899, as a senior jurist in the matter.[68]

The service of Bowen can be seen as the last step in the evolving Monroe Doctrine policy of the United States. In prior years Venezuela had sought help on the basis of the doctrine and even anticipated the development of U.S. policy. The United States, however, had pursued a fitful course.

In 1904, the year following Bowen's action, the Roosevelt Corollary to the Monroe Doctrine came into being. In the case of the Dominican Republic and its outside debts, the United States would intervene directly in the fiscal affairs of a nation for debt payment. That is, marines and accountants went in. Venezuela had wanted this earlier, perhaps excepting the marines, but the northern republic had not yet been ready. Now, in the eyes of a Venezuelan of the time, Domingo B. Castillo, "The New World is the property of the United States, according to the new interpretation of the elastic [Monroe] Doctrine." And for a number of years that seemed to be the case.[69]

6

PERU

Dominance of Private Businessmen

Lawrence A. Clayton

IN THE 24 DECEMBER 1824 issue of *The American Farmer*, its editors noted that when the U.S. warship *Franklin* docked at Baltimore earlier that year, after a long cruise on the Pacific station, one of its midshipmen off loaded "amongst other valuable and curious things . . . a small quantity of that celebrated manure, Guano dung, possessing such astonishing fertilizing properties."[1] Undoubtedly the young naval midshipman also brought back other, more appropriate gifts— possibly fashioned of famed Peruvian silver—for his mother and sweetheart perhaps. But the guano sample was, by far, the most interesting from a scientific and commercial perspective. Little did our midshipman realize how long and deep would be the shadow cast by bird droppings on the relations between Peru and the United States in the second half of the nineteenth century.

Indeed, before midcentury it can be said that relations between the United States and Peru were of relatively small import to either nation. From the 1840s onward, however, the discovery of guano by U.S. and European farmers changed the face of these relations. The Guano era had commenced, and Peru began its own takeoff into the modern era. By 1850 almost a hundred thousand tons of guano were being shipped to England alone, while the depleted tobacco fields of Virginia, Maryland, Delaware, and North Carolina were being similarly rejuvenated. A majority of the ships, mostly downeasters or medium clippers, calling at the Chincha Islands by midcentury were U.S. owned and operated. This period also happened to coincide with the heyday of U.S. guano imports. In 1857, for example, more than 213,000 tons of the fertilizer were shipped to the United States, while only 205,000 tons went to Great Britain.

General trade between the United States and Peru benefited from the prosperity induced by the Guano era. Between 1851 and 1861 Peru's exports to the United States doubled in value, while U.S. exports rose sevenfold compared to those of the previous decade. The disruptions produced by the U.S. Civil War also failed to reverse this trend, for trade between 1861 and 1871 doubled again from the previous ten-year period. The balance of trade between 1840 and 1870 favored the United States by nearly two to one.

In addition, whaling continued to be a big business into the mid-nineteenth century. Whaling ships from Nantucket, New Bedford, and other New England towns regularly called at Peruvian ports such as Paita in the north.

With such an increase in the contacts between the United States and Peru, collisions of interests increased at midcentury. Guano was at the center of one of the first public controversies between Peru and the United States. The confrontation centered around the guano-rich islands, such as the Lobos, located about fifteen miles off the north coast of Peru. Visited only occasionally in the past, in 1852 they became the target of ambitious U.S. guano entrepreneurs, who claimed that Peru exercised no sovereignty over them and that thus guano could be freely taken. The issue finally was resolved in Peru's favor in late 1852.[2] Elsewhere, the large U.S. presence at the Chincha Islands—more than thirty or forty vessels at any one time loading guano—provoked a rash of other controversies and disturbances in the 1850s between U.S. interests and Peruvians on the islands.

An Informal Relationship

In addition to the guano island controversies, the opening of the great Amazon River and its tributaries to international navigation also attracted U.S. attention. Brazil and Peru were determined, however, to exclude international navigation of the Amazon. In May 1850, Secretary of State John Clayton asked the navy to send a war vessel to explore the Amazon, but the Brazilians refused permission. Undeterred, a year later the U.S. Navy ordered its officers William Lewis Herndon and Lardner Gibbon to explore the river. They climbed the Andes together before splitting up. Herndon's party struck northward to the Huallaga River valley (today one of the leading sources of coca plants) and from there descended down the Huallaga to the Marañon, the Amazon's main branch, and then drifted on the Amazon for eleven months before reaching Par, on the Atlantic coast of Brazil. Gibbon turned south to Bolivia, where he was received most amicably, and then proceeded leisurely to descend the Madeira River to its union with the Amazon and thence to the sea. The subsequent two-volume report prepared for the navy was followed in 1853 by a commercial edition, which delighted readers.

The possibility of steam navigation on the Amazon—one of the elements in Herndon's report—excited U.S. interests but put the Brazilians and Peruvians on the defensive. Meanwhile, Lieutenant Gibbon, still in La Paz, convinced Bolivia in 1853 to commit itself to open navigation on those of her rivers feeding into the Amazon and Paraguay river basins. The jockeying continued for several years before both Brazil and Peru declared the Amazon open to international navigation in 1867 and 1868.

By the mid-nineteenth century, the upper Amazon region—called the *montaña* by the Peruvians—became the objective of intense interest on the part of Peru, which feared the annexationist tendencies of Brazil. Conscious of the *mon-*

taña's potential natural resources—forest products, minerals, and fertile lands—the Peruvians understood that in order to develop the region, it would need a transportation infrastructure of steamboats, roads, and communications to allow the entrance of colonists, soldiers, and bureaucrats. Toward that end, in 1867 Peru established a Hydrographic Commission and appointed a U.S. citizen, John Randolph Tucker, as its head. Tucker, an ex-Confederate naval officer, left for the jungle in 1867 with a small group of U.S. and Peruvian naval officers in tow, including Tucker's son and Leoncio Prado, the Peruvian president's son. Several friends made by Tucker and his staff during their eight years in the Amazon became equally prominent in Peruvian life. These friendships subtly knit the fortunes of Peru and the United States into a tighter weave as the nineteenth century progressed.

From Iquitos, Tucker's entourage undertook several expeditions into the Amazon. Among the groups' most important results were the works of Dr. Francis Land Galt, whose treatise, "Medical Notes on the Upper Amazon," received international attention. Galt's scientific curiosity transcended medicine. He made detailed meteorological observations, compiled a lexicon of Quechua and English, and wrote extensively of the Indian culture he encountered in his travels. The Smithsonian Institute published Galt's article "The Indians of Peru" in the Institute's annual report in 1877. It is considered one of the first creditable ethnographies of Amazonian Indians published in the United States and symbolized the new developing cultural relations between the United States and Peru. Galt's work, along with the reports of the naval officers Herndon and Gibbon, and the paintings of Andean landscapes rendered by U.S. artists such as George Catlin and Frederic Church, provided U.S. readers with an awareness of Peru's diversity.[3]

The Peruvians also learned about the United States. In 1854 a new show opened in Lima, La cabaña del tio Tom (Uncle Tom's Cabin). It was adapted for the theater from the antislavery novel of the same name by Harriet Beecher Stowe. The eternal theme of man's cruelty toward his fellow man made poi gnant by Uncle Tom's Cabin played well in Lima. In 1854, slavery was abolished in Peru, and antislavery feelings and convictions were intensified by this imported U.S. drama.

Peruvian society also experienced other U.S. cultural expressions. In July 1860 a company of four U.S. blacks, styled the Alleghanians, made their debut in Lima playing English and U.S. songs, opera arias, and some lighter music on their sixty-two-bell carillon and a xylophone. One of the members of the troupe was a woman. In November 1860, a U.S. minstrel group called the Ethiopian Minstrels delighted Lima audiences. The minstrels, formed in New York in 1854 and made up entirely of whites in blackface, played and danced the melodies and steps originated by the black culture of the United States, still largely slave. The minstrels returned in 1871 to Lima audiences that welcomed them enthusiastically.

Peruvian travelers to the United States were few, but they produced widely read impressions. In 1845, one of Peru's most famous travelers, Juan Bustamante, wrote Viaje al neuvo mundo. A mestizo born along the shores of Lake Titicaca, Bustamante set sail in 1841 on a three-year trip around the world. The trip included a great deal of time in the northeastern United States, with stopovers in the cities of

Boston and New York, where he noted the hustle and bustle of urban crowds. His book went through several editions.

Bustamante learned about his own homeland by being away from it, a lesson common to most travelers. He encouraged his fellow Peruvians to learn about people of vastly different character, education, and ideas, many of which were good, useful, and even grand, a quality manifestly lacking in Peru in many cases. Ironically, Bustamante, who would become one of the great defenders of Indians in his homeland, waxed almost lyrical on European civilization: "the Europeans, born in the most enlightened part of the world, naturally can show us the luminescence we lack in the arts and in the sciences, and our efforts ought to be aimed at putting us on the same level as these cultured nations; otherwise, independence will have been a waste."[4]

Imperialism: Old and New

During the 1860s, the political and military fortunes of the United States and Peru intersected seriously for the first time since the independence era, in a curious episode triggered by the dwindling fortunes of the old mother country, Spain.

In 1863 two immigrant Spaniards working in northern Peru on a plantation named Talambo in the province of Chiclayo were murdered in an attack instigated by the Peruvian overseer. The already strained relations between Spain and Peru intensified as Spain demanded indemnification and an apology on behalf of its citizens. Peru wavered, and Spain seized the Chincha Islands with its Pacific naval squadron in April 1864. That led to war a year later. Peru was joined by Ecuador, Bolivia, and Chile in rebuking Spain's actions. On 21 March 1866 the Spanish squadron bombarded Valparaíso, and on 2 May, Callao. Old fort San Felipe, defender of Callao Harbor, was far outgunned, but the Peruvians responded to the Spanish naval bombardment with spirit. The noisy, smoky, battle—called the Battle of *Dos de Mayo*—satisfied everyone's honor, and Admiral Castro Mendez Núñez of Spain withdrew his fleet after five hours. Thereafter there were no more hostilities. Part of the Spanish fleet retired across the Pacific to Manila, and the rest left for ports in the Atlantic. An armistice, however, was not formally achieved until 1871, when the United States presided over a peace conference in Washington, D.C.

Throughout the period, the United States had sought to resolve the conflict. Despite a claim to be neutral, U.S. sympathies rested clearly with Peru and its allies. In the minds of many, and certainly in the mind of Secretary of State William Seward, the Monroe Doctrine had been challenged by the Spanish, whose aggression threatened the independence and sovereignty of an American state. Furthermore, Peru's minister in Washington, Federico L. Barreda, successfully enlisted U.S. sympathy and assistance.

Barreda had represented Peru in Washington since the reestablishment of formal diplomatic relations in 1860. A brilliant young businessman only in his late thirties, he developed a natural affinity for life in the United States, where he amassed a sizable fortune in his business enterprises. Barreda symbolized an important element in the development of U.S.-Peruvian relations: the diplomat whose business, scholarly, or professional interests wound his nation's fortunes more tightly into the fabric of U.S. affairs. These diplomats frequently returned to Peru with messages of solidarity and cohesiveness to preach to skeptical audiences less convinced of the common interests of Peru and the United States.

Barreda had been busy from 1862 to 1866 acquiring war materiel in England and France because the Union prohibited the export of arms during the Civil War. He returned from London to Washington in April 1866 with instructions to find a U.S. naval leader to head the combined Chilean-Peruvian navies. This extraordinary decision by the Chilean and Peruvian governments was intended to avoid incessant wrangling and feuding among naval officers now linked in an unnatural alliance against Spain. Barreda enlisted the former Confederate Commodore John Randolph Tucker as a rear admiral in the Peruvian Navy—the same Tucker who also headed the Peruvian Hydrographic Commission from 1867 to 1874. Tucker assembled a small staff of other former Confederates, all of whom had served in the U.S. Navy before the Civil War and were professional naval officers. They arrived in Peru in mid-June 1866, the first U.S. naval mission to that country.

The next nine months in Peru were marked by an extraordinary round of balls, intrigues, jealousies, and political and military maneuvering. Tucker's problem was not of his own making. Peruvian naval officers were jealous of his appointment in the face of their victory over the Spanish in the Battle of *Dos de Mayo*, and they worked to bring about his removal. Meanwhile, Tucker and his staff were wined and dined in Lima, Santiago, Callao, and Valparaíso by supporters such as Peruvian President Mariano Ignacio Prado.

Tucker took his mission seriously and worked to make his command battle ready. Using a combination of tact and sensitivity, he sought to overcome Peruvian prejudice against his appointment while he worked to make long-lasting improvements. Ships were dry-docked and repaired to higher standards, armament was improved, and Tucker and his officers pushed Peru's sailors to meet his high professional standards. Naval regulations were modernized in the areas of ordnance and signals and fleet tactics, and Tucker's presence pushed the Peruvian Navy to a higher standard. Nonetheless, the commission was to be short-lived, undermined not only by Peruvian and Chilean professional jealousies but by his own countrymen serving in the U.S. Navy's Pacific Coast squadron. In the end, the bitterness and rancor produced by the U.S. Civil War forced Tucker to resign his post in March 1867.[5]

Meanwhile, in Washington, Seward and Barreda developed a rapport that helped keep Peru's views in the minds of U.S. policymakers. In October 1866, Seward pushed for peace negotiations, arguing that Spain had lost all incentive to keep the conflict alive and that Peru and its allies would have to sacrifice a great deal truly to defeat Spain. In other words, neither side had much to gain from war.

Barreda admitted as much to Seward, but he pointed out that the war raised patriotism to new levels in Peru and united all parties in defense of the homeland. Barreda agreed that peace was desirable, but only under highly honorable terms and only if the peace encouraged some form of American continental unity in the face of European aggressions and interventions in America.

Seward concurred that a peace settlement needed to guarantee the independence and sovereignty of the South American republics and clearly to repudiate Spanish or any other European intervention in their internal affairs as violations of the Monroe Doctrine. The "Republican system which is accepted by the people in any of those States shall not be wantonly assailed, [nor] subverted . . . by European powers," Seward wrote. If Europeans overstep the bounds of the Doctrine, such as "the French war in Mexico," then the United States reserves the right to intervene on the side of the Latin American republics.[6]

In the summer of 1866, when Spain threatened to retake the Chincha Islands, Seward noted that the seizure would be "injurious to many neutral states, and especially so to the United States," and warned that "if the Spanish doggedly persisted in this strategy, then the United States would find it difficult to remain neutral in the wars which had been carried on between Spain and the South American republics."[7]

In the end, the Battle of *Dos de Mayo* proved to be the last action of the war. Thereafter, an honorable way to end the war proved to be the thorniest issue. Both sides, especially the Spanish and Chileans, were prickly about satisfying honor. The Peruvians, with the Battle of *Dos de Mayo* to crow about, were less sensitive. The efforts of Seward and his successor Hamilton Fish culminated in an armistice signed in April 1871 in Washington. Although separate peace agreements were not signed for several years by the various nations, the armistice formally concluded the hostilities.

Expanding Commercial Interests

By 1867 a trade boom had sprung up between Peru and the United States, and this boom continued uninterruptedly until the outbreak of the war in 1879.[8] In the first half decade of the 1870s, all previous trade records were broken, with a heavy balance of trade in favor of the United States. The chief export from Peru to the United States remained guano until 1875, when sodium nitrate took the lead. More significant, however, was the export of U.S. steel, iron, and wood products to Peru for railroad construction. The Peruvians were seeking to modernize and transform their country, and the railroads were the keys to this effort.

No other Peruvian was more articulate and powerfully committed to the railroads than Manuel Pardo, who became president in 1872. "Who denies that the railroads are today the missionaries of civilization?" he wrote. "Who denies that Peru urgently needs those same missionaries: without railroads today there cannot be real material progress; and without material progress there can be no moral progress among the masses because material progress increases the people's well being and this reduces their brutishness and their misery; without the railroads civilization can proceed only very slowly." Pardo and his liberal, progressive followers expected too much from the railroads, these "missionaries [of] material progress."[9]

But the railroads were the avatars of modernization, and they were built in Peru largely through the activities of one of the most controversial, dynamic U.S. entrepreneurs to influence U.S.-Peruvian relations, Henry Meiggs.

A native New Yorker, born in the Catskills, Meiggs was drawn by fortune across the continent to California during the gold rush of 1849 to speculate in real estate. He went bankrupt and departed for Chile one step ahead of his creditors and the law. In Chile he converted his winning charm and organizational abilities into railroads and the flamboyant lifestyle of the newly rich. He bribed politicians liberally, treated his workers with unprecedented respect, and also made numerous conquests among the ladies of Chile.

In Peru, Meiggs was the "man of the hour, the true power in the political, social, and economic milieu" of the country in the 1870s.[10] When he was not doing business, he was helping Peruvians in other ways. After the earthquake of August 1868, Meiggs donated more than 50,000 soles (about $50,000) to the victims. He helped build churches and houses of charity. A Christian, he nonetheless donated land for a Jewish cemetery. He equipped the offices of *La Bolsa* newspaper in Arequipa. He was a patron of artists and writers. He was generous in the extreme, but his generosity extended far beyond simple philanthropy. He also distributed immense amounts of money to public officials in Chile, Peru, and Bolivia, to newspapermen, and to other influential citizens. Meiggs was, above everything else, a charmer. He doffed his wide-brimmed sombrero to rich and poor alike, a message that did not go unnoticed in Peru, where the class structure still divided rich and poor, white and Indian. He loved money, but more than money, he loved power and influence, although he was not demonstrative or arrogant in its use or display.

Between 1868 and 1871, Meiggs signed seven contracts to build over a thousand miles of railroads in Peru. These were financed by revenues generated from the guano boom of the past thirty years. As a result of complex financial negotiations, guano and nitrate revenues were pledged to pay off the immense loans contracted in Europe to pay for Meiggs's railroad construction projects. While the spirit of Meiggs prevailed, Peru traveled higher and higher on the thrilling roller coaster of success. Not only did railroads begin to penetrate the mineral-rich mountainous interior, vast public works were initiated to beautify and modernize Lima and Callao with broad boulevards, modern housing, new port facilities, and the other trappings of a modern metropolis. But Peru slowly went bust in the 1870s, revenue being too low to service the debts incurred in building the railroads.[11]

Meiggs died on 30 September 1877. He was not rich nor was he bankrupt, but his visions had turned into nightmares. While individuals pass away, nations tend to persist. Peru did not die, but it faced bankruptcy as it searched for a way out of the financial morass created in part by the high-flying—and now deceased—Meiggs.[12]

Yet Meiggs was not the only foreigner with influence in Peru during these tumultuous times. In stark contrast to the flashy Meiggs stood William Russell Grace, an Irish immigrant to Peru. He slowly and steadily built a commitment to Peru that endured for more than a century. Like Meiggs, Grace came to Peru to make his fortune. Unlike Meiggs, he stayed many years, built up his commercial house, and then kept his interests in Peru long after he left to live in New York and manage his growing affairs from the United States. W. R. Grace & Company became a fixture in U.S.-Peruvian relations for the next century. Through the "Casa Grace" Peruvians came into contact with more U.S. institutions and products than through any other U.S. company.[13]

William Grace came to Peru in 1852. He left Ireland because it was poor and starving and offered little opportunity, and he was drawn to the Americas because they promised to be everything that Europe was not. He ended up on the desert coast of Peru, rather than in New York City, because his father bought a tract of land from an Irish landowner in Peru. Once in Peru, young Grace quickly disassociated himself from the other Irish immigrants who had gone to work on the sugar plantation of Dr. Gallagher. He introduced himself to a small firm of importers named Bryce Brothers that was doing a booming business by servicing the guano fleet anchored off the Chincha Islands. Grace joined Bryce Brothers in 1852, and by 1856 the name of the firm was changed to Bryce-Grace Company.

Grace put into practice two key business principles. He would provide better service for his customers than his competitors, and he would do it more economically. It was no accident that Grace was soon well known by the many Yankee skippers of the guano fleet. They liked him, and the friendship was reciprocated. Grace married a ship captain's daughter from Maine, further drawing him into the U.S. economic and cultural orbit. All the while he was learning to know and respect Peru and Peruvians and was making a small fortune in doing so. For Grace, arrival on the coast of Peru during the guano boom had turned into a felicitous crossroads in his life.

One of Grace's first employees was a young Peruvian named Miguel Llaguno, who came well recommended as the nephew of the governor of the province of Pisco adjoining the Chincha Islands. Llaguno became the first in a long line of Peruvians who joined "Casa Grace" over the next hundred years. Grace treated Llaguno like any of the multitude of his family—brothers, cousins, nephews—who crossed the seas to work with Bryce-Grace in this formative period in the company's development.

Aware of the advantages a merchant who knew the language of his host country would have, Grace also learned to read and write Spanish, and he demanded that all who joined his company learn the language of Peru. If they expected to be successful in the company, it was a sine qua non of their job.

In 1866 Grace transferred his family and his headquarters to New York, leaving his brother Michael in charge of the business in Peru. Coincidentally, at the time Henry Meiggs was negotiating the first of several major railroad contracts with Peru. Such an immense entrepreneurial undertaking naturally attracted the Graces. By the end of the decade they were Henry Meiggs's chief buyers of railroad supplies in the United States. William Grace made good friends with Joseph Spinney, Meiggs's agent in New York, while brother Michael vigorously pursued Meiggs and his business in Peru. The fortunes of Meiggs, the Graces, and Peru seemed inexorably intertwined as the decade of the 1870s progressed. Immense loans from Europe enabled Peru to pay Meiggs well for the awesome, and expensive, challenge of penetrating the Andes with his railroads.

William Grace expanded his business in many other areas during the 1870s. In 1873 he established the Merchants Line, predecessor of the Grace Line, to take advantage of the increasing flow of men and materials between the East Coast of the United States and the West Coast of South America. Within a few years, the Merchants Line was ahead of its competitors in serving this traffic. The company expanded into sugar in 1879, with the acquisition of *Hacienda Cartavio* after its owners, the Alzamora family, went bankrupt, and also into shipping, ship owning, investing, and even sugar mill operations. By the late 1870s Michael Grace had acquired the exclusive right to distribute Peruvian nitrates in the United States.

Meiggs and the Graces were of course not working in a vacuum. They were encouraged and welcomed by Peruvian capitalists, nascent industrialists themselves who sought to modernize the economy by taking advantage of export-led development and modern economic and political institutions (banks, trusts, transportation infrastructures, laissez faire economics, and liberal politics). To do this, they often needed to rely on capital, ideas, and entrepreneurs from abroad, and they found immensely willing participants in Meiggs and the Graces. What few foresaw, however, were the disastrous implications of this rapid, unplanned economic development, especially the impact of Meiggs's costly railroads.

The commercial beachhead established by William Grace at midcentury had been considerably expanded by the late 1870s, but just as the Graces stepped into the lucrative nitrates market, the world collapsed on the Peruvians. The activities of those very entrepreneurs and merchants represented by Henry Meiggs and William Grace had brought the United States into much closer contact with Peru.

The War of the Pacific

In April 1879 the War of the Pacific erupted over disputed boundaries in the Atacama desert region shared by Bolivia, Peru, and Chile. They went to war in large measure because the Atacama had taken on new value in the preceding decades with the discovery of guano, nitrate, and even silver deposits there. A naval arms race between Peru and Chile contributed to the escalation of the conflict. When Bolivia attempted to impose new taxes in one of its provinces, largely developed by Chilean and English capital, Chile challenged the Bolivians. Bolivia declared war on Chile. Peru joined its old ally Bolivia.

When the war ended in 1883, Peru and Bolivia lost huge chunks of their national territory to the victorious Chileans. Bolivia was stripped of its coastline along the Pacific and turned into a landlocked nation, while Peru—whose capital city was captured and sacked by the Chileans—was humiliated by the defeat. Many consider it the transcending event in Peru's modern history, perhaps only matched by the Peruvian Institutional Revolution of 1968. While the war was won and lost by the combatants, the United States played a role, although not a decisive one.

It was not unexpected that the United States would side with the Peruvians in the conflict. Two factors brought the United States into the war, and both of them presaged greater involvement of the United States in Peruvian affairs. The first was increasing U.S. commercial activity along the West Coast of South America, and the second was the U.S. desire to play a greater role in regulating international politics in the Western Hemisphere. That the United States was spectacularly unsuccessful in mediating the war and enforcing its will on the combatants—especially on the victorious Chileans—was frustrating and embarrassing and an indication that the resources and strength of the United States in Latin American affairs was certainly not yet equal to the other great power in the region, Great Britain.[14]

The war went disastrously for the Peruvians. From the perspective of the United States, which had tried six times to mediate the war largely on behalf of Peru, the war represented a failure of U.S. diplomacy. In fact, one historian of the U.S. role in the conflict wrote that "if the results had not been so tragic and harmful to the prestige of the United States, the activities of the diplomatic corps could well be described as high comedy."[15] For the Chileans on the other hand, military and naval triumphs were matched by diplomatic successes at the negotiating table.

The war itself was not high comedy for any of its actors. The Chileans took control of the sea by October 1879 and thereafter pursued a relentless military campaign against the Bolivians and Peruvians. The Bolivian army, sent to the coast in 1879, was knocked out of the war very early. Peru maintained a military presence there until January 1881, when the Chilean armies captured Lima. Thereafter, some rear-guard, guerrilla-style activities marked the war until the Treaty of Ancón ended it in 1883. This summary cannot do justice to a war that was, in the opinion of many, the defining event for almost a century in the modern history of Peru.

The United States vacillated in its policy toward Peru and Chile during these crucial years. Domestic politics in the United States had much to do with this indecisiveness. The war broke out during the final two years of the Hayes administration, and Secretary of State William Evarts was cautious and neutral.[14] When James G. Garfield was inaugurated president in March 1881, Secretary of State James G. Blaine took a much more active role in attempting to mediate the war on behalf of Peru. By then, however, Chile's naval and military triumph over Peru was complete.

Among the several diplomatic initiatives taken by the United States was to sponsor an October 1880 meeting of the belligerents aboard the U.S.S. *Lackawanna* in the harbor of Arica. Secretary of State Evarts supported the initiative taken by U.S. diplomats posted in Lima and Santiago only after it became clear that the European powers—especially the governments of Great Britain, France, and Italy—might step in. Evarts acted on the basis of the Monroe Doctrine, which continued to be the dominant statement of principle governing the affairs of the

United States vis-à-vis Latin America. The meetings on the *Lackawanna* ended in a stalemate because the Chileans demanded more than the Peruvians were willing to concede and the U.S. diplomats could find no middle ground.

Peru was a field of competition between U.S. and English merchants and investors. British investments would prosper from a triumph of Chilean arms; conversely, the same could be said for U.S. investments in Peru. It was, obviously, not all that simple. Other European nationals—from France, Holland, Germany, and Italy, for example—had invested in both Chilean and Peruvian guano and nitrates through purchases of bonds and other notes of indebtedness based on the successful exploitation of these resources. These Europeans were interested principally in finding a quick adjudication of the war, for their investments became precarious and lost immense value during protracted periods of conflict. Nonetheless, the principal foreign actors were the English and U.S. interests.

The basic sympathy of the United States for Peru in the conflict was born not only on larger, international considerations based on power bloc politics but also on the interests of U.S. citizens in preserving the integrity and sovereignty of Peru. While Chilean and English capital had been invested heavily in the guano- and nitrate-rich Bolivian province of Antofagasta, similar resources in the Peruvian provinces of Tarapaca, Tacna, and Arica were developed by a combination of Peruvian, U.S., and European capitalists. The Peruvian government had expropriated the nitrate fields in 1875, and by the end of the decade was benefiting from the exploitation of nitrates in its southernmost provinces. Michael Grace had contracted in 1879 to distribute Peruvian nitrates in the United States, and it was natural for Grace and others to try and protect their investments.

Because of the immense profits to be made, the provisioning of arms to the combatants drew U.S. citizens into the war as well. Not surprisingly, the Graces and their young colleague Charles Flint were soon helping Peru buy arms and munitions abroad. W. R. Grace & Company was, after all, a commercial and trading company with contacts across the United States and Europe, and its sympathies were with the Peruvians.[16]

As the war progressed, U.S. diplomats promoted peace initiatives and mediation while Peru's military fronts crumbled before the victorious Chileans, culminating with the capture of Lima in January 1881. In the end, the United States delivered little relief or help to Peru. The Chilean victories put Santiago in the driver's seat, and the Chileans kept the territories they had captured during the war. This put Secretary of State Blaine—a partisan of Peru's position—in an even more antagonistic position to the Chileans.

Blaine named new envoys, both veterans of the Civil War, to Peru and Chile in May 1881. General Stephen A. Hurlburt was posted as the U.S. minister to Lima, and General Judson A. Kilpatrick went to Santiago. Both Hurlburt and Kilpatrick became partisans of the countries to which they were posted, creating some confusion in U.S. policy in 1881 and early 1882.

Blaine's instructions to Hurlburt and Kilpatrick emphasized the desire to maintain Peru's territorial integrity, but he also instructed both to encourage Peru and Chile to achieve a peace as soon as possible, even if that meant some loss of territory by Peru. Chile was urged to moderate its demands.

Hurlburt, in his enthusiasm, led Peruvians to believe that intervention by the United States against Chile was quite possible. On behalf of the United States, he issued a "Declaration to the Notables of Lima" opposing the dismemberment of Peru, and he personally gave a memorandum to the Chilean commander in Lima, Admiral Patricio Lynch, warning Chile not to take territory unless Peru refused to pay an indemnity. Hurlburt even signed an agreement with the García Calderón government to establish a U.S. naval base at the spacious port of Chimbote on the northern coast of Peru. It seemed as if the Garfield administration was poised to jump in and save the Peruvians from the rapacious Chileans. The astonished British minister in Lima, Spenser St. John, thought Hurlburt had far exceeded his instructions by, essentially, taking Calderón and Peru under his protection. Later that month Blaine censured Hurlburt for taking such extraordinary initiative in defending the Calderón government, although the secretary of state sympathized with the spirit of Hurlburt's actions, calling the Chimbote project "desirable but not opportune." In Peru, Hurlburt's partisan behavior raised the hope of U.S. intervention. But Blaine was in better touch with U.S. political realities and possibilities than his enthusiastic diplomats in Lima and Santiago. There was one possibility, however, that Blaine certainly had not counted on. President Garfield was assassinated, and the new president, Chester Arthur, replaced Blaine with Frederick T. Frelinghuysen.

Before leaving office in December 1881, Blaine attempted to force the belligerents to agree on a peace. With President Arthur's apparent approval, he appointed William Henry Trescot, a former assistant secretary of state, as a special envoy to Peru and Chile. His instructions were to pressure the Chileans to submit to U.S. mediation on favorable terms to Peru: that is, no cession of territory and the guarantee of neutral property rights in those territories now controlled by Chile. Trescot was accompanied by Blaine's able son, Walker, on his mission.[17]

Trescot was told to terminate diplomatic relations with Santiago if it turned out the Chileans had deliberately insulted the United States when they arrested President Calderón of Peru in November 1881. That is the way Hurlburt had reported the incident to Blaine. The secretary of state was outraged when he read of the arrest, which Hurlburt reported "to be understood by the people of Lima at large as the reply of Chili to the known support of that [Calderón] government by the United States." Blaine also advised Trescot that if Chile insisted on taking large portions of Peruvian territory, the United States would appeal to other Latin American countries in mediating the peace.[18]

After a late-December stop in Lima, where he got a warm welcome from the Peruvians, Trescot arrived on 7 January 1882 in Santiago, where he was received with frostiness. Subsequently, Foreign Minister José M. Balmaceda assured Trescot that the Chileans meant no offense to the United States when they arrested Calderón and that they welcomed the good offices of the United States in the search for a viable and just peace. Conversations continued through the month. Trescot unsuccessfully pushed for a more conciliatory position on the part of Chile. The conversations abruptly ended on 31 January, when Balmaceda told Trescot that his instructions from the new secretary of state, Frelinghuysen, superseded those of his predecessor, Blaine. Trescot was astounded. He had not received any word from Washington.

What happened? The best answer is U.S. politics. What unfolded in Washington in December 1881 and the early months of 1882 is a good example of how domestic politics can very deeply influence the course of foreign policy.

Blaine had a lot of political enemies, not all of them in the Democratic party. In 1882 a House committee investigated accusations that Blaine stood to profit financially from supporting Peru in the war, allegedly having secret financial interests in guano and nitrate companies. Although the charges were never proved, it was a good way to embarrass Blaine, one of the most prominent Republicans of his time.

Blaine's political rivals in the Senate had asked for publication of the diplomatic correspondence regarding the War of the Pacific. Blaine only allowed a portion to be made public before he left office. Then, on 26 January 1882, Frelinghuysen released all of the correspondence, including Blaine's original instructions to Trescot, and, more important, revised instructions that Frelinghuysen had sent Trescot early in January, which Trescot had not yet received.[19]

Frelinghuysen now advised Trescot that "the President does seek . . . to extend the kindly offices of the United States impartially to both Peru and Chili," reversing the firm pro-Peruvian tone of the Blaine instructions. In all fairness to Frelinghuysen, he had twice telegraphed Trescot on his way to South America, but Trescot did not receive the messages and therefore was unaware of the sweeping reversal of his instructions. When the Senate published the full correspondence on 26 January, the Chilean legation in Washington informed Balmaceda, enabling him to confront the mortified Trescot on 31 January. One student of U.S. foreign policy has observed, "to such a ludicrous pass had America's makeshift diplomacy arrived in the spring of 1882."[20]

The inability and unwillingness of the United States to intervene in defending Peru against Chile became painfully obvious to astute political observers such as Michael Grace. The results of such vacillation and pusillanimity were equally obvious. Michael—whose brother William was by then mayor of New York, having been elected to that office as a reform Democrat in 1880—talked with President Arthur late in 1881. Michael Grace was convinced of the total lack of resoluteness in the U.S. policy toward Chile. And he was disgusted. "Am. Intervention is all a humbug . . . Uncle Sam has backed down," Michael wrote one of his colleagues, Noel West, in Santiago. To his cousin Edward Eyre in Lima, Grace expressed himself with even greater vehemence: "The United States will be thoroughly hated on the West Coast, will be jeered and laughed at by all the foreign legations, will be made fun of by the Chilean press, and will be thoroughly despised by the Peruvian people, who will blame them to a very great extent for the present trouble."[21] What galled Michael even more was the invocation of the Monroe Doctrine by the

United States to block European attempts to mediate in 1880–81, which was an implicit promise to Peru that the United States would arrange matters itself. After raising the hopes of the government and people of Peru, the United States then abruptly withdrew and left Peru open to the mercies of a victorious army.

When Trescot tried to save face by pushing the Chileans to be moderate in their demands, Balmaceda simply refused to discuss the matter of Tarapaca further. "Tarapaca," Balmaceda bluntly told Trescot, "is now irrevocably Chilean territory and if the United States wanted Tarapaca for Peru, then it must fight for it."[22]

Trescot packed his bags and left for Lima in March. He arrived in the Peruvian capital on the 28th, just one day after the U.S. minister to Peru, General Hurlburt, suddenly died. Hurlburt was remembered by thousands of grieving Peruvians, who "lined the streets and decked his bier with flowers as it moved to the railway station." An English eyewitness remarked that Hurlburt "was looked upon by the natives as the Champion of the country," provoking such an outpouring of grief at his passing.[23] Hurlburt's death was the perfect symbol for the bankruptcy of U.S. policy in the War of the Pacific.

Trescot, ever the diplomat, made one last effort in Peru to persuade the Peruvians to accede to Chilean demands for the smaller provinces of Tacna and Arica as well as Tarapaca. Trescot traveled into the mountains and there met with Admiral Lizardo Montero, who headed an interim government recognized by some Peruvians while García Calderón was being held by the Chileans in Santiago. Montero asked Trescot what the United States was prepared to do to reduce the onerous Chilean demands for the cession of Peruvian territory. The last Peruvian Congress had stated unequivocally that there would be no transfer of territory. Montero was equally obstinate on this point. So was García Calderón. Both were being unrealistic, for the Chileans held all the cards, and the United States could do nothing.

Trescot concluded that "current policy was an embarrassment to all parties concerned and should be terminated as soon as possible."[24] When Trescot's mission ended in failure, Peru was left on its own. Chile proceeded to push for a final settlement on its terms. Since both García Calderón and Admiral Montero proved intractable on the issue of ceding territory, a new Peruvian government organized by General Miguel Iglesias in late 1882 was recognized by the Chileans in 1883. Iglesias accepted the onerous and unpopular task of meeting the Chileans' demands.

The Treaty of Ancón was signed at the seaside resort of Ancón just south of Lima on 10 October 1883, and it was ratified on 10 March 1884. Peru gave up its southern province of Tarapaca, rich in guano and nitrates. Two smaller provinces just north of Tarapaca—Arica and Tacna—were to be occupied by Chile for a period of ten years. A plebiscite would then be held to determine their future. The winner of the plebiscite would pay the loser $10 million and keep the territories.

Peru lost not only territory rich in natural resources that produced fiscal revenues, it also lost a significant number of people. Tacna and Arica were so wedded to the Peruvian sense of national territory that the Chileans were forced to make some concessions for the sake of the peace. They would have preferred outright annexation, but Peru, even under the presidency of Miguel Iglesias, adamantly resisted the unconditional loss of Tacna-Arica. The plebiscite solution agreed to in the Treaty of Ancón helped assuage the immense sense of loss in Peru. Ultimately, Tacna would remain Peruvian and Arica would go to Chile, with U.S. mediation contributing to the final settlement in 1929.

The war also unraveled Peru's social and economic fabric. In the mountains, for example, guerrilla warfare flared off and on through 1882 and 1883 and took on strong racial overtones. Bands of Indian guerrillas raided and attacked the homes and haciendas of Peruvian whites and *mistis* (*mestizos*) just as often as the camps and armies of the invading Chilean forces. A Chilean commander was stunned by what he saw in November 1883: "All the Indians of Huanta and Huancayo are in revolt. The few with whom we could make contact declared that their objective was not to fight the Chileans or the Peruvian peace party, but the entire white race." [25] The specter of social rebellion was not confined to the highlands. In some of the more populous coastal valleys, blacks massacred Chinese and whites indiscriminately. As the Chilean army gradually withdrew from Peru, scattered violence flared up and directly threatened the interests of the propertied class. Accommodation and agreement with the Chileans—no matter how onerous the terms with respect to the loss of territory—seemed to be the only way of preserving the interests of those who still ruled Peru. [26]

What was the legacy of the war with respect to relations between Peru and the United States? That the United States would refrain from outright military intervention was made clear in President Arthur's message to Congress in late 1882.

> The power of Peru no longer extends over its whole territory, and in the
> event of our interference to dictate peace it would need to be supplemented
> by the armies and navies of the United States. Such interference would al-
> most inevitably lead to the establishment of a protectorate, a result utterly
> at odds with our past policy, injurious to our present interest, and full of
> embarrassments for the future. [27]

On the other hand, Peru needed the support of the United States if it expected to recuperate from the massive losses inflicted upon it by the war. Not only did the oligarchy need to reestablish its authority in Peru, it needed foreign capital and assistance to do so. The immense debt inherited from the prewar loans and war-year expenditures—in the realm of $260 million—made it imperative that Peru look abroad to reestablish its credit.

So the legacy was mixed. On the one hand, many Peruvians were embittered by what they considered the unrealistic and ultimately worthless encouragement of the United States to resist Chilean demands. On the other hand, the United States was called upon to mediate and lobby on behalf of Peru in future settlements with Chile. If British interests were closely associated with Chile's fortunes, then many considered Peruvian interests to be favored by the United States.

The ambiguity that so often characterized relations between the United States and Peru was underscored by the War of the Pacific. While the U.S. government had proved to be a most unreliable patron, U.S. private investors and capitalists had not given up on Peru. In the next half century U.S. capital and U.S. liberal economic ideals found fruitful ground in Peru, as the country sought to reconstruct and modernize its economy in the face of the trauma of war and its consequences. In many ways, the war cleansed away much of the conservative, unchanging ways of the past and opened the path to the true modernization of Peru.

The Ascendant American Eagle

The period in U.S.-Peruvian relations from the end of the War of the Pacific to 1903 was transitional, marked by some subtle changes and some changes that were a good deal more obvious. Some of the most important changes were triggered by internal developments in each country as the process of modernization transformed ways of life.

In the case of the United States, modernization was manifested most strongly as industrialization and urbanization. In the case of Peru, recuperation from the ravages of the War of the Pacific dominated national life until the end of the century. Then, from the end of the nineteenth century and continuing well into the twentieth, Peru was more closely integrated into the world economy. Increased exports of primary materials such as silver, copper, oil, and tin and agricultural commodities such as sugar and cacao drove this export development.

The Grace Contract

For Peru, the legacy of war meant not only an immense debt incurred in waging the war itself but also a debt inherited from the halcyon days of railroad building under Henry Meiggs. Complicating the problem was the loss of Tarapaca with its reserves of guano and nitrates. These natural resources had been intended in prewar years to service the railroad debt and other internal developments. Not only had the war left a deep psychological scar on the national psyche of Peru, it also left the country in a financial morass. Attempts by the Peruvians in the 1880s to raise new loans in the European bond markets all failed. Bondholders, principally the British, wanted their prior investments in Peru guaranteed before allowing fresh new loans.

To break this logjam, the ubiquitous Michael Grace devoted his considerable charm, determination, and financial genius to helping Peru. The negotiation of the Grace Contract of 1890 was complicated and aroused considerable passion in Peru. In effect, Peru's future came to depend in part on what foreign capitalists and diplomats decided in the boardrooms and chancelleries of Europe and the United States. The entire second half of the nineteenth century and the early decades of the twentieth century witnessed the increasing economic and commercial penetration of Latin America by European—especially British—and U.S. capitalists. In this "second conquest of America," nothing symbolized the trend in Peru more than the Grace Contract.

The unfinished railroads were at the heart of the old debts. To be truly productive, the principal railroad from Lima into the central highlands needed to reach the rich Cerro de Pasco mining region. To revive and rehabilitate these once productive silver mines, where copper ores also were thought to exist in abundance, a drainage tunnel, called the Rumillana, had to be constructed. Meiggs and his heirs controlled many of the claims in the Cerro de Pasco region, as well as the rights to build the Rumillana. In 1885 Michael Grace bought all of these properties, franchises, rights, privileges, and obligations from the Meiggs heirs and agreed to finish the railroad and the tunnel.

To raise capital for his projects, Grace turned to the U.S. money market rather than the traditional source of capital, London. The flow of capital in the nineteenth century had been largely from east to west, for the great natural resources of America—both North and South—were frequently exploitable only with large injections of British capital. The development of finance capitalism was an essential stage in the growth of the U.S. industrial state, and Michael Grace's ability to tap this source demonstrated the growing maturity of U.S. capitalism.

In 1886 Grace formed a syndicate, the Cerro de Pasco Syndicate, to exploit the railroad and mining concessions he had acquired from Meiggs's heirs. The members of the syndicate represented an impressive lineup of the capitalist elite at the time: three—Arthur Twombley, W. Seward Webb, and W. D. Sloan—were sons-in-law of William H. Vanderbilt, while John J. Mackay of the Comstock lode, Robert Payne of Standard Oil, Frederick Billings of the Northern Pacific Railroad, Joseph W. Drexel of Drexel, Morgan & Company, and Michael's brother William R. Grace were also contributors. Once the syndicate was formed, Michael brought a team of mining engineers to Peru to investigate thoroughly the Cerro de Pasco region. He continued to operate the railroad, making necessary repairs, and prepared for the extension of the railway and the construction of the drainage tunnel. Meanwhile, the principal holders of Peru's foreign debt—bondholders in Great Britain—were pursuing their interests, which, like Michael Grace's, were inextricably linked to Peru's financial problems and promises.

The bondholders' dilemma was how to retrieve their investments. In response to Peru's rapidly deteriorating position in the late 1870s, the principal bondholders formed a committee to look after their interests. They viewed the railroads—pledged by the Peruvians in earlier loans as collateral—as legitimate compensation for loans the Peruvians had defaulted on. So did some Peruvians. Early in 1880, the administration of President Nícolas de Pirola issued a decree granting the bondholders the ownership of all the national railroads. Although the bondholders did not avail themselves immediately of this concession, it was a tacit admission of their right to the railroads.

There followed a complicated series of negotiations between the bondholders and the governments of Chile, Peru, and Great Britain. The bondholders wanted the Chileans to recognize bondholder claims to guano and nitrate deposits once formerly in Peru but now claimed by Chile. When Michael Grace bought the old Meiggs railroad concessions in 1885, an impasse existed. The Chileans were not interested in giving away what they had won in war. The Peruvians had little to negotiate with. The bondholders could not persuade London to intercede against Chile on their behalf. And the United States was undecided on how to intervene, if at all, on Peru's behalf. Grace offered his services to the bondholders and in 1886 became their principal representative before the government of Peru.

Grace sought both his fortune and that of Peru. He did not consider these mutually exclusive goals. If Peru were to recover her financial and commercial footing, Grace stood to prosper. If the country remained yoked with debt and subordinate to Chile, Grace would fail to prosper. His plan was simple, but its negotiation was complicated. Grace placed himself between the bondholders and the Peruvian government and sought to forge an agreement that both sides could live with. The key to his various proposals was the insistence that any agreement between the bondholders and Peru should relieve Peru of its entire debt; a final arrangement could come only "in exchange for an absolute acquittal of all claims of its foreign creditors."[27] Grace's gifts as a natural mediator were complemented by his ability to understand both the hard commercial mentality of the bondholders and the fierce national pride of President Andres Cacerés of Peru.

"How," President Cacerés queried Eyre, perhaps rhetorically, "are we going to give them our railroads which cost us so dearly?"[28] That was a question that troubled many other Peruvians, who split on the issue as the debate heated up in national forums. The initial demands of the bondholders included not only ownership of the railroads but also concessions to coal and mercury mines, oil fields, and territory to establish colonies as well as a monopoly on all subsequent guano exports and the right to collect customs duties at Mollendo, the Southern Railway terminus on the Pacific Ocean. Outraged opponents claimed that the demands were gross infringements of Peru's sovereignty.

The colonization clauses of the proposed contract were among the most interesting. European colonization had been sought eagerly by nineteenth-century Latin Americans who wanted U.S. citizens or Europeans to help "whiten" and "civilize" Latin America. Peruvians had tried to attract Irish, Spanish, and German colonists at one time or another. The results, however, had been lackluster. Now the champions of the Grace Contract were once again heralding the promise of rejuvenation through immigration. But many found the rationale specious and unrealistic.

Jose María Quimper, a leading opponent of the contract, said that "the projected colonization project was but a farce since the age of miracles had long ago passed," and he condemned it roundly.[29] Quimper's pessimism proved right in the long run, for no great wave of European or U.S. settlers swept into Peru to infuse society with whiteness and enrich it with the promise of Old World work habits, blood, and capacity for industrialized labor. The subject of immigration stirred imaginations and fired debate within the context of the bondholders' proposals. A strong nationalist sentiment was voiced in these debates, and these sentiments just as clearly colored relations between the United States and Peru as those—represented by Michael Grace and his Peruvian supporters, for example—that favored increasing collaboration at almost any cost.

Another critic, Manuel Atanasio Fuentes, the interim attorney general, cynically observed that all the promises inherent in Michael Grace's contract were chimerical. "Colossal enterprises," Fuentes said, were promised upon the conclusion of the contract and the settlement of the debt. "Here is a position," he continued, "that all debtors would certainly favor: a creditor's representative [Grace] who not only gives his debtors generous terms, but [promises] work and bread as well." He added, "we must be wary of dealing with those not born in this land."[30]

In addition, old President Cacerés and his Council of Ministers had come around by 1887 to supporting the contract, especially as Michael Grace worked to moderate the bondholders' original demands. When Cacerés addressed Congress in early 1887, he argued persuasively for the contract in four major areas: first, the necessity of reestablishing not only the external but also the internal credit of the nation to release economic forces, to get the currency moving again and to create new and more powerful fiscal resources; second, the necessity of completing the construction of the railroads and repairing and returning to regular service those in a lamentable state of deterioration; third, the importance of studying and then exploiting the riches of the principal mining centers; and, fourth, the utility of creating new centers of population to facilitate and stimulate immigration further.[31]

Negotiations continued through 1887, complicated by the Chilean opposition to any agreement that infringed on their newly acquired territories, for the bondholders continued to insist that part of their legitimate claims had to be met by nitrate and guano deposits once held by Peru but now by Chile. In September 1887, the Peruvian Congress complicated the complicated situation even further by authorizing the nationalization of certain Peruvian railoads. This brought the United States into the equation, pressured by its citizens to protect their railroad rights in Peru.

On behalf of themselves and other U.S. railroad concessionaires in Peru, the Graces petitioned the U.S. Department of State to intervene and protest the nationalizations. Secretary of State Thomas F. Bayard remonstrated with the Peruvian government, but the Peruvian Congress, especially the Chamber of Deputies where much of the opposition to the Grace Contract centered, did not back down. William Grace claimed that the seizures were illegal. He also ventured a criticism heard with more frequency in the late twentieth century than in the late nineteenth century with respect to public versus private management of industries. Grace lectured the secretary of state that "the Peruvian government well knows that if the roads should be taken by them and fall into the hands of government administrators, the result would be that within a few years they would not only not be extended, but the probability is that they would not be in existence."[32] Here we find summarized one of the principal elements in the making of modern relations between Peru and the United States—the debate over the propriety and effectiveness of public versus private enterprise in the economic development of nations. The determining forces and moods within the United States and Peru in the late nineteenth and early twentieth centuries tended to favor private enterprise.

Meanwhile, Michael Grace had to deal with the railroad nationalizations. He argued with his Peruvian supporters that even though the nationalizations may have been justified, the image abroad that Peru was politically unstable was reinforced by such forced seizures. "It gives another pretext," Grace said, "to the many enemies of the country to expound their theory that the country is unstable and unsafe to invest capital in."[33]

Next Grace worked to get the U.S. government more directly involved in protecting U.S. investments in Peruvian railroads. A special Peruvian envoy, Félix Cipriano Zegarra, was sent to Washington in 1888 to represent Peru's interests. Grace worked closely with Zegarra, Secretary of State Bayard, and President Grover Cleveland to gain his ends.

Grace held little hope for direct U.S. intervention in Peru. The United States, like Great Britain, was unwilling to intervene in what it considered a private dispute between investors and a foreign government. Bayard argued that the consequences of entering into contractual obligations with an unstable government should be borne by the investors. The U.S. government was not in the business of bailing out citizens who made bad investments or suffered the consequences of unsound business decisions. On behalf of the Peruvian government, Zegarra assured Grace and Bayard that his country would fight rather than yield on its right to nationalize the railroads. For his part, Bayard knew that the United States had little leverage on Peru.

William Ivins, Grace's representative in Washington during most of the negotiations, candidly told his boss that "the thing that staggers Mr. Bayard most, in case the worst comes to the worst, is the futility of attempting to coerce so weak and puny a state as Peru, as he fears it would only result in a long and ultimately fruitless occupation of the country and would on no account restore the values of the railroad properties."[34] Zegarra clearly played his strength—the very weakness of Peru—quite well.

The incident highlighted the asymmetrical nature of relations between Peru and the United States, but in this instance it happened with a different twist. Instead of power dictating to the weak, the power found itself quite unable to bring that power to bear. The relations between nations are not always governed directly by power and size. If fact, these determinants can often have the least influence in major decisions, whereas long-term goals, political principles and ideals, and a careful consideration of the desire or ability of internal public opinion to sustain intervention are often more important.

While negotiations in Washington slogged on through the hot summer months of August and September 1888, they moved more quickly in Lima, smoothed along by the reduced demands of the Bondholders' Committee. Their rights to the oil

fields in the north were dropped along with their effort to install their own cus-
tomhouse officials in Mollendo to collect duties. The railroad concession was reduced from seventy-five to sixty-six years, and some other terms were made more
favorable to Peru. The crisis over the seizure of the railroads was left in temporary
abeyance. It was recognized that if the new contract was ratified, railroad concessionaires such as Michael Grace would deal directly with the corporation—the Peruvian Corporation—that was slated to succeed the bondholders and carry out the
terms of the contract.[35]

The Grace Contract was finally ratified by Peru's Congress in late October
1889, although the debate was intense. When opposition members of the Chamber
of Deputies stormed out of one session in early 1889, President Cacerés simply declared their posts vacant and held new elections. With a majority of supporters,
Cacerés pushed through the contract.

By April 1890 the Peruvian Corporation was in operation, and Peru passed
into a new era. With the settlement of its debt, the road was opened not only to
recovery from the War of the Pacific but also to new economic development across
a broad spectrum of activities, from mining to agriculture to banking and beer
making. The Grace Contract remained, however, an issue of some controversy
among Peruvians for several generations.

The most balanced assessment of the Grace Contract was made by Peru's premier historian of the twentieth century, Jorge Basadre. Basadre felt that the contract represented the best arrangement under bad circumstances. The railroads
were in a state of deterioration, the bondholders were blocking Peru's access to
moneys abroad, the Chileans were in opposition, and the English Foreign Office
and the U.S. Department of State waxed hot and cold. The contract broke this impasse and by the vary nature of its solution invited foreign capital into the country.
In one sense—Michael Grace's point of view certainly—it was a liberating, progressive act that enabled Peru to draw freely again upon U.S. and European capitalists. According to Quimper and its critics, especially those subscribing to perspectives formed by Marxism and dependency theory in the twentieth century,
those very ties with capitalism enabled by the contract reinforced neocolonialism
and economic dependency, and thus the contract was a step toward the loss of national and economic sovereignty.

Between these two extreme points of view, Basadre's analysis of the contract
stands out for its balance. On the one hand, Basadre observed that "the unique
alliance predicted between Peru and her creditors to make the country flourish
dramatically did not develop." But, on the other hand, as Basadre noted, "nor did
the pessimistic vision of the Contract's more furious and hotheaded adversaries
come to pass." What happened was that "the past was liquidated and the country,
thinking itself free of her overwhelming foreign debt, confronted the future in
pursuit of reconstruction."[36]

In the overall scheme of relations between the United States and Peru, the
Grace Contract identified Peru's aspirations more closely with those of the United
States, challenging the predominant commercial and diplomatic weight of Great

Britain in Latin America. That Chilean destinies were perceived to be closely tied to British commercial interests furthered the Peruvian orientation of the U.S. government.

Developing Mutual Interest

During the protracted contract proceedings, the United States called the First International American Congress to meet in Washington, D.C. This was the predecessor to the Pan-American Union and, later, the Organization of American States and as such marks one of the initiating moments in the Pan-American movement. That it was called at a time when Peru was attempting to regain control of its lost provinces to Chile and that one of the items on the agenda was the peaceful resolution of disputes and conflicts between American states through international arbitration made the conference of interest and importance to Peru. Perhaps the conference, presided over by U.S. Secretary of State James G. Blaine, could be used to further Peruvian interests.

Peru's minister in Washington, Félix Cipriano Zegarra, then also negotiating closely with Michael Grace on the Grace Contract, was appointed to represent Peru. Andrew Carnegie and Charles Flint were two of the U.S. representatives.[37] William Grace was left off the U.S. delegation because it was thought his close ties to Peru and Latin America would create a conflict of interest.

The conference opened in Washington on 2 October 1889 with a gala banquet preceded by a reception given by President Harrison in the White House. The visiting delegates then embarked on a six-week junket across the United States on a special train that carried them as far north as Maine and as far west as Nebraska. Niagara Falls, Mammoth Cave, and other natural and man-made wonders were on the route. The tab—$150,000—was picked up by the United States. Presumably impressed by the wonders and warmed by the hospitality, the delegates convened once again in Washington in November 1889 and did not adjourn until 19 April 1890.

For Peru and the United States, little was accomplished. Indeed, other than agreements on some commercial and customs matters, nothing of importance approved by the conference was ratified by a majority of the participants. But the act of cooperating in pushing Chile to agree to accept arbitration in the Tacna-Arica matter promoted a sense of shared objectives between the United States and Peru. Chile and Argentina balked at U.S. initiatives. The Chileans would not submit Tacna-Arica to international arbitration, and the Argentines chaffed at the presumed leadership of the United States in affairs of the Western Hemisphere.

In the main, the conference underscored the basic alignment of the United States with Peruvian interests as Chile and Argentina pushed for greater influence not only in the Southern Cone but also in all of South America. Zegarra was certainly not in the pocket of or subservient to U.S. interests at the conference. Differences on how to negotiate a growing quarrel with Ecuador, for example, prompted Peru not to agree to a first draft of the proposed arbitration treaty, and in 1889

Peru's proposed nationalization of the railroads led to a mini-crisis between Peru and the United States over the propriety of such an action.

Interest in Peru on the part of the United States was more than commercial and diplomatic. It included the possible acquisition of a naval base on the north coast of Peru in the late nineteenth century.

The Chimbote Naval Station

The U.S. Navy almost acquired a major naval station at the port of Chimbote on the north coast of Peru at the turn of the century. The subject first came up during the War of the Pacific when the García Calderón government and the U.S. minister to Peru, Hurlburt, negotiated an agreement to allow the United States to establish a coaling station and naval base at the spacious port of Chimbote.[38] Nothing came of this initial agreement, borne largely out of Hurlburt's sympathy for Peru and the wartime exigencies and pressures on Peru to gain U.S. favor.

In 1889 the United States again parlayed with Peru on the Chimbote naval base. The United States was expanding its naval and commercial presence in the Pacific, and it was thought opportune to have a station on the West Coast of South America whose range would extend, naturally, into the South Pacific as well. The navy had maintained a small squadron along the West Coast since the independence era, largely patrolling between Callao, Valparaíso, and ports to the north as far as Central America and even California before the Mexican-American War. As the United States modernized its navy in the 1880s and 1890s and expanded its commercial horizons, the West Coast of South America gained its share of attention among U.S. planners.

Neither Peru nor the United States was ready in 1888 or 1889 to make the necessary commitments and concessions to establish the Chimbote naval station. The Peruvians would not give the United States territorial jurisdiction, including the right to fly the U.S. flag, and the United States would not yield to an absolute statement of Peruvian territorial integrity. Besides, in 1889, Secretary of State Blaine was launching the First Pan-American Conference, and it was thought inopportune to be negotiating territorial transfers when one of the goals of the conference was to guarantee the territorial integrity of all American nations.

In 1891 and 1892, largely at the behest of the U.S. minister in Lima, John Hicks, President Harrison approved further talks, although Secretary of State Blaine remained cool to the subject. Coincidentally, relations between the United States and Chile were reaching a nadir over various disputes. Hicks thought this would be a propitious time to deal with the Peruvians, who provided a counterweight to growing Chilean hegemony along the West Coast.[39] But Hicks was no more successful than Hurlburt, and the issue subsided until after the turn of the century, not to be laid to rest until 1910.

While the drive for a U.S. naval station at Chimbote waxed and waned, private U.S. commercial and industrial interests were growing in Peru. From the 1890s onward U.S. entrepreneurs became involved in a variety of activities in Peru, especially in the extractive industries of mining, rubber, and petroleum, even while continuing to invest in railroad building and in new ventures such as sugar plantations, beer making, and other commercial enterprises.

Peru was poised at the turn of the century to receive U.S. capital and investments in ever-increasing amounts, having recovered from the War of the Pacific and reestablished its good name in international financial circles. Investors from the United States found a congenial and stable environment, and capital—such as that made available through the Cerro de Pasco Corporation—revitalized and modernized some of Peru's most lucrative mining enterprises, especially copper and silver.

The relationship between the United States and Peru was developing into one of the closest that the United States would have in the early twentieth century with a South American country. An amalgam of factors—guano and Grace, Tucker and Meiggs, war and peace—combined to draw these two American nations into an interesting relationship. While Peru was no more part of the U.S. public's mind in 1903 than it was in 1850, the United States certainly had grown in influence in Peru. By the time of the First World War, the United States had displaced Great Britain as Peru's leading foreign investor and trader.

7

ARGENTINA

Clash of Global Visions I

Joseph S. Tulchin

R ELATIONS BETWEEN ARGENTINA AND the United States in the half-century
after 1850 fall into two distinct periods. The first, which began before 1850
and lasted until 1865 when the U.S. Civil War ended, was characterized by mutual
disinterest. The second period, which lasted until the end of World War I, was
characterized by a divergence of global visions on the part of two countries enjoy-
ing dramatic economic growth that drove them along similar and competitive
tracks and pushed them further and further apart. The period ended with the
United States as the dominant economic and military power in the world and Argentina relegated to minor status in world affairs.

Following the episode on the Malvinas in which U.S. naval forces had clashed
with Argentine officials on the islands over whaling rights, the United States and
Argentina entered a prolonged period of mutual disinterest. In both, the central
cause of their quite conscious failure to exert any effort to strengthen ties was a
determined focus on internal affairs, which included territorial expansion and civil
war. Throughout much of this period the U.S. government seemed as if it simply
could not muster the energy to do more than insist on its friendly disposition toward the Argentine republic. Despite repeated requests, it did not bother even to
send a diplomatic representative to Argentina to replace Francis Baylies, who left
in 1832, until 1844 or to send a minister until 1854. The lack of representation in
Argentina rendered U.S. diplomacy ineffective during the period of French and
then Anglo-French pressure against the government of Juan Manuel de Rosas.
This pressure included a naval blockade that interrupted U.S. commerce in the Río
de la Plata, which for some implied the threat of European intervention. Despite
provocation, the U.S. government never thought of invoking the Monroe Doctrine
or of doing more than protecting the rights of U.S. citizens under difficult circumstances. It declared its strict neutrality and ignored suggestions or requests for a
more active role. The Polk administration even went to the point of disavowing
aggressive actions by local naval officers and disciplining Captain P. F. Voorhees,

who had actually captured some Argentine vessels, which he accused of violating the rights of U.S. shipping during the blockade of Montevideo. By contrast, both the Buchanan and the Johnson administrations declared their willingness to use naval force to secure their short-term diplomatic objectives in the Río de la Plata, especially against the López regime in Paraguay; this belligerence appeared totally out of place in the region and was almost totally ineffective.

The Foundations of Expansionist Policies

Argentine foreign policy throughout most of the period was extremely defensive. Until 1862, when the nation was reorganized under the centralizing hegemony of the Province of Buenos Aires, the foreign affairs of the United Provinces were conducted by the province of Buenos Aires in the name of all of the provinces, or, after 1854, when the province seceded from the confederation, by the province for itself. Once the question of independence and recognition had been settled, the international relations of the new nation were conceived essentially as a matter of international trade on the one hand and as a matter of defining its boundaries on the other.

In 1852 Justo José de Urquiza overthrew Rosas. Urquiza began his campaign by attacking an ally of Rosas in Uruguay, Manuel Oribe, in 1848 and then offering recognition to Carlos Antonio López in Paraguay. Finally, in conjunction with López, he offered the European powers free navigation of the inland waterways. He also joined forces with Brazil, so that by the time he flushed Rosas out onto the field of battle at Caseros in 1851, it was an international campaign. In the succeeding decade Urquiza, as head of the Argentine Confederation, attempted to use foreign powers to break the resistance of the province of Buenos Aires and force the province to join the new union. In one sense he failed, and the consolidation of the nation was realized under the hegemony of the province of Buenos Aires when the governor of the province, Bartolomé Mitre, became president in 1862. In another sense Urquiza was successful as a transitional figure crucial to the evolution of his nation in the new international system. Himself a rancher and *saladero* in the mold of Rosas, although from an interior province, he recognized that the regime Rosas represented had stagnated and that it was necessary to open Argentina to the outside world and to accommodate the nation to the changes already occurring in the United States and Europe. To achieve those changes, universally called progress, it was necessary to establish internal order and to adopt a diplomatic style more congruent with the dominant style in Europe.

For the most part, the United States remained aloof from international intrigues in the Río de la Plata. In 1866 Secretary of State William Seward tried to mediate the War of the Triple Alliance, in which Paraguay faced Brazil, Argentina, and Uruguay, but he backed away when his offer was spurned, despite the urging of the U.S. minister in Rio, James W. Webb, who insisted that it was in the Latin Americans' "interest and their duty to look to the United States for protection and advice," and that the United States should assume "her right to interpose in all international conflicts on this continent."[1]

These were brave words in 1866. They would be echoed thirty years later by Secretary of State Richard Olney, to greater effect in the dispute over the boundary between Venezuela and British Guiana. Seward knew that U.S. trade in the Río de la Plata region was not significant and that U.S. capital was virtually absent from the early stages of the economic development that had begun following national consolidation. There was no direct steamship link between the two countries. And to make matters worse, when Congress began to impose protective tariffs on a growing list of products, one of the first, in the law of 1867, was wool, then the primary export of Argentina. The Argentine government protested the terms of the tariff, and the minister in Washington exerted considerable effort in Congress and in the national press to change the provisions of the bill. No changes were made. The executive did nothing to prevent damage to Argentine interests or national pride. Apparently the State Department did not consider the trade and the goodwill of Argentina. These attitudes would change rapidly in the remaining years of the century.

The explosive growth that Argentina experienced in the half century after 1860 is one of the great success stories in the history of capitalist economies. There are no records of any other economy growing so much, so fast. The only comparable case is that of the United States. The size of the U.S. economy was greater, both at the beginning of its most rapid growth and at the end. But by all the traditional measures of growth, those that focus on rates or percentages of change, the Argentine record was more dramatic than its counterpart in the United States, and it has been the subject of many studies.[2]

The fascination of the Argentine case stems not only from its startling initial success but also from its classification as a land of relatively new settlement and an export economy. The latter has provided the basis for comparisons with other lands of recent settlement, especially the United States, Canada, Australia, and New Zealand. Most of these comparisons, at least those made since 1960, have been unfavorable to Argentina, since they have focused on the prolonged stagnation of the economy over the last half century. The comparisons have spawned an entire literature concerned with the question, "What went wrong?" or, to extend the facile aphorism of W. W. Rostow, "Why did Argentina crash after taking off?" Of course, the comparison is too easy and the question false, but that has not blunted the interest of Argentines searching for explanations for the difficulties their nation has experienced since the Great Depression.

Whether the nature of Argentina's growth was healthy or unhealthy is not our subject, although it is of interest. The point is that the nature and timing of Argentine growth fostered a set of attitudes among the nation's elite and the public at large as to the appropriate role of the nation in world affairs. The success of Argentina's growth model, consciously adopted by the landed oligarchy, led directly to a widespread consensus as to how the nation should comport itself in the international arena and how it should structure its relationships with other na-tion-states. That consensus held in the face of serious social and political tensions that rocked the public order at various moments in the first two decades of the twentieth century and that might have prompted profound questioning of the dominant model and of the consensus on international relations. It held in the face of significant changes in the international system, particularly with reference to the relative power wielded by the dominant actors. It held until well after the mid-dle of the twentieth century, in the face of serious negative consequences in the form of hostile reactions by one or another foreign state. Even when the negative consequences proved painful and debilitating to the economy, as they did during both world wars and the depression, there was very little questioning of the view of the world lying behind the basic consensus. Instead, there were repeated efforts to justify and defend the view, despite the fact that after both wars, it appeared unusual, even singular, among the community of nations.

The world view adopted by Argentina as a reflection of its growth and devel-opment specifically sought to distance Argentina from the United States and to distinguish as clearly as possible between the national experiences of the two coun-tries. It was not that Argentina set out to compete directly with the United States or to confront U.S. power in the international arena. Rather, Argentine leaders sought to establish for their nation an image, a role, a niche as trading partner of Europe that obviously and deliberately differed from that of the United States. If circumstances brought the two nations together, either in the same forum or the same marketplace, then Argentina was willing to run counter to the policies or objectives of the United States, should that prove necessary, in order to avoid any semblance of domination by that country and in order to avoid any action that would embarrass its commitments to Europe. Those commitments were perceived as the chief cause of the economic benefits that flowed to Argentina during its period of expansion and as the guarantor of the nation's privileged position in world affairs.

From the perspective of the governing elite in the United States, the rise to world-power status of their nation in the half century after the Civil War did not bring them or the public to think often or hard about Argentina. There were num-bers of occasions on which the government was sensitive to differences with the Argentine government, and several efforts were made to reduce the structural in-compatibilities between the two economies, but Argentina never figured in policy planning or the thinking of the policy elite in the United States to the same degree or in the same manner as the United States figured in the thinking of Argentines. That asymmetry would lead to repeated confrontations and complicate the rela-tions between the two nations even when there were no specific problems or issues dividing them.

Both the United States and Argentina had been expansionist powers since they gained their independence, but with different results. While it may be argued that, in the case of the United States, the first increments to national territory were defensive moves designed to fix vague boundaries or to remove from the frontier the threat of European influence that the colonists' experience had shown would lead sooner or later to hostilities, there is no period during the nineteenth century, except perhaps during the Civil War, when the U.S. government was not interested in or actively seeking new territory and when U.S. population was not moving out beyond the nation's borders and exerting pressure on the government of neighboring states and territories. Until the Civil War, such territories were contiguous to the nation's boundaries and on the continent of North America. After the war, successive governments sought to project U.S. influence beyond the boundaries of the nation and outside the continent. The nature of this imperialist urge has been the subject of intense debate for generations, but no one today would deny that it was imperialistic and that it was shared by broadly based groups within the society, supported, if not led, by the government.[3]

One of the first comprehensive strategic visions of an imperial United States with responsibilities and opportunities around the world was put forward by Secretary of State William H. Seward. His was the integrated plan, the grand design.[4] He wanted to take possession of islands in the Caribbean in order to protect the Isthmian trade route to the Pacific. He wanted Alaska and the Aleutians to lead the way to Asia; he wanted Hawaii as a stepping stone to Asia. Of these, he managed to acquire only Alaska. He also participated in joint efforts with European powers to keep Japan open to western trade, lent his support to the unsuccessful effort to open Korea to western trade, and supported the open-door policy in China. Most of these efforts were frustrated or ended in failure. People in the United States could not muster much enthusiasm for global visions when their attention was focused on the settlement and development of the vast tracts of land within their own continent. This would change. Little more than a decade later, Naval Captain Alfred Thayer Mahan added a geopolitical or strategic dimension to the grand design for U.S. global expansion. Mahan's writing in the 1880s and 1890s on the influence of sea power in history served two distinct but closely connected purposes. The first was to influence opinion leaders and key members of Congress to support the naval building program that had been initiated in a desultory fashion at the end of the 1870s. The program, in Mahan's view, was necessary to take advantage of important advances in naval technology and to ensure that the United States did not fall too far behind the major European industrial powers, which had begun to build and buy modern warships. The second was to link naval power with trade and so provide the ultimate justification of sea power in time of peace. In this way, he secured support for the active projection of the nation's influence beyond its borders from groups that had not previously been supportive of such assertive policies.

In Mahan's view, it was unthinkable to expand the nation's international trade without planning on the naval strength to protect that trade. It was natural for nations to compete with one another. In order to compete successfully, it was necessary to possess and display all the elements of national greatness displayed by the other competitors. Without the naval might to back it up, the nation's export trade would suffer discrimination or even exclusion from foreign markets. Mahan argued that, unlike European nations that might use military power for its own sake or gobble up territories in Asia and Africa merely for the game of imperialism, the United States was not naturally imperialistic. Imperialism for him was the nineteenth-century equivalent of the predatory behavior of monarchies observed by the founding fathers in the eighteenth century. Territorial imperialism for Mahan was frivolous, the fruit more of dynastic rivalries than of legitimate national interests. Nevertheless, to survive in a competitive world, the United States needed the basic elements of power, and those included a strong navy. Central to both of Mahan's purposes was the notion that the oceans had ceased to be protective barriers behind which the United States could hide from pernicious European influences. They now were seen as highways for trade. Islands were stepping stones on these highways, facilitating contact between societies and states.

Although Mahan never expressed an interest in what he referred to pejoratively as the European imperialistic desire for territory, he did spell out the minimum territorial requirements for U.S. access to markets and for coaling stations that were necessary to supply the navy patrolling the seas in defense of U.S. trade. Thus, over a period of nearly two decades, in articles, lectures at the Naval War College, and conversations with the high and mighty in Washington, Mahan identified the strategic points around the world that the United States should control or at least guarantee access to, in order to protect what now were called the nation's strategic interests.

As Seward had before him, Mahan focused on the approaches to the isthmian route. He made it perfectly plain that any canal built across the isthmus—and it was only a matter of time before one was built—would have to be controlled by the United States. Just as important as the isthmus and access to trade in the Caribbean was trade in the orient. The fabled China market had begun to work its magic on the imaginations of people in the United States. The strategic question was how to maintain equal access to the fabulous markets in China in the face of selfish, exclusionary empires fighting for influence on the Asian mainland and even fighting for control over strategic points of access to the continent. Mahan remained optimistic that the United States would not have to imitate the territorial acquisitiveness of the European powers and Japan. But, in order to protect U.S. interests, it would be necessary to insist on equal access to the China market. To make good on that demand, it would be necessary to maintain a significant naval presence in the area and secure the coaling stations necessary to make that presence credible.

Parallel to Mahan's efforts, intellectuals such as Brooks and Henry Adams influenced opinion leaders in favor of expansion by stressing their apocalyptic visions of world history. Twenty years after Seward first put forward his grand design, it was the accepted wisdom that the United States was about to or already had run out of empty spaces on the continent of North America. Frederick Jackson Turner announced the closing of the frontier as if it were the death knell of civilization as their generation had known it. Brooks Adams warned that unless the country turned overseas to continue its expansion it would run out of energy and soon collapse. The nation required strong leadership to galvanize the society to action and ensure the success of its salvation. For Adams, history indicated that it was necessary for the United States to enter the new stage in its development or die.

These intellectual formulations had significant impact on political action and government policies. Their impact was extended by popularizers who took them beyond the fairly small circle of opinion leaders concerned with foreign affairs and won the support of the broader public for U.S. involvement in international adventures, even wars and colonialism.[5] A generation of writers, among whom Josiah Strong and John Fiske were the most prominent, popularized the ideas of Social Darwinism that lay behind all of the more esoteric justifications for imperialism and colonialism, combining the frontier thesis with a fervent belief in Anglo-Saxon missionary Manifest Destiny. According to this view, it was important, even critical, for the United States to lead in spreading Protestant civilization throughout the world. This was the Americanization of the racist concept of the white man's burden that had convinced so many liberals and social progressives in Europe, who had opposed wars and colonialism for nearly a century, to support the projects of their governments to spread their influence around the world. European liberals and conservatives applauded the spread of civilization, as it was called, to areas of the world not yet exposed to its benefits. The proponents of empire in the United States put forward a curious combination of faith in Social Darwinism and an assertion of U.S. exceptionalism that hearkened back to the Puritan concept of the City on the Hill. Fiske, Strong, and others made a moral case for the good expansionism, the good imperialism. They and public figures such as Theodore Roosevelt believed that the strong should moderate their competition with one another and should assume control over the weak for their mutual benefit.

By summarizing the principal arguments in favor of expansion and imperialism we run the risk of conveying the impression that the public discussion of the issue was one-sided or that the proponents of expansion were a monolithic, well-organized group. Such was not the case. The contrast with the movement supporting territorial expansion in the 1840s is striking. There was considerable debate and confusion over the means to be used for expansion and over the desirable ends to be sought. There also was a popular group and a large number of influential public figures who were opposed to any expansion and to all forms of imperialism. This strong dissent and the confusion among proponents of expansion delayed the emergence of a clear consensus and inhibited the formulation of clear policies and severely limited the nature and the extent of the expansion that occurred.

Throughout the public debate over expansion during the 1880s and, more vociferously, in the 1890s, the leaders of U.S. public opinion were influenced by and sensitive to European currents of thinking and to events in Europe or in which the European nations were protagonists. Those events and those ideas played an important part in shaping the thinking of the attentive, influential U.S. public. Whatever their attitude toward expansion, writers and public figures in the United States displayed a broad consensus in seeing for their country, "nothing less than the moral and material leadership of the world."[6]

From the very beginning, strategic thinking in the United States was global. The country was to form part of a world order in which major states competed for influence or power. There was no geographical limit to the scope of potential U.S. interest or influence. The global reach of U.S. aspirations was reflected in every aspect of the discussion of the nation's expansion—its naval power, its trade, its missionary zeal, and its Manifest Destiny. The United States was to be a protagonist in the worldwide spread of civilization. Progress was inevitable; it was linear. Those nations such as the United States that were fortunate enough to be well advanced on the road to progress were destined to carry the benefits of that progress to all areas of the globe. There never was the slightest doubt among U.S. leaders that the nation would participate in this process, although the nature of that participation was the subject of considerable debate.

But, acceptance into the club of civilized nations was not automatic. Many Europeans expressed skepticism about U.S. capacities and about U.S. will, and it was common sport among European intellectuals in the last decades of the nineteenth century to emphasize the rough qualities of U.S. culture and to deprecate the virtues of U.S. society. The United States was portrayed as being composed of a race of frontier yokels or country bumpkins. Europe was the center of civilization.

The tone of European commentaries on the United States changed abruptly and permanently after the short war with Spain. The successful, energetic use of national power quieted the critics and earned the respect of the continent's leaders. As the new century dawned, the United States was accepted into the restricted elite of the world's powers. It may well be, as one author has suggested, that the United States had greatness thrust upon it, but it was true nevertheless that it had accumulated national power and that its power was recognized by the industrialized nations of Europe and Asia.[7] The United States was admitted as a player on the global stage.

The nature of the game being played is of concern to us. All of the industrialized nations of Europe were engaged in it or attempted to participate in it as best they could. Within Europe, the nations displayed their power through industrial production, public works, and increasing numbers of larger and larger naval vessels. Those ships represented industrial capacity, technological advances, financial security, and military power. Their construction went along with public pronouncements declaring the will to use these symbols of the nation's power. The diplomacy of the last quarter of the nineteenth century and the first decade of the twentieth focused on the jockeying for advantage among the members of what slowly evolved into two great contending blocks of nations. The rhetoric of competition between the blocks as well as the labyrinthine commitments and arrangements among their members ultimately led to violent conflict, first in the Balkans and then, tragically, throughout Europe.[8]

Competition for Markets

Until the Great War, the fearsome energy and zeal for competitive confrontation among the European states was played out for the most part away from the European landmass. It was expressed as a race to plant the flag of empire in as many places as possible around the world. The British talked proudly of having established an empire on which the sun never set. The Germans, entering the race somewhat late, concentrated on establishing their influence at strategic points on the continent of Africa and on scattered islands in the Pacific. The Italians focused on the African hinterland across the Mediterranean from them. The French consolidated their hold on West Africa and the littoral of Southeast Asia, as well as portions of the North African coast. The Russians confined their attention to the rim of the Pacific, where they had the misfortune to run up against the Japanese, themselves determined to exercise their newly accumulated industrial and military power rather than allow themselves to be acted upon by Western nations, as they had been since Admiral Matthew Calbraith Perry had forced them to join the international market. The Dutch, Belgians, Spanish, Portuguese, and Danes also held territories over which they exercised imperial control.

The flag of empire was planted as the result of agreement with local authorities. That agreement might be the result of peaceful negotiations, of coercive negotiations in which the presence of an army or navy might have played a vital role, or of outright military conquest. Two decaying or decayed empires, the Ottoman and the Chinese, were simply carved up into zones or spheres of influence by the European powers. In the case of China, control over territory was not attractive. What the imperial powers wanted in China was access to the fabulous market. Visions of millions of Chinese wearing shoes, shirts, or what have you, manufactured in England, France, Germany, or the United States danced in the heads of manufacturers, bankers, and government leaders. In the 1890s, Great Britain, Germany, France, Russia, and Japan used force or the threat of force to negotiate special privileges in or control over one or more ports on the coast of China. The United States did not join in this mad rush to take over the coastal cities of China. People in the United States were made nervous by the penchant for exclusion displayed by the imperialists. While remaking the map of Africa and the Middle East by itself was not disturbing to the United States, the possibility of projecting the same nefarious policies of exclusion to Asia, particularly to China, or even to Latin America definitely was. The question for discussion in several administrations was how the United States could realize its will, how it could protect its national interests in such a competitive, Darwinian international environment.

Of course, none of these arguments or discussions would have been of any value or of political significance without the massive growth of the U.S. economy after the Civil War and the almost inexorable shift away from agricultural exports to manufacturing. By the end of the nineteenth century, the United States was the principal industrial power in the world. In a matter of years, it would cease to be a debtor nation and become the world's principal creditor. The export of its manufactures increased constantly, providing persistent justification for the opening of new markets as well as powerful demand for more and more labor. If the frontier had closed in 1890, which suggested that the nation no longer was rich in wide-open spaces, there was never the suggestion that the nation should stop immigration from abroad. The new settlers would be absorbed by the factories in the cities and by the expanding service industries complementing the nation's industrial might.

The consensus that international trade was vital to the nation's well-being emerged only slowly over many years. The idea had been central to Seward's grand design, but few had shared his vision in the 1870s. Still, time was on his side. Exports from the United States increased from $316 million in 1860 to $1,370 million in 1900. Total foreign trade remained at a fairly low 6.7 percent of gross national product. But, by the 1890s, it had grown to such significance—per capita exports increased threefold from 1860 to 1900—that it was impossible to ignore in the political sense and had spawned national organizations, such as the National Association of Manufacturers (1895), to lobby on its behalf, to support it, and to legitimize it in the eyes of the public.

Throughout the 1890s, advocates of stimulating international trade as the principal means of ensuring the nation's health and enhancing its influence in the world focused on Latin America and China as areas of U.S. concern. The first was envisioned as an area of U.S. hegemonic influence, while the best the United States could aspire to in the second was equal access, to avoid being excluded by the European and Asian powers that had gotten there first. Trade with Latin America increased from $90 million in 1860 to $300 million in 1900. Exports from the United States to China rose from $4 million in 1890 to $6.9 million in 1896 and to $11.9 million in 1897. Exports to Japan went from $3.9 million in 1894 to $7.6 million in 1896 and $13 million in 1897. By comparison, exports to Argentina at the same time were $4.68 million in 1885, $4.46 million in 1895, and $11.6 million in 1900. Industrialists themselves were convinced that they had to go outside the United States to capture markets for their survival. In supporting the idea of a Pan American meeting in Washington, in 1889 Andrew Carnegie wrote Secretary of State James G. Blaine, "Let the country be told it will cost money, but that the time has arrived when the republic must . . . secure the greater portion of the trade of its southern neighbors."[9]

The investment of U.S. capital outside the country was slow to follow trade. By the 1890s, U.S. capitalists had established significant positions in the Caribbean basin and were negotiating with great energy, even passion, to get involved on the mainland of Asia. Within the Western Hemisphere, the degree of financial involvement seemed loosely correlated with distance, although distance clearly was not a factor in deterring or stimulating the interest of investors in China. By the end of the nineteenth century, U.S. investors had ventured into every country in the hemisphere, although they were the primary national group only in Mexico and the Caribbean. They and their government noted the inferiority of their stake to that of the European powers, especially Great Britain. That inferiority was a source of preoccupation by the government. It was a form of European influence that could not be accepted easily. After the Civil War, as U.S. manufacturing capacity and trade increased rapidly, successive administrations began to consider how to counteract European influence in the hemisphere. The first concrete proposal to deal with the threat was put forward by Secretary of State James G. Blaine in 1881.

Blaine understood Seward's grand design. There was little that he could do in Asia, though he did raise the status of the U.S. mission in Hawaii. His principal concern was European influence in Latin America. He was convinced that the United States had to act purposefully in the region to forestall European penetration. In 1881, he proposed that the United States host a conference of the nations in the hemisphere, with a view to establishing a customs union among them and improving communications between North and South America so that the United States would be assured of advantages over its European competitors. Blaine had the ear of President Garfield, but when the latter was assassinated on 2 July 1881, Blaine fell from power. He was replaced by Frederick T. Frelinghuysen, who immediately killed the plan. Certainly the personality clash between Frelinghuysen and Blaine is sufficient to explain the sudden end to the government's interest in a Pan American conference. However, it is relevant to add that neither Congress nor public opinion was prepared to second an aggressive foreign policy in the region. The major reason for this reticence was the lack of commercial interest in the region, the lack of investment there, and the lack of a local military presence. At the beginning of the 1880s, the United States simply was not ready to play an imperial role in the hemisphere. By the end of the decade, the mood in Congress and in the Executive branch was more aggressive.

When he returned to the Department of State in 1889, Blaine was delighted to find that Congress had resurrected his plan for a Pan American Conference and had ordered that invitations be sent to all nations of the hemisphere. The agenda was ambitious. The ultimate objective was a customs union that would facilitate trade among the nations of the hemisphere and leave the Europeans in an inferior position. As steps to the desired goal, the U.S. delegation would place before the representatives of the other American republics proposals to establish common weights and measures, a common monetary unit, a juridical mechanism to settle disputes, a transportation network, and the creation of a central office or bureau that would collect and disseminate information of interest and value to the membership. Any progress on any of these would improve the U.S. position in the hemisphere vis-à-vis their European competitors.

The U.S. delegation did not anticipate much debate or any significant opposition to these proposals. They were not so naive as to expect dramatic progress; they merely wanted to put some of these ideas on the table and refer them to technical commissions that would work out the details of future agreements within the framework of the new bureau that they hoped to establish in the course of the meeting. The delegation was not prepared to bring discussion on any of these topics to closure. In fact, the delegation was not particularly well prepared to do anything. It scarcely met before the opening session and left the initiative in discussion to Secretary of State Blaine, who was not even an official delegate.[10] None of them, nor even Secretary Blaine, was in the slightest prepared for the persistent contrariness of the Argentine delegates, who from the opening session did their best to scuttle every initiative by the U.S. delegation. Virtually single-handedly, they managed to nullify or reduce to the barest minimum every proposal put before the conference. Their declared purpose was punctilious concern for procedural consistency and propriety. Through their interventions, which ran the gamut from parliamentary maneuvers to filibustering, it was patently obvious that they were simply opposed to any multilateral arrangements in which, by virtue of its superior size and power, the United States would have a significant role. They would not participate in any such programs, and they did their best to make sure that nothing could come into existence on a hemispheric basis without Argentine participation.

The U.S. government was surprised by the behavior of the Argentine delegation, which it considered bloody-minded and negative for the sake of being negative. The U.S. delegation and government should not have been surprised. The behavior was entirely consistent in both style and substance with Argentine behavior at recent international conferences. It was consistent, too, with the public statements of the Argentine government and by Argentine leaders concerning Argentina's international relations and the image they had of their nation. So certain was he that there would be confrontations between the Argentine delegation and the representatives of the U.S. government during the conference, that the Argentine minister to Washington, Vicente G. Quesada, requested permission to take a leave of absence from his post so that he would not attend the sessions and become associated with the attacks on the United States. Such an association would make it impossible for him to continue as minister. Taken aback by the aggressiveness and persistence of the Argentine attacks, the U.S. delegates retreated and contented themselves with submitting most of their proposals to further study by standing committees and securing acceptance of the idea of holding a second Pan American Conference in Mexico City.

The Argentine delegates to the conference in Washington, Roque Saénz Peña and Manuel Quintana, represented the thinking of the newly consolidated oligarchy that was firmly in power in Buenos Aires. Their speeches during the conference and their later reflections on the experience define clearly and give public expression to the emerging consensus concerning the Argentine position in world affairs and the consequences for the international relations of the nation of its recent reinsertion in the world market. The sense of national self articulated by Saénz Peña and Quintana in Washington defined the basic elements of Argentine foreign policy, which continued to guide the nation for more than half a century and which remain to the present as echoes of principles of action or assumptions that influence the formulation of policy.

These principles or assumptions were that Argentine well-being required fluid and open relations with the nations of Europe, which represented the principal market for their exports; that Argentina did not have or need particularly close relations with the rest of Latin America and was in some vague way superior to those nations; and that the United States represented a competitor. It was a competitor whose material accomplishments could not be denied and might even be emulated, but one, somehow, not worthy of respect. This meant unremitting opposition to any projects that accentuated the U.S. presence in Latin America and that might promote Latin American cooperation to the benefit of the United States and/or to the exclusion of Europe. Just before the centennial, Saénz Peña reflected on this policy to the historian Adolfo Saldías:

> I tell you that to the bottom of my heart—and without intending to alien-
> ate us from America, my leanings are toward Europe, in the sense of our
> cordiality toward the great powers of the Old World, from whom we have
> nothing to fear and much to hope. This tendency naturally will not prevent
> continental solidarity if we should be confronted by aggression from Europe;
> but that is so remote as to be considered impossible in the present state of
> affairs. So, we must not subject ourselves to an imaginary danger, adapting
> the use of scare tactics in the full enjoyment of peace and harmony.[11]

The focus on Europe and the confidence with which Argentina fixed the pattern of its relations with the other nations of Latin America and with the United States were both consequences of the remarkable pattern of growth and development experienced by Argentina in the half century after 1860. By 1889, the pattern was clear. By 1910, when the nation celebrated the centenary of its independence and fifty years of national consolidation, the dimensions of its success were evident, and the entire world was invited to participate in the celebration of that success.

The growth experience was not without its difficulties. Even as the Argentine people celebrated their centennial, there were serious social disturbances that forced the government to declare a state of siege for several months. There were frequent acts of violence, generally attributed to anarchists and to labor unions attempting to bring the claims of the working class to the attention of the nation's leaders. And, even as books were filled with accounts of the glory that was theirs and the glory that was still to come, there were a few, isolated voices that attempted to point out that the growth model, so proudly trumpeted by the oligarchy, was, in fact, not being carried out in several crucial aspects, both on the land and in the city.

On the land, the model called for widespread ownership. The model or ideal to which the oligarchy referred was the yeoman farmer-citizen whose ownership of property made him a responsible citizen of a functioning democracy as well as an energetic entrepreneur benefiting the common good while maximizing the profits of his own enterprise. That had been the vision put forward by Alberdi and his generation from which there never had been dissent. The process of settling the Pampas was well advanced before the government attempted to correct the tendency toward concentration of ownership and tenancy by passing laws aimed at creating a Jeffersonian pattern of land ownership. The laws were late and never enforced.

At the time of the centennial, official studies by the Ministry of Agriculture confirmed what was widely known, that the most productive land on the Pampas was in the hands of a relatively few owners and that there was throughout the country a massive class of renters and tenants working in miserable conditions with little or no hope of ever achieving ownership of their own land. The land-tenure pattern was such that the organization of production permitted profit maximization by the landowners without necessarily expanding production or benefiting the common good, and certainly without exhibiting innovating entrepreneurial zeal.[12] The lame response to these studies indicated that while the facts presented might be accurate and that it might be lamentable that the original goals had not been achieved, the great success of the development model was so apparent that the society really could not become exercised over these shortcomings and that the studies could be ignored as counsels of perfection.

In the city, the social problems were evident to every visitor and to every sensitive observer. The industrious, racially homogeneous population anticipated by Alberdi had not come forward, despite aggressive recruiting by the state. Instead, the alluvial mass that had arrived in Buenos Aires and passed through the Hotel de Inmigrantes, the Argentine version of Ellis Island, were the poorest of the poor, a lumpen proletariat from Southern and Eastern Europe that came to the new world, south and north, with no capital and precious few skills. Many of them did not care for life in the country, especially when they learned that they could not aspire to land ownership and that the promises made to them by colonization companies were empty or false. A growing majority of the new immigrants either stayed in the capital or soon drifted back into one or another of the major urban areas after a brutal and disillusioning experience on the land. In the city they crowded into slums and lived in the most inhuman, insalubrious conditions. Many of those who managed to find work joined the unions attempting to ameliorate the cruel conditions of the workplace and improve their abysmal salaries. Indeed, the first leaders of the unions were often themselves immigrants who had learned the principles of working-class solidarity in Italy or Spain, or Germany or Russia. The high incidence of immigrant leadership in the labor movement at the end of the nineteenth century and the beginning of the twentieth made it easy for the native oligarchy to blame social tensions on foreigners and to make xenophobia its initial response to the organized efforts of the working class to improve their lot. The so-called Residence Law of 1903 was the most draconian of a series of measures designed to curb the labor movement.

The defects in the growth model were as obvious in the city as in the countryside, and stated just as clearly in official reports, as well as in the Congress, the press, and in a long series of works by social analysis. The usual response was that the "social question," as these problems were called, was the result of nefarious foreign influences, that the wrong sort of immigration had been allowed, and that the crowding and other evidence of social inequalities would be eliminated in due course through the workings of the marketplace. The important thing was to eliminate the anti-social influences from the body politic and allow time for the marvelous healing process of growth and increasing national wealth to solve the social question. Anyone who thought otherwise was anti-national. The vast majority accepted the idea that their nation's golden future was guaranteed by the exports of meat, grains, wool, and hides.[13]

The expectations of Argentine greatness were shared by foreign observers. *Harper's Weekly*, at the end of the century, forecast that Argentina "promises soon to become the greatest wheat producing country in the world."[14] By 1909, Argentina was exporting more grain than any other nation. Four years earlier, its meat exports to Great Britain exceeded those by the United States for the first time. Argentina did not produce more than any other country, but it exported a higher portion of its production than any other nation, and by 1910, it had the highest per capita international trade in the world. Argentines' projections of their nation's greatness anticipated that they would equal or even surpass the level of material accomplishment in the United States. Former president Domingo F. Sarmiento predicted in 1888 that "We shall be America, as the sea is the ocean. We shall be the United States."[15] Just a year later, Alois E. Fliess assured the Sociedad Rural Argentina, the nation's leading cattlemen's organization, that "Argentina had material conditions superior to the United States of America, and would some day be greater than that nation."[16] At the end of the centennial, Argentine statesman and intellectual Estanislao Zeballos wrote somewhat testily that Argentina was destined to be "the colossus of the southern continent," and therefore did not need any tutelage or help from the United States.[17] Going further, some Argentines felt that they had the same missionary destiny, the same civilizing mission in the other nations of Latin America, that the United States asserted for itself in the Caribbean. In 1896, *La Prensa* asserted on behalf of the Argentine nation, "This powerful land is destined to undertake in the southern continent a democratic and humanitarian mission as great as that of the country of Washington."[18]

Most Argentines were content to see themselves as becoming a part of the civilized world. When reflecting on their nation's accomplishments and power, they adopted the language of discourse then in vogue in Europe. They spoke of being "a factor in human affairs" and serving as "a directing force in civilization."[19] It was important to Argentines that they had become or were becoming one of the civilized nations of the world. Through their trade, they expected to participate in the march toward progress. As an editorial in *La Nación* put it, "The Argentine Republic now has an established personality in the civilized world. From this moment forward one may say that Argentina will be highly esteemed because we have made known the rich products of our soil, of our industry, and of our intelligence."[20] Repeatedly, Argentine leaders insisted that they must not be lumped in with the other nations of Latin America in the eyes of Europe and that they must not allow themselves to be treated like the nations of Africa and Asia. The aggressive assertion of U.S. hegemony in the hemisphere in the Venezuelan boundary dispute (1895) and the revolution in Cuba (1895–98) elicited strong criticism from many Argentines and unequivocal insistence that the nations of South America were different from those of the Caribbean basin.[21]

The foreign policy designed to facilitate the achievement of these goals sought to preserve the conditions in which Argentines could maximize the export of the largest quantities of their agricultural products at the best possible prices. In return, the nation would import the manufactured goods it required or wanted and the capital it needed to expand its infrastructure and execute the public works that would make life in the cities and countryside more pleasant. In the terms of such a foreign policy, trade relations were "natural." Political relations were not. The latter must not be allowed to confuse or complicate the former. No commitments with other nations in the hemisphere or with any nation must be made that would encumber or embarrass the commercial links with the nation's customers. Publicly, the government declared its adherence to the "principles" of international relations, principles that favored the peaceful settlement of disputes between states.[22]

This should have been familiar to officials in Washington. It echoed the thinking and the very language used by the Founding Fathers in formulating a foreign policy for the newly independent United States, expressing their lack of faith in the political commitments of other states while pointing to the commercial relations between states as the better or more accurate indicator of a nation's interests. Of course, in the case of the United States in the eighteenth century, the nation's leaders had indicated their distrust of monarchies. They considered republics more responsible to their citizens and therefore more worthy of political relations. The Argentines came to the distinction between natural and unnatural relations without reference to the type of government a state might have. One writer, Joaquín V. González, recognized the historical parallel to the United States by defending Argentina's international posture as nothing more than following the precepts of George Washington's Farewell Address.[23]

The global scheme of which Argentines saw themselves an integral part was an international market that functioned smoothly on the basis of a division of labor. Nations produced or should produce the goods or products for which they had a comparative advantage. With its seemingly inexhaustible supply of fertile land and its rapidly expanding supply of cheap labor, Argentina appeared destined to produce foodstuffs cheaply and efficiently for the expanding urban markets of the industrial nations. If the United States, one of those nations, also produced the same goods in surplus, then Argentina would sell to the nations of Europe, whose demand for Argentine products seemed to be as unlimited as the fertility of the Pampas.

The division of labor appeared natural in the sense that the European customers also were those nations that produced the surplus capital Argentina needed to finance the expansion of its agricultural activity as well as the industrial goods that Argentina did not produce. Among the European customers, Great Britain was far and away the best. Not only did the British buy more of Argentina's cereals and beef than anyone else, they also had more capital for investment than any of the others. They had more cheap fuel for sale in exchange for foodstuffs, and they had the most developed merchant marine to dedicate to the commercial exchange between the two countries. The sense of naturalness or comfort in the bilateral relationship was reinforced by the British policy of avoiding involvement in Argentine domestic politics. After playing a prominent role in the overthrow of Rosas, the British consciously sought to remain neutral in internal disputes and to settle commercial differences as commercial issues, although the British diplomatic representative never was shy about expressing his support for British firms.[24]

Given the existing pattern of Argentine trade, the widespread attitude toward Europe, and the seemingly divine order of the international division of labor, it should not be surprising that Argentina's leaders reacted with something less than enthusiasm to the U.S. efforts to create a Pan American Union and enhance its own influence in the hemisphere through the operations of such an organization. The U.S. initiative was more than a nuisance or a maneuver from a potential rival for influence in the hemisphere. It was a real threat to Argentine national interests. What could the United States offer Argentina? Aside from the fact that they appeared to be rivals, the United States did not make any serious effort to improve trade between the two. The U.S. protective tariff structure seemed to operate with particular prejudice against Argentine products. Wool, Argentina's principal export for most of the second half of the nineteenth century, was virtually excluded from the U.S. market. When Argentine representatives urged the Department of State to intervene to lower the wool tariff and improve trade, the officials of the executive protested their inability to move Congress from its protectionist stance. In 1884, the United States sent a trade commission around Latin America. It stayed only twelve hours in Buenos Aires. A year later, trade between the two nations amounted to ten million gold pesos. At the same time, Argentine trade with Great Britain amounted to 48 million gold pesos, out of a total trade of 176 million. That year, more than a thousand steam vessels arrived in Buenos Aires from England or departed from Buenos Aires for British ports. None arrived from or departed for U.S. ports.

If U.S. economic diplomacy in dealing with Argentina in the 1880s and 1890s proved ineffective or worse, private business methods were also less than adequate. The U.S. minister frequently lamented that, in comparison with representatives from the European countries, U.S. businessmen came to Argentina unprepared. They did not know their own products well, they did not know anything about the market in which they wanted to operate, and they did not come willing to offer the short-term credits indispensable to open trade with Argentine customers. To make matters worse, there were no U.S. branch banks in Argentina until 1914 and few direct investments by U.S. capital until the early years of the new century.

The most persistent complaint by Argentines was that there was no direct shipping link between the two countries. When the U.S. delegations to the first and second Pan American conferences called for improved trade relations among the nations of the hemisphere, the Argentine delegates countered by asking if the U.S. government was prepared to subsidize a line that would serve the entire east coast of South America. Partly as a response to these protests, a link was established in 1896, but it was provided by British companies and British ships. It was not until 1908 that regular service was provided by a U.S. flag line between ports in the United States and the Río de la Plata.

Privately, Argentines were less blasé and expressed considerable hostility toward the United States. In January 1909, U.S. minister to Argentina Edward O'Brien approached Ricardo Pillado, an official in the Ministry of Agriculture and a confidant of President de la Plaza, with an informal inquiry as to how their two nations might improve the trade between them. Pillado's response was scathing, describing the triangular trade involving Great Britain, Argentina, and the United States and inquiring in a sarcastic tone why the United States purchased goods in Europe that it could purchase more cheaply in Argentina. He closed by informing the minister that if the United States wanted to improve relations, all it had to do was buy more from Argentina.[25] When former president Theodore Roosevelt visited Buenos Aires in 1910, he was lionized publicly, but privately many Argentines took his visit as an occasion to express their disdain for the United States. María Rosa Oliver, then a young girl, was much taken by the charismatic Roosevelt, although she found him ugly. When she expressed her opinion, her grandfather chided her, shouting, "Don't you know that those people want to swallow us?"[26]

After 1895, U.S. exporters appeared to take more interest in the Argentine market. Not by accident, Argentine exports to the United States increased significantly for a few years at the end of the decade when the duty on wool was cut. This era of commercial good will culminated in the years just prior to the First World War, when, in 1913, the U.S. tariff was amended to allow the import of Argentine beef, including chilled beef, the most profitable of the Argentine exports. U.S. exports also increased that year, as did direct investments. In 1914, the first U.S. branch bank was opened in Buenos Aires. These were the natural relations of which Saénz Peña and Quintana had spoken in Washington twenty-five years earlier. The war aborted this beginning, so it is impossible to say what might have happened had trade between the two countries continued to expand.

Argentine foreign policy remained remarkably coherent and consistent throughout the period of rapid economic expansion, right up to the beginning of the war. That policy, which asserted as the nation's highest priority the maintenance of fluid and open commercial ties to its natural markets in Europe, implied potential conflict with the United States. Curiously, that conflict was not understood in the terms normally used to describe interstate rivalry. The nation's leaders assumed that successful execution of the policy would lead inevitably to the nation's achievement of greatness and recognition as an international power or player. This is curious because, having demonstrated on innumerable occasions that they understood the European discourse on the nature of national power and its use, Argentine leaders never worked to provide their nation with the universally recognized symbols of that power, nor attempted to project Argentine influence on the global scale, in competitive terms. When they complained of a lack of maritime connections between ports in the United States and Argentina, they asked the U.S.

government to provide the subsidies necessary to create such a link. They never proposed building their own merchant marine or providing subsidies for vessels bearing the Argentine flag to carry Argentine products to ports in the United States or anywhere else. Argentine leaders aspired to greatness and to influence in world affairs, but they refused to acquire or to compete with the other great powers in terms of the usual measures of national power. As a consequence, the Argentine view of world affairs became unrealistic.[27]

The principal index of progress among the civilized nations was industrial capacity. And yet, the Argentine government deliberately and repeatedly rejected all proposals to diversify the economy through the development of national industries. They also refused to face the very serious issue of the persistent cyclical illiquidity of the agricultural economy. The liquidity necessary for the successful functioning of the economy was provided by British banks and banks from other European countries. Efforts to create Argentine banks that could provide the necessary liquidity and thus facilitate the process of capital accumulation in Argentina were systematically rejected by the oligarchy. In this and in countless other ways, Argentine leaders appeared strangely out of step with the thinking in the rest of the world on how greatness was measured and appreciated. They recognized that the European nations were powerful because of their industrial and financial capacity as well as their military might, and that even the United States had become great through the acquisition of these characteristics or capacities. But they did not consider it necessary for Argentina to acquire coaling stations for its navy or to build a navy to protect the nation's trade. The trade would be protected by the self-interest of the buyers, which included the most powerful nations in the world. They never had a global sense of their national interest. Of course, there is no rule that says nations must aspire to greatness or to global influence. But Argentine leaders did, and they wanted to play a role in world affairs commensurate with the influence of a powerful or great nation.

The confidence with which they contemplated the workings of the international system appears to have been a consequence of the timing of their insertion into the international market and the dizzying speed with which they had conquered their niche in it. It had left them with an almost religious faith in the international division of labor that they expected to increase their wealth and, somehow soon, create for them a role in the international arena no less significant than that of the United States or of any of the other major powers. How this was to come to pass is not discussed during the period. Even opponents of the regime and those few critics of the liberal growth model failed to deal explicitly with this problem.

The curious form taken by Argentine aspirations for influence in world affairs was manifest in the campaign to buy—not build, buy—modern naval vessels. The decision in 1908 to buy two Dreadnoughts for the Argentine navy at a time when the country had virtually no merchant marine was the manner in which Argentine leaders adapted the rules of the international power game to their perspective and to their understanding of the nation's strategic interests.[28] The timing and the nature of the Argentine arms buildup was a reaction to developments in Brazil. For a brief period, between 1906 and 1909, the two nations engaged in an arms race and a rhetorical escalation that brought them to the brink of war, just as the European nations were competing with one another and would soon go to the brink of hostilities and then cross beyond the brink. But Argentina backed away from the confrontation, refusing to participate in a regional or continental balance of power. They considered theirs to be a European or global role and refused to define their international status in terms of their relations with other American states.

The only European balance-of-power element lacking in the Southern Cone episode was the interlocking set of alliances and negotiations that set nation against nation. That element existed at the beginning of the period, when Argentine Foreign Minister Zeballos attempted to tie Chile to his policies and create a bloc of nations against Brazil. The Chilean government would not cooperate. This led Zeballos to raise the level of his rhetoric, even insisting on the need for a preemptive attack on Rio, if the government of Brazil did not agree to moderate its plans for a naval buildup. President Figueroa Alcorta would not follow the lead of his flamboyant minister and had him ousted from the cabinet. To calm relations with Brazil, the president dispatched one of Zeballos's political allies, Saénz Peña, to Brazil. Removing Zeballos seems to have been all that was needed. Various political groups rallied to the president's side. Saénz Peña soothed the ruffled feathers in Rio. He convinced the Brazilians to suspend their purchase of a third Dreadnought and to accept without response the acquisition by Argentina of its two naval fortresses.[29]

At no time in the debate over the naval arms race did the influential public in Argentina propose or contemplate the use of the naval power to open new markets to Argentine products or to force access to coaling stations in far-flung oceans so that Argentine trade would be assured of naval escort. Zeballos was a prominent exception to this consensus, appealing repeatedly for an assertive foreign policy. He attempted to proselytize his colleagues among the oligarchy on behalf of an expansionist policy, a policy that would place Argentina among the civilized, imperialistic nations of the world on the same terms as the United States was being accepted and was participating in world affairs. His voice, while not totally alone, found little echo.

For more than thirty years, Zeballos wrote and spoke in favor of an aggressive foreign policy, a policy of "vision and firmness."[30] He held a chair in the Faculty of Law at the University of Buenos Aires, wrote editorials on foreign policy for *La Prensa,* and founded, edited, and wrote extensively for the journal *Revista de Derecho, Historia y Letras.* He was a founding member of the Club de Progreso, a forum for discussion of contemporary issues among a portion of the oligarchy. In addition, he sustained an active correspondence with countless members of the elite. His writings suggest a man of keen intellect, prodigious energy, and passionately held views. He was foreign minister three times. His published writings and his private correspondence indicate clearly that he and his colleagues were intimately familiar with the writings of Mahan, the Adams brothers, and the European theoreticians of power politics. The thrust of Zeballos's writings was, put simply, to adapt Mahan's strategic views to the Argentine context. Zeballos wanted to accumulate economic and military power for Argentina and use that power to make explicit the nation's influence over its neighbors and throughout Latin America. He told the British ambassador, Sir Reginald Tower, that Argentina would absorb Uruguay and Paraguay and that Brazil did not have the power to prevent it.[31] He shared his colleagues' mistrust of the United States and their desire to compete with it for preeminence in the hemisphere. He wanted to use the same instruments of power as the United States, including a strong navy and a developed industry. He was one of the most cogent proponents of a protective tariff and gradually convinced the editors of *La Prensa* to advocate a policy of industrialization.

Although Zeballos served in the cabinet of three different presidents and enjoyed the confidence and friendship of powerful members of the oligarchy, including Saénz Peña, he never managed to bring any other major figure to his way of thinking. His writings and his correspondence make it impossible to sustain the argument that the generation of 1880 was oblivious to events that did not touch directly upon trade with Europe or that they did not understand the implications of power politics. They did. They chose consciously and deliberately to follow a line of policy that would keep Argentina at the margin of the international power struggle. And yet many indicated their belief in a strong nation. That was their error and the fundamental error of Argentine foreign policy in the twentieth century: to aspire to the exercise of power in world affairs and to insist on the recognition of its role as a powerful and influential nation when it had little power and scant influence.

All of the leading figures of the oligarchy were Europeanists, in the sense that they agreed that Argentine economic growth depended upon fluid trade with Europe and access to European capital. While they disagreed among themselves as to how long the international division of labor would hold to the form it had assumed during the period of the nation's explosive growth, they agreed to take a passive attitude toward the structural situation, to avoid rocking the boat, and to adjust the nation's policy to maintain the international status quo to the extent possible. In so doing, this dominant majority was prepared to claim for Argentina a role in international affairs in which the nation pretended or aspired to full participation in the club of civilized world powers but on very special terms. They insisted on recognition of Argentina's civilization, but they were not interested in having the nation participate in the international competition for influence or power as were the other members of the club. They did not want the responsibilities of world power. They did not want to take up the white man's burden in Africa or Asia. Quite a few appeared willing to shoulder it in South America, but all but a very few backed away immediately when asked to deal with the consequences of such a posture as in the conflict with Brazil. They confided in the support and even the protection of the European powers who were their best customers. That support or protection, they believed, would come to them when necessary in order to preserve the international division of labor that benefited their customers as much as it benefited them. In this way, the oligarchy constructed the relations of dependency that would distort their nation's development for the next century. Even in this early period, it is clear that the Europeans did not expect Argentina to become a world power, in the sense that the United States had been admitted into the club. The British, whose relations with Argentina were the most intense, revealed in their foreign policy that they expected Argentina to remain a faithful supplier and market, a role that assured Argentina the status of subordinate in the international scheme of things. Argentines did not see their role in the same light.

In a sense, the Argentine oligarchy was prepared to march slightly out of step with the other nations of the western world, but they believed that such a position would not prejudice their security or their national interests. It almost certainly would bring them into conflict with the United States, but they believed that the confrontation would be held within acceptable limits, either by the deterrent of their own growing power in the marketplace, or by the deterrence of their European customers and natural allies. Until that time, Argentine policy would be directed toward frustrating U.S. ambitions in South America and preventing any hemispheric projects that might compromise Argentine commitments to Europe and the international division of labor. The war in Europe would demonstrate painfully the limits of such a policy, the extent of Argentine dependence within the international market, and the considerable costs of confronting the United States in a situation in which the colossus of the north was disposed to use its overwhelming power.

8

CHILE

Clash of Global Visions II

William F. Sater

O N THE WHOLE, BETWEEN 1850 and 1905, Chile and the United States enjoyed correct but not particularly cordial relations. There were occasional in-
terludes of harmony, but more often than not, both nations viewed the other with
a disdain that sometimes degenerated into moments of real anger: twice, in 1882
and in 1892, the two countries almost went to war. Happily the passions cooled,
and by the early twentieth century Washington and Santiago, like an old married
couple, had learned to coexist. Problems might arise, but the disputes ceased en-
gendering the kind of anger that leads to violence.

The hostility of the mid-nineteenth century owed its origins more to the two
countries' similarities than to their differences. Like its northern neighbor, and in
contrast to its Latin brethren, newly independent Chile was a relatively well-organized nation. Following an 1830 civil war, a series of powerful presidents, all tied to
the local aristocracy, ruled Chile with authority, if not wisdom: domestic order
became the goal of the Moneda, the Chilean equivalent to the White House, a goal
that it often achieved albeit sometimes at the expense of its citizens' civil liberties.

Like the United States, Chile also depended on its exports of raw materials,
first agricultural products and then minerals, to generate revenues. Its reliance on
tenant farmers, the infamous system of *inquilinaie* certainly resembled the "peculiar institution" in the United States in substance if not form. Like the United
States, Chile also had a hostile Indian population, the Araucanians, that menaced
its frontier. After decades of bitter conflict, Santiago managed to subdue the Indians, opening Chile's southern hinterland to development just as Washington had
opened the West.

Finally, Chile had its own vision of its place in the international community,
or at least the South American community. Early in its history, the Moneda had
formulated the not necessarily novel notion that it alone should control the nation's future, and that, if required, it would use force to ensure that no foreign

country threatened its integrity. This policy first became clear in 1836 when Diego Portales, the *eminence gris* of Chile, declared war on the newly created Bolivian-Peruvian Confederation. Certainly economic considerations influenced Portales: the newly created Confederation, by levying selective taxes, threatened Valparaíso's commercial interests as well as those of its wheat producers. Worse, the Confederation's size and therefore its potential military power seemed to jeopardize Chile's very existence. Thus, Santiago seized on an excuse to launch a surprise attack on its enemy, eventually defeating it after a struggle of three years. Chile did not rest on its military laurels: it expanded into the Strait of Magellan to ensure its economic lifeline to the North Atlantic; it spilled over the Andes into the Argentine Patagonia; and it slyly inched across its northern borders as well.

An assertive Chile, willing to use force to achieve its goals, would eventually collide with the equally bold United States. Not unexpectedly, the Monroe Doctrine distressed Santiago's rulers. Portales considered Washington's exclusionary policy a threat, warning his countrymen that the United States wished "to conquer America, not only by force but by influence in every sphere." "Take care," he exhorted, "not to escape one domination to fall under another."[1] His fears proved premature: the same distance that made Chile a remote outpost of the Spanish Empire also insulated it from Washington's intrusions, although time and the steamship would whittle away the miles.

Economic competition increased the possibilities for disagreement. Chile produced wheat for the Pacific Coast nations of Latin America, later selling cereals to California and Europe. In the late 1830s, Santiago also began to export silver and copper to Europe and the United States. In short, as Chile became integrated into the North Atlantic economy, the potential for a U.S.-Chilean confrontation increased because both competed for the same markets.

The California Gold Rush roiled U.S.-Chilean relations. Initially the Chilean economy prospered because California's population became a market for food that agrarian Chile could sate. Enticed by the high prices, Chilean *hacendados* cultivated additional farmland, and millers modernized their equipment. Between 1848 and 1850, the amount of Chilean wheat and flour exported to California soared by almost 1,000 percent.[2] Seeing a potential market, U.S. grain producers began shipping their kiln-dried cereals to California. Because these farmers paid lower transportation costs, they easily underpriced their Chilean competition, driving them first out of the California market and then, when California farmers began to raise grain, challenging Chile's control of the Pacific markets, including Australia.[3] By 1855, the market collapsed, causing the Chilean agrarian sector substantial economic losses and thus earning U.S. interests a substantial enmity.

Other noneconomic issues contributed to the anti-American animus. Some U.S. entrepreneurs saw themselves as the paladins of a pure Anglo-Saxon people who enjoyed a God-given mandate to dominate the supposedly mongrel peoples of the south. James Buchanan's ranting about the superiority of "Anglo Saxon Blood" and the belief that the same "necessity that has carried us to the Gulf of

Mexico and to the Pacific Ocean, will continue to impel us forward," rightly made the Chileans anxious if not afraid.[4]

The Gold Rush experience exacerbated existing ill feelings. Many of the U.S. forty-niners passing through Chile acted in an inelegant if not utterly uncivilized fashion. These U.S. transients, described by one contemporary Chilean as "the garbage of the world," seemingly violated every Chilean social custom and in some cases abused the local inhabitants.[5] Thus, their departure, while perhaps working an economic hardship on Valparaíso's merchants, saloon keepers, and bordello owners, doubtless brought relief to the city's more refined inhabitants, who equated these U.S. transients with barbarians.

Predictably, large groups of Chileans, including a covey of prostitutes, flocked to California in search of their fortunes. While the total number of migrants remains unknown—although the 1852 U.S. Census counted at least 5,571 Chileans residing in California[6]—apparently so many departed that Chile's mines and fields remained silent or fallow; the nation's merchant marine, decimated by the desertions, almost ceased to function. The local newspapers and the occasional legislator resented that the nation was losing its best citizens.

To staunch the demographic hemorrhage, the press warned potential emigrants about the dangers of California living. Their concerns proved quite valid: in July 1849, a San Francisco mob, apparently angered by the presence of so many aliens, including Chileans, drove them from their community. The following year, other disgruntled Californians expelled Chileans from the local gold fields.

The San Francisco riots outraged Chileans. The U.S. envoy admitted that the stories of their persecution "keep alive the slumbering enmity which seems so inherent in the Spanish race towards our people." The issue angered enough deputies that they urged the Moneda to dispatch a warship to the United States in order to protect Chilean lives;[7] others advocated deporting any U.S. citizen residing in their nation. While the Chilean government did not take this step, the California episode had economic repercussions: when the U.S. Senate refused to enact legislation protecting Chilean citizens involved in mining, Santiago refused to renew its commercial treaty with the United States.[8]

If Chileans suffered in California, those U.S. citizens who unwisely became involved in Santiago's internal struggles also had cause for regret. In 1851, backers of the Liberal cause, including approximately seventy U.S. citizens, rebelled against the heavy-handed government of Manuel Montt. When captured, the insurgents, including the U.S. mercenaries, received the death penalty. Happily for the dissidents, the Moneda commuted their sentences. Various Chileans proved less forgiving, persecuting innocent U.S. colonists because some of their countrymen supported the rebel cause. The government, the public, and the press became vocally anti-American; "There is," as U.S. Minister David Starkweather observed, "widespread talk of expelling all Americans from Chile."[9]

Another rebellion erupted eight years later, and among those who died or lost their property were anti-government U.S. residents who sided with the unsuccessful insurgents. Again, U.S. citizens who had not participated in the rebellion suffered property losses as well. Their demands for compensation were simply added to the already substantial number of outstanding U.S. claims, some of which had been accumulating literally for decades.

Relations between the United States and Chile also deteriorated when some rebel fugitives received asylum in the home of William Trevitt, the U.S. consul. Chilean authorities violated international law when they searched Trevitt's residence, maltreating him and his wife. Although the State Department reprimanded Trevitt for granting asylum, it criticized the Chilean police for violating the principles of extra-territoriality. Far more than the issue of property damage that occurred during the rebellions, the Moneda's refusal to apologize for this incident caused ill feelings between the two governments.[10]

Chileans often complained about Washington's relations with the rest of Latin America. The U.S. decision to annex Texas and the subsequent war with Mexico, for example, deeply disquieted Chileans. Manuel Carvallo, a former Chilean minister to Washington, warned that Chile, "so rich in agriculture and mining would suffer the same fate at American hands as did Mexico."[11]

Carvallo's fears seemed to materialize when, in 1854, the United States made an offer to Ecuador to guarantee its integrity and to pay a substantial fee in exchange for the right to mine the guano deposits on the Galapagos Islands. Chile worried that the U.S. loan would make Ecuador so strong that it would threaten the prevailing balance of power on the Pacific Coast. The Moneda also opposed the U.S. offer, fearing that it might give the United States a toehold from which it would eventually attempt to absorb South America. The U.S. involvement in Ecuador, a Chilean statesman observed, so "introduces . . . a disturbance which can have pernicious consequences" that Santiago tried to organize international opposition to Washington's plan. The Moneda's fears proved exaggerated: the loan deal never materialized, but Santiago's response indicated that it would intervene in the affairs of its neighbors in order to ensure its hegemony.[12]

Two years later, in 1856, William Walker, acting on behalf of U.S. slaveowning interests, invaded Nicaragua. Many Chileans depicted him as the advance guard of a U.S. invasion of the hemisphere. El Mercurio saw the United States as a "threat to everything that you touch and surrounds you. . . . This is the danger for Chile and all of the Spanish American republics."[13] One of Chile's leading intellectuals stated that "Walker is the invasion, Walker is the conquest, Walker is the United States . . . the prophetic voice of a filibustering crusade which promises to its adventurers the regions of the South and the death of the South American initiative."[14]

Relations between Santiago and Washington warmed, however, when Washington sent Thomas Henry Nelson to serve as the new U.S. envoy to Chile. Nelson reached Santiago in October 1861, soon after the onset of the U.S. Civil War. Chile would favor the Union during the conflict. Many Chileans despised slavery, which they considered a medieval institution incompatible with a modern state. Moreover, they identified slavery with filibusters and the Democratic party, which, they feared, wanted to extend the "peculiar institution" into the Caribbean and perhaps beyond. President James Buchanan's bombastic 1859 presidential address, indicating that he favored intervention in any Latin American nation that threatened U.S. economic interests, caused Chileans to believe that the United States was preparing plans for the forcible annexation of Mexico and all of the Central and South American states. Chileans rightly fretted that a Democratic victory in the 1860 presidential election might unleash another spasm of U.S. imperialism. "If Douglas wins," warned *El Mercurio,* South America would suffer from "the terrible effects of an annexationist and invasionist policy."[15] Whatever President Lincoln and the Republicans might do, the Chileans, at least, did not have to worry about a revival of U.S. filibusters.

Nelson capitalized on the emerging pro-Union sentiment to improve the U.S. reputation. Thanks to the new envoy much of the Chilean press chose to blame the U.S. expansionist past not on the Union and the Republican party but on the Confederacy and the Democrats. He further enhanced his reputation by resolving a diplomatic dispute between Chile and Bolivia as well as by settling some outstanding financial claims involving U.S. citizens. When, at great personal danger, Nelson and various other Americans helped rescue some people from a burning Santiago church, the reputation of the United States soared. To show its appreciation to the U.S. colony, the Chilean government ordered special festivities, including the serenading of the minister with massed military bands, processions, and a mass, to celebrate U.S. Independence Day, 4 July 1863.

Private Chileans also showed their enthusiasm for the Union by celebrating its capture of Richmond and the peace at Appomattox. Lincoln's assassination provoked public grief, the Moneda proclaiming a day of national mourning, ordering the flying of some flags at half-mast and the firing of certain naval salutes. Although Nelson deserved no small portion of the credit for improving relations, he would have to deal with a particularly difficult issue: the French invasion of Mexico.

European Intervention

Yearning for a transatlantic empire, Louis Napoleon hoped to use Mexico's chronic indebtedness to create a French enclave in the New World. In October 1861, Napoleon invaded Mexico and installed a puppet emperor, Archduke Maximilian of the Austro-Hungarian Empire, to rule as its surrogate. Soon after Napoleon's army had landed in Mexico, Chile's new minister of foreign relations, Manuel Tocornal, inquired how the United States would respond to France's involvement in Mexico. The ongoing Civil War obviously consumed Washington's resources: Secretary of State William Seward had to struggle to keep Europe, including France, neutral while trying to isolate diplomatically the Confederacy; Mexico would have to wait.

It fell to Nelson to deliver the unpalatable message that Washington would not respond to French imperialism. The minister attempted to defuse the issue, explaining that although the United States could not afford to enforce the Monroe

Doctrine, it still adamantly opposed European intervention in the Hemisphere. Perhaps Chileans recognized the fundamental problem that the Civil War limited U.S. options. Santiago, of course, could also afford to be generous: Napoleon's intervention occurred so far from its shores that it did not have to worry. It would change its mind.

In 1861, a Spanish scientific expedition appeared off Peru. Since Madrid had never recognized Lima's independence, the arrival of the squadron doubtless caused some apprehension. The Limeños had valid cause for concern: the Spanish court had secretly authorized the expedition's commander, Admiral Luis H. Pinzón, to intervene on behalf of any Spaniard claiming property damages.

Pinzón finally had a chance to flex his muscles when he learned that a dispute between Spanish workers and the owner of the hacienda "Talambo" had erupted into violence that took the life of a Spaniard. Peru's courts had adjudicated the matter, finding in favor of the local landowner. But Pinzón nonetheless intervened, precipitating an incident that ultimately pitted Spain against most of South America's Pacific Coast nations.

Conceivably a crisis could have been avoided but for the activities of the Spanish representative, Eugenio Salazar y Mazzardo. Although Madrid had instructed Salazar to resolve peacefully the "Talambo" incident, the envoy decided to capitalize on the episode in order to advance his own career and presumably his nation's interests.

Lima, however, refused to discuss anything substantive until the Spanish Crown first recognized Peru's independence. The truculent Salazar, who did not place restoring peace high on his agenda, used this response to justify ordering the Spanish fleet to seize Peru's Chincha Islands. Madrid, he subsequently claimed, was still technically at war with Lima, thus, Spain had not invaded Peru. It had merely "revindicated" or repossessed what was once its territory.

Normally, few people coveted the desolate Chincha Islands. The tons of nitrogen-rich guano that coated these otherwise wretched islets made them a valuable economic asset. For decades Lima derived most of its revenue by levying an export tax on the sale of this noxious product. The loss of these islands, therefore, threatened to bankrupt Peru. Lima, which had no choice if it wished to survive economically, reacted in three ways: it began to rearm in case the dispute lead to war; it agreed to negotiate with Spain in order to resolve peacefully the issue; and it convoked an international congress in Lima to forge a Latin American response to the threat of European intervention.

Although Santiago traditionally evinced little fondness for Peru, it possessed even less for Spain's activities. The Moneda officially criticized Spanish policy, sending a delegate to the Inter-American meeting in Lima to protest Spanish imperialism. As the Chilean public's outrage became more vitriolic, the government prohibited the sale of Chilean coal or victuals to any Spanish naval vessel. The Moneda, moreover, increased the size of its fleet.

The international crisis abated slightly when Madrid agreed to recognize Peru's independence and renounced its claims to the Chincha Islands. The latter concession, however, was window dressing: Spain might abandon its claims to the islands, but it still refused to relinquish them until Peru satisfied its nationals' financial claims.

The Inter-American delegates to the conference, including the Chilean, advised Peru to try to reach a peaceful settlement with Spain but also to prepare itself for war. The arrival of a second Spanish fleet, under the command of Admiral José Pareja, convinced Peru's leaders that they could not act truculently. Pareja warned Lima that he would not return the islands unless it first settled the outstanding Spanish claims, as well as pay three million pesos to defray the cost of Madrid's naval expedition. Lima had little choice: in January 1865 it capitulated to Madrid, ransoming back its islands. The Peruvian Congress, infuriated by President Juan Antonio Pezet's craven behavior, rejected the treaty; the Peruvian public later deposed him.

Spain, having vanquished Peru, turned its hostile eye on Chile. Santiago had been one of the leaders in the anti-Spanish crusade. Not only had Chile refused to coal Spanish ships, it permitted aid to reach Peru, and it had allowed a Santiago newspaper, the *San Martín,* to print some particularly indecent opinions about Spain's Queen Isabel and her people.

Initially it appeared that Madrid's envoy to Santiago, Salvador de Tavira, could settle these issues peacefully. In September 1865, however, the Crown replaced him with the ever-belligerent Admiral Pareja. The latter apparently disliked the Santiago government because his father had died fighting against Chile's independence. Consequently, he added two fillips to the negotiations: to atone for its earlier insolence, Santiago must indemnify Madrid and fire a twenty-one-gun salute to its flag. If after five days the Moneda refused to comply, he threatened to use force. The admiral had placed the Chilean government into an impossible situation: given the insolent wording of Pareja's demands, the Moneda had to reject the Spanish ultimatum. Pareja reacted as expected: he blockaded Chile's coast. The Moneda responded by declaring war on Spain.

The U.S. Reaction

Chileans might carp about the Monroe Doctrine, but they nonetheless turned to the United States for assistance to repel the Spanish. The journalist Benjamin Vicuña Mackenna traveled to the United States to purchase weapons and to recruit a contingent of Chilean and Peruvians to attack Cuba from the United States. He failed on both counts: he could not enlist an exile army, and the U.S. authorities confiscated the weapons he managed to buy.

Vicuña Mackenna did succeed in cultivating some influential friends and founded a Spanish-language newspaper, *La Voz de America,* to justify the Moneda's cause. Perhaps the high point of his propaganda campaign was a January 1866 meeting in New York that was attended by various important individuals, some of whom soundly denounced Spanish imperialism and called for enforcing the Monroe Doctrine, "if need be . . . at the mouth of the cannon."[16] Secretary Seward did not share these opinions: "The war [between Chile and Spain] has no object," he noted. "Spain has no reason to cause it nor Chile any motive to accept it. For reasons of etiquette, great harm will befall commerce."[17] The secretary's unsympathetic reaction was not completely without reason. Seward feared that if he invoked the Monroe Doctrine, Madrid would grant the Confederacy either belligerent status or, worse, diplomatic recognition, and thereby cripple the Union cause. Consequently he tried to placate Spain. The Monroe Doctrine, Seward casuistically argued, only applied if the European intended to occupy an American nation. And, since Spain specifically stated that it did not seek to annex Chilean lands, Washington would remain neutral.

Even the defeat of the Confederacy did not modify Seward's opinion. In order to win Spanish assistance to build a trans-Caribbean telegraph system, Seward continued to cultivate Madrid, eulogizing it as "the only European power that has any right to a footing in America."[18] Seward went so far to placate Spain that he dismissed Nelson, replacing him with Judson Kilpatrick.

Since Santiago believed that Spain had pushed it into war, the Moneda expected Washington to stand by it just as it had stood by Washington during the Civil War. The U.S. minister privately sympathized with Chile, informing the government that President José Pérez had to respond as he did: if he adopted a more conciliatory policy, the minister observed, the Chilean public would have deposed him.

As the diplomats debated, the war become more active. The outnumbered Chilean squadron managed to repel Madrid's fleet, even capturing one of its vessels, the *Covadonga*. The loss of that ship so mortified the bombastic Pareja that he petulantly committed suicide. It became increasingly clear that the Spanish fleet could not operate so far from its base of supplies. Consequently, Madrid ordered Admiral Castro Mendéz Nuñez, Pareja's replacement, to suspend the blockade, but only after he punished Santiago for its supposed insolence. Mendéz Nuñez complied: he informed the Moneda that if it did not accept Madrid's conditions, including firing a twenty-one-gun salute, he would bombard Valparaíso.

Nelson, along with Commodore John Rodgers, the U.S. naval commander, and the newly arrived Kilpatrick, tried to persuade Mendéz Nuñez to modify his conditions. The Spaniard relented, accepting U.S. mediation and agreeing that Chile did not have to salute the Spanish flag unilaterally. Instead, he proposed that both nations exchange reciprocal salutes. Chile, however, would have to fire the first cannonade.

Because it had to act in concert with Peru, the Moneda rejected the U.S. compromise. Washington's representatives tried to win Spain's permission to include Peru in the offer. But, since Lima's minister had left Santiago, Minister Alvaro Covarrubias requested that Mendéz Nuñez extend the deadline before bombarding Valparaíso. The Spanish naval officer refused. Mendéz Nuñez had his orders: he must open fire at 8 A.M. on 31 March.

Only the vessels of the British and U.S. navies, lying at anchor in the harbor, could save the Valparaíso. Both the U.S. and British commanders were willing to intervene, but the British minister was not. Rather than take on the Spanish alone, the U.S. fleet joined the British fleeing Valparaíso, leaving the port unprotected. On 31 March 1866, after inflicting approximately fifteen million pesos in damage, mainly to foreign-owned property, the Spanish fleet heroically returned to its home port.

Washington's failure to defend Valparaíso seemed to infuriate the Chileans more than the Spanish bombardment; it also undid what Nelson had so painstakingly accomplished. Certainly the Chileans had ample reason to agree with Vicuña Mackenna, who denounced the Monroe Doctrine as a "cruel chimera" and to conclude that the United States used force to protect its investments; materialism, in short, always took precedence over issues of morality. The Chileans, however, had confused rhetoric with *realpolitik:* the United States, like most nations, acted only when it was in its self-interest, and clearly invoking the Monroe Doctrine at that particular moment, much as it might please Santiago, did not benefit Washington.

The Era of Ill Feelings: 1882–1893

The late 1870s mark the beginning of more than a decade of intermittent but invariably heartfelt loathing between the United States and Chile. In late 1878, the predatory Bolivian dictator Hilarión Daza raised taxes on a Chilean company mining nitrates, or *salitre,* in the Atacama Desert. Chile had once claimed a portion of this area. In 1874, however, Santiago renounced its claims to the disputed territory in return for a Bolivian promise not to raise the taxes on any Chilean corporation exploiting the desert's resources.

Since Daza's unilateral tax increase violated the 1874 agreement, he recognized that Chile might retaliate. But, because Santiago was embroiled in a boundary dispute with Argentina, he believed he could act with impunity. If he miscalculated and Chile retaliated, Daza had a trump card: in 1873, Bolivia and Peru had entered into a secret alliance against Chile. Hence, should Santiago became unruly, La Paz could call upon Lima for military help.

Chile did react: under severe domestic political pressure, in February 1879, President Aníbal Pinto ordered his troops to occupy the lands that his nation once claimed. For almost two months, Peru played a double game, preaching mediation but arming. Eventually, when pressed by Santiago, Lima admitted that a secret treaty tying it to Bolivia existed and that Peru would honor it. On 5 April 1879, Chile declared war on both nations.

The ensuing struggle, the War of the Pacific, pitted Chile against two neighbors with a larger population and military. Given the great distances separating Santiago's heartland from the theater of operations, Chile hesitated to initiate the land war; it first must win control of the sea in order to invade the north. Rather than attack the Peruvian fleet, Chile blockaded Iquique, the port through which Peru exported nitrate and thus earned its revenue. At first, this tactic had little success. Finally, in two decisive battles, Iquique (21 May 1879) and Angamos (8 October 1879), Chile destroyed Peru's two ironclad warships, opening the way for the land war to begin.[19]

Santiago landed troops at Pisagua in October 1879, and within weeks it had conquered the province of Tarapaca. Seven months later Chile attacked what are now the provinces of Tacna and Arica, capturing both after a series of arduous and extremely bloody encounters. By October 1880, the Moneda had made its plans to attack Lima and end the war, but then the United States became entangled in this struggle, an involvement that achieved nothing but alienating the Chileans.

Reconciling the belligerents proved a formidable task. Chile, after having spent its treasure and blood, wanted Lima to cede Tarapaca as payment for the cost of fighting the war. But neither Peru nor Bolivia would surrender their territory; they would consider paying only a monetary indemnity. Since the differences between the two sides seemed so enormous, Washington perhaps might have remained on the sidelines. But, believing that certain European powers, whose citizens had made enormous investments in Peru, might intervene, Secretary of State William Evarts ordered his ministers in Chile and Peru to offer the good offices of the United States.

Regrettably Washington's envoys—Isaac Christiancy in Peru, Thomas Osborn in Chile, and Newton Pettis in Bolivia—maimed Evarts's diplomatic initiative. Christiancy, for example, had learned that Chile's president considered Peru's cession of Tarapaca a prerequisite for entering into negotiations. Inexplicably, the U.S. diplomat did not pass this information on to his colleague in Bolivia or to the Peruvian government. This gaffe became particularly egregious because Christiancy and Pettis knew that neither Lima nor La Paz would permit Chile to retain Tarapaca or the Atacama.

Thus, when in October 1880 negotiators met on board the U.S.S. *Lackawanna,* they were playing roles in a Hispanic-American version of a Greek tragedy. The Chilean delegate insisted that Bolivia relinquish the Atacama and that Peru renounce its 1873 alliance, give up Tarapaca plus pay reparations of twenty million pesos, return all Chilean property and prizes seized in the war, demilitarize the port of Arica, and permit the Moneda's troops to occupy Tacna and Arica until Lima met all these conditions. Since neither of the Allies would accept these terms, the Moneda was baffled, and Osborn, who believed he had reached some understanding with Christiancy, was furious. The parley, of course, ended acrimoniously, with both sides turning from the peace table to the battlefield.

In December, Chile landed troops south of Lima and by early January 1881 had captured the capital. The Moneda's victory was incomplete: the Chilean general, Manuel Baquedano, failed to envelop the city and as a consequence let Nicolás Piérola, the Peruvian president, as well as a portion of the Peruvian army, escape into the Andes.

At the time, the activities of a handful of Peruvian diehards seemed unimportant. Santiago had won, and the Bolivians, no longer militarily important, sulked in the *altiplano* while the remnants of the Peruvian army fragmented into three groups: the force led by Piérola; a second band directed by General Andrés Cacerés; and, finally, the small army holed up in the Andean town Arequipa, 10,000 feet above sea level, commanded by a beached admiral, Lizardo Montero.

Initially, no Peruvian appeared willing to cede territory to the Chileans. In 1881, however, a rump legislature selected a lawyer, Francisco García Calderón, to replace Piérola. García Calderón's election initially delighted Santiago, which saw him as someone who would end the war and let Chile repatriate its disease-plagued army. García Calderón might indeed have proved to be a savior for the Moneda but for the intrusion of James G. Blaine, the Plumed Knight of Maine, President James Garfield's secretary of state.

Utterly lacking in diplomatic experience and insight, Blaine was a poor choice for secretary of state. Two notions dominated his geopolitical thinking: the world was a large marketplace in which the United States should play an important role; and that Latin Americans—"a race . . . of hot temper, quick to take affront, ready to avenge a wrong whether real or fancied," Washington's "younger sisters"— needed U.S. help to save them from themselves and the threat of non-hemispheric intervention.[20]

The War of the Pacific seemed ready made for the warrior from Maine: the fratricidal struggle, Blaine concluded, was fundamentally "an English war on Peru with Chili as the instrument . . . Chili would never have gone into this war one inch but for the backing of English capital."[21] Consequently, Blaine felt duty-bound to end the struggle and restore peace while repelling the British intruder.

Blaine's goals appeared simple. He did not begrudge Chile its pound of flesh. As the victor, Santiago deserved whatever financial spoils it could amass. The secretary, however, opposed its demand for Allied land. As the Franco-Prussian War had demonstrated, annexation simply generated revanchism, which created an inhospitable business climate. Santiago should settle for money rather than insist upon territory.

If Blaine's policy was myopic, his choice of envoys proved blind. The two principal U.S. ministers seemed uniquely unsuited for their posts. Judson Kilpatrick, who had married a Chilean, eventually became more an advocate of Santiago than a representative of the United States, and addiction to drink warped the already diminished thought processes of his colleague in Lima, Stephen J. Hurlburt.

For some reason Hurlburt made saving Peru into a personal mission, transforming himself from Washington's envoy into Lima's paladin. He told the Chilean authorities, for example, that the United States would not tolerate its annexation of Peruvian lands; he warned Admiral Patricio Lynch, Santiago's military governor of occupied Peru, that the Moneda's insistence on implementing its draconian policies would make Chile an outcast nation. Both statements, made without the Department of State's authorization, infuriated Chile. Worse, Hurlburt supported García Calderón in his struggle with Nicolás Piérola over the Peruvian presidency. The U.S. envoy even went so far as to lobby his diplomatic colleague in Buenos Aires to recognize García Calderón as Peru's chief executive.

Hurlburt further damaged the U.S. position when he convinced Garcia

Calderón to grant the U.S. fleet a coaling station in Chimbote, a port on Peru's coast. This act, which personally profited Hurlburt, compromised the United States in the eyes of Santiago. Chileans believed that Hurlburt would not have taken any step without Blaine's permission, permission that the secretary granted because he too would profit financially from the Chimbote scheme. Others suspected that Washington would use the War of the Pacific as a pretext for establishing a protectorate over Peru, an act that would bring the United States uncomfortably close to Chile.

Chile had new cause for anger. García Calderón, taking encouragement from Hurlburt and Blaine, decided to try to find the funds to pay reparations to Santiago rather than cede it territory. The Moneda had long argued that any Peruvian offer of funds lacked credibility because Lima had no money. This allegation was, of course, perfectly correct: without the revenues from Tarapaca's nitrate mines, Peru could not raise the money to pay reparations. And since Lima would never have money, the Chileans should keep Tarapaca.

Suddenly a financial angel appeared: a French corporation, the *Credit Industrial,* promised not only to advance Peru the money needed to placate the Chileans but also to pay off Lima's other debts and even provide it an income as well. The *Credit Industrial,* moreover, had some powerful backers—the brother of the speaker of the U.S. House of Representatives and the president of France, Jules Grevy—who used their influence to get the United States to back the deal.

The *Credit Industrial* was not Peru's only angel. A naturalized U.S. citizen, John Landreau, assigned his economic claims against Lima, which he inherited from his brother, to the newly formed, U.S.-based Peruvian Company. That corporation's president was Jacob Shipherd, a U.S. speculator with a reputation for striking a sharp deal and for having important political friends. Like the *Credit Industrial,* Shiperd's company promised to pay reparations to Chile in return for the privilege of mining Tarapaca's guano and nitrate.

The sudden offer of financial support so emboldened García Calderón that he balked at giving Tarapaca to Chile. In reprisal, Admiral Patricio Lynch, still Chile's governor of occupied Peru, first seized the paltry contents of García Calderón's treasury and then disarmed his troops. When García Calderón continued to affirm that he would not cede Tarapaca to Santiago, Lynch ordered his arrest and deportation to Chile's south.

Exiling García Calderón, however, did not end the war. Operating from mountain redoubts and the slums of Lima, Peruvian irregulars ambushed Chileans as they operated in the field as well as in urban streets. Although less violent, Chile's relations with the United States also suffered. Infuriated by what he perceived as Chile's maltreatment of García Calderón, Hurlburt became more brazen in his defense of Lima's interests: he attempted to convince the guerrilla leader, Andrés Cacerés, to support Montero as Peru's de facto president; he also told Peru's legislature that Washington would resist Chile's attempt to dismember it.

Hurlburt's unauthorized deal for the Chimbote coaling facility and his public advocacy of Montero converted him into a diplomatic loose canon. Yet, few U.S.

diplomats or statesmen seemed capable of restraining him. Certainly Kilpatrick could not: he was literally dying. (Some believed that his Chilean wife was running the embassy during his final illness, which might well account for his pro-Chilean policies.) With one envoy who had gone native and the other virtually moribund, Blaine ordered his son, Walker, and a seasoned professional diplomat, William Trescot, to determine what was going on in Chile and Peru.

In addition to the fact-finding, Trescot had orders to discover Chile's reasons for jailing García Calderón and for its attitude toward the U.S. offer to mediate the question of annexation. Blaine also authorized Trescot to warn Chile, in the most diplomatic fashion, that the United States contemplated declaring war if Santiago rejected U.S. good offices.

Chile, quite understandably, could not fathom Washington's motives. Why, after dismembering Mexico in the late 1840s, did the United States now wish to deny Santiago the right to do the same to Peru? Clearly Washington did not occupy the moral high ground. Increasingly, Chileans concluded that various sordid U.S. financial interests were anxious to exploit Tarapaca. Others described the United States as trying to swallow the entire continent. Washington, they claimed, planned to make Peru into a base of "North American power and wealth" from which it could control Latin America. Thus, Chile could argue that its decision to stand up to the United States, even at the cost of despoiling Peru, made it the protector of the Hemisphere.[22]

Should the Moneda become belligerent, Washington would have great difficulty prosecuting a war against Chile. Vowing to avoid the type of humiliation that it suffered at the hands of Spain in 1865, Chile had modernized its navy. It had done such a good job of rearming that by 1877 Admiral Porter of the U.S. Navy observed, "What a miserable condition we would be in [if the United States went to war with Chile]. . . . You might send our whole Navy out there and those Chilean ironclads would wipe the whole of them off the ocean."[23] Now, in 1879, with three armored ships commanded by seasoned officers, Santiago obviously had even more of an advantage over the U.S. South Pacific squadron, which consisted of four aged wooden vessels. Not surprisingly, Admiral C. R. Perry Rodgers informed a journalist that "we are not now in a position to menace the Chilean government." "It is manifest," stated a U.S. congressman, "that in a conflict with this small nation [Chile], the United States would be helpless to resist the first attack."[24]

Happily, it did not come to war. Chester Alan Arthur, who became president following Garfield's assassination, replaced Blaine with Frederick Frelinghuysen, who wanted no involvement in Chilean affairs. He canceled Trescot's instructions: the United States would not try to dictate the peace terms nor would it threaten Chile with war.

Frelinghuysen's *volte-face* left Trescot and Blaine's son swinging in the wind. Since the State Department sent the change in their instructions by surface mail, both Chile's minister to Washington and its foreign minister, José Manuel Balmaceda, learned about the policy shift before the envoys from the United States.

Thus, when the U.S. diplomats arrived in Chile, they discovered that Kilpatrick had died and that Washington had changed its mandate. Worse, it was Balmaceda who informed them of these unpleasant facts.

Although Balmaceda began his meeting stating that the Moneda never sought to offend Washington when it seized García Calderón, he made it clear that Chile would not budge. Indeed, he not only vehemently defended Chile's right to annex Tarapaca, he upped the ante: Peru's intransigence, he argued, had proved so costly that Chile now insisted that it retain, for a period of ten years, Tacna and Arica, and that it would mine Lobos Island's guano fields until it collected a twenty-million-peso indemnity.

The U.S. envoys meekly accepted his terms. The three diplomats crafted the Viha del Mar Protocol, named in honor of the seaside resort where they met, effectively ending U.S. involvement in the War of the Pacific. Chile would accept U.S. mediation in return for the right to annex Tarapaca and to occupy Tacna and Arica for ten years. In a moment of generosity, it promised Lima that it would share the revenues from the Lobos Island guano pits and that it would lower its demand for monetary reparations. The Moneda had triumphed because the United States lacked the military muscle to enforce the State Department's policies.

Trescot's task remained incomplete. He had to convince the Peruvians to accept the Viha del Mar Protocol, a particularly daunting task because Peru still had no government. Thus the U.S. envoy first had to find someone willing to form a national administration and then convince him to become an accomplice to the dismemberment of his country.

To help Trescot in his task, Secretary of State Frelinghuysen assigned new envoys, all men with experience in Latin America. Dr. Cornelius Logan, who had served in Santiago earlier, went to Chile; James Partridge went to Peru; and George Maney went to Bolivia. Whereas Logan urged Chile to moderate its appetite, Partridge, like Hurlburt before him, became Lima's champion. Even after President Arthur indicated that he would not help Peru, Partridge tried to encourage a joint European-U.S. intervention to save the country from mutilation. Because Partridge's proposal violated Arthur's instructions and virtually repudiated the Monroe Doctrine, Frelinghuysen discharged him. Partridge's dismissal had one positive benefit for Washington: it forced Peru to recognize that the United States would not protect it.

Admitting that Peru had to cooperate, General Miguel Iglesias offered to form a new government in Lima. With the assistance of Chile and the recognition of the United States as well as other European nations, the fledgling president seemed to prosper. Still, only one side of the equation was balanced: Iglesias had to negotiate a peace settlement.

Happily for him, Chile, fatigued by the costly and bloody guerrilla war, became more generous. It agreed to annex only Tarapaca and to occupy Tacna and Arica for ten years, when a plebiscite would determine eventual ownership. The winner would retain the land, and the loser would receive ten million silver pesos as compensation. This agreement remained moot until late 1883, when Chilean troops finally wiped out the last Peruvian guerrilla army of General Cacerés. With his last domestic opposition eradicated, Iglesias signed the Treaty of Ancón, ending Peru's involvement in the War of the Pacific.

Chile emerged from its War of the Pacific dispute with Washington a stronger and more confident nation. Clearly Santiago held the trump cards, which it played with such disdain that one U.S. writer noted, "In all the diplomatic history of the United States I know of no greater personal humiliation to which one of our envoys was subjected."[25] Various U.S. observers warned that the annexation of Tarapaca consisted of but the first stage of a Chilean master plan. "It is but a question of years," warned one writer, "when not only Peru, but Bolivia will become a part of Chili, and the aggressive nation will want to push her eastern boundary back of the Andes, and secure control of the sources of the Amazon, as she has of the navigation of the strait."[26]

Chile had become the bogeyman of the Pacific. Its naval power so emboldened a Chilean flag officer, noted one U.S. congressman, that he "simply told the American admiral, and the American government through him, that if he did not mind his own business they would send him and his fleet to the bottom of the ocean." Some legislators even feared that Chile "could come right into San Francisco, levy tribute on its people, burn down the town, and you have nothing in this world to keep them outside that harbor." Theodore Roosevelt fumed, "It is a disgrace to us as a nation . . . that our rich cities should lie at the mercy of a tenth rate country like Chile."[27]

The United States soon had additional reasons to fear Chile. Santiago purchased three new cruisers, the *Esmeralda,* the *Pinto,* and the *Errazuriz,* as well as the torpedo boats *Lynch* and *Condell.* It also hired Captain Emil Korner, a German General Staff officer, who organized Chile's General Staff and a war college, ordered new artillery and small arms, and restructured its land forces. Although the Moneda doubtless took some of these steps to ensure its security from its nearest neighbors, the developments nonetheless gave the United States pause.

Certainly the Moneda acted more confidently. President Domingo Santa Maria (1881–86) suggested that Chile and the United States divide up the hemisphere using the Isthmus of Panama as the demarcation line between their respective spheres of influence. Santa Maria's successor, José Manuel Balmaceda, was even more explicit: the nation "should be able to resist on its own territory any possible coalition, and if it cannot succeed in attaining the naval power of the great powers, it should at least prove, on the base of a secure port and a fleet . . . that there is no possible profit in starting a war against the Republic of Chile."[28]

The 1888 annexation of Easter Island—a speck of earth lacking any value, except to archaeologists, approximately 2,000 miles west of the mainland Chile coast—demonstrated the Moneda's aggressive foreign policy. Various Chileans espoused taking the island, arguing that it would enhance Chile's trade with Australasia and serve as a base to alert the country in case of an impending raid. Annexing the island, of course, made Chile an imperial power, establishing its claim to the South Pacific. Benjamin Vicuña Mackenna declared, "is it not fitting that we should implant [on Easter Island] . . . a flagpole on which would fly the white-starred symbol of our conquests of terra firma?"[29] Santiago's newly found naval prowess proved galling, since U.S. interests also visualized their nation as in the vanguard of the economic penetration of the Pacific Basin.

If the United States needed additional cause for concern, it was not long in coming. In April 1885, a rebellion erupted in Panama, then a province of Colombia. Washington, operating under the 1846 treaty with Bogota guaranteeing free transit across the Isthmus, sent naval units and troops to quell the disturbance, to ensure transit, and to protect U.S. property.[30] Colombia, which feared that the United States might linger, invoked its treaty arrangement with Santiago, requesting that Chile send naval aid to keep the U.S. troops at bay. The Moneda compiled: the newly commissioned *Esmeralda* arrived off the Panamanian coast; its captain, Juan E. López, carried secret orders that essentially permitted him to take any action needed to blunt U.S. imperialism.

Although he arrived after the worst of the crisis, the Chilean remained offshore, declaring that he would not abandon Panama until the forces of the United States evacuated Colón. López may have exaggerated his importance because there was nothing to indicate that the U.S. government had any intention of annexing Panama. Besides, he had a rival for fame: the French boasted that they, not the Chileans, forced the U.S. forces to abandon Panama. The *Esmeralda* subsequently sailed to Ecuador, where the United States had also sent the *Wachusett* in order to protect Julio Santos, an Ecuadorian-born but naturalized-U.S. citizen whom the authorities had arrested for supposedly plotting against the Quito government. The U.S. commander, the soon to be famous Alfred Thayer Mahan, concluded that the matter was not worth a candle and departed. López, however, had feared that the United States would use force to protect Santos, and he remained there until sure that the U.S. fleet would not bombard Guayaquil. In neither case did López have to act, but the point had been made: simply the presence of Chile's strong navy limited the U.S. fleet's options.[31]

Many U.S. observers recognized that the Panama crisis revealed their fleet's inadequacies. *The Army and Navy Journal* came to the same conclusion, warning that "Chili has today the finest, fastest, and most perfectly equipped fighting war ship of her size afloat . . . the *Esmeralda*. She could destroy our entire Navy, ship by ship, and never be touched."[32]

Having staked out its claim to the Pacific by annexing Easter Island, Santiago worked to preserve its power base. The United States tried to acquire a coaling station on the Galapagos Islands, but the Moneda successfully interceded to stop it. President Jorge Montt, who led the successful rebellion against Balmaceda and who became chief executive in September 1891, told the British minister in 1893 that Chile would always do its utmost to keep the United States out of the South Pacific, of which Chile was the natural defender. *La Ley* subsequently argued for the permanent stationing of a Chilean warship in Colombian waters for the purpose of "duly protecting those interests and exercising the influence which clearly is ours." In that same mood, Chile considered buying the Galapagos Islands from Ecuador. Two motives prompted this decision. By making the islands into a maritime refitting station for ships sailing from Panama to Oceania, Chile's economy would prosper. Owning the islands, moreover, would enhance Chile's ability to defend the Pacific from U.S. incursions, particularly after it completed the Panama Canal. The Moneda never purchased the Galapagos, but it sent a military and naval mission to Ecuador to bolster its influence in the region and to ensure that the United States would not acquire them either.[33]

Eventually, the United States reacted to what it perceived as a series of humiliations. The Panamanian incident helped convert Mahan into an advocate of a larger and stronger U.S. Navy.[34] By 1900, Washington's fleet of twelve capital ships and eighteen cruisers dwarfed that of Chile.

Other events, some involving the United States, seriously weakened Chile. In 1886, José Manuel Balmaceda became president. Although his administration began with promise, by 1890 Balmaceda had alienated most of the legislature. To force him to change his government, the Congress refused to authorize a spending bill for 1891. The president responded by stating that he would use the legislature's 1890 budget authorization for 1891. This act clearly violated the constitution and, in January 1891, his legislative foes, supported by the navy, rebelled.

The ensuing struggle was a strange one. The insurgents had managed to capture the northern port of Iquique, giving them access to revenues generated by the nitrate trade as well as to manpower from the mining population. But since the rebels had no army, they could not challenge Balmaceda's hold on the Chilean heartland. Conversely, Balmaceda, who possessed a large army, lacked the sea power he needed to eradicate the rebels' base. Thus for weeks both sides labored to remedy their peculiar deficiencies: Balmaceda tried to take immediate delivery of two cruisers that were nearing completion in French ports, and the rebels frantically sought to find the weapons needed to equip an army. Unfortunately, the United States would become involved in some of these schemes.

Balmaceda's foes, the Congressionalists, sent agents, including a Yale graduate, Ricardo Trumbull, to the United States to purchase small arms. Thanks to the good offices of the Grace Company, Trumbull acquired some rifles and munitions, which he sent to California for transshipment to Chile. Trumbull's actions had not passed unnoticed. Chile's minister to the United States asked Washington to prevent the export of Trumbull's arms cache. Once the Chilean legation's lawyer warned Washington that the United States might be held liable for any damage these weapons caused—certainly a distinct possibility—Secretary of State James G. Blaine, serving his second term, ordered a weapons embargo on Chile.

Blaine's edict did not stop Trumbull. He charted a coastal ship, the *Robert and Minnie,* to take the weapons from San Diego to a Chilean vessel, the *Itata,* which would transport them to Iquique. The U.S. authorities put a federal marshal on the *Itata* to prevent its sailing. They were also prepared to keep the *Robert and Minnie* in port but could not do so because that vessel remained outside U.S. territorial waters. In violation of the federal injunction, the *Itata's* captain steamed out of San Diego with the marshal in his custody, off-loaded the U.S. lawman and weapons from the *Robert and Minnie,* and set sail for Chile.

Washington was not pleased. The Chileans had kidnapped a federal official and flouted a court injunction. Consequently, it ordered the warship *Charleston* to catch the *Itata* and seize its cargo. It was no contest: the *Itata* reached Iquique before the U.S. warship, but Chile's Congressionalist foreign minister, fearful of antagonizing Washington, ordered it to return to the United States. The Congressionalists became furious, accusing the United States of piracy and claiming that it sought to sabotage their cause. Regrettably, they would have additional causes for complaint.

In August 1891, a Congressionalist invasion force landed off Valparaíso. Admiral George Brown, on board the U.S.S. *San Francisco,* ventured out to sea to discover where the rebels had landed. Once he determined the invasion site, he returned to port and informed Washington, in a coded message, of the rebel action. The insurgents claimed that Brown had passed this information to Balmaceda, thereby permitting the president to respond more effectively to the Congressionalist landing. This allegation lacked any substance: the loyalists knew of the invasion site long before the *San Francisco* returned to port. Still, suspicion hardened into fact. The rebels claimed that because Brown leaked information, the insurgents sustained higher-than-expected battlefield casualties. Even after the defeat of Balmaceda, rebel sympathizers continued to pillory Brown for his supposed duplicity.

The actions of some U.S. corporations compounded the problem. The U.S.-owned Central and South American Cable Company had sought a concession to lay a cable between Chile and Argentina. Balmaceda agreed but only if the company would restore service between Chile and Peru, service that the rebels had interrupted when they cut the cable at Iquique. The corporation accepted his conditions. Of course, in the course of connecting Santiago and Lima, the cable company had left the insurgent capital of Iquique without access to the outside world.

The combination of the *Itata* incident, Brown's supposed betrayal, and the cable episode seemed irrefutable proof that the United States sided with the Balmaceda government. In one sense, this allegation contained some truth: the U.S. minister, Patrick Egan, did favor Balmaceda. Egan, an Irish-born naturalized U.S. citizen, had personal ties with the president. Like Blaine in 1879, Egan saw Perfidious Albion behind all things malevolent. Thus he was sure that British capitalists, who had suffered at Balmaceda's hands, fomented the rebellion to topple him from power. Paradoxically, although Egan liked the president, he opened his embassy to Congressionalist refugees fleeing the Balmaceda government. And neither the Moneda's entreaties nor its threats could move Egan: the Congressionalists remained until he could arrange their safe conduct out of Chile.

Egan backed the wrong horse. The rebels defeated Balmaceda's army and occupied the capital in September 1891. Despite being declared an open city, Santiago still suffered widespread looting, and some of the president's most prominent supporters died at the hands of the mob or of rump court martials. Rather than endure such a fate, Balmaceda committed suicide; his less-dramatic followers fled, some of them reaching the sanctuary of the U.S. embassy. Just as Egan had granted asylum to anti-Balmaceda figures, he took in those who supported his regime.

Egan at least was consistent: he refused to turn over the *Balmacedistas* just as he had rejected earlier demands for the heads of the Congressionalists. Paradoxically, many of those same Congressionalists who had fearfully crouched in Egan's legation as Balmaceda's police brayed for their blood now demanded that Chilean authorities surround the U.S. legation with uniformed as well as plainclothes policemen, stopping individuals and even arresting Egan's son. Believing that his guests would be murdered if they left the embassy—not an unwarranted fear given the level of postrevolutionary violence that swept Santiago—Egan tried to arrange safe conduct for these people. He succeeded but literally had to sneak some of them onto the U.S.S. *Yorktown*. The State Department, furious at this blatant disregard of diplomatic immunity, delicately warned Santiago that it would use force to repel any embassy invasion.

For Chileans, Egan's actions seemed the culmination of Washington's deliberate program to frustrate the Moneda. Since 1880, many Chileans felt antagonistic toward the United States. First Washington had tried to deprive Santiago of its right to annex lands, then it had attempted to intervene in the South Pacific, in Panama, and Ecuador—all within Chile's self-proclaimed sphere of influence. During the 1891 revolution, however, U.S. intervention had become egregious: it had taken sides in the struggle, relayed intelligence, and openly favored the Balmaceda cause, even protecting its criminal officials. The "feelings of animosity against Americans is very decided," observed one U.S. diplomat, "in social gatherings and in groups of Chileans on the street concerns, when I have passed, I have heard chants of 'abajo los Yankees' (down with the Yankees.)"[35] The diplomat erred: the feeling of animosity would increase.

The *Baltimore* Incident

In October, less than a month after Balmaceda's suicide, the crew of the U.S.S. *Baltimore* landed in Valparaíso for a liberty call. Given the strong anti-American feelings following the 1891 revolution, the ship's commander, Admiral Winfield Scott Schley, should not have let his men go ashore. An argument between some of Schley's crew and the local denizens of the True Blue ended in the murder of three sailors and the beating of seventeen of their shipmates. The police eventually intervened, jailing some thirty U.S. servicemen.

Various Chileans minimized the attack on the *Baltimore*'s crew, noting that the incident had "nothing to distinguish it from the frequent brawls in sea-port towns." The Chilean trial judge, Enrique Foster, concurred: the disturbance, he argued, had been blown out of proportion and the police had acted correctly.[36]

Washington categorically rejected these conclusions. A U.S. Navy board of inquiry, meeting in Chile, faulted the Valparaíso police for not protecting the sailors from the mob and for apparently abusing them once they were in custody. Consequently, in December, President Benjamin Harrison demanded an apology and compensation for the injured and families of those killed. Despite private warnings, the Chilean government appeared to trivialize the U.S. president's concerns. Worse, the Moneda's foreign minister, Manuel Matta, in a wire to Pedro Montt, Chile's minister to the United States, described Harrison's conclusions as "erroneous or deliberately incorrect." Had Matta restricted his opinion to diplomatic circles, the situation might not have escalated. Instead, he read his telegram to Montt into the proceedings of the Chamber of Deputies. Then, the newspaper *El Ferrocarril* reprinted the entire message for all of Santiago, including Egan, to read. Once the U.S. envoy authenticated the newspaper's story, he forwarded a copy to Washington, which was not amused.

The situation worsened in January 1892, when the Chilean authorities published a magistrate's report that concluded that the U.S. sailors had precipitated the riot, that Valparaíso's police had acted in an exemplary manner, and that, whatever killed the sailors, it was not a police bullet. Although the court sentenced three Chileans to jail for trivial amounts of time, it also sought to indict various U.S. sailors for their role in the riot. Montt, who had the unhappy task of presenting Foster's report to Washington, had the good grace, and wisdom, to add some vapid expressions of regret.

Harrison, still fuming over Matta's behavior, demanded that the minister of foreign relations withdraw his earlier intemperate statements. Chile not only refused to apologize for Matta's remarks, it also asked Washington to recall Egan. Harrison, armed with a second report written by a U.S.-based naval board of inquiry—which confirmed Schely's original conclusions—became furious. He instructed the secretary of state to inform Chile that Washington would break diplomatic relations unless it repudiated Matta's statements, tendered an apology, and offered reparations for the attack on the *Baltimore*'s crew.

When Chile did not respond, Harrison informed the U.S. Congress about the Moneda's failure to protect U.S. citizens. The crisis, he concluded, had reached a critical point: "we must protect those who, in foreign ports, display the flag or wear the colors of this Government against insult, brutality, and death, inflicted in resentment of the acts of their Government, and not for any fault of their own."[37] Clearly the United States might declare war if Chile did not respond.

Santiago's situation was precarious. Although it had acquired three new ships, the United States could concentrate eight modern cruisers in Chilean waters. Chile faced other threats: Peru and Bolivia might capitalize on any U.S. intervention to launch another war. Argentina, in the spirit of Hispanic fraternity, offered to provide Washington bases to facilitate an attack on Chile. Already weakened by the 1891 revolution, potentially threatened by Balmaceda's supporters, who yearned to overthrow the new administration, and without European allies, Chile could ill afford another war.

Recognizing this new reality, the Moneda retreated. In a face-saving statement it implicitly recognized Matta's blunder, admitted its failure to protect the *Baltimore*'s crew, and offered compensation to the victimized crewmen. While the Chilean response did not placate Harrison, it satisfied the chairmen of the Foreign Affairs Committees of the House and Senate, who accepted the Moneda's telegram as a full apology. Lacking congressional support to punish Chile more, Harrison agreed to arbitrate any additional claims. The *Baltimore* crisis had ended.

A series of mistakes almost brought the two nations to war. Since *The Nation* dismissed the *Baltimore* dispute as one precipitated by "an hysterical Harrison administration" trying to "satisfy an excited and ignorant population that their Government was not eating dirt," we can perhaps understand why the Chilean government initially seemed to underestimate the gravity of the situation.[38]

In some respects, the Moneda's failure to take seriously the U.S. posturing seemed understandable. Twice Chile's leaders had seen the United States back down: in 1866, when it refused to implement the Monroe Doctrine in order to prevent Spain from bombarding Valparaíso; and in 1882, when Washington retreated before Santa Maria's threats. But the situation had changed in the intervening decade. The U.S. Navy had grown so dramatically that one of its officers boasted that we "can reasonably expect that the successes of our former memorable sea wars will be repeated, even against so gallant a foe as Chili."[39] The Chileans did not realize that this time, unlike 1882, the dispute centered not on the annexation of territory but on the right of safe passage for U.S. citizens. The Moneda should have recognized the different circumstances: if in 1876, Chile had vigorously denounced Bolivia for maltreating its citizens, it expected the United States to react similarly when Chile failed to protect its uniformed servicemen.

Santiago had become a victim of its own mythology; it still believed Americans to be Anglo-Saxon barbarians. But even barbarians were not without feelings, and it should have expected that they too, once provoked, would react. The Americans, noted one Chilean statesman, "are very dangerous and it is necessary to treat them with formality and care. . . . For that reason, I believe the best policy toward them is to have the best possible relations, but always, with the strictest formality and maintaining possible cordiality." Still some Chileans admitted that the "conduct of Washington was not so rude as was then said, and behind the habitual peculiarities of its justice, function a diplomatic technique sufficiently courteous and tolerant—above all with the expressions of Matta—than it used in dealing with any other South American nation."[40]

Regardless, the *Baltimore* incident tainted Chilean-U.S. relations for decades. The situation degenerated to such a point that some Chileans fabricated the myth of Lieutenant Carlos Peña. The United States, the tale went, demanded that a Chilean warship should strike its colors as penance for the *Baltimore* incident. No Chilean sailor would perform this onerous duty until Lieutenant Peña struck his nation's flag and then, to atone for this act, committed suicide on his ship's deck. The story was apocryphal: there was no Lieutenant Peña, but it still illustrated Chile's attitudes toward the United States.[41]

Even after the settlement of the *Baltimore* claims—which cost some $75,000—Santiago still had to face a laundry list of U.S. financial claims against Chile. As a consequence of various revolutions, including those of the 1850s as well as the War of the Pacific, U.S. citizens claimed that they had suffered some $26,000,000 in damage to property. Some of these, like the North Claims—which involved a $6,000,000 dispute between U.S. railroad developers and Balmaceda—lacked much substance. (This, however, did not stop the U.S. citizens from enlisting Washington in their cause and forcing the Chilean government to pay $150,000.) A more expensive and infinitely more complex issue was that of the Alsop Claims. A Brazilian citizen had transferred his claims against the Bolivian government to a U.S. corporation, the Alsop Company. When Chile conquered the Atacama, it assumed responsibility for Bolivia's debts, including that of the Alsop.

In 1893 Chile agreed to establish a three-member arbitration committee to resolve the various economic claims. Much of the Chilean public resented this action. Indeed, the Chamber of Deputies forced the resignation of Minister of Foreign Relations Isidoro Errázuriz and his colleagues for acceding to the arbitration convention. Political differences also continued to plague U.S.-Chilean relations.

Egan's continued presence in Chile certainly polluted the diplomatic climate. In 1893, the U.S. minister granted sanctuary to Colonel Exequiel Fuentes and Anselmo Blanlot Holley, who, for the second time, had unsuccessfully tried to overthrow the Montt government. The new Cleveland administration proved less supportive than Harrison: Washington demanded that Egan pull in the welcome mat. But the envoy, arguing that expelling the two men would expose them to certain death, temporized, allowing Fuentes and Blanlot to escape. Despite his efforts, the police arrested Fuentes, but Blanlot, dressed as a woman, managed to evade capture. Egan, however, had gone too far, and the State Department ordered him to return home. Although the White House had sided with Montt, the incident did not encourage closer ties between the two countries. Chile, claiming economic constraints, rejected an invitation to join the Hampton Roads naval review. It also refused to participate in the Chicago World's Fair.[42]

Washington's rediscovery of the Monroe Doctrine would afford Chile additional opportunities to take other moral stands. The United States adopted a more aggressive foreign policy, protesting England's position in an 1895 dispute with Venezuela over the latter's border with British Guiana. Washington's new stance deeply displeased Chileans. A newspaper, *La Nueva República,* for example, questioned why, after years of ignoring the Monroe Doctrine, the "practical, selfish, and utilitarian" United States would become embroiled in Venezuela's boundary dispute with Great Britain; clearly there had to be an ulterior motive. Unable to find any moral imperative, some Chileans concluded, "we have more to fear from United States' protection than from European aggression."[43]

The Spanish-American War confirmed these apprehensions. *El Ferrocarril* denounced the conflict as part of a larger Anglo-Saxon, meaning U.S., plot, with the goal being "the absorption or conquest of Latin America."[44] Ironically, approximately thirty years after Spain had bombarded Valparaíso, and thirty-two months after Santiago's crowds almost physically attacked Madrid's legation to protest its Cuban policy, a bewildered U.S. minister Henry Lane Wilson noted that the Chileans had now become "strongly and overwhelmingly in sympathy with Spain."[45]

Officials from the United States had cause to fear more tangible expressions of local hostility. Wilson learned that local Spanish residents planned to sabotage the warships U.S.S. *Oregon* and U.S.S. *Marietta* when they put into Valparaíso. To ensure the *Oregon's* safety, Wilson secretly ordered it to refuel at Coronel, a port in Chile's south, and bypass Valparaíso. While wishing to avoid another *Maine* incident, Chilean authorities took special precaution to protect the *Marietta* from possible attack. The Moneda also rebuffed Spanish attempts to purchase its newly acquired cruiser *O'Higgins,* in part because it did not wish to alienate the United States and in part because it could ill afford to give up a ship needed to protect Chile from possible Argentine aggression.[46]

Santiago's preoccupation with the adjacent countries was not new. After 1891, the Moneda's international situation became increasingly precarious not just vis-à-vis the United States, whose presence distance tempered, but also its neighbors: Peru, Bolivia, and especially Argentina.

By 1900, Buenos Aires had emerged as a continental power. Its population dwarfed that of Chile; it could field an army of 8,000 and possessed a fleet with more modern ships than its neighbor to the east. The much stronger Argentine republic planned to use this force to address certain outstanding issues. Since the 1870s, the two nations disputed the location of their common border. Not only were some 90,000 square kilometers at stake, but also if the Argentine interpretation carried the day, Buenos Aires would win access to the Pacific Ocean.

Santiago could ill afford an armed confrontation with Buenos Aires. Even its generals admitted that the armed forces they commanded did not seem up to the struggle. Additionally, the Moneda still feared that Bolivia and Peru might join any potential conflict on the side of Argentina. Faced with such unpleasant possibility of a two-front war, the Moneda reluctantly went to the bargaining table.[47]

The 1902 agreement between Argentina and Chile, the *Pactos de Mayo,* theoretically settled the issue by accomplishing two goals. It stopped the arms race by restricting the size of Chile's and Argentina's navies, and it authorized the King of England to fix the boundary line between the two countries. Perhaps of more importance, the treaty divided Latin America into two spheres of influence, confining Argentina to the Atlantic seaboard and restricting Chile to the Pacific.

Nor did Santiago's control of South America's Pacific Coast go unquestioned. Bolivia and Peru had embarked upon expensive rearmament programs. By 1903, La Paz could field an army of almost 3,000 men, equipped with Krupp field guns. Peru, because of its naval power, once again posed a threat. Thus, Chile's geopolitical situation in 1900 uncomfortably resembled that of 1879: six million recently armed northern neighbors angrily eyed Chile while Argentina belligerently loitered in the background. Regrettably, each of these nations nurtured a grievance against

Chile. Bolivia, which still yearned to regain an outlet to the sea, had suspended but not ended its state of war with Chile; Peru still pined for the return of its lost provinces, Tacna and Arica; and Argentina insisted upon settling its boundary.

While Chile squabbled with its neighbors, Washington wisely sat on the sidelines. Eventually, despite the warnings of its minister to Santiago, the United States did become ensnared in Chile's dispute with Argentina over the Punta de Atacama. Covering some 80,000 square kilometers, the Punta de Atacama lay in the area captured by Chile during the War of the Pacific. Although Santiago controlled the Atacama, it did not possess legal title to the territory because Bolivia had never formally ceded it to Chile. Twice, in 1889 and in 1893, La Paz secretly, and doubtless not without some malice, transferred its interest in the Atacama to Argentina. Bolivia's conveyance accomplished two goals: La Paz acquired territory that it wanted in Tarija, and in the process it gave Argentina another reason to exasperate Chile.[48]

The two nations quarreled over this wretched piece of land to no avail. Finally, in 1899, after yet another war scare, Argentina and Chile submitted the issue to the judgment of William Buchanan, the U.S. minister to Buenos Aires. Following a prolonged series of arguments, Buchanan granted a majority of the territory to Argentina. Predictably, the envoy's decision angered many Chileans, who blamed it on Buchanan's pro-Argentine bias and "a colossal ignorance." This sense of outrage increased when Argentina requested that Chile pay a portion of the £20,000 fee that Buchanan submitted for serving as mediator. Paying Buchanan for despoiling the country, particularly since he had given the lion's share of the land to Argentina, clearly added insult to injury.[49]

Although Chileans resented Buchanan's decision, their hostility toward the United States slowly abated. The members of the elite *Club de la Union* feted the U.S. envoy, Henry Lane Wilson, as "a gentleman of the highest Anglo-Saxon type" and praised the nation he represented as one "to which we have always looked with kind regard and respect." Chile permitted the battleship *Iowa* to use its naval dry dock at Talcahuano and generously refused payment for these services. Some newspapers even described the U.S. occupation of Cuba as part of its mission to regenerate that benighted island. "Yankee influence, which some alarmed chauvinists attempt to present as a danger to America, cannot be, for progressive and liberal spirits, anything else but a healthy and beneficial influence since it will never be anything but a pacific and civilizing character."[50]

The Chileans recognized that Argentina or the increasingly bold Europe menaced Santiago and the hemisphere more than the United States. After all, it was Germany, not the United States, that bombarded Venezuela when it failed to pay its debts. Indeed, according to Wilson, Chileans "are learning rapidly in these days how closely their interests are identified with those of the United States, and how important it is that they should lend their moral and political support to the policy of our Government relative to South American republics."[51]

Henry Lane Wilson may have been correct when he observed that Chileans regarded the Monroe Doctrine and the Roosevelt Corollary more as a shield against European aggression than as an excuse to intervene. Their nation was stable, not some Central American banana republic perpetually wracked by internal unrest. Hence they could ignore Theodore Roosevelt's jingoist bombast because, as one newspaper noted, his statements "bode danger only to those republics that live in a complete state of anarchy and that are never at peace either internally or externally." Since Chile was one of the "well organized countries," it had nothing to fear.[52]

Chilean *amour-propre* suffered a blow when, in 1903, rioting erupted in Valparaíso. Some of the Chilean press worried that the United States might follow the British example and send its fleet to protect its interests. Minister Wilson, who called such action "hasty and ill considered," cautioned Washington to act with restraint. In a brilliant gesture that soothed Chilean sensitivities, he not only showed Chile's minister of foreign relations a copy of his telegram requesting Washington to keep its fleet in home port but also informed the Santiago press of his action. Washington, of course, had no reason to become distressed because the Valparaíso rioting did not seriously threaten U.S. interests. Regardless, Washington's inaction delighted the Chilean press, which praised the United States on its independence day in 1903.[53]

Thus, anti-American sentiment moderated. The Santiago daily *El Ferrocarril,* which earlier excoriated the United States, defended the U.S. desire to build the Panama Canal and a proposed Pan-American railroad, projects that, it claimed, would ultimately benefit Chile. It praised Washington's occupation of Panama, arguing that the White House's actions, which were in accord with international law, had forestalled European intervention. The Conservative paper *El Diario Ilustrado* ruefully admitted that Chile, by refusing to send a warship to help Colombia as it had in 1885, had betrayed its treaty obligations to Bogota, but it nonetheless found solace in the proposed economic benefits of the Panama Canal.[54]

Still, the U.S. seizure of the isthmus revolted some Chileans. One legislator denounced the Moneda's failure to defend Colombia and urged his colleagues to forge a Chilean-Brazilian-Argentina alliance to "defend their interests [against] the imperialist countries who seek their commercial welfare without stopping to think [about] . . . respecting the sovereignty of other nations."[55] Complaints such as these forced the Moneda to act carefully. Thus, while Chile's foreign minister verbally informed Wilson that he approved of U.S. intervention, neither he nor his government would do so publicly. Similarly, the Moneda, anxious to placate Colombia, hesitated before diplomatically recognizing the new Panamanian regime.[56]

Even prior to the Valparaíso riots and the occupation of Panama, Wilson informed the State Department that Chileans had learned that "their interests are identified with those of the United States, and how important it is that they should lend their moral and political support to the policy of our Government relative to South American republics."[57] Although he may have exaggerated, Chile and the United States did share a common purpose: protecting their territory.

This new mutuality of interests developed because of the rise of the Pan-American movement. Initially, Chileans feared this new diplomatic initiative because the principal architect was the much loathed James G. Blaine, "the representative and embodiment of a false and corrupt system of politics."[58] Quite logically, the Moneda feared that the same man who had tried to stop Chile from annexing territory during the War of the Pacific would now force it to return Tacna and Arica. Hence it balked at attending any meetings of the Pan-American nations.

When Blaine promised the Moneda that the proposed conference would not discuss the status of the lost provinces of Tacna and Arica, Santiago agreed to attend. The Plumed Knight from Maine, however, quickly discovered that he could not control the meeting's agenda: Argentina and Brazil used the conference first to denounce any nation that had used force to annex land and then demanded compulsory arbitration of all outstanding boundary problems. Since the proposal seemed to be directed at the victors of the Mexican-American War and the War of the Pacific (it generously ignored the 1870 Luso-Argentine dismemberment of Paraguay) it propelled Chile and the United States into a temporary, but heartfelt, alliance to oppose this proposal.

Ironically, it would be Blaine who preserved the fruits of Chile's earlier conflict. He managed to pass a proposal requiring arbitration, but on the condition that it could not be applied retroactively. Thus, since Chile had signed the Treaty of Ancón in 1883, it was safe. The Moneda's respite proved brief. At the 1902 Pan-American Conference the Peruvian, Bolivian, and Argentine delegates again sponsored a measure requiring the arbitration of any outstanding hemispheric disputes.[59] Mexico, which had earlier opposed compulsory arbitration, changed its stance, favoring a modified version. Happily for Chile, the United States, involved in a dispute with Mexico, joined Chile in rejecting the call for mandatory arbitration.

Eventually, Mexico withdrew its proposal. In its place, Ecuador, the United States, and Chile introduced a plan suggesting that member states accept the Hague Convention of 1899. This treaty established the Permanent Court of Appeals, which only upon the request of the interested parties would arbitrate international disputes. Thus, once again the United States and Chile acted in concert first to oppose compulsory arbitration and then to adopt the Calvo Doctrine—which stipulated that foreigners had to accept the jurisdiction of local courts in financial disputes.

Having settled its dispute with Argentina, Chile finally resolved its outstanding issues with Bolivia. Without a potential ally in Argentina, La Paz had to bite the bullet of territorial concessions. In a 1904 peace treaty, Bolivia formally ceded the Atacama to Chile. La Paz, however, was not supine. It demanded and won important concessions—concessions which, years earlier, Santiago would never have granted. Chile, for example, had to fund and construct for Bolivia a railroad connecting the port of Arica with La Paz. Bolivia not only could use this rail line, but La Paz could also charge import duty on goods entering the nation on the railroad. Fifteen years after its completion the rail line reverted to La Paz. In addition, Santiago had to pay La Paz a cash settlement plus guarantee its loans.

Pacifying Bolivia, however, proved easy in comparison to the dilemma facing the Moneda: resolving the Tacna and Arica dispute. The Treaty of Ancón had stipulated that an 1894 plebiscite would determine the ownership of the two provinces. In truth, Chile considered the Ancón agreement as anything but a face-saving device that permitted the hapless Iglesias to end the war. The Moneda, however, never intended to return either Tacna or Arica to Peru.

Unfortunately for Chile, Lima took the provisions of the Ancón agreement literally. It insisted that Santiago hold the plebiscite, something the Moneda would not do because the Peruvian population of the two provinces exceeded the Chilean. In order to coax the Chileans, Lima offered compromises, even suggesting a ploy that would allow Chile to retain Arica while Peru regained Tacna.

Rather than negotiate, the Chilean government tried a variety of tactics to perpetuate its control. Santiago encouraged Chileans, particularly veterans, to migrate to the area. It also attempted to limit, if not eradicate, Lima's influence by placing control of the local clergy under Santiago's ecclesiastical authority, deporting Peruvian priests, banning Peruvian newspapers and social clubs, and forbidding the commemoration of any of Peru's national holidays or the display of any symbols associated with that country. When "gentle persuasion" did not work, Chile used gangs of toughs to beat the more obdurate Peruvians into line.

Lima protested the Moneda's action. Sometimes it either limited or severed diplomatic contacts. In 1901, for example, Peru recalled its minister when a newspaper published secret documents revealing the Moneda's blueprint to "Chileanize" Tacna and Arica. Simply breaking diplomatic relations could not convince Santiago to change its policies. Peru did try a different approach. It hired a French mission to train its army and purchased equipment for its army and navy. Developing a military option to pressure Chile, however, would take time and time was what worked against Lima's interests.

Since the *Pactos de Mayo* effectively deprived Peru of an important ally, Lima turned north to the United States for support. Anxious to win U.S. support for a plebiscite, Peru tried to seduce Washington into becoming its advocate by offering the U.S. fleet a coaling station at Chimbote; it also hinted that it might buy warships from the United States. Some Peruvians even suggested that their nation become a U.S. protectorate. Much as the U.S. fleet might have coveted the coaling facility, Washington did not take up Lima's offer.[60]

By 1905, relations between Chile and the United States seemed more cordial than before. The U.S. fleet once again put in for liberty at Valparaíso, where it was warmly welcomed. This time the authorities were prepared to avoid problems. When the crews, with "three months' pay to spend and three months' suppressed energy to be given an outlet," became unruly, their commander immediately ordered the sailors back to their ships.[61] There would not be another Lieutenant Peña to bedevil the United States and Chile.

Chileans might dislike the Monroe Doctrine, but newspapers such as *El Mercurio* increasingly saw it as a "guarantee [of] the territorial integrity of the American Republics against the pretensions of the great powers." Rather than oppose reflexively all U.S. initiatives, the journal suggested that Chile turn to the United States for capital to develop its natural resources and instruction on how to organize its public services.[62] As the nitrate industry gyrated, Chileans argued that the country develop alternatives, and hence they called for the *gringos,* among others, to develop its copper resources. Later, of course, they would bemoan this fact, but at the time they welcomed the investment and praised the U.S. businessman as a humane employer and a harbinger of progress.[63]

By 1905, Chile's relations with the United States had improved dramatically. In part this change resulted from a confluence of mutual interests: neither Washington nor Santiago wanted to give up the land it had annexed. In part it resulted because of Chile's increased vulnerability. After 1900, the Moneda came close to being friendless in South America. Not merely Peru, Bolivia, and Argentina but also its former ally, Brazil, opposed Santiago's "conquest policy"; even Ecuador seemed on the verge of joining this emerging anti-Chilean coalition.

Given this estrangement, Chile had to mend fences with Washington for fear that an alienated Washington would deepen its isolation or, worse, that it would precipitate U.S. involvement in resolving the status of Tacna-Arica.[64] The United States, whatever its many faults, at least did not covet Chilean territory. Thus, the Moneda tolerated, and even appeared to accept, Washington's Big Stick, its intervention in Panama, and its involvement in the British-Venezuelan boundary dispute. The arrangement was not a happy one. As Chile's Foreign Minister noted, "we have been very far from accepting United States' policy . . . and only a sense of discretion has limited us to a silent protest."[65] Nevertheless, the arrangement did introduce a period of calm into what had been a stormy relationship.

In a sense, geopolitical realities had caught up with Chile. It was a small country that, thanks to its ability to ensure domestic order and to exploit its resource base, became the first Latin American nation to enjoy a degree of political stability. Thus, while its larger neighbors wallowed in domestic chaos, Chile prospered. The United States might have constituted a menace, but it was so far from Santiago that the threat seemed ineffable.

Chile's time as hemispheric power proved limited. Once the other Latin American nations also began to enjoy peace, they too progressed and eventually surpassed Santiago. Unfortunately, the steamship, economic competition, and U.S. and Chilean imperial impulses brought the two countries into unhappy proximity just as Santiago's enemies became more bold. Chile, facing the more proximate threat from its immediate neighbors, had to pacify Washington, and thus, however unhappily, it recognized the U.S. preponderance.

9

BRAZIL

On the Periphery I

Joseph Smith

B Y THE MIDDLE OF THE NINETEENTH CENTURY diplomatic relations between the United States and Brazil were mostly concerned with transacting routine commercial and consular business. The modest relationship reflected Brazil's lack of strategic significance and the fact that the activities of such faraway countries rarely impinged upon the U.S. consciousness.[1] Nevertheless, Brazil was not completely unknown to people in the United States. Indeed, a positive image generally existed of the one Latin American country whose huge territorial extent and reportedly abundant natural resources invited direct comparison with the United States. "Brazil is, next to ourselves, the great power on the American continent," stated the U.S. minister to Brazil, James Watson Webb, in 1867.[2] In terms of actual size and potential some U.S. writers ranked Brazil ahead even of the United States. According to a best-selling travel account by the Protestant clergymen Daniel F. Kidder and James C. Fletcher, Brazil "embraces a greater territorial dominion than any other country of the New World, together with natural advantages second to none on the globe."[3]

Kidder and Fletcher urged U.S. businessmen to seize the immense commercial opportunities presented by Brazil. This was hardly a new idea, but the authors believed that the economic climate of the 1850s was particularly propitious. The 1857 edition of their book included a statistical appendix emphasizing that Brazil had not only become the most prosperous country in South America but also represented "the largest and the last undeveloped field of trade now left open to the industry and enterprise of man."[4] Although Kidder and Fletcher thought primarily in terms of U.S. merchants seeking business in the established and rapidly growing cities of Rio and São Paulo, the most exciting economic "frontier," potentially a "new Texas," was farther away to the north in the vast Amazon region.[5] The marvels of the River Amazon had been revealed to the U.S. public in 1853 by the report of an exploratory geographical survey undertaken on behalf of the Department of the Navy by Lieutenants William L. Herndon and Lardner Gibbon. The findings endorsed the promotional activities of Herndon's brother-in-law, Lieutenant Matthew Fontaine Maury, who was energetically engaged in writing articles and organizing public meetings in the southern United States designed to arouse U.S. commercial interest in the region. Maury glowingly predicted that the area was so fertile that it was "capable of supporting with its produce the population of the whole world."[6]

The U.S. public was also informed by the contemporary travel literature that Brazil was "different" from the Spanish-American nations. This was a reference to the fact that Brazil was a monarchy and its people were Portuguese-speaking. The feature that most impressed U.S. travelers, however, was that, in marked contrast to its neighbors, Brazil was a model of political stability and respectability. Kidder and Fletcher attributed this to the skill of Emperor Pedro II, who had ruled since 1840 and had become greatly admired not just in Brazil but throughout the world. It was unusual for U.S. citizens to praise a monarchical system, but they readily acknowledged its suitability for Brazil. In 1866 Professor Louis Agassiz of Harvard University visited the country and concluded that Brazilians were fortunate to be ruled by "a sovereign as enlightened as he is humane."[7]

Agassiz had been drawn to Brazil by his professional interest in exotic flora and fauna. The travel account compiled by his wife and published in 1868 confirmed the popular image of Brazil as a tropical paradise. Another contemporary U.S. traveler, Thomas Ewbank, engagingly described the country as "the land of the cocoa and the palm"[8] whose inhabitants were gentle, courteous, and hospitable. Such colorful portraits of Brazil were undermined, however, by reports of negative experiences. For example, the sheer size of Brazil was considered to be a liability rather than an advantage. Beyond the capital city of Rio de Janeiro, the rest of the country was perceived as an enormous and intimidating wilderness. Large areas were unmapped and virtually inaccessible. Agassiz observed that even Brazilians knew little about the geography of their country. He warned that a journey into the interior was "no light task" and required "a vast deal of forethought."[9]

An additional hazard both for inhabitants and for visitors was the reputedly unhealthy climate and the constant dread of infectious diseases such as malaria, smallpox, typhus, cholera, and especially yellow fever. The latter was transmitted from Africa in 1849, and epidemics had become a regular occurrence. In Rio alone it was estimated that yellow fever had claimed more than 50,000 lives by the end of the century. Visitors from the United States often attributed the spread of disease to low standards of hygiene. A typical impression was recorded by William E. Curtis, who briefly visited Rio in 1885 as the secretary of the Latin American trade commission. Approaching Rio by sea, he viewed the city as "a fragment of fairyland," but "the illusion is instantly dispelled upon landing, for the streets are narrow, damp, dirty, reeking with repulsive odors, and filled with vermin-covered beggars and wolfish-looking dogs."[10]

It was hardly surprising therefore that relatively few U.S. citizens traveled to Brazil during the nineteenth century. These included mainly individual explorers, geographers, entrepreneurs, and Protestant missionaries attracted to the tropics by scientific curiosity, an appetite for exotic adventure, and a desire to spread the Gospel. With the exception of a few thousand Confederate exiles who settled in São Paulo immediately after the Civil War, organized emigration from the United States was unknown. The Confederate scheme began auspiciously, but the Anglo-Saxon Protestant newcomers found it hard to relate to a society with a Latin and Catholic culture. It was also perplexing to discover that social conventions between whites and blacks were less restrictive than in the United States. Moreover, whereas Brazilians were hospitable to travelers, they generally manifested a suspicious and unfriendly attitude to foreign settlers. Consequently, the Confederate settlements soon fragmented, and their well-publicized failure virtually terminated U.S. interest in immigrating to Brazil. In 1888 rumors of an attempt to organize a similar venture prompted Secretary of State Thomas Bayard to discourage the participants by reminding them of "the unfortunate results attending the emigration of citizens of some of the Southern States to Brazil in 1865."[11]

Commercial Relations

The most frequent and enduring contact between U.S. citizens and Brazilians was through trade. Attracted by the economic potential of Brazil, U.S. merchants had energetically entered the Brazilian market when it was legally opened to foreigners during the early nineteenth century. Despite high initial expectations, the resulting trade turned out to be very modest. The economic reality was that both countries were primarily agrarian economies that produced similar products and had therefore little to sell to each other. From the beginning of the nineteenth century the actual balance of trade was invariably in Brazil's favor. Merchants from the United States imported sugar, cocoa, and tobacco from northeastern Brazil, coffee from Rio and especially São Paulo, and hides from the Plate region. Brazilians bought dairy products from New England and flour milled from the winter wheat of Maryland and Virginia and shipped via Baltimore. During the 1830s annual trade amounted to less than $10 million and rose to $25 million by 1860. These figures represented no more than 3 to 4 percent of total U.S. trade. Nevertheless, a reasonably profitable commercial relationship was established in which Brazil ranked along with Cuba and Mexico as one of the largest trading partners of the United States in Latin America.

European countries, however, dominated the export trade to Brazil. Indeed, U.S. merchants were particularly envious and critical of the powerful influence exercised by Britain in all aspects of Brazilian commercial activity. For most of the nineteenth century, however, they could do little to upset the British economic preeminence, which rested not so much on Britain's capacity to extract unfair commercial advantages but on the ability of "the workshop of the world" to supply, transport, and offer credit facilities for the manufactured goods Brazilians wanted. By contrast, U.S. companies were notoriously deficient in providing shipping services and credit to finance trade. In the earlier age of sail power, "Yankee" clippers had been more than a match for any European rivals, but U.S. shippers were reluctant to adapt to the introduction of steam power. The resulting lack of direct steamship lines between the United States and Brazil meant that both passengers and freight usually had to travel between the two countries via a European port. Kidder and Fletcher described communications with Brazil as "exceedingly difficult" and lamented that Britain "is reaping golden harvests" while "our Government and our merchants, notwithstanding their boasted enterprise, have done next to nothing to foster trade with Brazil."[12]

Conducting business in Brazil was not so straightforward as Kidder and Fletcher implied. For the small number of U.S. merchants who were willing to try, there were many practical difficulties. A pertinent example was provided in 1866 by John Codman, who took his steamer to ply the coastal trade of southern Brazil. Not only was the market many times smaller than Codman had been led to expect, but also he was constantly infuriated by the attitude of local officials. In attempting to transport a cargo, his goods would be subject to numerous official inspections, and he might be required to fill out several documents—in one transaction he completed ninety-six separate forms in one day! The "vexatious impediments" to trade quickly persuaded Codman to abandon his Brazilian enterprise and to conclude that the accepted standard reference work on Brazil by Kidder and Fletcher had been written "through glasses of couleur de rose."[13]

Although U.S. merchants complained of frustrating difficulties in exporting to Brazil, Brazilian sales to the United States encountered far fewer obstacles. Quite simply, the United States was becoming a nation of coffee drinkers who showed a clear preference for the good quality and mild flavors of Brazilian coffee. From the middle of the nineteenth century onward shipments of coffee steadily increased from Brazil to the United States, but the pattern of trade in the other direction was markedly different as there was no similar lucrative item that Brazilians desired in return. The result was a further widening of the trade balance in Brazil's favor to more than $20 million annually during the 1860s and 1870s. Businessmen from the United States and their political allies argued that Brazil should redress the imbalance by granting tariff concessions to U.S. goods. "We are her best customer and friend," affirmed Lieutenant Maury in 1853, and he called upon Brazil to show "her appreciation of this patronage and friendship by some sign or token at least that she too would be liberal in her policy."[14]

In matters relating to customs duties and commercial regulations, U.S. merchants looked to the diplomatic and consular officials of the State Department for assistance. A trade treaty negotiated in 1828 had defined the rights of U.S. merchants, but its provisions had lapsed in 1841. It was official U.S. policy to negotiate a new commercial agreement, but the Brazilian government was unwilling to comply. This did not signify any particular hostility toward the United States because a similar attitude was shown by Brazil toward Britain, whose commercial advantages gained by treaty in 1810 were not renewed in 1844. From that year onward a wide range of foreign imports were subject to rates of duty, rising to as much as 60 percent. In fact, higher duties brought increased revenue and made the Brazilian government resistant to concluding trade treaties containing tariff reductions.

Although this was irritating to U.S. officials, it was not particularly detrimental to commerce because U.S. goods were placed on an equal footing with those of Britain and other nations competing in the Brazilian market. Nevertheless, a succession of U.S. ministers in Rio continued to point out that the United States was Brazil's best customer and that this entitled U.S. goods to preferential tariff treatment. The appeal to Brazil's sense of commercial justice was often accompanied by hints of an imminent increase in the U.S. tariff on coffee. A duty on imports of coffee had been originally introduced in 1862 as part of an emergency measure to raise revenue for the Union during the Civil War. After 1865 there was domestic political pressure in the United States to reduce if not abolish the duty, but U.S. officials saw the ability to alter the rate of duty as a valuable bargaining tool in commercial negotiations with Brazil. The U.S. minister, James Partridge, believed that a commercial "understanding" could be reached "easily" if the duty was reduced. This strategy, however, was crucially undermined by the decision taken unilaterally by Congress in 1872 to make coffee imports free of duty without requiring anything in return. It would not be the first time during the "gilded age" that diplomatic considerations would be subordinated to the complexities of the tariff question. "We acted with undue liberality," regrettably summed up Partridge.[15]

Diplomatic Relations

Officials from the United States in Brazil often hindered rather than helped the promotion of trade by assuming a superior and forceful approach in their personal dealings with the Brazilian foreign office. Invariably appointed for political reasons in accordance with the dictates of "spoils politics," they lacked diplomatic or consular experience and rarely possessed either a knowledge of Portuguese or an acquaintance with Brazilian affairs. The most notorious example during the second half of the nineteenth century was James Watson Webb, who did not disguise his personal disappointment at being offered a posting to Brazil in 1861. On his arrival at Rio, Webb freely admitted that he had no knowledge of Portuguese and had no desire to learn. It was a foretaste of the insensitive and controversial style that would characterize his stay in Brazil.

The Brazilian government demonstrated, however, that it could resist and even retaliate against foreign diplomatic pressure. For example, Brazil steadfastly refused U.S. requests to open the River Amazon to foreign trade. Although Lieutenant Maury emphasized that he advocated a "policy of commerce" and not "the policy of conquest," his lobbying activities aroused concern in Brazil that a filibustering expedition to seize the region was being prepared in the United States. In a series of well-publicized letters Maury roundly condemned what he described as Brazil's "Japanese spirit." He warned, "It may well be imagined that the miserable policy by which Brazil has kept shut up, and is continuing to keep shut up, from man's—from Christian, civilized, enlightened man's use the fairest portion of God's earth, will be considered by the American people as a nuisance, not to say an outrage."[16]

Ironically, the activities of Maury, Herndon, and Gibbon had stimulated Brazilian awareness of the commercial possibilities of the Amazon. But nationalist sensitivity prevailed over financial consideration. Any immediate prospect of the river being opened to foreign shipping was effectively eliminated by what Kidder and Fletcher described as Maury's "offensive language."[17] Indeed, the tactic of issuing threats invariably proved counterproductive and only provoked latent Brazilian fears of "Yankee imperialism." The result was a vigorous declaration of Brazil's sovereignty over the Amazon region, resulting in the closure of the river to foreign shipping until 1867. The political furor created by Maury also adversely affected U.S. commercial interests in Brazil. Kidder and Fletcher believed that it was responsible for Brazilian reluctance to discuss a new commercial agreement with the United States.

Brazil's independent spirit and latitude of diplomatic maneuver was further underlined in 1861 by its declaration of neutrality in the U.S. Civil War. Like the European governments, Brazil granted belligerent rights to the Confederate states. Consequently, Confederate ships were able to enter Brazilian ports to refit and take on supplies. The Lincoln administration was annoyed but did not regard the Brazilian government as unfriendly. In fact, Emperor Pedro II privately expressed his wish that the Union would be victorious. Therefore U.S. diplomacy was more concerned with European infractions of maritime neutrality and paid little attention to Brazil. The appropriate diplomatic protests, however, were made by the State Department whenever Confederate ships entered Brazilian ports. In one instance in October 1864, Brazil's sovereign rights were infringed when a U.S. warship, the *Wachusett,* captured the Confederate cruiser *Florida* at dock in Salvador da Bahia and towed the vessel from the port. The incident was a sobering demonstration to Brazilians of how the United States could project its superior naval power with virtual impunity in Latin American waters. Nevertheless, the Brazilian government resolutely declared that the national flag had been insulted and demanded that the United States make an official apology. Secretary of State Seward was conciliatory and explained that the naval action had been unauthorized. But Brazilians were unhappy that the *Florida* had been sunk en route to Hampton Roads, Virginia, and could not be returned. Anti-American feeling was also aroused over the long delay in firing a naval gun salute to honor the Brazilian flag at Salvador da Bahia. This was promised by Seward at the beginning of 1865 but was not carried out until July 1866.

Seward was not motivated by any desire to annoy Brazil. In reality he was preoccupied with other hemispheric issues relating to European intervention in Mexico and his own schemes to purchase Alaska and to conclude an isthmian canal treaty. Despite his "expansionist" image, Seward sought to prevent the United States from becoming diplomatically entangled in South American controversies such as the War of the Triple Alliance, in which Argentina, Brazil, and Uruguay fought against Paraguay from 1865 to 1870. This contrasted with his minister-on-the-spot James Watson Webb, who was fearful of European diplomatic meddling in the war and proposed U.S. mediation to bring the belligerents together to discuss peace. "We should impress all the American governments with a conviction that it is alike their interest and their duty to look to the United States for protection and advice," affirmed Webb.[18] But Seward was more circumspect. He believed that the United States should not interfere unless formally requested to do so by the belligerents. "It is not within the province of the United States," he informed Webb, "to pronounce an opinion upon either the original merits of the war, or upon the wisdom or necessity of its longer continuance."[19]

Seward's diplomacy indicated that Brazilian affairs had marginal strategic significance for the United States. In fact, aside from a modest trading relationship, U.S. citizens had relatively little contact with Brazil during the period from 1850 to 1875. The barriers of language and geographical distance ensured that both nations were culturally and physically kept apart from each other. For Brazilians, the "Old World" of Portugal, France, and Britain remained their exemplar and spiritual home. Nevertheless, as communications improved throughout the second half of the nineteenth century, Brazilians became more aware of the existence and achievements of the United States. They were particularly impressed by that country's dynamic economic growth and technological advances. Foremost among Brazilians who desired to know more about the United States was Emperor Pedro II. The centennial celebrations planned for 1876 gave him an opportunity to make a personal visit.

Emperor Pedro II landed at New York in April 1876 and stimulated a wave of public interest both in himself and in the country that he represented. Although the emperor was officially received at the White House by President Grant, he characteristically displayed disarming modesty by requesting that state formalities be reduced to an absolute minimum. The main purpose of the visit was to attend the centennial exhibition at Philadelphia and afterward to travel by railroad across the length and breadth of the United States. Unaccustomed to Brazilian visitors and even less accustomed to royalty, the U.S. public was intrigued and impressed by the tall, fair-complexioned and blue-eyed Dom Pedro, who appeared in a plain black suit rather than ornate imperial regalia. He could also speak and understand English and was genuinely delighted and fascinated to be visiting the United States. Although bemused by the king's personal appearance, observers in the United States resolved the puzzle by calling him "Our Yankee Emperor" and considering him like themselves. As Agassiz had remarked a decade earlier, Brazilians were regarded as fortunate to have such an enlightened and dignified ruler.

Dom Pedro came to the United States primarily to indulge his personal passion for scientific discovery and foreign travel. Political motivation was lacking. He did allude, however, to the desirability of closer commercial ties between the two countries. In the United States the emperor had a meeting with the entrepreneur John Roach, who was a leading advocate of the need for regular steamship service between New York and Rio. Roach sought to take advantage of the favorable publicity arising from Dom Pedro's visit. In order to finance his own fledgling steamship line and to compete against well-established European competitors, he lobbied Congress for subsidies to carry the U.S. mail to Brazil. The issue of steamship communication, however, was just as politically controversial in the late 1870s as it had been some two decades earlier. After considerable debate in Congress, Roach's proposals were eventually defeated in 1879. The most determined opposition arose from the merchants of Baltimore, who traditionally controlled the import-export business with Brazil and were determined to prevent trade passing to rival East Coast ports such as New York. Moreover, the fact that Roach received Republican backing prompted the Democrats to seize upon the issue for partisan political advantage. The desire to improve shipping links with Brazil was denounced as a ruse to plunder the public purse. "The American people," remarked James Blount, the Democratic congressman from Georgia, "have been cheated and deceived and millions have been taken out of the treasury under the false delusion of aid to American commerce."[20] Without government subsidies, however, U.S. shipping lines could not compete with their bigger and more efficient European rivals. Roach struggled on and eventually formed the United States and Brazil Steamship Company (USBSC) in 1882. His lack of success was appropriately reflected in the nickname given to the company: the "Unusually Slow and Badly Managed Steamship Company."[21]

One of Roach's favorite arguments was that U.S. exports would benefit from regular steamship communication with Brazil because "trade follows the flag"; this innovation would significantly reverse the long-standing imbalance of trade between the two countries. But Roach did not adequately address the question of what exactly would be sold to Brazil. Furthermore, his optimism could not hide the fact that the economic fundamentals of the 1850s were still in place thirty years later. Consul-General Christopher Andrews explained that the Brazilian market remained as limited as ever: "Though a field of much attention and enterprise, she [Brazil] has not the capacity for that rapid commercial development which her resources would at first seem to indicate. Her situation is not favorable for the rapid accumulation of wealth. With a population of some 13 million scattered over a region nearly as large as the United States, her territorial extent is a source of weakness. Her resources, though undoubtedly imposing and calculated to ensure for her an important future, are yet inferior to what is commonly supposed."[22]

It was also debatable to what extent U.S. interests were sincerely concerned over the trade deficit with Brazil. "If the trade relations between the two countries are badly balanced," remarked a British diplomat, "the Americans are in great measure to blame." In his opinion, U.S. merchants needed "to establish commercial houses in this country, manufacture expressly for Brazil, introduce capital, etc."[23] But such advice had long gone unheeded. In 1879 the U.S. chargé d'affaires at Rio, John White, deplored the lack of U.S. businessmen in Rio and remarked that "foreigners and foreign capital control the trade of this country."[24] Only a few years later, in 1885, William Curtis similarly reported the absence of his fellow countrymen in the local business community. Yet U.S. officials were not entirely free of blame for the lack of commercial presence. The members of the Latin American trade commission spent only a few days in Rio in June 1885. After reading their official report and its brief mention of Brazil, the U.S. chargé d'affaires at Rio, Charles Trail, concluded that "one is led to infer that Brazil is the least important of all the countries in this Hemisphere south of the Equator."[25]

Whatever its deficiencies, the actual dispatch of a trade commission to tour Latin America was a remarkable event and indicated that the United States was attaching a new importance to developing commercial links with its hemispheric neighbors. The policy was particularly associated with Republican politicians, notably James G. Blaine, and became increasingly a subject of U.S. political debate during the 1880s. Most attention was directed to Mexico and the nations of Central America and the Caribbean. As usual the more distant countries such as Brazil were generally neglected. From 1887 onward, however, Brazil became an integral element of U.S. commercial diplomacy. Surprisingly, the initiative came from the Democrats rather than the Republicans. As part of his electoral strategy to win reelection in 1888, President Grover Cleveland decided to stress the promotion of U.S. overseas commerce. The inclusion of Brazil in his plans was revealed in a private interview with the Brazilian consul-general at New York, Salvador de Mendonça. After praising Brazil as the most important nation of South America, Cleveland suggested the formation of a customs union or German *zollverein* between the two countries.[26] The president's proposal was studiously vague, but he wished it to be communicated to Rio.

For more than thirty years the U.S. legation at Rio had frequently raised the question of concluding a new commercial treaty between the two countries. The Brazilian government had steadfastly resisted entering into substantive discussions for a variety of reasons ranging from a reluctance to give up valuable customs revenue to a concern over the reaction of local merchants and foreign interests to preferential advantages being granted to their U.S. competitors. In 1887, however, the whole question acquired a new significance as a result of the unexpected intervention of the U.S. president and his singling out Brazil for special consideration. Brazilian officials viewed Cleveland's initiative as a reflection of the growing economic and political power of the United States. Cultivating closer links was not only sensible but would also offset Brazil's dependence on the great European powers. Moreover, it would boost sugar exports and thereby reverse the worrying decline of the Brazilian sugar industry. A confluence of interests was taking place. For the first time since the signing of the original trade treaty in 1828, both the Brazilian and U.S. governments wanted to conclude a formal commercial treaty. "Altogether, it seems to me," noted the U.S. consul-general at Rio in late 1888, "that we now have an opportunity such as seldom occurs for extending our trade."[27]

While Brazilian officials pondered their course of action, Cleveland was defeated by Benjamin Harrison in the 1888 presidential election. The Republican victory did not, however, signify a reversal of U.S. policy. Although no specific reference to Brazil was made during the campaign, both candidates endorsed the desirability of increased commercial contact between the United States and all the countries of Latin America. This was confirmed in their respective party political platforms and by the wide degree of bipartisan congressional support given earlier in the year for the president to organize a Pan-American conference. The meeting was scheduled to assemble at Washington in October 1889.

The Brazilian government saw the conference as a convenient opportunity to send a delegation empowered to enter into formal discussions on a bilateral commercial treaty. Cleveland's electoral defeat meant, however, that the Brazilian delegates would have to deal with the newly elected Harrison administration, in which James G. Blaine was secretary of state. In fact, Blaine's appointment was considered advantageous to Brazil because he had been an active supporter of John Roach and had once written that "Brazil holds in the South much the same relationship to the other countries that the United States does in the North." The Brazilian chargé d'affaires in Washington reported Blaine's cordial attitude and hinted that he was disposed to make commercial concessions.[28]

Recognition of the Brazilian Republic

The Pan-American Conference convened briefly in Washington at the beginning of October 1889 and then adjourned to allow the delegates to be taken on a deluxe railroad tour of the United States. Just before the resumption of the conference the sensational news arrived from Rio that a military coup had overthrown the Brazilian empire on 15 November. Suddenly Brazil was front-page news in the United States, and attention was focused on the question of when the United States would recognize the provisional government of the new republic. Recognition was quickly forthcoming from Uruguay and Argentina, and most of the other Latin American countries followed suit in December. The United States, however, adopted a cautious and legalistic response and acted in the style of a European rather than a Latin American government. A recurring problem that U.S. officials faced in dealing with remote countries like Brazil was their slight personal knowledge of the countries and lack of up-to-date information on conditions. Moreover, even experienced diplomats were genuinely astounded by the events of November 1889. The U.S. minister in Rio, Robert Adams, viewed the revolution as "the most remarkable ever recorded in history."[29] He reported reassuringly that no U.S. lives or property were in danger. Convinced that the imperial era was definitely over, Adams wished to establish official relations immediately. But the dictates of diplomatic procedure and propriety persuaded his superiors at the State Department to act with caution. While maintaining friendly relations with the new rulers of Brazil, the Harrison administration decided to withhold official recognition until such time as its minister in Rio reported sufficient evidence of popular support for the regime.

The delay was especially puzzling because U.S. politicians and press opinion clearly welcomed what was regarded as a signal victory for republicanism in the "New World." "Nothing so grand or so excellent has ever been achieved in the history of any nation," declared Senator John T. Morgan of Alabama.[30] But U.S. delight was moderated by the existence of genuine sympathy and sadness for the much-admired Dom Pedro. News reaching the United States from Brazil only reaffirmed the exceptional qualities of the "Yankee Emperor." It was reported in detail how he had peacefully and unselfishly yielded to the ultimatum presented by the leader of the coup, Marshal Deodoro da Fonseca, that he and the imperial family leave immediately for exile in France.

Moreover, the conservative instincts of U.S. politicians were alarmed at the overthrow of a symbol of authority and stability by military violence. This was underlined in the Senate on 20 December, when a resolution calling for recognition of the new republic was defeated. Democratic senators urged that Congress should welcome "this new sister into the family of republics." Further hesitation would only encourage "despotic" influences to plan a restoration of the monarchy. But Republican senators argued that caution was necessary. Senator John Sherman of Ohio acknowledged the coup as "one of the greatest events in our times," but he also regretted Dom Pedro's deposition. The majority of his Republican colleagues shared this feeling and voted that recognition be delayed to soften the blow to the old emperor. Indeed, without Dom Pedro Brazil was no longer seen in U.S. eyes as so special or even different from the politically turbulent Spanish-American countries. Considerable disquiet was also expressed in the Senate over the exact nature of the new regime. It was known that the coup had been engineered by army officers and that the provincial government had already interfered with freedom of the press. Senator Edward Teller of Colorado critically observed, "We have had in the past some experience with republics in South America that were republics only in name, unworthy even of the name of republic, and that brought disgrace upon republican government the world over. We do not want to make that mistake. Whenever the people of Brazil say that there is a republican government in that country, then we are for Brazil."[31]

With the exception of the *New York World*, which consistently praised the new Brazilian government, the New York press mirrored the wary attitude shown by the Senate. "What at present confronts us in Brazil," declared the *New York Sun*, "is a military dictatorship."[32] The *New York Times* argued that "our indorsement" would be given "an undue cheapness by tossing it to the first claimants" and recommended that U.S. recognition should not be accorded "until it has been shown by experience that the Brazilian Government is a responsible one, and can perform its part in any agreement that may be made with it."[33] Such U.S. apprehensions were further confirmed by the continuance of unsettled political conditions in Brazil and the declaration of a state of siege at the close of 1889. "The Republican leaders are finding," observed the *New York Times*, "that it is not so simple a matter to overturn an empire and establish a settled Government in its place as their easy success first seemed to indicate."[34]

The attitude of the United States was a matter of concern to the provisional government in Brazil because it regarded U.S. recognition as a useful means of strengthening its domestic authority. Moreover, Foreign Minister Quintino Bocaiúva knew the United States from personal experience and was particularly eager to cultivate close relations. The policy was ably supported and greatly facilitated by the newly appointed Brazilian minister in Washington, Salvador de Mendonça, who had served for almost fifteen years as Brazil's consul-general in New York. Salvador was married to a U.S. citizen and was already an established and popular figure in Washington society. Moreover, his personal access to U.S. political leaders was most unusual for a Latin American diplomat, many of whom tended to be either ignored or treated with condescension. Most notably, Salvador was able to cultivate a close working relationship with Secretary of State Blaine.

The question of U.S. recognition, however, was complicated by Republican party politics, in particular Blaine's own presidential ambitions. Salvador believed that Blaine was hesitant to recognize the new government for fear of annoying prominent Republicans such as Senator Sherman. Throughout January 1890 Salvador campaigned persistently, either by means of personal interviews or through the use of his Republican friends as intermediaries, to convince the secretary of state that speedy recognition was vital if the republic was to survive. Seeking to exploit Blaine's well-known antipathy toward Europe, Salvador raised the specter of Old World intrigue. The Brazilian minister argued that the present state of uncertainty in Brazil only encouraged European thoughts of interference, although, with somewhat inverted logic, he also declared that the European powers were awaiting U.S. action and would not themselves recognize the republic until the United States had done so.

One weekend toward the close of January, Blaine's hesitation was suddenly overcome, and he called Salvador to his office to tell him that U.S. recognition was approved. The reasons for Blaine's action are unknown, but the whole episode was characteristic in that it reflected his swings of behavior between vacillation and impulsiveness. No embarrassment was shown over the apparent contradiction with the administration's earlier policy of allowing its minister in Brazil to judge the correct moment to recognize. In fact, the decision was taken without the knowledge of Adams, who, according to British reports, was "much hurt" especially since he had only very recently denied that such a step was being contemplated by his government.[35] The decision was made so casually and unexpectedly that the U.S.-owned weekly, the *Rio News,* was unprepared for the news and initially doubted its accuracy: "Had the United States taken so important a step as to officially recognize a republic . . . it is certain that the Legation here would have been at once advised to that effect. . . . But no such message has been received, nor even the slightest intimation that such a policy was under consideration."[36] Adams confided to his British colleague that it was a mistake to recognize a regime that had regrettably deteriorated into a "military dictatorship."[37] Under the circumstances his position became untenable, with the result that he felt compelled to resign and leave his post in March 1890.

The shabby treatment of Adams underlined how little influence U.S. ministers in Brazil exercised upon their own government's policy. But there were no damaging repercussions. In fact, the formal decision to recognize attracted little notice in the United States, and Congress gave its approval without dissent in February. It was considered that a sufficient interval had elapsed as a mark of respect to Dom

Pedro and, if the United States had acted ahead of the European governments, so much the better. Some apprehension still lingered that a military dictatorship was being imposed upon Brazil. This concern, however, was greatly diminished during the summer of 1890, when it was reported that a new Brazilian constitution had been drafted. In fact, U.S. political observers were flattered to discover that it rejected the European parliamentary system and proposed a federal government openly modeled on that of the United States. The *New York Daily Tribune* called it "the best possible augury for the future of the country," whereas the *New York Times* predicted that "the future of the republic is regarded as most encouraging."[38] These articles, however, were merely minor items of political news. After the drama of the 1889 coup, the U.S. public quickly lost interest in Brazilian affairs. At the official level, however, serious discussions were in progress between U.S. and Brazilian diplomats designed to expand the commercial relationship between the two countries.

Reciprocity

The question of trade had been high on the agenda of the Pan-American Conference, which continued meeting in Washington until April 1890. Although the U.S. proposal of a *zollverein* found little favor among the Latin American delegates, the conference did ultimately approve the idea of negotiating commercial treaties. In fact, preliminary discussions designed to produce just such a treaty had actually commenced between Blaine and Salvador de Mendonça independently of the Pan-American Conference. But these talks were suspended in February 1890 when the whole question became entangled with the Republican party's domestic political priority of preparing a new congressional tariff bill. Only a few months earlier, Congress had frustrated attempts to recognize the Brazilian republic. It now similarly put at risk the Pan-American commercial ambitions of Harrison and Blaine.

Sugar was the most contentious issue. Although Republican congressmen endorsed the drive for increased exports, they were also politically committed to making sugar imports free of duty. A reduction in the price of sugar was an essential element of the strategy of the "free breakfast table" aimed at winning votes in the forthcoming 1890 congressional elections. The Harrison administration pointed out, however, that "free sugar" would remove its vital bargaining lever in commercial negotiations with Latin American countries. Brazil assumed importance because it was cited as a pertinent example of a country that was prepared to grant important tariff concessions on U.S. goods in return for free sugar. The worry of Harrison and Blaine was that Congress appeared intent on simply abolishing the duty on sugar without requesting anything in return, just as it had done in the case of coffee in 1872.

Despite strenuous lobbying, Harrison and Blaine could not secure the removal of sugar from the "free list." Nevertheless, a satisfactory compromise eventually emerged. In October 1890 an amendment was added to the tariff bill that allowed

President Harrison the discretionary authority to manipulate the free list in order to secure the negotiation of commercial arrangements with foreign countries. Latin American countries would enjoy the provisions of the free list only if they "reciprocated" by granting tariff reductions on their imports of U.S. goods. The use of the term "reciprocity" was misleading because the Harrison administration would essentially be giving away nothing beyond the items on the free list already drawn up by Congress.

Talks were immediately resumed between the United States and Brazil. For John W. Foster, the principal U.S. negotiator, the treaty with Brazil was fundamental to the success of the reciprocity policy. He later recalled that it "was to be the test case of success or failure and we awaited the result not without some misgivings."[39] This did not result in a weak bargaining position because Salvador de Mendonça wanted a treaty even more than Foster. By responding positively the Brazilian minister hoped to give his country a virtual monopoly of imports into the U.S. sugar market. A treaty also possessed significant diplomatic benefits because it would highlight U.S. support for the republic and demonstrate to the other South American countries that Brazil enjoyed a privileged relationship with the United States.

Salvador's objectives were not easily obtained. The delay caused by the congressional tariff debate had resulted in a tougher U.S. bargaining mood than earlier in the year. Congress had extended the "free list" to contain not only sugar but also coffee, tea, hides, and molasses. Accordingly, Foster told Salvador that the United States expected extra tariff concessions from Brazil. Salvador replied by agreeing to remove duties on various U.S. goods including wheat, flour, and certain manufactured items such as tools and machinery. Despite these substantial U.S. gains, Foster curiously argued that it was Salvador who had secured "a great triumph." Seemingly forgetful of how crucial the treaty was for the future success of the administration's reciprocity policy, Foster stated that the significant concessions had been made by the United States. He added, "Nothing but the earnest desire of the rulers and people of the United States of America to extend to the new republic of Brazil hearty sympathy and encouragement, and to give as little embarrassment as possible to its much needed revenues, could have influenced the President and Secretary of State to agree to accept as satisfactory the reciprocity arrangement proposed."[40]

Salvador traveled to Rio with the draft agreement in November 1890. After some weeks of secret discussion with government officials, he was able to return to the United States and give his government's formal adherence to the treaty on 31 January 1891. It appeared that U.S. merchants had finally secured the commercial advantages that they had sought for so long and that the United States and Brazil were on the threshold of a new and mutually beneficial economic relationship. The new U.S. minister in Rio, Edwin Conger, sent his congratulations to Blaine and predicted enthusiastically that the "successful reciprocity negotiations have opened the doors of Brazilian trade to wonderful opportunities for our people." But only a few weeks later he was writing that public reaction was "by no means as cordial as we had a right to expect." In April he confirmed sadly that local opinion was adverse to the treaty and that Congress would vote its repeal.[41] The *Rio News* summed up: "The Brazilian press, Congress, the foreign mercantile houses, and even the Brazilians themselves, are almost unanimous in condemning the recent commercial treaty with the United States."[42]

Evidently U.S. officials had not expected that the treaty would receive a hostile response. Unfortunately, the reciprocity question coincided with a period of acute political controversy in Brazil arising from President Deodoro da Fonseca's arbitrary style of leadership. When Deodoro threatened to enforce the reciprocity agreement by executive decree, his critics accused him of high-handedness and insisted that the arrangement required congressional approval. A diplomatic issue was therefore swiftly transformed into a battle over the constitutional authority of the executive power. A succession of congressional debates demonstrated the unpopularity of both Deodoro and the reciprocity treaty. Criticism was redoubled in May 1891 when it was learned that the United States had concluded an identical arrangement with Spain on behalf of Cuba. The fact that Cuban sugar would now also have free entry into the United States effectively destroyed Brazilian expectations of capturing a monopoly of the U.S. sugar market. Conger relayed Brazilian annoyance to Washington but only drew the comment of Second Assistant Secretary of State Alvey Adee that President Harrison would regard any move by Brazil against the treaty as "most unfortunate for the good relations of the two countries."[43] In June the Brazilian government instructed Salvador to express officially its misgivings and state that Brazilian public opinion "requires good ground to sustain the agreement before the country."[44] But a sympathetic response was not forthcoming. Foster answered that Harrison was "taken greatly by surprise by the attitude of Brazilian government." Any insinuation that the U.S. government had not acted in good faith was curtly dismissed by the assertion that the arrangement with Brazil did not preclude the United States from negotiating a similar agreement with Spain. Moreover, Foster ominously declared that failure of Brazil to ratify the treaty "will be interpreted as an unfriendly act to the United States" and that the "consequences to the future relations of the two countries cannot fail to be most unfortunate and dangerous."[45]

A sense of grievance existed in Rio that Salvador had been tricked into making the agreement by the promise of "free sugar," but in the light of the rather unyielding though correct attitude of the Harrison administration, the Brazilian government could hardly do otherwise than stand by the arrangement. In fact, the Brazilian government was firmly committed to the treaty because it had been transformed from a commercial matter into a test of Deodoro's political strength. The government proceeded to mobilize all its resources of persuasion and patronage to win congressional ratification by a close vote in September 1891. Edwin Conger had special praise for Deodoro's leadership and described the marshal as "a true friend of the policy of reciprocity."[46] But Conger's delight was short-lived. A military coup had been predicted for some time, and it eventually materialized in November 1891 when a naval squadron commanded by Admiral Custódio José de Melo threatened to bombard Rio. Fearful of unleashing civil bloodshed, Deodoro resigned.

Alarmed by Deodoro's fall from power, Edwin Conger was relieved that the new regime headed by former Vice President Floriano Peixoto made no move against the reciprocity treaty. But government support could no longer be taken for granted. On his departure for a period of leave in January 1892, Conger reported that Floriano was believed to be an opponent of the treaty. When he returned to Rio in August, the U.S. minister remarked that there was only "a little improvement in the feeling" in favor of reciprocity.[47] British dispatches suggested that the Brazilian government found the arrangement "very unpalatable" and that abrogation could not be ruled out. "The present Government in this country," commented the British minister in Rio, "does not wish to surrender itself to the 'Pan American' policy of the United States."[48]

Conflict with the U.S. government was cleverly avoided by Brazilian resourcefulness. An argument employed to secure ratification of the arrangement had been that, if Brazilian goods were adversely affected by preferential reductions given to U.S. products, then the Brazilian tariff should be raised to restore the original price differential. Floriano responded to the growing protectionist mood of the Brazilian Congress by adopting this tactic in the form of an *expediente* tax added to the 1892 tariff. This increased import duties by up to 60 percent and thus restored the competitive advantage of the home producer. Although the action was clearly against the spirit of the treaty, U.S. merchants could hardly complain because the margin of their preferential privilege over foreign goods remained intact.

The critics of reciprocity in Brazil were therefore effectively disarmed, and the issue became much less politically controversial. Not only could Brazil apparently alter the arrangement to its own satisfaction, it was also evident that Brazilians stood to gain more than the U.S. interests. Within one year of the treaty being put into effect, the *Rio News* asserted "that Brazil is thus far getting nearly all the benefits."[49] The continuation of this trend was confirmed by Secretary of State Gresham's comment in 1894 that reciprocity had increased U.S. purchases from Brazil by nearly $17 million while U.S. exports to Brazil had risen by less than $500,000.[50] Even with tariff advantages, U.S. merchants were still unable to supply Brazilians with the goods they wanted. "While we may hope for a gradual increase of American exports to Brazil," remarked former U.S. consul-general, Christopher Andrews, "any high expectations in that direction are not likely to be realized."[51]

The persistence of the adverse trade balance was annoying to U.S. officials, but the treaty with Brazil had important compensations. Indeed, Brazil's consent had been crucial to the success of the reciprocity policy. By guaranteeing adequate supplies of sugar, coffee, and hides to the U.S. market, it lent substance to Harrison's threat of retaliation against other raw-material producers should they decline to enter into similar reciprocal arrangements. A British official summed up that Brazil's "surrender" had "crippled" the other Latin American governments.[52] The United States subsequently signed similar treaties with the countries of Central America and with Britain and Spain in behalf of their Caribbean possessions. The flowering of the reciprocity policy was pleasing to the Harrison administration and beneficial to the U.S. consumer, but it failed to revive the Brazilian sugar industry and therefore defeated Brazil's original purpose in signing the arrangement. Only with a tariff advantage could Brazilian sugar exports hope to compete with the more efficient Caribbean sugar producers. To make matters worse, Brazilian protests to Washington were treated in an unsympathetic manner. Despite the bruised feelings of Brazilian diplomats, the arrangement proved advantageous for Brazil. Although the reciprocity treaty failed to halt the decline of the Brazilian sugar industry, it gave a boost to coffee exports and thereby assisted the development of the fastest growing sector of the Brazilian economy. Consequently, "free coffee" replaced "free sugar" as the dominant issue in commercial relations between the two countries.

The conclusion of the reciprocity arrangement in January 1891 marked the high point of diplomatic cooperation between the United States and Brazil during the second half of the nineteenth century. Brazil soon diminished in importance in the eyes of U.S. officials, who gave more attention to events in other Latin American countries such as the Baring Crisis in Argentina and the *Baltimore* Incident in Chile. Furthermore, by 1893 both Blaine and Harrison, the leading architects of the reciprocity policy, had departed from office. In keeping with the politics of the "gilded age," the incoming Cleveland administration carefully considered lists of "deserving" Democrats for jobs in the foreign service. Brazilian affairs were relegated to a state of limbo until the newly appointed U.S. minister, Thomas L. Thompson, took up his post. Only a few days after Thompson arrived in Rio in August 1893, a major political disturbance erupted that required a diplomatic response and, if only temporarily, made Brazil newsworthy once again in the United States.

The Brazilian Naval Revolt

Despite Deodoro's resignation in November 1891, political peace had not materialized in Brazil. Floriano Peixoto had succeeded to the presidency, but his hold on power was precarious. A serious split emerged within the military as naval officers grew resentful of the political prominence accorded to the army since the fall of Dom Pedro. On 6 September 1893, Admiral Custódio de Melo took command of the fleet in the harbor of Rio and demanded Floriano's resignation under threat of naval bombardment of the city. Contrary to Custódio's expectation, Floriano refused to surrender power as Deodoro had done in almost identical circumstances only two years previously. The result was a military stalemate in which Custódio commanded all the Brazilian warships in Guanabara Bay while Floriano controlled the batteries on shore. What had been originally intended as no more than a brief demonstration of naval power became transformed into a prolonged siege lasting from September 1893 to March 1894.

The naval revolt attracted diplomatic attention as a result of its damaging effect upon trade within the harbor. The governments of the United States and the

European powers were presented with the delicate questions of how to protect their commerce and whether belligerent rights should be granted to the rebels. For U.S. officials there was the additional concern that the revolt might represent ulterior motives adverse to U.S. commercial interests. Allegations that foreign nations, especially Britain, were covertly supporting the rebels in order to restore the monarchy and bring an end to the reciprocity treaty were assiduously propagated in Washington by Salvador de Mendonça, who called almost daily at Secretary of State Gresham's house during the revolt. U.S. officials were naturally suspicious of European intrigues in the New World, but State Department policy toward the revolt was pragmatic and stressed legalistic rather than commercial or ideological considerations.

The wily Floriano also sought foreign assistance in a more direct form. Although it would take weeks or months before they could arrive, orders for warships were placed with private companies in the United States. In the meantime, Floriano attempted to compensate for his lack of a navy by persuading the foreign powers to use their ships in the harbor against Custódio. At the beginning of the revolt he requested that all the foreign diplomats at the capital come to the presidential palace and discuss measures to safeguard merchant shipping. But the diplomatic corps were not so easily manipulated. Thompson joined with his European colleagues to refuse the invitation on the ground that compliance would be a departure from his instructions to observe strict neutrality.

The foreign representatives and their naval commanders did not give serious consideration to the idea of withdrawing and letting the Brazilians fight among themselves. Instead, they decided to present a series of notes to both Floriano and Custódio stating that merchant ships flying foreign flags should continue to go about their legitimate business in the bay and would be protected by their respective national warships. The policy was legally correct although its enforcement would tend to restrict Custódio's operations and consequently favor the established government. Approval came from Secretary of State Gresham, who instructed Thompson that U.S. goods should continue to be landed at Rio with naval assistance if necessary, provided that this did not interfere with military operations in the bay.[53]

The actual implementation of the guideline was the responsibility not of Thompson but the commander of the U.S. naval squadron. No U.S. warships were actually present at Rio when Custódio declared his revolt. "For many years now," explained the *Rio News*, "this port has been almost wholly abandoned by the naval forces of the United States."[54] Two cruisers, the *Newark* and the *Charleston*, arrived in October. On entering the bay, Commodore Oscar Stanton followed normal naval protocol and ordered an exchange of salutes and visits with Custódio. This provoked a diplomatic furor in which Floriano accused the U.S. commander of collusion with the rebels. Stanton had not sought to interfere in the revolt, but he had acted unwisely. He was recalled by the Navy Department, and the next-ranking officer, Captain Henry Picking, was placed in temporary command.

Placed in the middle of two warring factions, Picking was confronted with an unenviable task. Although Custódio refrained from bombarding the city, the frequent outbreak of sporadic firing between the rebel ships and the harbor batteries made commercial operations hazardous and at times impossible. Despite their earlier declaration that they would support their own merchant ships, all the foreign naval commanders adopted a passive role. The U.S. commander faced the same dilemma. In answer to complaints about lack of protection, he stated that forceful action on his part must inevitably assist one side against the other and would be construed as a departure from the policy of noninterference in the domestic affairs of Brazil. No doubt, the example of Stanton's recall also persuaded Picking to avoid taking any controversial initiative.

Adding to the difficulties of the foreign officials on the spot was the continued uncertainty as to the exact legal status of the rebels. When Custódio realized that the revolt would be prolonged, he sought to strengthen his position by forming an alliance with separatist forces already active in southern Brazil. On 24 October Custódio announced the formation of a provisional rebel government with its headquarters at Destêrro in Santa Catarina. The foreign powers declined, however, to confer the desired recognition. Thompson's dispatches were particularly dismissive of the rebels. Two days before Custódio's announcement, the U.S. minister had telegraphed Gresham that the position of the insurgents in the harbor at Rio was "becoming desperate." On 24 October he reported that the Uruguayan government had refused to receive a deputation sent by the rebels. On the basis of this information, Gresham judged that recognition by the United States of the provisional government was not justified.[55]

The sagging morale of the rebels was, however, given a considerable boost in December when the head of the prestigious naval academy, Admiral Luís Saldanha de Gama, joined their cause. Saldanha took command of the rebel fleet in the harbor and announced his determination to institute a more vigorous prosecution of the siege. It now became extremely difficult for the foreign naval commanders to find a safe landing place for their merchant shipping. British merchants complained in particular of the inadequate protection afforded to them by their own naval commander. Saldanha's monarchist sympathies were well known, and the fact that his entry into the struggle coincided with rumors of the withdrawal of naval protection by the British commander revived suspicions of British complicity in plots to restore the Brazilian monarchy.

The charge made by the Floriano government that the rebels intended to destroy the republic was designed to win support primarily within Brazil, but it was realized that this might also sway U.S. opinion. Thompson had meager knowledge of Brazilian affairs and was susceptible to official propaganda. As early as 3 October he relayed government statements to Washington that the true aim of the revolt was to bring back the monarchy. Two months later he informed Gresham that the Brazilian foreign minister claimed to possess proof that British naval forces were giving material support to the rebels.[56]

The secretary of state showed little immediate concern. Uppermost in his mind was not the question of monarchist intrigue but how to resolve the practical difficulties posed to U.S. merchant shipping by the naval siege and now made worse by Saldanha's much more energetic policy. Conditioned by his legal training and conservative instincts, Gresham could only suggest a continuation of the very same thing that the foreign diplomats and naval commanders had been trying to achieve since the beginning of the revolt. On 9 January 1894 he instructed Thompson to cooperate with Picking to find a docking place "where neutral vessels may receive and discharge cargoes in safety without interference with military operations." The next day, the minister was informed that unless all foreign shipping suffered common restrictions "no substantial interference with our vessels, however few, will be acquiesced in."[57]

Coincidental with the dispatch of these instructions, Admiral Andrew Benham arrived in Rio. The Department of the Navy had ordered three additional ships to Rio and wished an officer more senior than Captain Picking to be in command. Benham assumed control of a squadron comprising five warships, the most powerful foreign fleet in the harbor. Moreover, the admiral's arrival came just at the time when Saldanha was demanding the right to stop and search all foreign merchant vessels in the bay. If allowed, such action would mean the establishment of an effective blockade by the rebels and a consequent *de facto* recognition of their belligerent rights. After consultation with his foreign naval colleagues, Benham informed Saldanha on 28 January that he would not tolerate interference with U.S. merchant shipping and would employ the force at his command to ensure the safety of U.S. ships. On the following day shots were exchanged between U.S. and rebel ships as Benham successfully escorted a U.S. merchant vessel to the docks. Benham claimed to be neutral, but his intervention indicated a refusal to allow Saldanha to establish the very blockade that would secure recognition of the belligerent rights of the rebels. Moreover, his firing on the rebel ships undoubtedly assisted Floriano. That this was not the purpose of U.S. diplomacy was evident in the frantically worded telegram sent by Gresham on 30 January instructing Thompson to "report fully and speedily present situation, what has occurred at Rio and in harbor."[58]

Although Benham's naval intervention resolved the immediate problem of the protection of neutral shipping in the bay, the rebel fleet still remained in the harbor. Furthermore, reports of military successes by the separatists in southern Brazil suddenly gave the question of recognition new urgency and significance. Thompson once again raised the specter of British plots. But Gresham was dubious. He outlined his views to the U.S. ambassador in London, Thomas Bayard, in January: "I do not believe Great Britain, or any other European Power, will attempt to re-establish the Monarchy in Brazil. The present state of things at Rio can not last much longer and I shall not be surprised at the result whatever it may be. I do not believe the Brazilian people are very patriotic. Perhaps a majority of them are indifferent to what is now going on."[59]

Gresham was typical of U.S. leaders who displayed a condescending attitude toward Brazil. In his opinion, the Brazilian republic was in danger not from external forces wishing to restore the monarchy but from the lack of virtue and patriotism among its own citizens. Most U.S. interests had welcomed the creation of the republic in 1889, but reservations had always been expressed concerning the new type of government. These doubts were reinforced as Brazil lurched from one political crisis to another. "The Brazilians care very little how or by whom they are ruled," observed the Rio correspondent of the *New York Times* in December 1889.[60] The naval revolt appeared as yet another example of military infighting in which the Brazilian people were reluctant to give support to either faction. In October 1893 Captain Picking described Brazilians as showing "little interest" in the naval revolt.[61] Gresham's allusion to "indifference" three months later demonstrated that U.S. observers no longer regarded Brazil as an example of political stability and order. In the circumstances the secretary of state formulated a policy identical to that of the European powers and stressed the principles of neutrality and noninterference in the domestic affairs of foreign states.

Nevertheless, U.S. independence of action was constantly emphasized. There was no formal attempt to concert policy with the European powers, and when the intervention by Benham took place, it was executed unilaterally. Gresham initially took alarm on receiving reports of fighting involving U.S. warships. His immediate anxiety was that the United States had been drawn into the conflict. He was therefore reassured to learn that Benham's objective was not to maintain Floriano in power or to crush the rebels but to assert the U.S. right to carry out commercial operations without hindrance. The fact that the intervention took place in Brazil was not particularly significant. This was underlined by Secretary of the Navy Hilary Herbert, who placed the whole matter in the broader context of the protective and humanitarian role pursued by the U.S. Navy in the world's trouble spots during the late nineteenth century. Commending Benham's action as meeting with "universal approval," Herbert declared that it would "have a far-reaching and wholesome influence in quite a number of countries where revolutions are so frequent as to almost constantly imperil the rights of American citizens."[62]

Whatever his exact intention, Benham had effectively demonstrated how the growing military power of the United States could be projected to assert U.S. rights in Latin America. Like the case of *Wachusett* thirty years previously, scant attention was given to local feelings. Indeed, the British minister in Rio reported that Benham's action had created "a very bad impression on shore."[63] Brazilian nationalist sensitivities were aroused by the deliberate act of interference in their affairs, but little adverse comment surfaced on this occasion because Benham had dealt a severe blow to the rebels for which the Floriano government was naturally very appreciative. Thwarted in his attempt to establish a legal blockade, Saldanha's position became untenable, and the rebel fleet withdrew from Rio in March 1894. Saldanha's death in June 1895 brought an end to the naval rebellion.

Floriano's triumph owed much to the rivalries and divisions among his enemies and to his own stolid refusal to give up power. Diplomacy was merely one of a number of instruments he used to gain assistance against the rebels. Floriano valued the material and moral support of the United States. However, he never directly requested U.S. military intervention nor did he propose any commercial deal between the two governments. Gresham was wary of becoming entangled in a quarrel for which he had little personal sympathy. He adopted a reactive policy that stressed neutrality. However, by its insistence on upholding the status quo, Gresham's legalistic approach actually assisted the established government and had the fortuitous effect of strengthening diplomatic relations between the two countries. Floriano was so grateful that he ordered 4 July 1894 to be observed as a Brazilian national holiday.

The Revival of Reciprocity

The departure of the rebel fleet led to the resumption of normal commercial activities in Rio, but this was of more immediate benefit to European rather than U.S. merchants. At the end of the siege, Thompson recalled that there were only five ships in the harbor flying the U.S. flag. At the same time, he counted over a hundred British vessels. In a plea reminiscent of those made by Kidder and Fletcher some forty years earlier and by Roach more recently, the U.S. minister urged that "something should be done to meet this already dominating and rapidly increasing European influence."[64] But Congress had consistently refused to vote financial subsidies to set up U.S. shipping lines. Similar political constraints had also hampered the reciprocity policy with Brazil in 1890 and would do so again with the passage of the Wilson Tariff in August 1894.

When the Cleveland administration came to office in 1893, its declared priority was to reverse the Republican policy of protection. A bill was prepared in Congress that proposed not only tariff reduction but also the abrogation of all the various agreements made under the 1890 tariff including the reciprocity arrangement with Brazil. The threat of congressional interference prompted Salvador de Mendonça to inform the State Department that his government regarded the reciprocity arrangement as a formal treaty and that there were agreed terms of giving three months' notice for its abrogation. Gresham privately devised a formula designed to accommodate the minister's objections by allowing time to terminate the treaty "in the proper manner." But Democratic congressmen were unsympathetic to diplomatic niceties and refused to accept the proposed compromise. The secretary of state was therefore compelled to reject Brazil's contention that there was an agreed procedure to terminate what he now described as a "so-called treaty."[65] It was clear that U.S. diplomacy enjoyed a latitude of maneuver not permitted to Brazil. Three years previously Salvador's hints that his government might not ratify the arrangement had met with a brusque reply from President Harrison. In 1894 President Cleveland abrogated the controversial arrangement by the simple statement that the U.S. Congress had passed a law to this effect.

Democratic politicians had no ill will toward Brazil; in the main, they were indifferent. Reasons of domestic politics rather than commercial calculation required that a duty be reimposed on imports of sugar. Fortunately for Brazil, no such political significance attached to coffee, which remained on the free list. Prior to the Wilson Tariff more than 99 percent of Brazilian goods entered the United

States free of duty. Afterward, the figure dipped only slightly to around 95 percent. Consequently, the 1894 tariff had little detrimental effect on Brazilian exports to the United States. Ironically, U.S. merchants stood to lose most from the action of their own government since the abrogation of the reciprocity arrangement removed the preferential tariff advantages that they had briefly enjoyed. British residents in Brazil were described as "greatly pleased" to learn of the demise of the treaty.[66]

Brazilian diplomats were annoyed at the imperious manner in which the reciprocity treaty was terminated, but they no doubt welcomed the opportunity to put aside what had long been a controversial matter. Considerably more importance was attached to President Cleveland's arbitration of the Misiones boundary dispute with Argentina. The failure of Brazil and Argentina to agree to a settlement in 1891 had resulted in the question going to the arbitration of the president of the United States. The respective cases were submitted to President Cleveland in February 1894. As months passed by, the president's delay in making his decision aroused growing apprehension in both Argentina and Brazil, but in February 1895 Brazilians were delighted by the announcement of an award that gave Brazil virtually all of the disputed territory. Any annoyance over the 1894 tariff was swept aside in the light of what was interpreted as a conclusive demonstration of U.S. friendship for Brazil. It was not surprising therefore in December 1895 that the Brazilian Senate sent a message of congratulations to President Cleveland for his handling of the Venezuela boundary crisis. A few years later Brazil was notably the only Latin American country to sympathize publicly with the United States during the Spanish-American War.

The U.S. government was pleased by the gestures of friendship but did not feel any need to court Brazil's favor. During the late 1890s Brazil experienced a succession of internal difficulties that greatly diminished the country's diplomatic prestige and activities. Commerce remained the most important link between the two countries, once again attracting diplomatic attention in 1897 when the Republicans returned to political power and passed the Dingley Tariff. The new law included the reinstatement of the 1890 reciprocity provision giving the president authority to negotiate reciprocal commercial arrangements and, at his discretion, to retaliate against those countries that pursued unfair practices against U.S. goods. The reciprocity policy was aimed at the whole of Latin America, but it was seen as especially applicable to Brazil because the balance of trade with that country was known to be notoriously adverse to the United States. In 1897 the difference was estimated to be more than $50 million in Brazil's favor and attracted more attention than in the past as a result of a lobbying campaign undertaken by the merchants of Baltimore. They pointed out that a reduction in the Brazilian tariff on flour was crucial for their city's commercial prosperity because that product made up more than 50 percent of U.S. exports to Brazil.[67]

Section 3 of the Dingley Tariff specifically empowered the president to impose a three-cent duty upon each imported pound of coffee. The State Department believed that this would provide substantial bargaining leverage against Brazil. Initially U.S. policy stressed, however, a desire for fair commercial treatment and re-garded retaliatory action as a threat only to be implemented after persuasion had failed. A willingness to be reasonable highlighted Secretary of State Hay's instructions to the U.S. minister in Rio, Charles Page Bryan. Hay pointed out that in 1898 the United States had imported more than $61 million of Brazilian products and that 95 percent of these were admitted free of duty. In return Brazil purchased U.S. goods valued at only $13 million out of which a mere 13 percent was admitted free. These "unequal conditions" greatly discouraged U.S. trade and had led to demands for retaliation against Brazilian coffee. "It is due," Hay remarked, "to the cordial friendship of which this Government has given many proofs to Brazil, to inquire whether that Government will not make such reasonably adequate concessions to the exports of the United States as to justify the continuance of our present free market for the important products of Brazil."[68]

After the controversial experience of the earlier reciprocity agreement, Brazil's response in 1897 was much less accommodating than in 1890. Prior to the passage of the tariff bill Salvador candidly informed the State Department that he could not see in the proposed measure "one single word which can attract Brazil."[69] In marked contrast to 1890, Brazilian officials could not perceive any obvious diplomatic or commercial advantages to be gained. Indeed, there was a disinclination to grant commercial concessions to the United States. The protectionist lobby in the Brazilian Congress, backed by influential state politicians and industrialists, urged an increase rather than a reduction in tariff levels. This course of action was attractive to the federal government for whom import taxes contributed more than half of total government revenue. Any reduction of duty would inevitably result in a decrease of income at a time when the Brazilian economy was on the verge of bankruptcy.

The hostile attitude of foreign governments was an additional complication. The 1891 agreement had drawn protests from several European countries, and these governments were unhappy that U.S. goods might once again enjoy preferential tariff treatment. The issue also coincided with pressure from Argentina for a commercial treaty. Argentine merchants especially hoped to increase their exports of flour and were acutely aware that this was the product on which the U.S. interests most wanted Brazilian concessions. In the opinion of the British minister in Rio, Brazilian commercial policy was "in an inextricable tangle in every direction."[70] Any concessions granted to the United States must inevitably provoke Argentine anger and vice versa.

One reason for U.S. patience with Brazil during the trying saga of reciprocity negotiations was awareness of the obstacles faced by that government in attempting to conclude a commercial agreement. "The difficulties now surrounding the Brazilian Government," wrote Secretary of State John Sherman in 1897, "deserve fair consideration and forbearance on the part of our Government."[71] Yet Sherman and his successor, John Hay, remained optimistic that an agreement would eventually be reached. It was their conviction that Brazilian diplomats recognized the anomalous nature of trade relations between their respective countries and that they would rectify this out of a sense of fairness. The stick of the retaliatory tax on coffee existed but was held in reserve because its use would indicate that diplomacy had failed. In addition, Brazilians queried whether the threat of retaliation was actually credible. "Almost the universal opinion among public men here," reported the U.S. chargé in Rio, Thomas Dawson, in 1901, "is that we have no such intention."[72] So well-established was the coffee trade that Brazilians were confident that U.S. consumers would continue to purchase substantial quantities no matter what the particular commercial policy pursued by the U.S. government. Indeed, any tax imposed on Brazilian coffee must inevitably lead to a higher price eventually being charged in the United States.

Because U.S. commercial policy was so unpredictable, Brazilian officials could never be completely certain that the threat would not be carried out. In June 1899 the new Brazilian minister in Washington, Assis Brasil, noted apprehensively that New York firms were buying up coffee stocks in apparent anticipation of the imminent imposition of a retaliatory tax on the product.[73] Another source of pressure arose from the persistent and forceful presentation of the U.S. case. Hay stressed fairness and reason, but his dispatches talked of the United States "demanding" and "insisting" on reciprocal concessions. On learning that the Brazilian Congress was considering an increase in the import duty on flour, Hay telegraphed the blunt warning that "this Government would regard it as an act directed against our commerce and justifying countervailing action on our part."[74] Charles Page Bryan later revealed that during 1900 he had "urged" Brazil to grant tariff concessions "at nearly every weekly audience" with the Brazilian foreign minister.[75]

It seemed that U.S. diplomacy had finally achieved success in 1900 when the Campos Sales administration undertook to grant tariff concessions on imports of U.S. flour. But the Brazilian Congress would not grant its approval. Retaliation by the United States was rumored but did not materialize. A State Department memorandum later disclosed that "we had tried to scare Brazil, but failed to do so, and that was the end of the matter."[76] Unlike 1890, the turn of the century was not a propitious time for the revival of the reciprocity policy. In fact, Brazil's resistance was not unique and was shared by the rest of South America with the sole exception of Ecuador. The U.S. diplomatic pressure on Brazil was considerable, but financial crisis and internal political divisions compelled the Brazilian government to proceed with circumspection. Hay confessed his inability to conclude an arrangement with Brazil, but this was only a temporary setback for U.S. diplomacy. So long as the United States remained Brazil's largest export market, the Brazilian government would remain vulnerable to changes in U.S. commercial policy.

The Acre Question

Whereas Brazilian officials could be difficult in commercial negotiations, they showed themselves at their most sensitive and awkward whenever the national territory was believed to be in danger from foreign encroachment. This had been evident in the intransigent response toward Maury's scheme to open the River Amazon to foreign commerce during the 1850s. A similar attitude was revealed at the end of the nineteenth century over the "Acre question." The Acre Territory was a remote area adjoining the state of Amazonas that suddenly acquired prominence during the 1890s as a result of the international demand for rubber. Reckoned to be the richest rubber region in the world, its ownership had long been a matter of dispute among the governments of Brazil, Bolivia, and Peru. In 1899 Bolivia attempted to assert its authority over the territory by taxing shipments of rubber. President Campos Sales retaliated by claiming that the Acre Territory belonged to Brazil.

The U.S. government became associated with the Acre question because it was rumored that Bolivia had secretly acquired U.S. diplomatic support. Brazilian suspicions of U.S. imperialist designs were later heightened by the unauthorized voyage up the Amazon in 1899 by the U.S. warship *Wilmington*. In Washington, Hay explained to Assis Brasil that the voyage was intended to be friendly and had no ulterior motive. When Hay complained of "unfriendly feeling" shown to the captain and officers of the *Wilmington*, however, the Brazilian minister quickly reminded him of "the perfect right of Brazil to establish that warships of friendly nations may not navigate the national rivers without special permission, asked for and granted in each case."[77] In 1902 anti-American sentiment in Brazil was further aroused after it was learned that the Bolivian government had definitely granted not only commercial rights but also virtual sovereign powers of administration in the Acre Territory to a syndicate of U.S. capitalists. The latter were reported to be already moving equipment and supplies to the disputed region.

Only a few years previously, Brazil had adopted a sympathetic attitude toward U.S. military intervention in Cuba. The emergence of what was now popularly referred to as "the American danger"[78] to Brazil's own territory caused a marked change of opinion. "There is so general a distrust of the United States," lamented a U.S. merchant resident in Brazil, "that the people grasp eagerly at the chance to make mountains out of molehills."[79] Brazil's displeasure was frankly expressed in July 1902, when Foreign Minister Olinto de Magalhaes informed the U.S. minister that he hoped that U.S. capitalists would be "discouraged" from involvement in "an undertaking which was sure to result in financial disaster to themselves and in discord between nations."[80]

Shortly before leaving office in November 1902, President Campos Sales ordered the closure of the River Amazon to foreign shipping. The action was intended to highlight his government's serious concern over the Acre question. It also effectively isolated the syndicate from its source of external supplies and underlined how much any exploitation of the rubber trade was dependent on Brazilian consent and assistance. The new Brazilian foreign minister, Barao Rio Branco, was determined to avoid any show of weakness and resolved to continue the demonstration of Brazil's sovereign power despite protests from Britain, France, Germany, and the United States.

The U.S. consul-general in Rio, Eugene Seeger, was incensed. In a style reminiscent of Maury some fifty years earlier, he condemned the closure "as a thrust against the United States." He believed himself justified in warning Rio Branco that the U.S. government "has always considered the navigation of the Amazon through Brazil as being free to all nations."[81] But Seeger's contention could not be sustained either by law or historical practice. It was rejected by his superiors in Washington, who had no desire to provoke a confrontation with Brazil. In contrast to the naval revolt, the legal rights of the U.S. members of the syndicate were uncertain, and there was no evidence that they were being infringed. Nor was there any collusion between the State Department and either the Bolivian government or the syndicate. Assis Brasil was informed that the syndicate was regarded as a purely private venture.[82]

The State Department not only acknowledged the strength of Brazil's claim to the disputed territory but also showed that it wanted good working relations with the Brazilian Foreign Office. This was underlined by the expression of pleasure at the news of Rio Branco's appointment as foreign minister in 1902. Officials in the United States "agreeably recalled" his residence in Washington at the time of the Misiones arbitration when he had been in charge of presenting Brazil's case.[83] The U.S. minister in Rio, David Thompson, also confirmed that the baron was "most friendly." Although he acknowledged that some Brazilians were suspicious of U.S. motives, Thompson stressed that Rio Branco "does not court this feeling, and wants to feel faith in our good intentions."[84]

The mood of goodwill helped Rio Branco to gain his first major diplomatic success as foreign minister. Deprived of outside supplies and of any real prospect of U.S. diplomatic support, the syndicate gratefully took up his suggestion that it discuss a financial arrangement with the Brazilian government. With the knowledge and approval of the State Department, negotiations commenced in Washington between Assis Brasil and representatives of the syndicate. In February 1903 the syndicate agreed to renounce its contract in return for an indemnity of $550,000 to be paid by the Brazilian government. The arrangement was confirmed during the following month, by which time the River Amazon had been reopened to foreign shipping and the draft of an agreement settling the territorial dispute had been concluded between Brazil and Bolivia. By the Treaty of Petropolis, signed in November 1903, Bolivia formally recognized Brazil's possession of more than 70,000 square miles of the Acre Territory.

The boundary question, however, was not yet completely resolved. The Peruvian government was annoyed at being excluded from the settlement and reaffirmed its own territorial claims to the area. Like Brazil, Peru was well aware of the critical value of U.S. influence and attempted to win Washington's favor by promptly recognizing the new republic of Panama in December 1903, ahead of similar action by Brazil and other South American countries. But Rio Branco was confident that U.S. opinion was firmly on the side of Brazil. He responded to Peru's intervention by encouraging the State Department to help bring about a settlement. The Brazilian foreign minister correctly interpreted the desire of the administration of President Theodore Roosevelt to act as a force for peace and stability in the hemisphere. This was confirmed by Hay's instructions to Minister

Thompson to work for an outcome "mutually honorable and advantageous" to both countries.[85] In fact, by deliberately not taking sides, Thompson implicitly reaffirmed the status quo and thereby dashed Peru's strategy of reopening the whole question. The diplomatic victory belonged to Rio Branco. Peru was effectively isolated and soon agreed to recognize Brazil's legal title to the Acre Territory.

End of an Era

The Acre question demonstrated that, at the beginning of the twentieth century, the United States was no longer a distant and indifferent spectator of South American affairs. Indeed, the interested parties in the dispute saw Washington as the decisive focal point of their diplomatic maneuvers, and each side competed to win U.S. support. Brazilian diplomacy had already, if only fitfully, reflected this development throughout the 1890s. Salvador de Mendonça had stressed the vital importance of U.S. recognition of the republic. Floriano Peixoto had appreciated the usefulness of U.S. support during the naval revolt. But it was Rio Branco who was credited with articulating the strategy of "approximating" Brazil's foreign policy as closely as possible to that pursued by the United States. Already appreciative of the significance of U.S. assistance in the Misiones boundary dispute, Rio Branco recognized that his country's diplomatic axis had shifted from Europe to the United States. Relations with the great European powers would continue to be important, but the friendship and support of the United States was now considered crucial to the realization of Brazil's own national interests.

Diplomats from the United States were conscious of Brazil's tilt toward their country and hoped that it would bring economic benefits. Charles Page Bryan was especially encouraged by the election in 1902 of Rodrigues Alves as president. He believed that there was a particular desire to expand trade with the United States and was confident of the "readiness to assist in our wishes for commercial reciprocity."[86] Bryan's prediction was borne out in 1904 when the Rodrigues Alves administration issued a presidential decree reducing the tariff on U.S. goods. The unilateral grant of commercial concessions by Brazil delighted the Roosevelt administration. Although U.S. officials never formally accepted the idea of "approximation," they genuinely wanted friendly and cooperative relations with Brazil, especially when that country once again became a model of political stability and economic progress in the first decade of the twentieth century. In 1905 diplomatic relations were upgraded to ambassadorial level and during the following year Secretary of State Elihu Root visited Rio to attend the Third Pan-American Conference. To the immense pleasure of Brazilians Root spoke publicly of the two countries acting as equal partners to maintain hemispheric peace and order. With the exception of the mutual delight arising from Dom Pedro's visit to the United States in 1876, diplomatic relations between the two countries had never been so amicable. The apparent convergence of national interests in 1906, however, disguised the historical record of the past half century, during which U.S. policy toward Brazil had been characterized more by neglect and insensitivity rather than by a particular desire for close diplomatic relations.

During the second half of the nineteenth century, the principal link between the two countries was trade. Companies in the United States were continually exhorted to take advantage of the boundless commercial opportunities offered in Brazil. The rhetoric scarcely altered from decade to decade, and it seemed that Brazil was always being "discovered." For example, in 1898 the former U.S. minister, Thomas L. Thompson, echoed the writings of Kidder and Fletcher in describing Brazil as a "treasure-house" waiting to be unlocked.[87] The reality, however, was that few U.S. companies wanted to do business or settle in Brazil. During the heyday of immigration to Brazil at the beginning of the twentieth century, only one-quarter of one percent of immigrants were from the United States. "The English dominate in all import traffic," Thompson lamented, "they know the market and cater to the demands of the trade."[88] Change would come about faster than Thompson anticipated and not as a result of diplomatic activity or individual U.S. enterprise. As Rio Branco perceived, an era of international relations was coming to an end. The European powers were in relative decline, while the United States was asserting its hemispheric preeminence. Adjusting to this geopolitical fact would be the principal theme of relations between the United States and Brazil for much of the twentieth century.

10

PARAGUAY AND URUGUAY

On the Periphery II

José B. Fernández and Jennifer M. Zimnoch

DIPLOMATIC RELATIONS BETWEEN THE United States and the two smallest republics of the Southern Cone, Paraguay and Uruguay, were marked by periods of interest and neglect for most of the nineteenth century.

Endowed by nature with magnificent forests and broad rivers but lacking in mineral wealth, Paraguay was an obscure, landlocked outpost of the Viceroyalty of the Río de la Plata. Unlike some of its South American neighbors, Paraguay achieved independence without bloodshed. In June 1811, a radical doctor of theology named José Gaspar Rodríguez de Francia announced to his people that the "unfortunate times of oppression and tyranny have ended at last."[1]

Known as "El Supremo," the austere Dr. Francia isolated his country from the rest of the world and the highly miscegenated Paraguayan population emerged as the most egalitarian society in the Americas. As a result of Francia's isolationist policy, Paraguay was virtually unknown to the U.S. public. In 1840, "El Supremo," the undisputed master of Paraguay, died, and the country's second man of destiny appeared on the scene. Carlos Antonio López, a rich *estanciero*, would rule Paraguay until his death in 1862.[2]

In a radical departure from his predecessor, "El Ciudadano," as López was popularly known, opened the remote and obscure country to the outside world. It was during this *apertura* that the United States became interested in establishing a presence in Paraguay. In 1845, the United States commissioned Edward A. Hopkins as special agent to Paraguay. Formal diplomatic relations, however, were not established until 1853, and from then until 1870, relations were marred by inconsistencies, misconceptions, and personality conflicts between U.S. envoys and the Paraguayans. Following Paraguay's defeat in the War of the Triple Alliance (1865-70), relations between the two countries were marked by a period of benign neglect on the part of the United States toward Paraguay. As a matter of fact, U.S. ministers to Uruguay and Paraguay were stationed in Montevideo rather than in Asunción, and Paraguay received only scant attention from the U.S. State Department. This policy would last well until the twentieth century as the United States was contented to allow Paraguay to be a "ward" of Brazil and Argentina.

As a result of the Treaty of Tordesillas in 1494 the colonial Banda Oriental formed a disputed wedge of approximately 250,000 square miles between the Spanish and Portuguese empires in the New World. The mighty colonial powers were dictated by geography to covet this sparsely populated territory of little economic significance. Strategically, the area was essential to the Spaniards for the defense of mineral-rich Upper Peru, and to the Portuguese the control of the area meant protection of the key settlements of São Paulo and Rio de Janeiro. Neither power won decisive control of the region, and the Banda Oriental remained a constant point of contention. The independence movement in the Viceroyalty of Río de la Plata (1810–16) brought no respite to the suffering *orientales*. Although the Río de la Plata was freed from the clutches of Spain by 1816, the Banda Oriental experienced more violence during the power struggle between Buenos Aires and Portugal and later an independent Brazil.[3] The conflict brought trade in the region to a standstill for the Brazilians, who initiated a blockade of the port of Buenos Aires in 1825. British equity in Buenos Aires was estimated at £1,536,411, and as a result of the blockade, England demanded that the belligerents negotiate a peaceful solution concerning the Banda Oriental. British statesman George Canning asserted in February 1826 that the city of Montevideo should become independent of both Brazil and Argentina and thenceforth brokered an agreement between the two countries in 1828 that made Uruguay an independent country.[4] But as Uruguay's first president, Fructuoso Rivera, observed, it was a precarious independence: "its cradle is like that of Hercules, two vipers surround it."[5]

Diplomatic relations between the United States and Uruguay began in 1834, but until the late nineteenth century they could be best described as superficial. In fact, the first U.S. minister to be stationed in Montevideo who had no additional duties in Buenos Aires was not appointed until 1870.

In the United States preoccupation with Manifest Destiny followed by the Civil War and Reconstruction largely accounted for this absence of interest in Uruguay. In the latter years of the nineteenth century, Uruguay attracted a bit of U.S. attention as a result of an increased U.S. interest in commerce with Uruguay and the Uruguayans' dream of weaning themselves from British commercial domination. This U.S. interest, however, was short-lived, as the British continued to maintain their commercial grip on Uruguay.

U.S.-Paraguayan Relations

A Period of Misconceptions and Misperceptions (1845–1862)

On 10 June 1845 President James K. Polk commissioned Edward A. Hopkins, the twenty-two-year-old son of the first Episcopal bishop of Vermont, as the U.S. special agent to Paraguay. With a salary of six dollars a day plus expenses, Hopkins was instructed to inform Secretary of State James Buchanan about the character of the people of Paraguay, their degree of intelligence, and the proportion of European, Indian, and mixed races among the population. Although on a fact-finding mission, Hopkins was more than a diplomat. He became a confidant of President Antonio López, charming him with lavish praise and withholding his usual arrogance. Hopkins advised "El Ciudadano" on the "danger of forming entangling alliances with other nations or conferring commercial advantages upon one nation at the expense of the rest." In other words, the U.S. expected most-favored-nation commercial status. Beyond his instructions, Hopkins bragged to López about his connections with U.S. businessmen who were willing to form a company to invest in Paraguay and add to the Paraguayan president's name and fortune.[6] Hopkins also wrote glowing accounts of Paraguay for publication in U.S. newspapers. On one occasion he described Paraguay as "the most united, richest, and the strongest nation of the New World," after the United States, a description that defied reality.[7]

Hopkins's unauthorized offer to mediate a possible Paraguayan conflict with Argentina in 1846 brought an immediate rebuke from Secretary Buchanan for violating a fundamental principal of U.S. foreign policy at the time: noninterference in the internal affairs of other nations in their controversies with each other. The angry Buchanan revoked Hopkins's commission and ordered his immediate return to the United States.[8] Hopkins's antics also were responsible for the delay in extending formal recognition to Paraguay until 1853.

The *Water Witch* Incident

After his return to the United States, Hopkins made several public appearances designed to stimulate interest in Paraguay. His address before the American Geographical and Statistical Society in 1851 prompted Secretary of the Navy John P. Kennedy to outfit an expedition to explore the La Plata river system that would, he hoped, lead to expanded commerce and navigation in the region. Kennedy typified the lack of U.S. understanding about Paraguay in his instructions to Lieutenant Thomas Jefferson Page. He advised the commander to establish friendly relations with the local "savages."[9]

The U.S. expedition coincided with the fall of President Juan Manuel de Rosas of Argentina. Following his defeat by the Brazilians at Monte Caseros, Uruguay, Rosas was exiled to England. As a consequence of these actions, the Río de la Plata system was opened to U.S. navigation. In March 1853, Argentina, Uruguay, and Paraguay signed fluvial treaties with the United States. Hoping to capitalize on these treaties, the Page expedition had begun. On 1 October 1853 Page docked the 375-ton sidewheel steamer *Water Witch* at Asunción, which became the first U.S. war vessel ever to enter the waters of the Paraguay River. Page and his crew received a cordial welcome from "El Ciudadano" and presented him with a twelve-pounder howitzer as a token of friendship. Under the terms of the 4 March 1853 U.S.-Paraguayan navigation treaty, Page was able to sail up the Paraguay River to Bahía Negra, but he was warned by President López not to enter the Brazilian territory of Matto Grosso, which Paraguay claimed as part of its nation and to which the Brazilian government had granted Page access. López's warning underscored the rising animosity between the two nations over the control of the Paraguay River.[10]

In October 1853, as Page prepared for his expedition, Hopkins returned to Asunción as U.S. consul accredited to Paraguay and as an agent of the United States and Paraguay Navigation Company. The company, chartered in Rhode Island in 1852 with initial assets of $100,000, sought to engage in river navigation and in the manufacture of bricks and cigars in Paraguay. President López, who still held Hopkins in high esteem, cordially greeted the agent and lent him $10,000 to cover the loss of equipment on one of the company's vessels, which was wrecked off the Brazilian coast en route to Paraguay. Hopkins's view of Paraguay had not changed since his visit in 1845 and 1846. In an early dispatch to Secretary of State William L. Marcy, Hopkins heaped lavish praise on López and pointed to the potential significance of Paraguay to U.S. commerce. But Hopkins did not have a kind word for Page. He wrote Marcy: "He [Page] has not seen fit to consult in the slightest degree my long experience in this peculiar country, nor treat my position with that public respect which our laws require—nor yet inform himself of important points of public etiquette by which he has wounded the fastidious resceptibilities [sic] of a people just opened to contact with the world."[11]

For his part, Page shared Hopkins's perception of López's greatness and his optimism about future commercial relations. He also wrote an encomiastic report on the character of the Paraguayan people and their auspicious disposition toward the United States. Page, however, was not favorably disposed toward Hopkins and charged that he had coerced López to make further concessions in the 1853 navigation treaty. Perhaps fearful that his own expedition was in jeopardy, Page unsuccessfully offered to act as the official U.S. representative to Paraguay in the exchange of the treaty's ratifications.[12]

With his ship fully outfitted, Page began his expedition on 7 November 1853. The *Water Witch* sailed from Asunción under the guidance of native Paraguayan Feliciano Ramírez. After collecting scientific information, the vessel arrived at Bahía Negra, where Page decided to ignore López's admonitions and proceed to Corumbá, Brazil.

The *Water Witch* returned to Asunción in December. Although Page was elated with the scientific results of his expedition, López was infuriated by his act of disobedience. The Paraguayan president was convinced that Page's action would entice Brazil to secure passage of her ships beyond Bahía Negra and present Brazil with the opportunity of exercising its hegemony over the La Plata region, including the Paraguay River. López's scolding of Page prompted a remorseful response: "In entering Brazilian territory, I had touched the dignity of the republic and periled its peace." Despite this incident López granted Page permission to conduct explorations on the Paraná River.

As the *Water Witch* headed south, relations between López and Hopkins deteriorated as a result of the former's greediness and the latter's arrogance. The dictator had been angered by Hopkins's refusal to make him a partner in the Navigation Company's cigar factory. The consul, however, was angered when he was not invited to attend a public ball given for President López by a group of prominent Paraguayan citizens. Soon after, Hopkins denounced the "Jesuitical intriguers of President López and his numberless parasites and spies" and referred to the Paraguayans as the "retrograde slaves of the Jesuits, an infernal mixture of all the original types of the human race."[13] Quite a change from Hopkins's earlier praise!

Tensions between the two heightened on 21 July 1854 when the consul's brother, Clement Hopkins, and the wife of the French consul, Mme. Jean Guillemot, rode through a herd of cattle as they returned to Asunción from the outlying town of San Antonio. The cattle herder, a Paraguayan soldier named Agustín Silvero, dealt Hopkins a blow with his saber for interfering with the herd's orderly movement. The incident sent the arrogant Edward Hopkins into President López's reception room with a whip in his hand demanding an apology from the president and punishment for Silvero. López condemned Silvero to 300 blows but refused Hopkins's demand to publicize the condemnation as a warning as to what the Paraguayans could expect if they committed offenses against any members of the U.S. community residing in the country.[14] The incident served only to exacerbate relations between the United States and Paraguay.

López obtained his revenge by immediately issuing a number of decrees providing for the confiscation of the company's cigar factory and virtually forbidding it from operating in Paraguay. In the ensuing verbal war with Paraguay's acting foreign minister, José Falcón, Hopkins demanded $300,000 in reclamations and expenses brought about by López's decrees against the company. Hopkins felt betrayed by the government he claimed to have defended before the world. Not to be outdone, Falcón angrily replied that "such service has never come to the knowledge of [this] government."[15]

On 1 September 1854 López revoked Hopkins's *exequatur* and withheld his passport until he repaid the $10,000 loan made to him in 1853. The furious Hopkins now labeled his former friend as "equal to Dr. Francia in insolence—his superior in ignorance." Hopkins also suggested to Secretary Marcy that he be retained as consul in order for the United States to intervene and punish López for his offenses against the U.S. representative. "It is high time," Hopkins wrote Marcy, "that the United States set aside that lamentable Don Quixote policy towards these barbarous *caciques.* . . . Talking with them is time lost, they want the specimen of our cannons."[16] Marcy dismissed the suggestion, but without a passport Hopkins remained in Asunción, where he continued to vent his anger on the Paraguayan authorities.

As the Hopkins-López controversy intensified, Page decided to come to the rescue of his former nemesis. He sailed on the *Water Witch* from its research site at Corrientes and arrived in Asunción on 20 September 1854 to request that Hopkins be permitted on the ship. To press the issue Page instructed the crew to aim the vessel's guns on the presidential palace. Page prevailed, and ten days after his arrival, the Paraguayans allowed Hopkins to board the *Water Witch* and return with it to Corrientes. Again in anger, López responded with yet another decree on

3 October 1854 that excluded foreign war vessels from navigating the republic's rivers and prohibiting the exploration of the upper reaches of the Paraguay River. The decree was obviously aimed at the armed *Water Witch*.

Shortly after arriving in Corrientes in mid-October to continue his scientific explorations, Page received word that he had been appointed agent to oversee the exchange of the ratifications of the 1853 navigation treaty. Page notified Falcón of his appointment, but he sent the document in English without the customary Spanish translation, an omission that angered Falcón, particularly in light of the well-known fact that Page had translators on his ship. But Page refused to budge. He would communicate only in English with the Paraguayan government. And, in a show of bravado, Page suggested to Secretary Marcy that the U.S. Navy's Brazilian squadron be sent to Asunción to ensure ratification of the 1853 treaty. As relations continued to deteriorate, the confident Page prepared for the exploration of the Argentine Chaco region in a smaller vessel.

In January 1855 Page instructed Lieutenant William Jeffers to proceed to the Upper Paraná River as far as the island of Apipe to collect scientific data, a clear violation of López's October 1854 decree. In early February 1855, Jeffers and the *Water Witch* approached the Paraguayan fort of Itapirú, located four miles beyond the confluence of the Paraná-Paraguay Rivers. Instead of heading for the main channel, which was on the Argentine side of the Paraná, the vessel veered toward the Paraguayan side directly in front of the Paraguayan garrison. The fort's commander, Colonel Vicente Duarte, informed Jeffers that he was in violation of the López decree. As Falcón had treated Page, Jeffers now rejected the Spanish-language note and ordered the crew to continue its course. In response Duarte had three blank shots fired, but the *Water Witch* continued. Duarte then ordered a round of live ammunition to be fired across the ship's bow, but it hit the wheel and killed helmsman Samuel Chaney. The *Water Witch* returned the fire and set sail for Corrientes from whence it had come.[17]

The encounter infuriated Page, who asked the commander of the U.S. South Atlantic Squadron in port at Buenos Aires, Commodore William D. Salter, to take punitive action on the Paraguayans. By the time the request reached Buenos Aires, Salter had departed the city for Rio de Janeiro, leaving behind a small gunboat, the *Germantown*, which had inadequate armament to inflict any punishment on the Paraguayans. Coupled with Hopkins's insolence and loss of favor in Asunción, the *Water Witch* incident only drove U.S.-Paraguayan relations to new depths and contributed to Paraguay's continued refusal to ratify the 1853 navigation treaty.

With his "honor" unvindicated, Page soon received orders to return to the United States, where he informed Congress that Paraguay's fluvial rights were an obstacle to U.S. commercial interests in the Río de la Plata region.

The *Water Witch* incident also opened the way for Brazilian probing of the Paraguay River. Less than three weeks after the firing at the *Water Witch* a Brazilian fleet sailed north away from Uruguay, stopping just a few miles from the Paraguayan fortress of Humaitá on the Paraguay River. President López blamed the

Brazilian probe on the *Water Witch* incident. The continued Brazilian presence forced Paraguay in 1858 to grant the Brazilians commercial navigation rights on the river.

U.S.-Paraguayan relations suffered another blow when on 6 April 1855 James A. Peden, the U.S. minister in Argentina, blamed Paraguay for refusing to ratify the 1853 treaty, for the expulsion of Hopkins, and for the attack on the *Water Witch*. He also demanded compensation from Paraguay for the death of helmsman Chaney and recommended that a U.S. naval force be sent to punish Paraguay. Peden apparently did not realize that Paraguay also had a number of grievances against the United States, particularly Hopkins's actions, which contributed to misunderstandings, his alienation of López, and Page's actions of bravado at Asunción and Itapirú, which had prompted the López government to seek retaliatory action.

In the tense atmosphere, the State Department sent Richard Fitzgibbons as special agent to Paraguay in November 1856. Fitzgibbons also was to oversee the exchange of ratifications of the 1853 treaty, which now contained thirty-two amendments added by the U.S. Senate that were expected to be accepted by Paraguay. No sooner had he arrived in Asunción, however, did Fitzgibbons learn that López had no intention of ratifying the treaty. López also requested that another envoy be sent for the sole purpose of solving the impasse. Fitzgibbons returned to Washington empty-handed. So upset was President James Buchanan that in his first state of the union message he called for a redress of grievances against the López regime. Congress, in a nationalist mood, acquiesced and granted the president authority to use all diplomatic and military measures necessary to correct Paraguay's affront.

Buchanan sent Judge James Butler Bowlin, who had diplomatic experience in Colombia, with an array of instructions, including a demand for a Paraguayan apology for the *Water Witch* incident, compensation for the Chaney family, ratification of a new commercial and navigation treaty, and submission of the Hopkins claim of $1 million for his Navigation Company to arbitration. To impress the Paraguayans with the U.S. determination, eleven steamers, seven frigates, one hospital ship, and four supply vessels carrying 2,000 soldiers under the command of Commodore William Shurbrik accompanied Judge Bowlin to Asunción. It was the largest naval force sent from the United States to any part of the world up to that time.

After nearly a year of preparation and sailing time, the fleet arrived at Buenos Aires in December 1854 and then proceeded up the Paraná River to the city of Paraná, where Bowlin met President Justo José Urquiza. The Argentine president agreed to sail with Bowlin to Asunción in order to help his friend López promptly settle with his U.S. friends. The entourage arrived at Asunción on 26 January 1859, and after several days of intensive negotiations the Paraguayans caved in to the U.S. demands. López apologized for the *Water Witch*, agreed to pay the Chaney family $10,000, signed a new commercial and navigation treaty that included all the provisos of the 1853 accord plus the thirty-two Senate amendments, allowed U.S. merchant vessels free access to all Paraguayan ports, and agreed to submit the Hopkins claim to arbitration.[18]

Buchanan's gunboat diplomacy had succeeded. A triumphant Bowlin reported to Secretary of State Cass: "In addition to the satisfaction of having thus converted a little enemy into a warm friend, we have exhibited to the world a memorable example of the beneficent and civilizing mission of true democracy, as well as of the magnanimity due from the strong to the weak."[19] Bowlin reflected the arrogance of U.S. power and the condescending attitude that characterized U.S. diplomats before him, neither of which did anything to improve the Paraguayan impression of the North Americans.

The Hopkins arbitration did not go well for him. On 13 August 1860 the arbitration commission ruled that Paraguay was not liable for any damages because Hopkins had an unrealistically inflated claim and because Hopkins himself had been largely responsible for the Paraguayan confiscation of the company's property. Furthermore, the commission rejected Hopkins's charge that its only mission was to determine how much Paraguay owed by asserting that its task was to decide between "zero and the highest amount." President Buchanan rejected the commission's decision, and his successor, Abraham Lincoln, pursued the case when he instructed the new U.S. emissary to Paraguay, Charles Ames Washburn, to persuade "El Ciudadano" to indemnify the company. Shortly after his arrival in Asunción on 14 November 1861, Washburn was rebuked by López. Following three months of futile efforts to win the Hopkins claim, the exasperated Washburn proposed sending yet another naval expedition. "It is useless," he cabled Secretary of State William H. Seward, "to attempt to negotiate with a government like this one unless prepared to back up negotiations with blows."[20] Beset by the Civil War, Lincoln did nothing. U.S.-Paraguayan relations remained on testy grounds.

Francisco Solano López and the War of the Triple Alliance

When "El Ciudadano" died on 10 September 1862, the Hopkins claim remained unresolved. The new president, Francisco Solano López, the thirty-eight-year-old son of "El Ciudadano," ignored Washburn's requests to meet with him concerning the Hopkins claims. From the start he reiterated that Paraguay would have nothing more to do with the United States and Paraguay Navigation Company claims. Still, Commissioner Washburn welcomed the change in leadership and wrote that in many respects López was better than his father, having traveled extensively in Europe and learned that Paraguay was not the hub of the universe.[21]

Francisco Solano López lost no time in consolidating his power. On 16 October 1862 the servile Paraguayan Congress elected him president for ten years. "El Brigadier General," as he preferred to be known, showed no signs of departure from the autocratic totalitarianism of his father. The single-party system created by his father allowed for no effective opposition, and the power of the president was supreme. Government, commerce, and the Church were subject to the direct supervision of the president. Unquestioned loyalty to the government was expected of all, and dissident elements were quickly exterminated or sent into exile. Government control and political espionage was so pervasive that Washburn believed that no concerted opposition existed.[22]

In spite of his despotism, López gave tangible evidence of being interested in Paraguay's material progress and cultural achievements. Building the Paraguayan armed forces, however, consumed most of the president's time and effort. By 1863 Paraguay had a standing army of 28,000, with 46,000 reservists. There was no indication that Paraguay was contemplating the idea of waging war with Brazil, but the nation's humiliating experience with Buchanan's gunboat diplomacy had caused "El Brigadier General" to make Paraguay a power in the region.

It was not until late October 1862 that López consented to grant an audience to Washburn. "El Brigadier General" expressed hopes of increasing commerce with the United States and bestowed accolades on the virtues of the people of that country. During the course of the interview López became inquisitive about U.S. naval vessels and "expressed his desire for information in regards to the cost and capacity of such war vessels as the *Monitor.*" The U.S. commissioner, aware of López's boundary dispute with Brazil and eager to entice Paraguay into commercial relations with the United States, jokingly "assured him [López] that if he wanted to whip Brazil, or any other of his neighbors, the Yankees would furnish him the tools to do it with great despatch, on more reasonable terms, giving at the time a more efficient article, than could any other nations or peoples."[23]

Relations between the United States and Paraguay cooled as a crisis developed between Argentina, Brazil, and Paraguay over fluvial rights and boundaries. For Paraguay the crisis became real on 16 April 1863, when exiled Uruguayan *Colorado caudillo* Venancio Flores, aided by his friend, President Bartolomé Mitre of Argentina, crossed the Uruguay River to lead a revolt against the rival *Blancos.* Unstable since its independence, Uruguay had long been a bone of contention between Brazil and Argentina, and López now feared that Argentina would try to create a puppet government in Uruguay or that Brazil would use the crisis to annex Uruguay and, consequently, encroach upon Paraguay.[24]

Alarmed by the intentions of its two powerful neighbors over Uruguay, President Solano López tempted the United States to invoke the Monroe Doctrine when he hinted to Washburn, who had been elevated to minister, about the possibility of a French intervention in the La Plata region similar to the one in Mexico. On 6 October 1863 Washburn described López's fears:

> There are so many French and English in Uruguay that in case of any serious or long war President López fears foreign intervention and that the imperial philanthropist Louis Napoleon may attempt to a similar part in the La Plata countries to what he has played in Mexico. He is exceedingly anxious that the rebellion in the United States may be speedily put down so that our government may be in a condition to interpose against monarchical aggressions in the Americas.[25]

Whether the French threat to Uruguay was real or not, the United States, still enveloped in its Civil War, was in no position to antagonize any European power by intervening in the La Plata region. Furthermore, a Union victory would not have allowed the establishment of a U.S. shield in the Western Hemisphere because of the anticipated postwar reconstruction problems.[26]

Washburn also believed that López was using the Uruguayan crisis to further his dreams of becoming an emperor: "My belief . . . is that he has asked the approval of Louis Napoleon in making himself Emperor of Paraguay and that the latter has proposed the matter to his royal neighbors." The worried Washburn insisted that the United States prepare a contingency plan to deal with "this unprecedented action on the American continent which would undoubtedly be repugnant to the government and people of the United States." As time progressed, Washburn became obsessed with the idea of "El Emperador López," who was building a palace of grand dimensions and had purchased a crown in Paris.[27]

As Washburn worried about López's intentions, the crisis in Uruguay worsened. In March 1864, in the midst of the Uruguayan civil war, the *Blancos* elected Dr. Atanasio Aguirre to the presidency. Aguirre started a repression of *Colorado* sympathizers, which included a number of Brazilian citizens living in the tiny nation. Aguirre's action infuriated Brazil, which threatened to send troops to Uruguay to protect its citizens.

Faced with the Brazilian threat, President Aguirre had no other alternative than to establish an *entente* with Solano López. Possessing a strong army and a burgeoning navy, "El Brigadier General" promised to help Aguirre thwart any hostile action against Uruguay and issued a proclamation to the effect that if Uruguay were to be invaded, Paraguay would declare war against Brazil. As the ominous war clouds were approaching the La Plata region, Secretary of State Seward instructed U.S. envoys to observe strict neutrality and noninterference in the affairs of these nations.

The impulsive López, however, did not plunge into war at the first moment. Instead, in July 1864 he offered Paraguayan mediation in collaboration with Emperor Dom Pedro II of Brazil. The offer was declined by both Brazil and Argentina. On 14 October 1864, when Brazilian troops crossed into Uruguay and occupied the town of Melo to join forces with Flores, López did not immediately declare war on Brazil. Instead, a war of words ensued between the Brazilian minister to Asunción, César Vianna de Lima, and Paraguayan Foreign Minister José Berges. But when the Brazilian steamer *Marqués de Olinda*, carrying Federico Carneiro, the new Brazilian governor of Matto Grosso, docked to coal at Asunción on 11 November 1864, López decided to act, ordering the Paraguayan gunboat *Tacuarí* to intercept the slower steamer after its departure from Asunción. Washburn condemned the incident "as a violation of all laws of war" and also as part of a deliberate plan by López to provoke an invasion of Paraguay and make Brazil look the aggressor. Seward reminded his minister to avoid any unjustified meddling that could result in an unnecessary war.

Despite the growing coolness toward each other, López was dejected when he learned that Washburn had applied for a leave of absence from his post. "El Brigadier General" was convinced that the U.S. envoy could be of service in any attempt at mediation of any crisis in the region since he "was the only minister of any nation to the countries of the Plata who would be acceptable to both parties. All others were hostile to Paraguay." The war that Solano López feared came on 26 January 1865, when Brazil declared war on Paraguay following the latter's invasion of Matto Grosso state.[28]

At the outbreak of hostilities President Bartolomé Mitre of Argentina declared his government's neutrality despite his displeasure with López's act of aggression. On 18 March 1865, however, Paraguay declared war on Argentina, and 30,000 Paraguayan troops entered Corrientes and occupied the province.

López's action precipitated the creation of an alliance between the *Colorados* of Uruguay, Brazil, and Argentina. On 1 May 1865 the Triple Alliance Treaty was signed. Under the terms of the treaty, the Allies were not to withdraw from the conflict until Paraguay had been defeated, but they agreed to respect the independence of Paraguay if victory were to be achieved.

Following the occupation of Corrientes the war went well for the soldiers of "El Mariscal" (López's newly acquired title), but on 10 June 1865 Paraguay lost half of its fleet at Riachuelo. The loss at Riachuelo meant that, except for the impressive fortress of Humaitá, Paraguay had lost control of the Paraguay River and would have to fight a defensive war in the future.[29]

In October 1865, in the midst of the conflict, Washburn returned to the La Plata region. Unable to reach Asunción, the envoy contented himself by sending dispatches to Seward seeking advice regarding the U.S. position in the War of the Triple Alliance. Seward remained committed to nonintervention: "This Government owes it to the belligerents as well as to its own dignity to abstain from everything that could be, or even could appear to be a departure from neutrality in the unhappy contest which is now going on between Paraguay and her Allied enemies. You will be expected to conform your proceeding rapidly to the late principle of non-interference."[30]

In November 1866 Washburn returned to Asunción and pleaded to Secretary Seward for U.S. intervention or mediation. Seward refused to sanction intervention but approved Washburn's offer to mediate, only to have it rejected by the Brazilian Marquis of Caxias, commander of the Allied army.

Following the failed mediation effort, a chagrined Washburn requested to be recalled from his post, but he was refused because his presence in Paraguay was needed to maintain the image of U.S. neutrality. In late December 1867, the Allies renewed their military offensive, prompting Washburn to warn Seward of the possible extermination of the Paraguayan population. With the United States unable to bring peace, Washburn called for European intervention. Seward welcomed the suggestion and informed his ministers in the La Plata region that the United States would not find it objectionable if other neutrals offered to help end the conflict.

That did not happen. In February 1868, the Marquis of Caxias, favored by a rise in the river's waters, ordered his navy's ironclads to pass Humaitá and head for Asunción. This forced the partial evacuation of Humaitá, "the Sevastopol of the South," and opened Paraguay to total invasion from the river.

As the Allies began their bombardment of Asunción, rumors circulated around the city that Washburn, because of his attempted mediation with the Marquis de Caxias, was a Brazilian spy. In July 1868, the spy charge became enmeshed with Washburn's granting of refuge in the U.S. Legation to George Masterman, a British pharmacist employed by "El Mariscal," and Porter Bliss, a U.S. journalist-historian and former employee of the Paraguayan government. Foreign Minister Gregorio Benítez demanded that both men be handed over to Paraguayan authorities on the grounds that they were under contract to the Paraguayan government. In refusing to do so, Washburn claimed that they were members of the legation staff. Angered by Washburn's obstinacy, López charged the U.S. diplomat with being the head of a conspiracy against his government that included Bliss, Masterman, former foreign minister Berges, and "El Mariscal's" two brothers, Benigno and Venancio. Furthermore, Washburn was charged with using his diplomatic post as a way of facilitating correspondence between the conspirators and the Brazilian enemy. It is difficult to ascertain if such a plot really existed. Possibly Solano López fabricated the story to divert attention from Paraguay's military predicament or to eliminate possible rivals.

Washburn left Paraguay in September 1868 only after he claimed that he had to be "rescued" by Commander William Kirkland of the U.S. gunboat *Wasp*, which had been sent to take the diplomat to Buenos Aires. Paraguayan security forces arrested Bliss and Masterman as they were accompanying the envoy to the docks, assuming that they could also board the *Wasp* to leave with him. The espionage charges against Washburn and his failure to protect Bliss and Masterman from arrest stirred public controversy in the United States. A number of newspapers chastised Washburn for leaving Paraguay without his two U.S. Legation employees, and there were calls for a congressional investigation of Washburn's duty tour in Paraguay. President Andrew Johnson did not consider Washburn's participation in the alleged conspiracy improbable, but he refused an intervention in the affairs of the Southern Cone, much less against Paraguay alone. When Johnson subsequently appointed General Martin T. McMahon as minister to Paraguay, he instructed the new envoy to cultivate friendly relations with López and to maintain U.S. neutrality.

When McMahon arrived in Paraguay on 20 October 1868, one of his first tasks was to liberate Bliss and Masterman. After obtaining Allied permission to do so, in late November 1868, McMahon, along with Admiral Charles Henry Davis, commander of the U.S. South Atlantic Squadron, sailed from Asunción to Angostura, a few miles from López's new capital at Prebebuy, on 3 December 1868. In subsequent negotiations López agreed to turn Bliss and Masterman over to Admiral Davis as proof of his friendship toward the United States, provided that the two men declare their guilt to the Paraguayans and that the declaration be witnessed by U.S. officials. On 8 December 1868 the nervous Bliss and Masterman "confessed" to their wrongdoing in front of the Paraguayans, after which they were released to the commander of the *Wasp.*

The Bliss-Masterman incident was a sideshow to the continued attack on Solano López's army. On 1 January 1869 Brazilian troops occupied the already abandoned capital of Asunción. As Solano López's army retreated northward, General McMahon followed the Paraguayans, offered his services as mediator, and suggested to the Paraguayan president that he should voluntarily go to exile in the United States. "El Mariscal," however, refused the U.S. envoy's offer.

U.S. presence in the region suffered another setback in May 1869 when McMahon was unexpectedly recalled. Although no explanations were given for the action, there was speculation that his close relationship with "El Mariscal" was objectionable to the Allies. More likely was the fact that McMahon's presence in Paraguay was offensive to Charles Washburn's brother Elihu, who had been named acting secretary of state at the time.

For the next year and a half, the war went badly for Paraguay. While López's depleted army fought for survival, the Paraguayan dictator appealed to the United States, hoping that previous offers of mediation would now bear fruit. López now recognized the need for U.S. presence in the region and requested a replacement for McMahon. The most intriguing appeal for U.S. help came from the Paraguayan chargé d'affaires in Paris, former foreign minister Gregorio Benítez. He wrote a number of letters to Secretary of State Hamilton Fish asking for his help in defusing Allied propaganda against Paraguay and petitioning for U.S. mediation. In his correspondence to Fish, the Paraguayan chargé stressed that an Allied victory would give Brazil a virtual monopoly over navigation in the La Plata region and also bring the French to the region because one of the daughters of Brazilian Emperor Dom Pedro II was married to the Comte D'Eau, and since the emperor had no male heirs, the count would undoubtedly succeed the emperor to the Brazilian throne. The count was a member of the French House of Orleans, and his presence in Brazil constituted a violation of the Monroe Doctrine.[31]

In January 1870 "El Mariscal" made one last attempt to enlist aid from the Grant administration. He sent his son Emiliano López to Washington, where he received friendly treatment but otherwise accomplished nothing. The United States "was not to interfere in a war which did not directly affect American interests."[32]

The war came to its bloody end on 1 March 1870, when Brazilian cavalry caught up with "El Mariscal" and shot him at point-blank range. "Muero con mi patria" (I die with the fatherland), López gasped with his last breath. The War of the Triple Alliance had finally ended.

The War of the Triple Alliance was the bloodiest and costliest war in Latin American history, resulting in more than 291,000 Allied deaths and an estimated cost of $3.5 million. For Paraguay the war meant virtual extinction, for at the end of the fighting there were only 28,746 males left in the country, while the country's monetary and property losses were immeasurable. During the War of the Triple

Alliance, U.S. noninterference and strict neutrality reflected the fact that the war did not affect U.S. interests.[33]

Postwar Relations

Until the end of the century, U.S.-Paraguayan relations shifted to the back burner except for the perennial Hopkins claim and other minor issues.

On 26 August 1870 John Lloyd Stevens presented his credentials to President Cirilo Rivarola as minister to Uruguay and Paraguay. He stayed briefly before settling in at Montevideo, but his stay was long enough for him to recognize the continued Brazilian threat to the beleaguered Paraguay. "It is hoped that Brazil," he informed Secretary of State Hamilton Fish, "having destroyed López and reduced the boundaries of the country in the future be content to expand its resources of men and money in developing its own immense domain."[34] The minister was not overreacting to what he saw in Asunción but was expressing a real concern about potential Brazilian hegemony in the Río de la Plata region. When Stevens returned to Asunción in July 1871, the threat to Paraguay's territory had intensified. During this brief visit, President Rivarola asked for U.S. support in placating the Allies' greed for territorial aggrandizement, "believing that an earnest word from the President [Grant] on behalf of a struggling people will be courteously received by the Brazilian and Argentine governments."[35]

Trade with Brazil by the United States, however, superseded concern over Brazilian hegemony. Washington refused to act. Nevertheless, U.S. ministers to Paraguay, who continued to live in Montevideo, repeatedly voiced their mistrust of Brazilian control over Paraguay through a series of "puppet" presidents.

Argentina and Paraguay became involved in a dispute over the Gran Chaco region, located between the Pilcomayo and Verde Rivers. In January 1877, both nations requested that President Ulysses S. Grant of the United States settle the dispute. Grant accepted the challenge, but the case was actually completed by president-elect Rutherford B. Hayes. He ruled on 12 November 1878 that Paraguay was "legally and justly entitled to the territory between the Pilcomayo and the Verde Rivers and to the Villa Occidental situated therein" but gave no reason for his decision. As a manifestation of its appreciation for the president's decision Paraguay changed the name of Villa Occidental to Villa Hayes.

For nearly twenty years after the Brazilian occupation of Asunción in January 1869, Edward A. Hopkins remained a thorn in the side of both the Paraguayan and U.S. governments. Ever searching for new opportunities, Hopkins opened a sawmill at Villa Occidental in the disputed Gran Chaco area. When on 28 September 1869 the Paraguayan government imposed license taxes on business enterprises to collect much-needed revenues, Hopkins asserted that the tax did not apply to his operation because it was on Argentine territory. When the Paraguayan government pointed out that it had granted him permission to operate the sawmill in Paraguayan territory, Hopkins turned to General Emilio Mitre, commander of the Argentine occupation forces at Villa Occidental. The feeble Paraguayans were unable to respond. Once again, the Vermonter had provoked an embarrassing incident for Paraguay.

On 13 August 1870, Hopkins persuaded the State Department to reopen the claims case of the United States and Paraguay Navigation Company. The Paraguayan government insisted that the case had been closed for some time and that all records relating to the case had been destroyed in the fighting over Asunción. In explaining this to Secretary of State Hamilton Fish, Stevens also suggested the case be dropped because Paraguay was too impoverished, as illustrated by the fact that the government could not collect sufficient monies to meet its own operating expenses. The issue should have been put to rest, but the persistent Hopkins was willing to accept land rather than the estimated $1 million the claim had escalated to because of accumulated interest.

In May 1886, U.S. chargé John Bacon and Hopkins held a series of meetings with Paraguay's foreign minister, José Decoud. As before, Decoud explained that Paraguay held that the case, now twenty-five years old, had been settled by arbitration. Not to be dissuaded, Hopkins proposed yet another form of settlement, $104,000 in gold. Decoud was not impressed and repeated his government's stance. After all, he told Hopkins, the United States never notified Paraguay of any objections to the 1860 award. If Hopkins was frustrated, Bacon was incensed. In a note to the State Department, Bacon described the atrocious acts committed against the company, insults heaped upon the U.S. government, and the millions of squandered dollars.

Still another attempt at settlement was made in July 1887. This time President Patricio Escobar of Paraguay and the new foreign minister, Benjamín Aceval, struck a deal with Hopkins to pay his United States and Paraguay Navigation Company $90,000 in gold, but the Paraguayan Chamber of Deputies defeated the measure by one vote. The Chamber's action reflected the rivalries of Paraguayan politics and also prompted Hopkins to demand again that his government use force to collect the claim.

While a dejected Hopkins continued to bombard chargé Bacon and the State Department with letters demanding support for his claim, Washington decided to put the matter aside as it set course for new directions in its relations with Latin America. Over the thirty years since Hopkins first presented his claim, U.S. taxpayers spent $7,000,000 in futile efforts to settle the issue.[36]

In the 1890s Paraguay received scant attention from the U.S. State Department. Few U.S. ministers to Paraguay and Uruguay visited Asunción. They preferred to stay in Montevideo, and their dispatches were limited to rather superficial briefings of their occasional visits to Paraguay. The quiescence changed in 1898 following the sinking of the cruiser *Maine* in Havana harbor. As the United States and Spain moved toward war, Washington concerned itself with possible Spanish moves in the Southern Cone. In the Río de la Plata area, U.S. diplomats were instructed to monitor the movement of the Spanish gunboat *Temerario* anchored at Montevideo. Three weeks after the outbreak of the Spanish-American War, the *Temerario* set sail for Asunción, where it subsequently docked for repairs. Spain offered to sell the vessel to Paraguay, a suggestion that prompted U.S. chargé d'affaires William R. Finch to propose that Paraguay buy the *Temerario* and sell it to the United States, which would lease it back to Paraguay for one or two years! Although no deal was struck, the *Temerario* remained at Asunción to make the necessary repairs under the watchful eye of Paraguayan naval officers. The worried Finch envisioned that the repaired *Temerario* would then be of assistance to the Spanish government by attacking U.S. vessels in the Río de la Plata. Once repairs were completed, Finch's vision never came to pass. On 20 July 1898, seventeen days after the U.S. naval victory at Santiago Bay, the *Temerario* left Asunción for Brazil with the understanding, imposed by the U.S. representatives, that it could not return to Paraguayan waters. Once again, Paraguay had been humiliated by the "Colossus of the North."[37] For some time thereafter, relations between the United States and Paraguay drifted as few U.S. citizens were interested in a humiliated and bankrupt Paraguay.

U.S.-Uruguayan Relations

Diplomatic relations between the United States and Uruguay commenced on 1 July 1834, when Washington issued an *exequatur* to Uruguay's consul-general, John Darby. Little more happened for the next generation as the United States preoccupied itself with westward expansion and domestic expansion. For its part, Uruguay was immersed in a continuous cycle of revolutions between the two traditional parties, the *Blancos* and the *Colorados*. Between 1850 and 1869 each nation slowly began to take account of each other. Their limited contacts established the groundwork for future discourse.

When Uruguay opened its rivers to the vessels and commerce of all nations on 10 October 1853 it resulted in increased information about Uruguay and the Río de la Plata system. But the reports were often as inaccurate as that filed by James B. Bowlin, the U.S. commissioner to Paraguay. On 20 December 1858, Bowlin informed Secretary of State Lewis Cass that in Uruguay, "I find two parties here, formed I presume by the titles they bear upon a difference of race and colour— They are known as the Blancas [*sic*] and the Colarados [*sic*], meaning no doubt, white and coloured races—and the Blancas [*sic*] are now in the ascendant in this Republic."[38] Bowlin did not understand that the *Blancos* were a traditionally conservative party and that the *Colorados* expressed a more liberal viewpoint. Race played no part in these political philosophies.

The first U.S. diplomat assigned to Montevideo was General Alexander Asboth, a veteran of the Civil War and an inexperienced diplomat who gave little attention to Uruguay. Instead he focused on Argentina and its role in the War of the Triple Alliance. Despite Asboth's aloofness, the Uruguayan government held out hopes that the assignment of a permanent diplomat to Montevideo would bring some benefits. The Uruguayans had to be disappointed. Before his death in January 1868, Asboth did little more than send a few reports about the country to the State Department.

Asboth's replacements, Henry B. Worthington and Robert C. Kirk, were equally disinterested. Each remained stationed for less than a year at the Buenos Aires legation and also showed greater concern for the War of the Triple Alliance than with the fate of Uruguay.[39]

As a result of these limited contacts, policymakers in Washington and Montevideo had little knowledge about the other when increased contacts began after the U.S. Civil War.

Developing Interests: 1870–1884

Events in 1870 created an environment more conducive for diplomatic discourse between Washington and Montevideo. For the Uruguayans and the rest of the Southern Cone region, the end to the War of the Triple Alliance provided the opportunity to look abroad for new contacts. With its Civil War over and industrial expansion beginning to take off, the United States also looked abroad for markets. Secretary of State Hamilton Fish took this opportunity to restate a long-standing U.S. objective: "close relations of geographical continuity and political friendship justly entitled the United States to a share of Latin American trade." John Stevens was appointed minister to Uruguay in 1870, but, unlike his predecessors, Stevens was stationed in Montevideo with no additional duties in Buenos Aires. He was the first person to hold such an assignment. When Stevens presented his credentials to President Lorenzo Batlle in July 1870, Uruguay's commercial possibilities appeared endless because of its unique location on the mouth of the Río de la Plata system. "The Republic of Uruguay occupies a significant and important position. . . . Its flourishing capital stands as a commercial base of one of the most commanding rivers of the continent and cannot fail to have an important future in population and in material wealth," Stevens told Batlle.[40]

Although Stevens and his successors, John Caldwell and William Williams, described Uruguay's business climate as hospitable, none of them really explored the possibilities or sought to exert an increased U.S. presence. In reality Uruguay's business environment was not so hospitable. The continuous rebellions and political instability exacted a high price on the Uruguayan economy, for the rebellions dealt successive shocks to the economic mechanisms. Even the minor disturbances frequently occasioned weeks of disquiet and alarm.[41] In 1875 President José Eugenio Elluari confronted a severe financial crisis. Public confidence waned and rumors of revolution circulated. In order to stabilize the economy and quiet the political arena, the government issued a new and devalued paper currency. This brought a strong reaction from the diplomatic community. An alarmed Caldwell wrote Fish, "The [Uruguayan] Secretary of Treasury proposes to pay the interest of the national debt in this irredeemable paper . . . [and] it will cause the ruin of many commercial houses which are large holders." Caldwell joined the diplomatic representatives from several European nations to protest the use of devalued currency to pay international debt obligations even though U.S. companies had a limited interest in Uruguay's treasury notes. Collectively, Caldwell and the ministers of Great Britain, Italy, Spain, Brazil, and the Germanic Empire issued a joint protest to Elluari and warned of dire economic consequences if Uruguay failed to alter course. Elluari caved in to the pressure but sought no other remedy to the nation's financial crisis, and as a result political instability followed the precarious economic situation, meaning Uruguay remained an unattractive spot for foreign investors and merchants.[42]

Following the crisis, relations between the United States and Uruguay reached a nadir until the mid-1880s. The U.S. representatives remained content to do little more than pass along occasional comments on the local political situation, but there were no tangible results.

Establishing a U.S. Presence: 1885–1903

In the latter part of the nineteenth century the United States pursued a more aggressive policy toward all Latin America. As enunciated in 1881 by Secretary of State James G. Blaine, the United States would seek to increase its economic activity and to lessen the European presence. To Blaine, "commercial expansion constituted only part of the grand task; it must be matched with skilled diplomacy to . . . block European intrusion in the hemisphere."[43] Diplomats like Judge John E. Bacon and William R. Finch in Uruguay from 1885 to 1903 used their offices to extend U.S. interests, and they registered a marked degree of success in reaching U.S. policy objectives.

Judge Bacon, who proved to be the first effective U.S. diplomat in Montevideo, was appointed chargé d'affaires in 1885, after a distinguished career that began as secretary in the St. Petersburg legation in 1857. An accomplished linguist, Bacon was eager to prove to the State Department that Uruguay had a significant place in the scope of U.S. policy objectives. In preparing for his assignment Bacon found that "the files of the State Department . . . were almost blank," a fact that influenced him subsequently to apprise the department of all facets of Uruguayan life. Bacon meticulously recounted the numerous revolts, cabinet shufflings, and cultural activities of the Uruguayan nation. His detailed communiqués not only informed about events in Uruguay but also encouraged further U.S. involvement along two lines. First, Bacon felt that economic opportunities in Uruguay should be exploited by U.S. capital, and, second, a stronger U.S. presence was necessary in order to protect its citizens and property from the constant civil strife between the *Blancos* and *Colorados*.

Although trade between Uruguay and the United States after 1880 had increased somewhat, Bacon asserted that the prospects in 1886 were even greater largely because of the nation's political tranquility. General Máximo Tajes, elected president of Uruguay in 1886, created a calm atmosphere in which political opposition did not seem to jeopardize the political arena. Bacon also pointed out that the substantial internal-improvement programs undertaken by Tajes expanded opportunities for foreign investors. Tajes also brought a sense of stability to the erratic Uruguayan economy. The sudden turn of the republic from practical bankruptcy to financial prosperity pleased businessmen in Montevideo and Buenos Aires.

But questions remained. Where could U.S. companies make prudent investments? How could they capitalize on trade opportunities? The problem of South American trade and investment was not a new one for the United States. For several years, the issue of direct trade with Latin America commanded the earnest attention of Congress and the president, but no definite or satisfactory solution could be reached.

In Uruguay, Bacon pointed to several opportunities: "Government securities has [*sic*] appreciated in the most wonderful manner. The real estate within the city limits . . . has appreciated in value in the ratio of 10 to 1 and land in the country have [*sic*] doubled and tripled in prices." In addition to selective investments within Uruguay, the United States needed to find manufactured items that could be exported to Uruguay at prices cheaper than those the European commercial houses offered. Here Bacon suggested the wool-processing and garment-making industries, because "woolen goods of all sorts can and will be manufactured in the United States cheaper than in England or Belgium, especially such articles as hats, clothing, blankets, etc."[44]

Although Bacon's endeavors led to an increase in the U.S. market share of manufactured goods, the United States still failed to end Great Britain's economic domination of the area. Bacon, however, remained confident that if the United States persevered it would pass the British in the not too distant future.

In addition to promoting U.S. economic interests, Bacon sought to protect U.S. property and lives, which were often endangered by the frequent political upheavals that plagued Uruguay. He was astonished by the number of U.S. citizens residing in Uruguay who claimed the protection of the stars and stripes. The legation's inability to protect U.S. citizens was illustrated by an incident at Paysandú in March 1886, when a revolt broke out against the government of President Máximo Santos. At Paysandú the U.S. enterprise Shufnagel and Company owned real estate and goods valued at approximately $350,000. The property was located at positions of strategic importance on the Uruguay River for both revolutionary and government forces in the area. The company appealed to Bacon for advice and protection of the property because the U.S. steamer *Nipsic* had left the River Plate and its replacement the *Talapoosa* was not yet halfway to the area, but Bacon could do no more than suggest the company have its property appraised and then "notify in writing anyone of the belligerents . . . that it was the property of American citizens and that they would be held strictly responsible for any loss or damage that might accrue thereto."[45] Bacon did find comfort, however, in the offer made by Vice Consul John Chaplin of Great Britain: "Should the necessity unfortunately arise Her Majesty's Ships 'Ready' and 'Stork' at present in this harbour are prepared to afford the same protection to your flag as to our own. Also furthermore that Her Majesty's ships above named would be open to receive refugees of the United States and their portable property."[46] The United States and Great Britain may have been economic competitors in the region, but Chaplin's offer indicated that it was at least a friendly one. The threat passed and the property and real estate of

Shufnagel and Company escaped damage and the British services were not needed, but the incident illustrated a U.S. weakness and the need for a greater diplomatic and military presence.

The numerous claims by U.S. citizens against the Uruguayan government further illustrated the need for a strong U.S. presence in Montevideo. Bacon felt overwhelmed with the number of claims, involving millions of dollars and also the most outrageous abuses of U.S. citizens and their property. One of the most prolific claims was that of R. R. Pearler. The claim dated to the destruction of his property during Colonel Lorenzo Latorre's successful 1875 revolution. Pearler tried to resolve the issue himself and, failing that, turned it over to the U.S. legation, which ignored it until Bacon's arrival in 1885. The Pearler claim was for $3 million. Even the State Department vilified the confiscation, describing it as a "lawless confiscation of Mr. Pearler's property . . . [and] by its confiscation of the property . . . the Constitutional government thereby made itself a party and participant in a gross act of oppression and injustice against an American citizen." Bacon labored on the case for two years until 1888, when it was finally settled. Pearler received $80,000 in gold, a mere fraction of the original $3 million claim.[47]

Unfortunately, Bacon's perceptions about Uruguay's political climate demonstrated his failure to understand local dynamics, which in turn misled policymakers in Washington. For example, he failed to comprehend the political manipulations and constitutional abuses of President Máximo Santos. In January 1886, Bacon described President Santos as an energetic young man who had done much for his country by providing it with a longer period of continuous peace than anyone before him. Such admiration did not reflect the political reality of Santos's presidency.

Bacon's contemporaries were more realistic. The German minister to Uruguay, Baron von Rotenham, noted that although Santos began his career with little financial assets, he had acquired over 7,000,000 pesos before he left the president's office. Many young Uruguayan intellectuals, especially José Batlle, denounced the Santos government as a negation of the whole spirit of democracy. Batlle asserted that the national sovereignty, honor, and dignity were crucified by his henchmen.[48]

Despite his lack of finesse and understanding of the Uruguayan political climate, Bacon gave the State Department the most comprehensive information to date and urged it to take a firmer economic and political stand in the region. He became the first U.S. envoy to put forth a comprehensive investment plan for Uruguay that showed tangible results. Despite his optimism and determination, Bacon failed to gain a prominent position for the United States. The State Department did not attach the importance to Uruguay that Bacon did and therefore denied his numerous requests for the stationing of a naval vessel at Montevideo to enhance his negotiating position. Also, Uruguay was not prepared to break its long-standing economic and political dependence that bound her to Great Britain. English capital and enterprise dominated the Uruguayan economy, with over £25 million in English sterling invested in the 1880s alone.

In the 1890s circumstances changed in Uruguay. The economic boom fostered by unrestrained English investment came to a grinding halt as British investors became wary of investing in the region. Uruguay, accustomed to the seemingly endless flow of credit sterling, found itself in a protracted financial crisis. Although some British investment continued, little new English capital found its way to Montevideo for more than a decade. Uruguay, shunned by her transatlantic partner, desperately needed new investment partners to remedy the current crisis. In this climate, Uruguay actively sought U.S. investment and requested to Washington that the United States play a greater role in the Southern Cone region.

The British economic abandonment of Uruguay had short-term significance in allowing other nations, including the United States, into a domain that had previously been viewed as exclusively British. More important though were the long-term effects. The financial crisis caused Uruguayans to evaluate British influence, which touched on almost every aspect of the republic. Peter Winn compared the office of the president of Uruguay to that of the manager of a great ranch whose board of directors is in London. The extent of involvement was deemed too intrusive, and the Uruguayan government sought permanent solutions to remedy British economic domination.

Also the delicate balance of power in the Southern Cone region was threatened by the reemergence of the Argentine-Chilean boundary dispute. Their common boundary had been settled by arbitration in 1884, but the vague terminology led to constant misunderstandings that threatened the peace in 1895 when Chile confronted Argentina over the issue, and Brazil made overtures to Chile for an alliance against Argentina. In this ambience, Argentina tried to lure Uruguay into an alliance, but the administration adamantly refused.

The Uruguayan government understood that an Argentine-Chilean conflict would bring Brazil across their common border. Minister of Foreign Affairs Jaime Estrazulas of Uruguay explained that Brazil had never become reconciled to the loss of Uruguay in 1828, and, in the event of war between Chile and Argentina, Brazil would reclaim Uruguay. Uruguay was too weak to enforce its self-professed neutrality, and in all likelihood it would become the battleground in the contest between Argentina and Brazil.

In hopes of preventing the seemingly inevitable, on 21 August 1895 the Uruguayan government suspended the rights of foreign warships to have gun practice within a three-mile limit of its shore or to land men for drill practice because it feared that Chile and Argentina would use those exercises on the Uruguayan coast as a cloak for an examination of landing places from which to establish a base of operations. Estrazulas apologized to Stuart because the decree also applied to the United States, but he begged the minister's understanding. Although Stuart understood the logic of Uruguay's action, unfortunately it did nothing to stop war preparations, as both Argentina and Chile increased their navies, drilled and equipped their national guards, and placed their respective countries on a war footing. But like many of his U.S. colleagues, Stuart failed to comprehend the nationalistic feelings that motivated the Latin Americans when he observed that the existing treaties between Chile and Argentina provided for the arbitration of all differences between them.

As the diplomatic war of words between Argentina and Chile continued for two more years, William J. Finch replaced Stuart in late 1897. Whereas Finch did much to increase U.S. economic activity and to challenge European influence, it was more important that he had a greater understanding of Uruguayan and South American politics than his predecessors.

Finch arrived in Montevideo just as the country was entering another period of political tranquility. Finch would find the presidency of Juan Lindolfo Cuestas a model of co-participation that ushered in political peace, whereas Stuart had resided in a republic governed by an arbitrary military oligarchy. The Uruguayan economy had also achieved a great degree of stability, but, unfortunately, it had become increasingly dependent on foreign investment and foreign loans, which allowed foreign companies, mainly British, to exploit the country.[49] Furthermore, the profits from the goods and services bought by the Uruguayans made their way to foreign banks.[50] The situation became so acute in 1898, that Senator José Batlle declared: "While we may have destroyed the colonial system in the political sphere, we did not destroy it in industry, in commerce. . . . The fact is that an immense amount of the country's wealth leaves it. . . . Its industries are like those fishing fleets that establish themselves along the coasts of desert islands. They carry off everything they can and weigh anchor."[51]

To counteract British economic domination, the Uruguayan government sought to increase its commercial and political ties with the United States. It hoped to ease the British stranglehold without disrupting the foreign-driven economy. The situation provided Finch with an opportunity to increase the U.S. presence in Uruguay, but he first needed to define the U.S. role in the Argentine-Chilean confrontation regarding Uruguayan neutrality. Three years had passed since the Argentine-Chilean problem first arose, and in the continuing tense atmosphere war always loomed on the horizon. He begged a State Department position in March 1898: "What will be the attitude of the United States with reference to the neutrality of Uruguay in the event of war between Chile and Argentina? Will the United States notify Argentina and Chile that they must keep off Uruguay's territory, or will the attitude of the U.S. be that of an indifferent spectator?" Finch preferred U.S. intervention and put forth the hypothesis many Uruguayans themselves had formulated, "England has large interests here and would gladly make Uruguay a part of her colonial possessions, and if she comes here to protect Uruguay's neutrality she may decide to annex her."[52]

In an effort to persuade the State Department into taking up Uruguay's cause, Finch commenced a campaign reminiscent of Bacon's regarding the attributes of the Uruguayan people. He also pointed out that Uruguay supported U.S. policy in the Spanish-American War. Furthermore, he indicated that President Cuestas permitted U.S. warships to be provisioned in Montevideo, while denying the Spanish a similar request. The Uruguayan government also granted a U.S. request to permit consular supplies to enter the country duty free but did not make it public because of President Cuestas's unwillingness to extend the same privileges to the other consulates in the city. As a result of these concessions Finch recommended that the United States support Uruguay's neutrality during the Argentine-Chilean crisis.

The State Department was not persuaded. Secretary of State John Hay concluded that the United States would not guarantee Uruguay's neutrality against encroachment of Argentina, Chile, or Brazil. Undaunted, President Cuestas persisted and on 9 December 1901 pleaded for the United States to provide Uruguay with a moral guarantee by maintaining two or three ships at Montevideo. Cuestas also played the British card and, according to Finch, preferred British assistance "if the Government of the United States is indisposed to lend a hand."[53] The United States refused to become involved, and the Argentine-Chilean boundary dispute was finally submitted to successful arbitration in 1902.

Despite its refusal to become embroiled in the conflict, the United States achieved a solid foothold because of the Uruguayan government's preference for the United States over Great Britain. The "Great Neighbor of the North" had been openly courted by Uruguay to help maintain the balance of power in the Southern Cone. It undermined British political influence in Uruguay that had been steadily cultivated since the British siege of Montevideo in 1806.

Uruguay also sought out the United States to supplant British influence in the economic market. Although U.S investors were not major players in the Uruguayan economy, in 1898 U.S. private landholdings in Uruguay reached $1 million. To lure U.S. investors, Uruguay assured Finch that they would be given preferential treatment with government contracts, which permitted Finch to secure several opportunities for U.S. financial investments at the expense of the British and other European powers. The most tangible benefit was the $15 million Montevideo Port Bill granted to U.S. companies in 1899.[54]

Like his predecessors, Finch found himself engaged in controversies between U.S. interests and Uruguayans. The most noteworthy incident centered around the visit of Methodist Bishop Charles C. McCabe to Uruguay, and Finch revealed his own naiveté regarding the strength of the Uruguayan conservative Catholic element. At McCabe's personal request, he introduced the bishop to the minister of foreign affairs and subsequently to President Cuestas. Finch viewed the short and pleasant meeting as harmless and routine; the Montevideo papers did not agree.[55]

The staunchly Catholic newspaper *El Bien* roundly criticized Finch for his act and questioned the motives of the introduction:

> The diplomatic representative of the United States personally presenting the Protestant ecclesiastic dignitary . . . without doubt offers a curious case in the relations of two sovereign States: the one Catholic, the other Protestant . . . there is no doubt that the arrival of the functionary is to reinforce the Protestant propaganda in our country, and, with it, to strengthen the moral conquest of . . . Spanish America, a conquest which we can but view with patriotic distrust.[56]

Bishop McCabe's response to the newspaper article fueled Catholic discontent. In a letter to and published by *El Bien,* McCabe asserted, "That the Methodists will be content if they obtain all the people over which the Roman Church has lost control: those who never go to mass, nor to confess, nor to the Church, and whose numbers reach ten millions; and we will make our greatest effort to obtain them."[57] Finch had made an error in judgment that resulted in open criticism of the U.S. diplomat. The outcry concerning McCabe's visit faded, but the incident again illustrated the diplomat's lack of understanding of Latin American culture.

Through the nineteenth and the beginning of the twentieth century, Uruguay was part of the British informal empire. "British capital dominated transportation, communications, utilities and insurance. . . . All seven of the international loans Uruguay had contracted during the preceding four decades had been floated in London, and Uruguay was linked to England by the highest per capita debt in South America."[58] U.S. diplomats in Uruguay recognized this point and some, such as Judge Bacon, tried to find niches in which U.S. merchants could successfully compete. But, without a significant commitment from the U.S. government to wrest Uruguay away from Britain and include Uruguay in its sphere of influence, all economic and political actions within the country were relatively insignificant. Not until the 1890s was the United States able to maneuver into position and begin to exert influence that would grow in the first decade of the twentieth century and eventually supplant the British in the aftermath of World War I.

Diplomatic relations between the United States and the two Guaraní-named republics of Latin America reflected a lack of interest and understanding on the part of the State Department. In the case of Paraguay, U.S. policy toward the landlocked nation through the War of the Triple Alliance was characterized by a lack of clear guidelines, which encouraged U.S. envoys to form their own style of personal diplomacy, oftentimes contributing to increased tension and friction between themselves and their hosts. After the War of the Triple Alliance, U.S.-Paraguayan relations entered into a dormant stage, characterized by a condescending U.S. attitude and indifference toward the vanquished nation.

Conversely, from 1834 until the late nineteenth century, diplomatic relations between the United States and Uruguay reflected Uruguay's insignificance for the State Department. Beginning in 1885 with John E. Bacon, and subsequently with William R. Finch, the United States started to increase its economic and political role in the country. Although the British remained the dominant outsider by the end of the nineteenth century, the United States found itself greatly favored by the Uruguayans. Unfortunately, the United States preferred to remain a distant and indifferent spectator concerning *La República Oriental.* Uruguay, like its neighbor Paraguay, continued to remain in the periphery of U.S. interest.

NOTES

Chapter 1. Mexico

1. The doctrine of popular sovereignty permitted the residents of each U.S. territory to determine the status of slavery in their area.

2. Thomas Ewing Cotner, *The Military and Political Career of José Joaquín de Herrera, 1792–1854* (Austin: University of Texas Press, 1949), 172–220.

3. The text of the Treaty of Guadalupe Hidalgo is in Antonio de la Pena y Reyes, *Algunos documentos sobre el tratado de Guadalupe y la situación de México durante la invasión americana,* 2nd ed. (Mexico City: Editorial Porrua, 1970), 114–37.

4. León C. Metz, *Border: The U.S.-Mexico Line* (El Paso: Mangan Books, 1989), 11–18.

5. Ibid., 20–29, 65–68; Oscar J. Martínez, *Troublesome Border* (Tucson: University of Arizona Press, 1988), 16–18. A commission appointed in March 1853 under the leadership of Major William Emory surveyed the Rio Grande portion of the boundary without encountering major diplomatic or technical problems.

6. The treaty is usually referred to as the Gadsden Purchase in U.S. history and the Treaty of La Mesilla in Mexican history. The standard, if dated, work on the treaty in English is Paul N. Garber, *The Gadsden Treaty* (Philadelphia: University of Pennsylvania Press, 1923). For the Mexican viewpoint on the treaty, see Luis G. Zorrilla, *Historia de las relaciones entre México y los Estados Unidos de America, 1800–1958,* 2 vols. (Mexico City: Editorial Porrua, 1965–66), 1:335–60.

7. Edward H. Moseley, "The United States and Mexico, 1810–1850," in *United States–Latin American Relations, 1800–1850,* edited by T. Ray Shurbutt (Tuscaloosa: University of Alabama Press, 1991), 128–44.

8. Charles H. Brown, *Agents of Manifest Destiny: The Lives and Times of the Filibusters* (Chapel Hill: University of North Carolina Press, 1980), 175–208.

9. Ibid., 191–93, 208–17; Marcy to Mexican minister to the United States Juan Almonte, 12 June 1854, in William R. Manning, ed., *Diplomatic Correspondence of the United States: Inter-American Affairs, 1831–1860,* 12 vols. (Washington, D.C.: Carnegie Endowment for International Peace, 1932–39), 9:164–65.

10. Gadsden to Marcy, 18 May 1855, Manning, *Diplomatic Correspondence,* 9:771–76.

11. Gadsden to Marcy, 5 December 1855, 4 October 1856, Marcy to Gadsden, 30 June 1856, Manning, *Diplomatic Correspondence,* 9:205, 803–6, 847–50.

12. Marcy to Forsyth, 16 August 1856, Manning, *Diplomatic Correspondence,* 9:209–10.

13. Donathon C. Olliff, *Reforma Mexico and the United States: A Search for Alternatives to Annexation, 1854–1861* (Tuscaloosa: University of Alabama Press, 1981), 49–51, 58–60.

14. Forsyth to Marcy, 8 November 1856, Manning, *Diplomatic Correspondence,* 9:9, 854–56.

15. Forsyth to Marcy, 1 and 15 January 1857, Manning, *Diplomatic Correspondence,* 9:877–78; Olliff, *Reforma Mexico and the United States,* 69–72.

16. Forsyth to Marcy, 2 and 10 February 1857, Manning, *Diplomatic Correspondence,* 9:888–93; Olliff, *Reforma Mexico and the United States,* 72–73.

17. Marcy to Forsyth, 3 March 1857, Cass to Forsyth, 11 March 1857, 17 November 1857, Manning, *Diplomatic Correspondence,* 9:219–20, 243–47.

18. Cass to Forsyth, 17 July 1857 (two communications), Manning, *Diplomatic Correspondence,* 9:223–38; Zorrilla, *Historia de las relaciones,* 1:375–77.

19. Forsyth to Cass, 15 September 1857, Manning, *Diplomatic Correspondence,* 9:929–36; Olliff, *Reforma Mexico and the United States,* 88–89.

20. Lerdo de Tejada to Forsyth, 12 September 1857, Manning, *Diplomatic Correspondence,* 9:926–27; Zorrilla, *Historia de las relaciones,* 2:377.

21. Walter V. Scholes, *Mexican Politics During the Juárez Regime, 1855–1872* (Columbia: University of Missouri Press, 1969), 20–24; Forsyth to Cass, 18 November 1857, 17 December 1857, 29 January 1858, 30 January 1858, Manning, *Diplomatic Correspondence,* 9:946, 962–63, 965–66.

22. Forsyth to Cass, 13 and 15 February 1858, 1 March 1858, Manning, *Diplomatic Correspondence,* 9:967–70.

23. Forsyth to Cuevas, 22 March 1858, 8 April 1858, Cuevas to Forsyth, 5 April 1858, Manning, *Diplomatic Correspondence,* 9:971–79.

24. Forsyth to Cuevas, 21 June 1858, Manning, *Diplomatic Correspondence,* 9:1000–6; Olliff, *Reforma Mexico and the United States,* 104–8.

25. Instituto Nacional de Antropología e Historia, *Colección de documentos inéditos o muy raros relativos a la reforma en México,* 2 vols. (Mexico City: Instituto Nacional de Antropología e Historia, 1957–58), 1:91–93, 105–18, 121–25, 140–43; *Congressional Globe,* 35th congress, 1st session, 735–36; James D. Richardson, ed., *A Compilation of the Messages and Papers of the Presidents, 1789–1897,* 10 vols. (Washington, D.C.: Government Printing Office, 1896–99), 5:511–14, 538–40 (hereafter Richardson, *Messages and Papers*).

26. Richardson, *Messages and Papers,* 5:513; Cass to Churchwell, 27 December 1858, Churchwell to Cass, 8 and 22 February 1859, Manning, *Diplomatic Correspondence,* 9:255–56, 1024–30, 1032–35.

27. Cass to McLane, 7 March 1859, McLane to Cass, 7 April 1859, Diez de Bonilla to U.S. Consul at Mexico City, 14 April 1859, Diez de Bonilla to Cass, 14 April 1859, Manning, *Diplomatic Correspondence,* 9:256–58, 1037–47; Instituto Nacional de Antropología e Historia, *Colección de documentos relativos a la reforma,* 2:111–29.

28. Cass to McLane, 24 May 1859, 19 and 30 July 1859, McLane to Cass, 21 April 1859, 12 July 1859, 7 December 1859, Manning, *Diplomatic Correspondence,* 9:260–64, 268–75, 1050–56, 1108–9, 1135–36.

29. McLane to Cass, 14 December 1859, Manning, *Diplomatic Correspondence,* 9:1137–45; Olliff, *Reforma Mexico and the United States,* 129–45.

30. Karl M. Schmitt, *Mexico and the United States, 1821–1973: Conflict and Coexistence* (New York: Wiley, 1974), 83–85; Scholes, *Mexican Politics,* 35–37.

31. McLane to Cass, 21 January 1860, 9 and 30 March 1860, Manning, *Diplomatic Correspondence,* 9:1156–58, 1167, 1170–73; Scholes, *Mexican Politics,* 29–30, 37–38.

32. Frank Lawrence Owsley, *King Cotton Diplomacy: Foreign Relations of the Confederate States of America,* 2nd ed. (Chicago: University of Chicago Press, 1959).

33. Ibid., 87–103; Thomas D. Schoonover, *Dollars over Dominion: The Triumph of Liberalism in Mexican–United States Relations, 1861–1867* (Baton Rouge: Louisiana State University Press, 1978), 25–47.

34. Ronnie C. Tyler, *Santiago Vidaurri and the Southern Confederacy* (Austin: Texas State Historical Association, 1973), 45–71; Owsley, *King Cotton Diplomacy,* 113–18; Schoonover, *Dollars over Dominion,* 24–25, 81–88.

35. Owsley, *King Cotton Diplomacy,* 108–12; Schoonover, *Dollars over Dominion,* 49–76; Corwin to Seward, 20, 24, and 28 March 1862, 28 April 1862, 20 May 1862, Seward to Corwin, 28 May 1862, 7 and 24 June 1862, in U.S. Congress, Senate, *Messages of the President of the United States,* 37th Congress, 3rd Session, 1:730, 732–34, 739–40, 747–49.

36. For an overview of the forces at work leading up to the French intervention, see Norman B. Ferris, *Desperate Diplomacy: William H. Seward's Foreign Policy, 1861* (Knoxville: University of Tennessee Press, 1976), and Ralph Roeder, *Juárez and His Mexico,* 2 vols. (New York: Viking Press, 1947), 1:269–380.

37. Alfred Jackson Hanna and Kathryn Abbey Hanna, *Napoleon III and Mexico* (Chapel Hill: University of North Carolina Press, 1971), 3–10, 126–27, 141–42.

38. Robert Ryal Miller, *Arms Across the Border: United States Aid to Juárez During the French Intervention in Mexico* (Philadelphia: American Philosophical Society, 1973), 1–11; Schoonover, *Dollars over Dominion,* 102–17.

39. Miller, *Arms Across the Border,* 8–12, 16–21, 36–37, 47–52.

40. Frank Averill Knapp, Jr., *The Life of Sebastián Lerdo de Tejada, 1823–1889* (Austin: University of Texas Press, 1951), 79–97; Schoonover, *Dollars over Dominion,* 175–77.

41. Miller, *Arms Across the Border,* 22–30, 37–41, 53–58.

42. Arnold Blumberg, *The Diplomacy of the Mexican Empire, 1863–1867* (Philadelphia: American Philosophical Society, 1971), 75–80; Hanna and Hanna, *Napoleon III and Mexico,* 221–35.

43. Blumberg, *Diplomacy of the Mexican Empire,* 81–82; Hanna and Hanna, *Napoleon III and Mexico,* 238–46; Miller, *Arms Across the Border,* 42–47.

44. Blumberg, *Diplomacy of the Mexican Empire,* 84–85; Hanna and Hanna, *Napoleon III and Mexico,* 264–68; Richardson, *Messages and Papers,* 6:368–69.

45. Blumberg, *Diplomacy of the Mexican Empire,* 107–14; Hanna and Hanna, *Napoleon III and Mexico,* 274–88.

46. Jack Autrey Dabbs, *The French Army in Mexico, 1861–1867* (The Hague: Mouton, 1963), 183–216; Blumberg, *Diplomacy of the Mexican Empire,* 127–40.

47. Colin M. MacLachlan and William H. Beezley, *El Gran Pueblo: A History of Greater Mexico* (Englewood Cliffs, N.J.: Prentice-Hall, 1994), 39–43, 48–78; Brian Hamnett, *Juárez* (London: Longman, 1994), 161–63.

48. Miller, *Arms Across the Border,* 13, 32–34, 45–52; Schoonover, *Dollars over Dominion,* 252–76.

49. Daniel Cosío Villegas, ed., *Historia moderna de México,* 9 vols. (Mexico City: Editorial Hermes, 1955–72), 4:17–18; César Sepúlveda, "Historia y problemas de los límites de México, I; La frontera norte," *Historia Mexicana* 8 (July–September 1958): 1–34.

50. Tyler, *Santiago Vidaurri,* 129–56; Jerry D. Thompson, ed., *Juan Cortina and the Texas-Mexico Frontier, 1859–1877* (El Paso: Texas Western University Press, 1994).

51. Metz, *Border,* 148–51; Martaelena Negrete Salas, "La frontera tejana y el abigeato, 1848–1872," *Historia Mexicana* 31 (July–September 1981): 79–100.

52. Zorrilla, *Historia de las relaciones,* 1:475–76.

53. Ibid., 1:481; Scholes, *Mexican Politics,* 149–67.

54. Martínez, *Troublesome Border,* 57–74; Mexico, Ministerio de Relaciones Exteriores, *Correspondencia diplomática cambiada entre el gobierno de los Estados Unidos Mexicanos y los de varias potencias extranjeras,* 4 vols. (Mexico City: Gonzalo A. Esteva, 1882–87), 2:1–2.

55. Zorrilla, *Historia de las relaciones,* 1:489–507; Stephen R. Niblo, "The United States–Mexican Claims Commission of 1868," *New Mexico Historical Review* 50 (April 1975): 101–21.

56. Laurens Ballard Perry, *Juárez and Díaz: Machine Politics in Mexico* (DeKalb: Northern Illinois University Press, 1978), 203–31, 413–28; Alberto María Carreño, ed., *Archivo del General Porfirio Díaz,* 30 vols. (Mexico City: Editorial Elede, 1947–61), 12:96–100.

57. Daniel Cosío Villegas, *The United States versus Porfirio Díaz*, translated by Nettie Lee Benson (Lincoln: University of Nebraska Press, 1963), 13–21; Robert D. Gregg, *The Influence of Border Troubles on Relations Between the United States and Mexico, 1876–1910* (Baltimore: Johns Hopkins University Press, 1937), 19–47.

58. Cosío Villegas, *The United States versus Porfirio Díaz*, 27–36; Gregg, *The Influence of Border Troubles*, 22–25.

59. Don M. Coerver, *The Porfirian Interregnum: The Presidency of Manuel González of Mexico, 1880–1884* (Fort Worth: Texas Christian University Press, 1979), 135–37.

60. Cosío Villegas, *The United States versus Porfirio Díaz*, 110–27; Zorrilla, *Historia de las relaciones*, 1:547–49.

61. Gregg, *The Influence of Border Troubles*, 68–80; Cosío Villegas, *The United States versus Porfirio Díaz*, 139–55.

62. Gregg, *The Influence of Border Troubles*, 81–103, 141–45.

63. Frelinghuysen to Morgan, 6 June 1882, Frelinghuysen to Romero, 6 July 1882, Davis to Morgan, 18 August 1882, in U.S. Department of State, *Papers Relating to the Foreign Relations of the United States* (Washington, D.C.: Government Printing Office, 1882), 390, 396–97, 425–26 (hereafter referred to as *FRUS* [date]).

64. Romero to Davis, 28 May 1883, Romero to Frelinghuysen, 17 January 1884, 11 and 18 July 1884, in Mexico, Legación, United States, *Notes from the Mexican Legation in the United States to the Department of State, 1821–1906*, vols. 30–31, 33–34; Mexico, Ministerio de Fomento, *Memoria presentada al Congreso de la Unión por el Secretario de Fomento, enero 1883– junio 1885*, 5 vols. (Mexico: Oficina Tip. de la Secretaría de Fomento, 1887), 1:32–33.

65. Don M. Coerver, "From Morteritos to Chamizal: The U.S.-Mexican Boundary Treaty of 1884," *Red River Valley Historical Review* 2 (Winter 1975): 531–38.

66. David M. Pletcher, "México, campo de inversiones norteamericanas: 1867–1880," *Historia Mexicana* 2 (April–June 1953): 564–74.

67. Mira Wilkins, *The Emergence of Multinational Enterprise: American Business Abroad from the Colonial Era to 1914* (Cambridge, Mass.: Harvard University Press, 1970), 113–29; Fred Wilbur Powell, *The Railroads of Mexico* (Boston: Stratford Co., 1921), 109–35; Mexico, Ministerio de Fomento, *Memoria*, 5:551; Jorge Espinosa de los Reyes, *Relaciones económicas entre México y estados unidos, 1870–1910* (Mexico City: Nacional Financiera, 1951), 50–54, 64–65.

68. Luis Pombo to General José G. Carbó, 9 March 1882, in *La colección General Porfirio Díaz*, legajo VII, document 889, Archivo General de la Nación, Mexico City; Fechet to Hunter, 13 May 1884, in *Despatches Received from United States Consuls in Ciudad Juárez (Paso del Norte), 1850–1906*, vol. 2, U.S. National Archives, Washington, D.C., United States Department of State (hereafter referred to as USNA).

69. MacLachlan and Beezley, *El Gran Pueblo*, 142–43, 158–63.

70. Ibid., 172–93; Roger D. Hansen, *The Politics of Mexican Development* (Baltimore: Johns Hopkins University Press, 1971), 20–23.

71. Linda B. Hall and Don M. Coerver, *Revolution on the Border: The United States and Mexico, 1910–1920* (Albuquerque: University of New Mexico Press, 1988), 12–15.

Chapter 2. Cuba

1. U.S. Congress, House, House Executive Document no. 93, 33rd congress, 2nd session, ser. 790 (Washington, D.C.: Government Printing Office, 1855), 127–32.

2. José García de Arboleya, *Manual de la isla de Cuba*, 2nd ed. (Havana: Imprenta Gobierno, 1859), 58; Robert E. May, *The Southern Dream of a Caribbean Empire, 1854–1861* (Baton Rouge: Louisiana State University Press, 1973).

3. The Grito de Yara has inspired a vast literature. Some of the most notable works include Ramiro Guerra y Sanchez, *Guerra de los diez años, 1868–1878*, 2 vols. (Havana: Editorial Ciencias Sociales, 1972); Enrique Collazo, *Desde Yara hasta Zanjón,* 2nd ed. (Havana: Editorial Ciencias Sociales, 1967); Francisco Ponte Dominguez, *Historia de la guerra de los diez años* (Havana: El Siglo XX, 1958); María Cristina Llerena, ed., *Sobre la guerra de los 10 años, 1868–1878* (Havana, 1973).

4. Thomas Jefferson to James Monroe, 24 October 1823, in U.S. Congress, Senate, Senate Document no. 26, 57th congress, 1st session, ser. 4220 (Washington, D.C.: Government Printing Office, 1902), 3–4.

5. John Forsyth to Aaron Vail, 15 July 1840, in U.S. Congress, House, House Executive Document no. 121, 32nd congress, 1st session, ser. 648 (Washington, D.C.: Government Printing Office, 1852), 36–37.

6. John M. Clayton to Daniel Barringer, 2 August 1849, Manning, *Diplomatic Correspondence,* 1:181.

7. Thomas Jefferson to James Monroe, 11 June 1823, in Paul L. Ford, ed., *The Writings of Thomas Jefferson,* 10 vols. (New York, 1898), 10:293; John Forsyth to Secretary of State, 20 November 1822, in U.S. Congress, House, House Executive Document no. 121, 32nd congress, 1st session, ser. 648 (Washington, D.C.: Government Printing Office, 1852), 4.

8. Ulysses S. Grant, "Annual Message to Congress," 7 December 1875, Richardson, *Messages and Papers,* 10:4293–94.

9. Allan Nevins, *Hamilton Fish,* 2 vols. (New York: Unger, 1957), 1:180.

10. Hamilton Fish Diary, 6 April 1849, Hamilton Fish Papers, Box 314, Manuscript Division, Library of Congress.

11. Emilio Roig de Leuchsenring, "La tregua revolucionaria del Zanjón al 95," *Bohemia* 57 (18 June 1965): 100–102.

12. H. E. Friedlaender, *Historia económica de Cuba* (Havana: Jesus Montero, 1944), 545.

13. William P. Pierce to John Davis, 20 August 1883, in "Despatches from U.S. Consuls in Cienfuegos, 1876–1906," General Records of the Department of State, National Archives, Record Group 59 (hereafter referred to as Despatches/Name of city or country).

14. Edwin F. Atkins, *Sixty Years in Cuba* (Cambridge, Mass.: Riverside Press, 1926), 30–137.

15. Ramon O. Williams to J. C. Bancroft Davis, 23 February 1882, Ramon O. Williams to James N. Porter, 18 December 1886, Despatches/Havana.

16. Jose R. Alvarez Diaz et al., *A Study on Cuba* (Coral Gables: University of Miami Press, 1965), 133–36.

17. Pulaski F. Hyatt to Secretary of State, 12 October 1894, Despatches/Santiago de Cuba.

18. *La Lucha,* 3 January 1895, 1.

19. Pulaski F. Hyatt to Secretary of State, 12 October 1894, Despatches/Santiago de Cuba.

20. "To the President of the Republic of the United States of America," enclosure in Fitzhugh Lee to Richard Olney, 24 June 1896, Richard Olney Papers, Manuscript Division, Library of Congress.

21. A Planter in Cuba, "The Argument for Autonomy," *Outlook* 58 (23 April 1896): 1012–14.

22. *New York World,* 22 March 1897, 1.

23. William H. Calhoun to William McKinley, 22 June 1897, in *Special Agents,* vol. 48, National Archives, Record Group 59.

24. Richard B. Olney to Enrique Dupuy de Lôme, 4 April 1896, *FRUS* (1897), 543.

25. Lyman J. Gage, "Work of the Treasury Department," in *The American-Spanish War: A History by the War Leaders* (Norwich, Conn.: C. C. Haskell, 1899), 367–91; John E. Wilkie, "The Secret Service in the War," in *The American-Spanish War,* 423–36.

26. Richard B. Olney to Grover Cleveland, 22 September 1895, Grover Cleveland Papers, Manuscript Division, Library of Congress.

27. Fitzhugh Lee to William R. Day, 17 November 1897, Despatches/Havana.

28. Alexander C. Brice to William R. Day, 17 November 1897, Despatches/Matanzas.

29. Fitzhugh Lee to William R. Day, 23 November 1897, Despatches/Havana.

30. *Washington Post,* 22 December 1897, 1.

31. *New York Herald,* 14 December 1897, 3.

32. Máximo Gómez to John R. Caldwell, 5 December 1897, *New York Herald,* 29 December 1897, 1; see also Máximo Gómez, *Diario de campaña del mayor general Máximo Gómez* (Havana: Impreso Centro Superior Technológico, 1940), 390–411.

33. *New York World,* 10 February 1898, 1; 6 March 1898, 3.

34. *New York Journal,* 24 February 1898, 1.

35. Calixto García to Editor, 18 December 1897, *New York Journal,* 5 January 1898, 4; Aníbal Escalante Beatón, *Calixto García en su campaña en el 95* (Havana: Editorial Caribe, 1978), 293–317.

36. Máximo Gómez to Gonzalo de Quesada, 10 March 1898, *New York Daily Tribune,* 10 April 1898, 5.

37. *New York World,* 17 August 1897, 1.

38. William R. Day to Stewart L. Woodford, 26 March 1898, *FRUS* (1898), 704.

39. William R. Day, "Recognition of Independence," William R. Day Papers, Manuscript Division, Library of Congress.

40. William R. Day to Stewart Woodford, 27 March 1898, *FRUS* (1898), 711–12.

41. Luis Polo de Bernabe to Secretary of State, 10 April 1898, in Spain, Ministerio de Estado, *Spanish Diplomatic Correspondence and Documents, 1896–1900, Presented to the Cortes by the Minister of State* (Washington, D.C., 1905), 121; William R. Day, "Interview with the Spanish Minister," 10 April 1898, William R. Day Papers, Manuscript Division, Library of Congress.

42. Ramón Blanco, "Suspension of Hostilities," 10 April 1898, *FRUS* (1898), 750.

43. Calixto García to Mario G. Menocal, 18 April 1898, in Calixto García, *Palabras de tres guerras* (Havana: Impreso Superior Technológico, 1942), 143–44; Gómez, *Diario de campaña del mayor general Máximo Gómez,* 354.

44. Richardson, *Messages and Papers,* 10:63–64.

45. *Congressional Record* 31 (18 April 1898), 3988–89.

46. *New York Times,* 5 August 1898; *Washington Evening Star,* 19 July 1898, 2.

47. Calixto García to Pedro Perez, 12 August 1898, in Juan J. E. Casasús, *Calixto García (el estratega)* (Havana: Oficina del Historiador, 1942), 284.

48. Calixto García to William R. Shafter, 17 July 1898, in García, *Palabras de tres guerras,* 107–10.

49. Calixto García to William R. Shafter, 17 July 1898, in García, *Palabras de tres guerras,* 107–10; see also Cuba, Ejercito Libertador, *Parte oficial de lugarteniente general Calixto García al General en Jefe Máximo Gómez, 15 de julio de 1898 sobre la campaña de Santiago de Cuba* (Havana: El Siglo XX, 1953), 22–23.

50. Elihu Root to John Hay, 11 January 1901, Elihu Root Papers, Manuscript Division, Library of Congress.

51. For the complete text of the Platt Amendment see *U.S. Statutes at Large,* vol. 21, no. 857–58.

52. *Commercial and Financial World* 9 (7 April 1906), 10.

53. Pulaski F. Hyatt and John T. Hyatt, *Cuba: Its Resources and Opportunities* (New York: J. S. Ogilvie, 1898), 95.

54. "Developing Oriente," *Cuba Magazine* 1 (September 1909), 4–7; George Reno, "Ori-

ente, the California of Cuba," *Cuba Review* 25 (August 1927): 14–20; Thomas J. Vivian and Ruel P. Smith, *Everything About Our New Possessions* (New York: R. F. Fenno, 1899), 112–19.

55. Isaac N. Ford, *Tropical America* (New York, 1893); Edward Marshall, "A Talk with General Wood," *Outlook* 68 (July 20, 1901), 670.

56. James L. Hitchman, "U.S. Control over Cuban Sugar Production, 1898–1902," *Journal of Inter-American Studies and World Affairs* 12 (January 1970): 90–106; Atherton Brownell, "The Commercial Annexation of Cuba," *Appleton's Magazine* 8 (October 1906), 409.

57. Antonio Calvache, *Historia y desarrollo de la minería en Cuba* (Havana: Academia de Ciencias 1944), 64; Lisandro Pérez, "Iron Mining and Socio-Demographic Change in Eastern Cuba, 1884–1940," *Journal of Latin American Studies* 14 (November 1982): 390–95.

58. Oscar Zanetti and Alejandro García, *Caminos para el azúcar* (Havana: Editorial Ciencias Sociales, 1987), 195–232.

59. U.S. Congress, Senate, *Cuban Sugar Sales: Testimony Taken By Committee on Relations with Cuba,* 57th congress, 1st session (Washington, D.C., 1901), 332, 339–41.

Chapter 3. Colombia

1. The republic was generally known as New Granada through the 1850s and as Colombia thereafter. The latter name will be used throughout this chapter.

2. E. Taylor Parks, *Colombia and the United States, 1765–1934* (Durham: Duke University Press, 1935), 170–75; Eugene R. Huck, "Colombian–United States Commercial Relations, 1821–1850" (Ph.D. diss., University of Alabama, 1963), 70–72.

3. Raimundo Rivas, *Historia diplomática de Colombia: 1810–1934* (Bogotá: Imprenta Nacional, 1961), 258. On the treaty, see Rivas, *Historia diplomática,* 263–84, and Joseph B. Lockey, "A Neglected Aspect of Isthmian Diplomacy," *American Historical Review* 41 (January 1936): 295–305. Relevant documents appear in Manning, *Diplomatic Correspondence,* 5:360–61, 630–38.

4. Germán Cavelier, *La política internacional de Colombia,* 2 vols., 2nd ed. (Bogotá: Editorial Iqueima, 1959), 1:210. Colombia's objections to British advances in Mosquitia were based partly on its own claim to that section of the Central American coast north to Cape Gracias a Dios. See Manning, *Diplomatic Correspondence,* 5:618–21.

5. John H. Kemble, *The Panama Route, 1848–1869* (Berkeley: University of California Press, 1943; rpt., New York: Da Capo, 1972), 181–89.

6. José Antonio Ocampo, *Colombia y la economía mundial, 1830–1910* (Bogotá: Siglo XXI Editores de Colombia, 1984), 52.

7. On nineteenth-century Colombia, see James W. Park, *Rafael Núñez and the Politics of Colombian Regionalism, 1863–1886* (Baton Rouge: Louisiana State University Press, 1985); Helen Delpar, *Red Against Blue: The Liberal Party in Colombian Politics, 1863–1899* (University: University of Alabama Press, 1981); Charles W. Bergquist, *Coffee and Conflict in Colombia, 1886–1910* (Durham: Duke University Press, 1978).

8. Ocampo, *Colombia y la economía mundial,* 105–15; William P. McGreevey, *An Economic History of Colombia, 1845–1930* (Cambridge: Cambridge University Press, 1971); Delpar, *Red Against Blue,* 14, 136.

9. Ocampo, *Colombia y la economía mundial,* 121–23, 127–29, 136–38, 162–63.

10. Ibid., 53; J. Fred Rippy, *The Capitalists and Colombia* (New York: Vanguard Press, 1931), 37.

11. Rippy, *Capitalists,* 56–57; Theodore E. Nichols, *Tres puertos de Colombia: Estudio sobre el desarrollo de Cartagena, Santa Marta y Barranquilla* (Bogotá: Biblioteca Banco Popular, 1973), 127–30, 187–88.

12. Ernest Dichman to William H. Evarts, 27 December 1880, Dabney H. Maury

to Thomas F. Bayard, 24 December 1886, Jacob Sleeper to Richard Olney, 30 August 1895, Charles B. Hart to John Sherman, 23 October 1897, Despatches/Colombia.

13. Frank Safford, *The Ideal of the Practical: Colombia's Struggle to Form a Technical Elite* (Austin: University of Texas Press, 1976), 147–65; Thomas R. Favell, "The Antecedents of Panama's Separation from Colombia: A Study in Colombian Politics" (Ph.D. diss., Fletcher School of Law and Diplomacy, 1950), 120; José Manuel Marroquín, *Don José Manuel Marroquín íntimo* (Bogotá: Arboleda y Valencia, 1915), 304.

14. Rafael Núñez, *La reforma política en Colombia*, 7 vols. (Bogotá: 1944–50), 2:326 (hereafter referred to as Núñez, *La reforma política*, with volume and page numbers).

15. Ibid., 4:79–87; Rafael Núñez, *La reforma política en Colombia: Colección de artículos publicados . . . de 1881 a 1884* (Bogotá: Imprenta de "La Luz," 1885), 631–32.

16. Núñez, *La reforma política*, 6:72.

17. See William George Wolff, "The Diplomatic Career of William L. Scruggs: United States Minister to Colombia and Venezuela, and Legal Adviser to Venezuela, 1872–1912" (Ph.D. diss., Southern Illinois University, 1975).

18. Isaac Holton, *New Granada: Twenty Months in the Andes*, edited by C. Harvey Gardiner (Carbondale: Southern Illinois University Press, 1967), 34, 109, 180, 204; Allan A. Burton to William Seward, 14 February 1866, Despatches/Colombia.

19. Hurlburt to Fish, 1 February 1870, 7 December 1871, Dichman to Evarts, 3 July 1880, Despatches/Colombia.

20. Antonio José Uribe, ed., *Anales diplomáticos y consulares de Colombia*, 6 vols. (Bogotá: Imprenta Nacional, 1900–20), 4:518–521; Bayard to Mary, 27 November 1888, 8 February 1889, in "Diplomatic Instructions, Department of State to Colombia, 1801–1906," National Archives, Record Group 59 (hereafter referred to as Despatches Instructions/Colombia); John G. Walker to Bayard, 7 April 1888, Maury to Bayard, 8 January 1889, 6 February 1889, 21 February 1889, Maury to James G. Blaine, 18 March 1889, 21 March 1889, Thomas Adamson to George L. Rives, 12 January 1889, 2 February 1889, 13 February 1889, Despatches/Panama.

21. Uribe, *Anales diplomáticos*, 4:598–601, 650–53; John T. Abbott to Blaine, 23 April 1891, 7 September 1891, 13 November 1891, 25 April 1892, Abbott to John W. Foster, 3 August 1892, Luther McKinney to John Gresham, 1 September 1894, Despatches/Colombia; see also Parks, *Colombia*, 267–71, and Stephen J. Randall, *Colombia and the United States: Hegemony and Independence* (Athens: University of Georgia Press, 1992), 74–76. For statistics on annual trade between Colombia and the United States, based on U.S. figures, see Miguel Urrutia and Mario Arrubla, eds., *Compendio de estadísticas históricas de Colombia* (Bogotá: Dirección de Divulgación Cultural, Universidad Nacional de Colombia, 1970), 143–46.

22. The riot and the conditions that brought it about are described in Mercedes Chen Daley, "The Watermelon Riot: Cultural Encounters in Panama City, April 15, 1856," *Hispanic American Historical Review* 70 (1990): 85–108; see also Parks, *Colombia*, 221–24, 286–302.

23. Manning, *Diplomatic Correspondence*, 5:388–408, 416–20, 731–37, 835–37, 849–66, 871–72; Rivas, *Historia diplomática*, 386.

24. Seward to Burton, 27 April 1866, 13 February 1867, Despatches Instructions/Colombia; Burton to Seward, 26 December 1866, Despatches/Colombia; see also Parks, *Colombia*, 303–4; Nathan L. Ferris, "The Relations of the United States with South America During the American Civil War," *Hispanic American Historical Review* 21 (1941): 71–72.

25. The *Rayo* had been purchased by the Colombian government to be turned over to Peru for use in its war with Spain, in violation of U.S. neutrality laws. This arrangement was part of a secret treaty signed in 1866 by Peru and the administration of Tomás C. Mosquera, who had recently returned to the presidency. Since the treaty was never submitted to the Colombian Congress, as required by the constitution of 1863, and violated Colombia's official policy of neutrality in the Peruvian-Spanish conflict, it became a source of contention

between Mosquera and his enemies in Congress and led directly to his deposition on 23 May 1867. His removal precipitated a conflict between his partisans and enemies in Bolívar and Magdalena in which the U.S. residents became involved. See Peter H. Sullivan to Seward, 12 August 1867, Despatches Magdelena; Rivas, *Historia diplomática*, 420–21, 432–34.

26. August Hanabergh to Seward, 30 April 1867, 2 July 1867, 3 September 1867, Despatches/Cartagena; Seward to Sullivan, 30 October 1867, 28 July 1868, 4 February 1869, Despatches Instructions/Colombia.

27. Cavelier, *La política internacional de Colombia*, 2:199–222. Only the highlights of this complicated affair can be discussed here. Additional details can be found in Rivas, *Historia diplomática*, 544–59, and in Eduardo Lemaitre, *La bolsa o la vida: Cuatro agresiones imperialistas contra Colombia* (Bogotá: Banco de Colombia, 1974), 166–200. There is, however, no exhaustive study of the case.

28. Bayard to Charles D. Jacob, 11 February 1886, Despatches Instructions/Colombia; Jacob to Bayard, 4 May 1886, Despatches/Colombia.

29. William R. Day to Sleeper, 11 June 1897, Sherman to Hart, 20 November 1897, Despatches Instructions/Colombia.

30. Lemaitre, *La bolsa o la vida*, 166; Lewis M. Iddings to State Department, 13 and 14 July 1898, 14 July 1898, Iddings to Day, 10 August 1898, in "Despatches from United States Ministers to the Italian States, 1832–1906" (hereafter referred to as Despatches/Italian States).

31. Hart to Day, 18 July 1898, Despatches/Colombia.

32. Iddings to Day, 14 and 25 July 1898, Despatches/Italian States; Hart to Day, 18 August 1898, Despatches/Colombia.

33. Iddings to State Department, 10 August 1898, William F. Draper to State Department, 25 November 1898, Draper to John Hay, 20 March 1899, 7 June 1899, Despatches/Italian States; Hay to Hart, 29 December 1898, 4 March 1899, 29 April 1899, 10 June 1899, Despatches Instructions/Colombia.

34. Kemble, *Panama Route*, 186–87; Michael L. Conniff, *Panama and the United States: The Forced Alliance* (Athens: University of Georgia Press, 1992), 27–40, 48–49.

35. Kemble, *Panama Route*, 182.

36. Manning, *Diplomatic Correspondence*, 5:414–15, 820–24, 876–80; William L. Scruggs to Bayard, 2 October 1885, Despatches/Colombia; Bayard to Jacob, 3 November 1885, Despatches Instructions/Colombia.

37. Conniff, *Panama*, 34.

38. Daniel H. Wicks, "Dress Rehearsal: United States Intervention on the Isthmus of Panama, 1885," *Pacific Historical Review* 49 (1980), 581–605. On the 1884–85 revolution, see Delpar, *Red Against Blue*, 127–32; Park, *Núñez*, 255–64; Gonzalo España, *La guerra civil de 1885: Núñez y la derrota del radicalismo* (Bogotá: El Ancora Editores, 1985). España's version of the events described here is somewhat different (168–74), as is Randall, *Colombia and the United States* (69–70), but both note the Colombian government's support for U.S. intervention in Panama in 1885.

39. Scruggs to Frederick T. Frelinghuysen, 23 December 1884, Despatches/Colombia; Frelinghuysen to Scruggs, 20 January 1885, Despatches Instructions/Colombia; Adamson to William Hunter, 23 March 1885, 6 April 1885, Despatches/Panama.

40. R. K. Wright to Hunter, 31 March 1885, 4 and 19 April 1885, Despatches/Colón.

41. Wicks, "Dress Rehearsal," 587–96; Kenneth J. Hagan, *American Gunboat Diplomacy and the Old Navy, 1877–1889* (Westport, Conn.: Greenwood Press, 1973), 173–75.

42. Hagan, *American Gunboat Diplomacy*, 179–87; Wicks, "Dress Rehearsal," 596–99; Adamson to Hunter, 25 April 1885, 5 May 1885, Despatches/Panama.

43. Scruggs to Bayard, 14, 20, 21, and 30 April 1885, 2 May 1885, Despatches/Colombia; Bayard to Scruggs, 29 April 1885, Despatches Instructions/Colombia.

44. Richard Collin, *Theodore Roosevelt's Caribbean: The Panama Canal, the Monroe Doctrine, and the Latin American Context* (Baton Rouge: Louisiana State University Press, 1990), 127–338; Eduardo Lemaitre, *Panamá y su separación de Colombia,* 2nd ed. (Bogotá: Italgraf, 1972); Dwight C. Minor, *The Fight for the Panama Route* (New York: Columbia University Press, 1940).

45. Parks, *Colombia,* 345–64; Minor, *Fight,* 20–30, 64, 117–18. Colombia requested Dichman's recall in 1881 on the grounds that he had meddled in its internal affairs. See Parks, *Colombia,* 369; Uribe, *Anales diplomáticos,* 4:133–35.

46. Minor, *Fight,* 385–86.

47. For divisions within the Conservative party and the War of the Thousand Days, see Bergquist, *Coffee and Conflict.*

48. Tomás Herrán, *La crisis de Panamá: Cartas de Tomás Herrán, 1900–1904,* edited by Thomas J. Dodd (Bogotá: Banco de la República, 1985), 115; H. A. Gudger to Hay, 21 November 1901, Gudger to David J. Hill, 25 November 1901, Oscar Malmros to Hill, 25 November 1901, Despatches/Panama.

49. Felix Ehrman to Hill, 22 September 1902, 13 October 1902, Despatches/Panama; Malmros to Hill, 26 September 1902, 7 October 1902, Despatches/Colón; Hart to Hay, 25 and 26 September 1902, 6 October 1902, Despatches/Colombia.

50. Minor, *Fight,* 183–95.

51. Ibid., 199; Bergquist, *Coffee and Conflict,* 210–13.

52. Favell, "Antecedents," 260–61.

53. A. M. Beaupré to Hay, 15 April 1903, Despatches/Magdelena.

54. Minor, *Fight,* 317.

55. Ibid., 319–20; Beaupré to Hay, 13 June 1903, 5 July 1903, 5 and 15 August 1903, Despatches/Colombia.

56. Collin, *Roosevelt's Caribbean,* 283–97; Joseph L. Arbena, "Colombian Reactions to the Independence of Panama, 1903–1904," *The Americas* 33 (July 1976): 13–47; E. Bradford Burns, "The Recognition of Panama by the Major Latin American States," *The Americas* 26 (July 1969): 3–14.

57. Herrán, *Crisis,* 388; Arbena, "Colombian Reactions," 147.

58. Joseph L. Arbena, "Algunos aspectos de la política exterior del Quinquenio," *Boletín de Historia y Antigüedades* 65 (January–March 1978): 142–60; Bergquist, *Coffee and Conflict,* 225–46. For relations between 1903 and 1921, see Richard L. Lael, *Arrogant Diplomacy: U.S. Policy toward Colombia, 1903–1922* (Wilmington, Del.: Scholarly Resources, 1987).

59. Parks, *Colombia,* 440–57.

60. McGreevey, *Economic History,* 257–59.

Chapter 4. Central America

1. John Lloyd Stephens, *Incidents of Travel in Central America: Chiapas and Yucatán,* 2 vols., rev. ed. (New York: Dover, 1969).

2. For a discussion of Manifest Destiny see Frederick Merck, *Manifest Destiny and Mission in American History: A Reinterpretation* (New York: Vintage, 1963); Albert Weinberg, *Manifest Destiny* (Chicago: Quadrangle, 1963).

3. Mario Rodríguez, *A Palmerstonian Diplomat in Central America: Frederick A. Chatfield, Esq.* (Tucson: University of Arizona Press, 1964). The Central American appeals to the United States can be found in Manning, *Diplomatic Correspondence,* 3:160–93. In the 1840s, not all Central Americans were favorably disposed toward the United States; this was particularly the case in Guatemala. President Rafael Carerra saw the United States as a

greater threat than Great Britain, and Juan José Aycinena suggested that the U.S. indifference to the Mexican seizure of Chiapas augured ill for future relations. Conservatives supported the Mexicans in their war with the United States for fear that once the war was over, the United States might attempt to compensate Mexico with Central American territory.

4. For a discussion of the events leading to the signing of the Clayton-Bulwer Treaty, see Charles L. Stansifer, "United States–Central American Relations, 1824–1850," in *United States–Latin American Relations,* edited by Shurbutt, 40–45; Wilbur D. Jones, *The American Problem in British Diplomacy, 1841–1861* (Athens: University of Georgia Press, 1974), chap. 5.

5. Nicaragua, Ministry of Foreign Relations, *Contracto de canalización: Celebrado entre el gobierno de Nicaragua y una compañia de ciudadanos de los Estados Unidos de Norte América* (León: Imprenta Nacional, 1849); Roger S. Baldwin, "Tarrying in Nicaragua: Pleasures and Perils of the California Trip in 1849," *Century Magazine* 49 (October 1891): 911–31 (quote); E. George Squier, "San Juan del Norte," *Harper's New Monthly Magazine* 10 (December 1854): 50–61.

6. Mario Rodríguez, "The '*Prometheus*' and the Clayton-Bulwer Treaty," *Journal of Modern History* 36 (September 1964): 260–78.

7. For a fuller discussion of the events of the 1850s, see Jones, *American Problem,* chaps. 6–9; Mary W. Williams, *Anglo-American Isthmian Diplomacy, 1815–1915* (Washington, D.C.: American Historical Association, 1916), chaps. 4–8.

8. Dean Kortge, "The Central American Policy of Lord Palmerston" (Ph.D. diss., University of Kansas, 1973), 25–45.

9. U.S. Congress, Senate, "Establishment of a New British Colony in Central America," Senate Document no. 407, 32nd congress, 2nd session, ser. 671, 27; John B. Moore, *The Works of James Buchanan: Comprising His Speeches, State Papers and Private Correspondence* (Philadelphia: J. B. Lippincott, 1911), 9:1–10; David Wadell, "Great Britain and the Bay Islands, 1821–1861," *Historical Journal* 2 (1959): 59–77; Clarendon quoted in Mary Z. Froncek, "Diplomatic Relations Between the United States and Costa Rica, 1823–1882" (Ph.D. diss., Fordham University, 1959), 105.

10. U.S. Congress, Senate, "Presidential Message Transmitting Reports on the Destruction of San Juan de Nicaragua," 33rd congress, 1st session, ser. 734, 19–25; James M. Woods, "Expansion as Diplomacy: The Career of Solon Borland in Central America, 1853-1854," *The Americas* 40 (January 1980): 399–416.

11. U.S. Congress, Senate, "Correspondence and Papers Relating to the Nicaraguan Canal," Senate Document no. 1615, 6th congress, 1st session, ser. 3853; Richardson, *Messages and Papers,* 5:328–31, 442–45; George M. Dallas, *Diary of George M. Dallas While Minister to Russia 1837 to 1839 and to England 1856 to 1861* (Philadelphia: J. B. Lippincott, 1897), 217–443.

12. Kortge, "The Central American Policy of Lord Palmerston," 130–49.

13. Wayne Clegern, "A Guatemalan Defense of the British Honduras Boundary," *Hispanic American Historical Review* 40 (November 1960): 571–81.

14. Craig L. Dozier, *Nicaragua's Mosquito Shore: The Years of British and American Presence* (Tuscaloosa: University of Alabama Press, 1985), 141–49; John Findling, "La diplomacia norteamericana y la reincorporacion Mosquitia," *Boletín Nicaragüense de Bibliografía y Documentación* 26 (November–December 1978): 15–24.

15. "Colonel Kinney Defends His Plan," *New York Times,* 15 December 1854, 1; James T. Wall, *Agents of Manifest Destiny: America's First Intervention in Nicaragua* (Washington, D.C.: University Press of America, 1981), 49–71; José Ramierez M., *José de Marcoleta, padre de la diplomacia Nicaragüense* (Managua: Imprenta Nacional, 1975).

16. For a discussion of Walker's life, see Brown, *Agents of Manifest Destiny;* Albert Carr, *The World of William Walker* (New York: Harper and Row, 1963).

17. William O. Scroggs, *Filibusters and Financiers* (New York: Macmillan, 1916), 9–17, 31–70; David I. Folkman, Jr., "Westward via Nicaragua: The United States and the Nicaraguan Route, 1826–1869" (Ph.D. diss., University of Utah, 1966), 119–48.

18. Randall O. Hudson, "The Filibuster Minister: The Career of John Hill Wheeler as United States Minister to Nicaragua," *North Carolina Historical Review* 49 (July 1972): 280–97.

19. May, *The Southern Dream of a Caribbean Empire*, 111–35; J. Preston Moore, "Pierre Soulé: Southern Expansionist and Promoter," *Journal of Southern History* 21 (May 1955): 203–23.

20. Folkman, "Westward via Nicaragua," 246–54; Froncek, "Diplomatic Relations Between the United States and Costa Rica," 95–103.

21. Buchanan quoted in *Congressional Globe*, 35th congress, 1st session, part 1, 216–17. For a discussion of the campaign against Walker, see Miguel Angel Alvaréz, *Los filibusteros en Nicaragua, 1855, 1856, 1857* (Managua: Editorial La Prensa, 1944); Rafael Obregon Lorla, *Costa Rica y la guerra del 56* (San José: Editorial Costa Rica, 1976).

22. *FRUS* (1862), 881; Thomas D. Schoonover, "Misconstrued Mission: Expansionism and Black Colonization in Mexico and Central America During the Civil War," *Pacific Historical Review* 49 (November 1980): 607–20; Warren A. Beck, "Lincoln and Negro Colonization in Central America," *Abraham Lincoln Quarterly* 6 (1950–51): 162–83.

23. *FRUS* (1862), 882–905; Charles Abro Barker, ed., *The Memoirs of Elisha O. Crosby* (San Marino: Huntington Library, 1945), 89–90; José Ramierez M., *José de Marcoleta, padre de la diplomacia nicaragüense;* Dade Sparks, "Central America and Its Relations with the United States, 1860–1893" (Ph.D. diss., Duke University, 1934), 30–61 (quote).

24. Charles N. Riotte to Secretary of State William H. Seward, 29 August 1861, Despatches/Costa Rica.

25. For colonial Central America see Miles L. Wortman, *Government and Society in Central America, 1680–1840* (New York: Colombia University Press, 1982). For the years from 1821 to 1829 see Andres Townsend Ezcurira, *Las Provincias Unidas de Centroamérica: Fundación la republica* (San José: Universidad de Costa Rica, 1973). For U.S. relations with the United Provinces see George P. Connick, "The United States and Central America, 1823–1850" (Ph.D. diss., University of Colorado, 1969).

26. Riotte to Seward, 24 September 1865, Despatches/Costa Rica; Ralph Lee Woodward, Jr., *Rafael Carerra and the Emergence of the Republic of Guatemala, 1821–1871* (Athens: University of Georgia Press, 1993), provides an excellent perspective on the Conservative period in Central American history.

27. Thomas D. Schoonover, *The United States in Central America, 1860–1911: Episodes of Social Imperialism and Imperial Rivalry in the World System* (Durham: Duke University Press, 1991), 46–61.

28. *FRUS* (1890), 28–146; (1885), 73–144; (1896), 367–71; Richardson, *Messages and Papers*, 10:178–79; Thomas L. Karnes, *The Failure of Union: Central America 1824–1960* (Chapel Hill: University of North Carolina Press, 1961), 164–73; Alberto Herrarte, *La unión de Centro America* (Guatemala City: Editorial del Ministerio de Educacion Publica, 1964), 154–64; Robert Ogden, "The Proposed Central American Union," *The Nation*, 27 July 1887, 47–53; A. F. Taylor, *The Foreign Policy of James G. Blaine* (Minneapolis: University of Minnesota Press, 1927), 16–17; Mary P. Chapman, "The Mission of Lansing Bond Mizner to Central America," *Historian* 19 (May 1957), 391–95; U.S. Congress, Senate, "First International Conference of American States, Minutes," Senate Executive Document no. 231, 51st congress, 1st session, ser. 3207.

29. Victor Miguel Díaz, *Barrios ante la posteridad* (Guatemala City: Tijos, 1935), 471–74.

30. Ralph Lee Woodward, Jr., ed., *Positivism in Latin America, 1850–1890* (Lexington: D. C. Heath, 1971).

31. Williams to Clay, 26 August 1826, Despatches/Central America; Savage to Livingston, 22 August 1832, in Consular Despatches/Central America; *FRUS* (1870), 260–61, 274–75; William M. Malloy, comp., *Treaties, Conventions, International Acts, Protocols and Agreements Between the United States and Other Powers, 1776–1904*, 4 vols. (Washington, D.C.: Government Printing Office, 1910–1938), 1:160–69; R. B. Campbell, "Henry Clay and the Emerging Nations of Latin America" (Ph.D. diss., University of Virginia, 1966).

32. Williamson to Fish, 16 October 1873, Despatches/Central America.

33. "Despatches Received from the Commission to Central and South America, 1884 and 1885"; Thomas D. Schoonover, "Imperialism in Central America: United States Competition with Britain, Germany, and France in Middle America, 1820s–1920s," in *Eagle Against Empire: American Opposition to European Imperialism*, edited by Rhodri Jefferys-Jones (Aix-en-Provence: Université de Provence, 1983), 41–58; Schoonover, "Costa Rican Trade and Navigation Ties with the United States, Germany, and Europe, 1840–1855," *Jarbüch Fur Geschichte von Staat, Wirtschaft and Gesellschaft Latein Americkas* 14 (1977): 269–307.

34. Kenneth V. Finney, "Precious Metal Mining and Modernization of Honduras: The Quest of El Dorado, 1880–1900" (Ph.D. diss., Tulane University, 1973); Finney, "Our Man in Honduras: Washington S. Valentine," *West Georgia College Studies in the Social Sciences* 17 (June 1978): 13–20.

35. Warren Kneer, *Great Britain and the Caribbean, 1901–1913* (East Lansing: Michigan State University Press, 1975), 134–63; J. Fred Rippy, "The United States and Guatemala During the Era of Justo Rufino Barrios," *Hispanic American Historical Review* 22 (November 1942): 595–605; Alister White, *El Salvador* (New York: Praeger, 1973); Watt Stewart, *Keith of Costa Rica: A Biographic Study of Minor Cooper Keith* (Albuquerque: University of New Mexico Press, 1974).

36. Wayne F. Anderson, Guatemala's Search for Deep Water Ports in the Nineteenth Century" (Ph.D. diss., Tulane University, 1986); John E. Findling, "The United States and Zelaya: A Study in the Diplomacy of Expediency" (Ph.D. diss., University of Texas, 1971), 60–61; J. Fred Rippy, "The United States and Costa Rica During the Guardia Era," *Bulletin of the Pan American Union* 77 (1943): 61–68; Edward D. Hernandez, "Modernization and Dependency in Costa Rica During the Decade of the 1880s" (Ph.D. diss., University of California at Los Angeles, 1980).

37. Rippy, "United States and Guatemala," 597–99.

38. Findling, "United States and Zelaya," 60–61.

39. J. Fred Rippy, *British Investments in Latin America, 1822–1949* (Minneapolis: University of Minnesota Press, 1959), 105–9.

40. Sanford Mosk, "Coffee Economy in Guatemala, 1850–1919," *Inter-American Economic Affairs* 9 (Winter 1984): 6–20.

41. Frederick Adams, *Conquest of the Tropics* (New York: Arno Press, 1976); Alfredo Suárez, *La situación bananera en los paises del Caribe* (San José: Imprenta Borrase hnos., 1928); Mario Plaza, *The United Fruit Company in Latin America* (Washington, D.C.: National Planning Association, 1958).

42. William D. Curtis, "Central America: Its Resources and Commerce," *Forum* 25 (April 1898): 166–67.

43. For a discussion of the various transisthmian canal projects see Gerstle Mack, *The Land Divided: A History of the Panama Canal and Other Transisthmian Projects* (New York: Knopf, 1944).

44. For a discussion of U.S. canal policy see Miles Duval, *From Cadíz to Cathay: The Story of the Long Diplomatic Struggle for the Panama Canal* (New York: Greenwood, 1968). The proposed French project is discussed in Cyril Allen, *France in Central America: Felix Belly and the Nicaraguan Canal* (New York: Pageant Press, 1966).

45. For a discussion of the Panama Railroad Company see Joseph L. Schott, *Rails Across Panama* (Indianapolis: Bobbs-Merrill, 1967). For Vanderbilt's effort see Wheaton J. Lane, *Commodore Vanderbilt* (New York: Knopf, 1942).

46. A good account of the various nineteenth-century canal projects is in Kemble, *Panama Route;* David Chandler, "Juan José Aycinena, Nineteenth Century Guatemalan Conservative: An Historical Survey of His Political, Religious, Educational and Commercial Careers" (M.A. thesis, Tulane University, 1965).

47. Malloy, *Treaties,* 2:1279–87.

48. Ulysses S. Grant, "The Nicaraguan Canal," *North American Review* 145 (February 1881): 71–80.

49. Jackson Crowell, "The United States and a Central American Canal, 1869–1877," *Hispanic American Historical Review* 49 (February 1969): 29–49.

50. U.S. Congress, House of Representatives, *Report of Historical and Technical Information Relating to the Problem of Interoceanic Communication by Way of the American Isthmus,* House Executive Document no. 107, 47th congress, 2nd session, ser. 2112 (1881).

51. Roscoe R. Hill, "The Nicaraguan Canal Idea to 1898," *Hispanic American Historical Review* 28 (May 1940): 190–92.

52. For a discussion of the DeLesseps project see David McCullough, *The Path Between the Seas: The Creation of the Panama Canal, 1876–1914* (New York: Simon and Schuster, 1977), 17–242.

53. Riotte to Fish, 26 January 1872, Despatches/Costa Rica. An excellent U.S. response can be found in Walter E. Lowrie, "France, the United States and the DeLesseps Canal: A Renewed Rivalry in the Western Hemisphere" (Ph.D. diss., Syracuse University, 1975).

54. U.S. Congress, House of Representatives, "The Interoceanic Canal and the Monroe Doctrine," 46th congress, 3rd session, ser. 1982, xi. For an early explanation of the link between a transisthmian canal and the Monroe Doctrine, see Lindley Keasbey, *The Nicaragua Canal and the Monroe Doctrine* (New York: Putnam, 1896).

55. Richardson, *Messages and Papers,* 10:4537–38; W. W. Pierson, "The Political Influences of an Inter-Oceanic Canal, 1826–1926," *Hispanic American Historical Review* 6 (November 1926): 219–20; U.S. Congress, House of Representatives, *Problem of Interoceanic Communication By Way of the American Isthmus,* 23.

56. *FRUS* (1881), 554–59; John Kasson, "The Monroe Doctrine in 1881," *North American Review* 149 (December 1897): 523–33.

57. John Whitley, "The Diplomacy of the United States in Regard to a Central American Canal," *North American Review* 165 (1897): 368–74.

58. "U.S. and Nicaragua Conclude Treaty," *New York Times,* 16 December 1884, 1; *New Orleans Times Picayune,* quoted in Karl Bermann, *Under the Big Stick: Nicaragua and the United States since 1848* (Boston: South End Press, 1986), 116.

59. *FRUS* (1883), 57–67; Richardson, *Messages and Papers,* 3:5958–60; J. Fred Rippy, "Justo Rufino Barrios and the Nicaraguan Canal," *Hispanic American Historical Review* 20 (February 1940): 193–95; Roscoe R. Hill, "The Nicaraguan Canal Idea to 1913," *Hispanic American Historical Review* 28 (February 1948): 201–4.

60. Nicaragua, *Gaceta oficial,* 25:19 (1887), 159–65; 25:62 (1887), 613.

61. Luís Fernando Sibaja Chacón, *Nuestros límites con Nicaragua: Estudio histórico* (San José: Comisión Nacional de Conmemoración Histórica, 1974).

62. Archibald R. Colquhoun, *Key to the Pacific: The Nicaragua Canal* (Westminster: Archibald Constable, 1895); William Simmons, *The Nicaragua Canal* (New York: Harper, 1900).

63. Quoted in Julius W. Pratt, "The Larae Policy of 1898," *Mississippi Valley Historical Review* 19:2 (September 1932): 219–42.

64. William R. Adams, "Strategy, Diplomacy and Isthmian Canal Security, 1880–1917" (Ph.D. diss., Florida State University, 1974).

65. Walter LaFeber, *The New Empire: An Interpretation of American Expansion, 1860–1898* (Ithaca: Cornell University Press, 1963); Emory R. Johnson, "The Nicaraguan Canal and the Economic Development of the United States," *Annals of the American Academy of Political and Social Science* 7 (January 1896): 38–48; Paul F. Scheips, "United States Commercial Pressures for a Nicaraguan Canal in the 1890s," *The Americas* 20 (April 1964): 333–58.

66. Richard Hofstadter, "America Was Engulfed in a Psychic Crisis," in *American Imperialism in 1898*, edited by Richard H. Miller (New York: John Wiley and Sons, 1970), 36–45.

67. Quoted in U.S. Congress, House of Representatives, "Report on United States Relations with Panama," House Report no. 2218, 86th congress, 2nd session (1960), 5. For a discussion of the growing national interest in a canal see Alfred C. Richard, "The Panama Canal in the American National Consciousness, 1870–1922" (Ph.D. diss., Boston University, 1966).

68. Charles S. Campbell, *Anglo-American Understanding, 1898–1903* (Baltimore: Johns Hopkins University Press, 1957).

69. Minor, *Fight*; Richard, "The Panama Canal in the American National Consciousness."

70. Findling, "United States and Zelaya," 105–33; McCullough, *Path Between the Seas*, 305–60; Minor, *Fight*, 75–156; United States Isthmian Canal Commission, *Report of the Isthmian Canal Commission, 1899–1901* (Washington, D.C.: Government Printing Office, 1904). An excellent brief analysis of Panama's independence can be found in Conniff, *Panama*, 63–70. The Panama issue in the larger context of Caribbean policy is explained in David Healy, *Drive to Hegemony: The United States in the Caribbean, 1898–1917* (Madison: University of Wisconsin Press, 1988), 77–94.

Chapter 5. Venezuela

1. The two most complete studies of the period are Benjamín A. Frankel, *Venezuela y los Estados Unidos, 1810–1888* (Caracas: Ediciones de la Fundación John Boulton, 1977), and Armando Rojas, *Historia de las relaciones diplomáticas entre Venezuela y los Estados Unidos*, vol. 1: *1810–1899* (Caracas: Ediciones de la Presidencia de la República, 1979).

2. Samuel Flagg Bemis, *The Latin American Policy of the United States: An Historical Interpretation* (New York: Harcourt, Brace, 1943), 29–30, 73, 99, 100; George Dangerfield, *The Era of Good Feelings* (New York: Harcourt, Brace, 1952), 299ff.; Dexter Perkins, *The Monroe Doctrine, 1826–1867* (Baltimore: Johns Hopkins University Press, 1933), 135; Frankel, *Venezuela*, 282.

3. Rojas, *Historia*, 46, 56; Venezuela, Ministerio de Relaciones Exteriores, *Tratados públicos y acuerdos internacionales de Venezuela* (Caracas: Imprenta Nacional, 1957), 28–39.

4. Bemis, *Latin American Policy*, 87ff., 104ff.; Weinberg, *Manifest Destiny*, 136ff.

5. Elke Nieschulz de Stockhausen, *Los periodistas en el siglo XIX, una elite* (San Cristóbal: Universidad Católica del Táchira, 1982), 55–56, 73–74; Stockhausen, *Periodismo y política en Venezuela: Cincuenta años de historia* (Caracas: Universidad Católica Andres Bello, 1981), 58, 62–63; Frankel, *Venezuela*, 282; Robert Paul Matthews, *Violencia rural en Venezuela, 1840–1858: Antecedentes socio-económicos de la Guerra Federal* (Caracas: Monte Avila Editores, 1977), passim; Venezuela, Congreso de la Republica, *Pensamiento político venezolano del siglo XIX: Textos para su estudio*, 3 vols. (Caracas: Congreso de la República, 1983), 12:359–78; Venezuela, *Leyes y decretos de Venezuela*, 5 vols. (Caracas: Biblioteca de la Academia de Ciencias Políticas y Sociales, 1982–), 2:80–84, 498–99; Francisco González Guinán, *Historia contemporánea de Venezuela*, 15 vols. (Caracas: Ediciones de la Presidencia de la República,

1954), 4:411ff.; F. Michelena y Rojas, *Exploración oficial por la primera vez desde el norte de la América del Sur* (Brussels: A. Lacroix, Verboeckhoven, 1867), passim.

6. Rojas, *Historia*, 93, 98–99, 108–9; Frankel, *Venezuela*, 74–79, 87, 227; Venezuela, *Tratados*, 164–65; Venezuela, *Leyes*, 2:447–49, 518–19; González Guinán, *Historia*, 5:153.

7. Allan Nevins, *Ordeal of the Union* (New York: Scribners, 1947); Nevins, *The Emergence of Lincoln* (New York: Scribners, 1947).

8. Rafael Castillo Blomquist, *José Tadeo Monagas: Auge y consolidación de un caudillo* (Caracas: Monte Avila Editores, 1987), passim; Venezuela, *Leyes*, 3:149–65; José María Rojas to Henry S. Shelton, 13 April 1858, Henry Shelton Sanford Papers, Sanford, Florida, Box 35.

9. Frankel, *Venezuela*, 94, 208; Rojas, *Historia*, 117, 302; González Guinán, *Historia*, 6:120–32; David Y. Thomas, *One Hundred Years of the Monroe Doctrine, 1823–1923* (New York: Macmillan, 1927), 54; Venezuela, *Leyes*, 3:141–42.

10. Frankel, *Venezuela*, 27; Albert Z. Carr, *The World of William Walker* (New York: Harper and Row, 1963), passim; Garber, *The Gadsden Treaty*, 97, 180.

11. William Lane Harris, *Las reclamaciónes de la Isla de Aves: Un estudio de las técnicas de las reclamaciónes* (Caracas: Universidad Central de Venezuela, 1968), 7ff.; James M. Skaggs puts it in humorous perspective in *The Great Guano Rush: Entrepreneurs and American Overseas Expansion* (New York: St. Martin's Press, 1994).

12. Harris, *Reclamaciónes*, 27; Rojas, *Historia*, 153ff.

13. Harris, *Reclamaciónes*, 57ff.; Sanford's Journal, Sanford Papers, Box 3.

14. Frankel, *Venezuela*, 95–96; Venezuela, *Tratados*, 215–28; Simón Camacho, *La vuelta del General J. A. Páez a Venezuela, 1858* (New York: John F. Trow, 1858).

15. Lisandro Alvarado, *Historia de la revolución federal en Venezuela* (Caracas: Ministerio de Educación, 1956), passim; Jacinto Pérez Arcay, *La guerra federal: Consecuencias* (Caracas: Editorial Genesis, 1974), 156.

16. For the myriad details of the war see E. B. Long, *The Civil War Day by Day: An Almanac, 1861–1865* (Garden City, N.Y.: Doubleday, 1971).

17. Frankel, *Venezuela*, 97–99, 281.

18. Charles Wilkes, *Autobiography of Rear Admiral Charles Wilkes, U.S. Navy, 1798–1877* (Washington, D.C.: Department of the Navy, 1978), 792–95; Harris, *Reclamaciónes*, 95ff.; Frankel, *Venezuela*, 100, 196; Perkins, *Monroe Doctrine*, 464ff.

19. Venezuela, *Leyes*, 4:375; Frankel, *Venezuela*, 116, 175, 199, 227ff.; Pascual Casanova, *Reclamaciónes internacionales: Aprobado in 1864* (Caracas: La Opinión Nacional, 1872); Venezuela, Ministerio de Relaciones Exteriores, Archivo, Estados Unidos, vol. 187 (hereafter referred to as AMREVEU); *The Emigrant's Vade-Mecum, or Guide to the "Price Grant" in Venezuelan Guayana* (London: Trübner, 1868), passim; Alfred Jackson Hanna and Kathryn Abbey Hanna, *Confederate Exiles in Venezuela* (Tuscaloosa: Confederate Publishing Co., 1960), passim.

20. Venezuela, *Tratados*, 276–79; AMREVEU, vol. 187; Frankel, *Venezuela*, 107ff.

21. González Guinán, *Historia*, 9:58ff.; AMREVEU, vol. 187 (1866–68); *Proceedings of the Mixed Commission under the Convention of April 25, 1866* (Washington, D.C.: Gibson Brothers, 1889), passim; José Gregorio Villafañe, *Informe dado al gobierno sobre los actos de la comisión mixta* (Caracas: Imprenta la Concordia, 1868), passim; Frankel, *Venezuela*, 110ff., 176, 245ff.

22. Frankel, *Venezuela*, 114ff.; González Guinán, *Historia*, 9:232ff.

23. Frankel, *Venezuela* ("La Pandilla de Caracas"), 241ff.

24. Antonio Guzmán Blanco, *Documentos para la historia. Memorandum del General Guzmán Blanco . . . en los años de 1870, 1871, y 1872* (Caracas: La Opinión Nacional, 1875), 175; Frankel, *Venezuela*, 124; Rojas, *Historia*, 217; Antonio Guzmán Blanco, *Glorias del ilustre americano: General Guzmán Blanco* (Caracas: Imprenta El Demócrata, 1875), 369.

25. Frankel, *Venezuela,* 125; see also Adolfo Salvi, *Dalla Costa guayanés Insigne* (Caracas, 1965).

26. González Guinán, *Historia,* 11:197–98; Frankel, *Venezuela,* 128–29, 257; T. R. Ybarra, *Young Man of Caracas* (New York: Ives Washburn, 1941), 36ff.

27. William L. Harris, *La diplomacia de José María Rojas, 1873–1883* (Caracas: Academia Nacional de la Historia, 1984), 73ff.; Rojas, *Historia,* 261ff.

28. Rojas, *Historia,* 234; see also the correspondence of Matchett, Pile, and Dalla Costa, by name and year, or in "Estados Unidos de América," in Caracas, Fundación John Boulton, Archivo Guzmán Blanco (hereafter referred to as FJBAGB).

29. Frankel, *Venezuela,* 131; Rojas, *Historia,* 233.

30. Rojas, *Historia,* 235ff.; Frankel, *Venezuela,* 261ff.; see in particular the Matchett letters in FJBAGB.

31. Thomas, *One Hundred Years,* 207ff.; Frankel, *Venezuela,* 133.

32. Venezuela, *Tratados,* 422–29, 432–36; Frankel, *Venezuela,* 138; Guzmán Blanco to Benjamín Qüenza, London, 30 June 1885, AMREVEU, vol. 188.

33. Harris, *Reclamaciónes,* 104; Francisco de P. Suárez, *Report of the Secretary of the United States and Venezuelan Claims Commission* (Washington, D.C.: Gibson Brothers, 1890), passim; Samuel Guy Inman, *Inter-American Conferences, 1826–1954: History and Problems* (Gettysburg, Penn.: Latin American Institute, 1965), chaps. 1–3; David S. Muzzey, *James G. Blaine: A Political Idol of Other Days* (New York: Dodd, Mead, 1935), 426ff.

34. Armando Rojas, *Venezuela: Limite al este con el Esequiba* (Caracas: Cromotip, 1968), 6ff.; Robert H. Schomburgk, *A Description of British Guiana, Geographical and Statistical: Exhibiting Its Resources and Capabilities* (London: Simpkin, Marshall, 1840); Pablo Ojer, *Sumario histórico de la Guayana Esequiba* (Caracas: Editorial Arte, 1982), 20ff.; Armando Rojas, *Los papeles de Aleio Fortique* (Caracas: Universidad Central de Venezuela, 1962), 40; Enrique Bernardo Núñez, *Tres momentos en la controversia de limites de Guayana* (Caracas: Imprenta Nacional, 1962), 15; González Guinán, *Historia,* 5:120, 132; Thomas, *One Hundred Years,* 54.

35. Frankel, *Venezuela,* 79, 207–8; Manuel Landaeta Rosales, *Gran recopilación geográfica, estadística e histórica de Venezuela* (Caracas: Banco Central de Venezuela, 1963), 60ff.; William Eleroy Curtis, *Venezuela: A Land Where It's Always Summer* (New York: Harper, 1896), 235.

36. Thomas, *One Hundred Years,* 54; Rojas to Sanford, 1863, Sanford Papers, Box 35; José María Rojas, *El Dorado of the Spaniards in Venezuela* (Paris: Clark and Bishop, 1903); Rojas, *Historia,* 283ff.; Frankel, *Venezuela,* 126, 210.

37. Frankel, *Venezuela,* 302; Harris, *Diplomacia,* chap. 5; Núñez, *Tres momentos,* 28–30; Rojas, *Historia,* 303.

38. *Diccionario de la historia de Venezuela* (Caracas: Fundación Polar, 1988), 1:498; Nazareno [Simón Camacho], *Cosas de los Estados Unidos* (New York: J. Durand, 1864), passim; Frankel, *Venezuela,* 132ff.

39. Núñez, *Tres momentos,* 34; Rojas, *Historia,* 305.

40. Frankel, *Venezuela,* 305–6; Charles Callan Tansill, *The Foreign Policy of Thomas F. Bayard* (New York: Fordham University Press, 1940), 630ff. (hereafter Tansill, *Bayard*).

41. O. E. Thurber, *Origin del capital norteaméricano en Venezuela* (Barquisimeto: Editorial Nueva Segovia, n.d.), 11ff.; Charles G. Jackson, "The Manoa Company, Limited" (M.A. thesis, University of North Carolina, 1957), 14, 25, 29; Venezuela, *Leyes,* 11:42–43, 98–99, 13:269–71; Frankel, *Venezuela,* 210.

42. Frelinghuysen to Jehu Baker (copy), Washington, D.C., 25 July 1884, AMREVEU, vol. 188; Rojas, *Historia,* 309.

43. Armando Rojas, *Las misiones diplomáticas de Guzman Blanco* (Caracas: Monte

Avila Editores, 1972), 153ff.; Venezuela, Ministerio de Relaciones Exteriores, Archivo, Gran Bretaña, vol. 144 (1884–85), passim; FJBAGB, José María Rojas (1884).

44. Tansill, *Bayard,* 636; Rojas, *Historia,* 319.

45. Tansill, *Bayard,* 637; Rojas, *Historia,* 167ff.; Antonio de Pedro Fernández, *La historia y el derecho de la reclamación venezolana de la Guayana Esequiba* (Caracas and Madrid: Editorial Mediterraneo, 1969), 244–45.

46. Venezuela, *Correspondence Between the Venezuelan Government and Her British Majesty's Government about the Question of the Frontier* (Caracas: La Opinión Nacional, 1887); Tansill, *Bayard,* 644; Rojas, *Historia,* 320; R. F. Seijas, *Venezuelan International Law: British Boundaries of Guayana* (Paris: Impr. C. Pariset, 1888).

47. Rojas, *Historia,* 322ff.

48. Muzzey, *Blaine,* 436; AMREVEU, vol. 233, 1, 5.

49. Wolff, "The Diplomatic Career of William L. Scruggs," 198; AMREVEU, vol. 233 (1891), passim.

50. Tansill, *Bayard,* 654; Rojas, *Historia,* 334.

5l. Tansill, *Bayard,* 672ff.

52. AMREVEU, vol. 233 (Spring 1893); Tansill, *Bayard,* 694; Bemis, *Latin American Policy,* 123ff.; John A. S. Grenville and George Berkeley Young, *Politics, Strategy, and American Diplomacy: Studies in Foreign Policy, 1873–1917* (New Haven: Yale University Press, 1966), 157.

53. William L. Scruggs, *The Venezuelan Question: British Aggressions in Venezuela, or the Monroe Doctrine on Trial; Lord Salisbury's Mistakes; Fallacies of the British "Blue Book" on the Disputed Boundary* (Atlanta: Franklin Printing, 1896), "Preliminary Note"; Dexter Perkins, *Hands Off: A History of the Monroe Doctrine* (Boston: Little, Brown, 1941), 173–74; John Bassett Moore, *A Digest of International Law* (Washington, D.C.: Government Printing Office, 1906), 6:535.

54. Perkins, *Hands Off,* 175; Rojas, *Historia,* 338–39.

55. Rojas, *Historia,* 334; Henry James, *Richard Olney and His Public Service* (New York: Houghton Mifflin, 1923), 114–22.

56. Tansill, *Bayard,* 736; J. Fred Rippy, *Latin America in World Politics: An Outline Survey* (New York: Knopf, 1928), 118–19; James, *Richard Olney,* 123. The commission published a nine-volume *Report and Accompanying Papers* (Washington, D.C., 1897).

57. AMREVEU, Documentos sobre Guayana, carpeta 3, expediente 12, indicates the flow of Scruggs documents. Marco A. Osorio Jiménez, *La Guayana Esequiba* (Caracas: Academia Nacional de la Historia, 1984), 10–11; Rojas, *Historia,* 350; Venezuela, *Historia oficial* (New York: Louis Weiss, 1896); Curtis, *Venezuela;* Bradford Perkins, *The Great Rapprochement: England and the United States, 1895–1914* (London: Victor Gollancz, 1969), 18–19.

58. Venezuela, *Tratados,* 681–85.

59. AMREVGB, vol. 186; José María Rojas to Venezuelan minister of foreign relations, Paris, 25 July 1899, 24 August 1899; Calvin DeArmond Davis, *The United States and the First Hague Peace Conference* (Ithaca: Cornell University Press, 1962), 126, 204.

60. Venezuela, Ministerio de Relaciones Exteriores, *Report on the Boundary Question with British Guiana Submitted to the National Government by the Venezuelan Experts* (Caracas: Cromotip, 1967), 17ff.; Federico Martens, *Rusia e Inglaterra en Asia Central* (Caracas: Academia Nacional de la Historia, 1981), contains extensive information on Martens.

61. Venezuela, *Report on the Boundary Question,* 42; Martens, *Rusia e Inglaterra,* 28ff.; Davis, *First Hague Conference,* 204–5.

62. Julius W. Pratt, *America's Colonial Experiment: How the United States Gained, Governed, and in Part Gave Away a Colonial Empire* (Englewood Cliffs, N.J.: Prentice-Hall, 1950), 39; Julius W. Pratt, *Expansionists of 1898: The Acquisition of Hawaii and the Spanish Islands* (Baltimore: Johns Hopkins University Press, 1936), passim.

63. Robert L. Gilmore, *Caudillism and Militarism in Venezuela, 1810–1910* (Athens: Ohio University Press, 1964), ix; Jackson H. Ralston, *Venezuelan Arbitrations of 1903* (Washington, D.C.: Government Printing Office, 1904), 1060ff.; Venezuela, *Tratados,* 539–41.

64. Pratt, *America's Colonial Experiment,* 13, 87ff.

65. Thomas, *One Hundred Years,* 211.

66. Ralston, *Venezuelan Arbitrations,* 483ff., 1063ff.; Calvin DeArmond Davis, *The United States and the Second Hague Peace Conference* (Durham: Duke University Press, 1975), 74; Comisión Mixta Venezolana-Francesa, Protocolo del 19 de Febrero de 1902, *Dictámenes del arbitro venezolano* (Caracas: J. M. Herrera Irigoyen, 1903), passim; Miriam Hood, *Diplomácia con cañones, 1895–1905* (Caracas: Universidad Católica Andres Bello, 1978).

67. Davis, *Second Hague Conference,* 80ff.; Holger H. Herwig and J. León Helguera, *Alemania y el bloqueo internacional de Venezuela, 1902/03* (Caracas: Ministerio de Relaciones Exteriores, 1976), 28ff.

68. Davis, *Second Hague Conference,* 82ff.; Ralston, *Venezuelan Arbitrations of 1903,* passim; Manuel Rodríguez Campos, *Venezuela 1902: La crisis fiscal y el bloqueo* (Caracas: Universidad Central de Venezuela, 1983), 345.

69. Pratt, *America's Colonial Experiment,* 123ff.; Castillo, *Memoria de mano lobo: La cuestión monetaria en Venezuela* (Caracas: Publicaciones de la Presidencia de la Republica, 1962), 19; *Diccionario de historia de Venezuela,* 1:617–18.

Chapter 6. Peru

1. *American Farmer,* 24 December 1824, 316–17, quoted in L. C. Nolan, "The Diplomatic and Commercial Relations of the U.S. and Peru" (Ph.D. diss., Duke University, 1935), 140.

2. Nolan, "Diplomatic and Commercial Relations," 155–76; Jorge Basadre, *Historia de la república de Perú,* 11 vols., 7th ed. (Lima: Editorial Universiteria, 1983), 5:82–83.

3. David Werlich, *Admiral of the Amazon: John Randolph Tucker, His Confederate Colleagues, and Peru* (Charlottesville: University Press of Virginia, 1990), 141, 255–56; Donald M. Dozier, "Pathfinder of the Amazon," *Virginia Quarterly Review* 23 (Autumn 1947): 554–67; Malvin C. Ross, ed., *George Gatlin: Episodes from Life Among the Indians and Last Rambles* (Norman: University of Oklahoma Press, 1959). Gatlin traveled through South America from 1852 to 1855, sketching a good deal along the Peruvian Amazon.

4. Basadre, *Historia de la república de Perú,* 4:333–34, 377, 388–89.

5. Nolan, "Diplomatic and Commercial Relations," 293; Werlich, *Admiral of the Amazon,* 86ff.

6. Nolan, "Diplomatic and Commercial Relations," 307–8, 318–19; George Baker, ed., *The Works of William H. Seward,* 5 vols. (New York: Houghton Mifflin, 1984), 5:444–45.

7. Nolan, "Diplomatic and Commercial Relations," 309–10.

8. Ibid., 217ff.

9. Heraclio Bonilla, *Guano y burguesia en el Peru* (Lima: Instituto de Estudios Peruanos, 1974), 58.

10. Basadre, *Historia de la república de Perú,* 5:136.

11. Ibid., 5:122.

12. Watt Stewart, *Henry Meiggs: Yankee Pizarro* (Durham: Duke University Press, 1946); Basadre, *Historia de la república de Perú,* 5:135–36.

13. For a full biography of William Russell Grace, see Marquis James, *Merchant Adventurer: The Story of W. R. Grace* (Wilmington, Del.: Scholarly Resources, 1993).

14. For a good summary of the failure of U.S. diplomacy in this war see A. Nayland Page, "United States Diplomacy in the Tacna-Arica Dispute, 1884–1929" (Ph.D. diss., University of Oklahoma, 1958).

15. Ronald Bruce St. John, *The Foreign Policy of Peru* (Boulder: Lynne Rienner, 1992), 112.

16. James, *Merchant Adventurer*, 115.

17. J. P. Christiancy to J. G. Blaine, 4 May 1881, *FRUS* (1881); 899–904; St. John, *Foreign Policy*, 119ff.; Charles S. Campbell, *The Transformation of American Foreign Relations, 1865–1900* (New York: Harper and Row, 1976), 94ff.; David M. Pletcher, *The Awkward Years: American Foreign Policy under Garfield and Arthur* (Columbia: University of Missouri Press, 1962), 49; Herbert Millington, *American Diplomacy and the War of the Pacific* (New York: Columbia University Press, 1948), 93.

18. Blaine to Hurlbut, 22 November 1881, Senate Executive Document no. 79, 47th congress, 1st session, 565–66.

19. Campbell, *Transformation of American Foreign Relations*, 96–98. For indictments of Blaine see Perry Belmont, *Reflections of an American Diplomat* (New York: Columbia University Press, 1941), chaps. 7–8.

20. Frelinghuysen to U.S. consul at Panama (for Trescot), 4 January 1882, Frelinghuysen to Trescot, 9 January 1882, *FRUS* (1882), 56–58; Campbell, *Transformation of American Foreign Relations*, 98.

21. James, *Merchant Adventurer*, 137–38.

22. Ibid.

23. Campbell, *Transformation of American Foreign Relations*, 98.

24. St. John, *Foreign Policy*, 121.

25. James, *Merchant Adventurer*, 138.

26. Heraclio Bonilla, "The War of the Pacific and the National and Colonial Problem in Peru," *Past and Present* 81 (November 1978): 92–118.

27. Quoted in Gumucio Granier, *The United States and the Bolivian Seacoast*, 84; M. P. Grace to chairman of Bondholders Committee, 18 May 1885, Grace Papers, Columbia University.

28. Edward Eyre to M. P. Grace, 10 July 1886, Grace Papers.

29. Basadre, *Historia de la república de Perú*, 6:2755.

30. James, *Merchant Adventurer*, 155–56.

31. Basadre, *Historia de la república de Perú*, 6:2754–57.

32. W. R. Grace to Secretary of State Bayard, 19 December 1887, Grace Papers.

33. M. P. Grace to Aurelio Denegri, 20 February 1888, Grace Papers.

34. W. Ivins to Edward Eyre, 9 July 1888, Grace Papers.

35. Basadre, *Historia de la república de Perú*, 6:2760–61; Rory Miller, "The Making of the Grace Contract: British Bondholders and the Peruvian Government, 1885–1890," *Journal of Latin American Studies* 8 (May 1976): 93.

36. Basadre, *Historia de la república de Perú*, 6:2770.

37. Information on conference is drawn from Basadre, *Historia de la república de Perú*, 7:23–25; St. John, *Foreign Policy*, 138; John Fagg, *Pan Americanism* (Makabar, Fla.: Robert Krieger Publishing Co., 1982), 23–25; Lawrence A. Clayton, *Grace: W. R. Grace and Co., The Formative Years, 1850–1930* (Ottawa, Ill.: Jameson Books, 1985), 235–36.

38. St. John, *Foreign Policy*, 119 passim.

39. Dale William Peterson, "The Diplomatic and Commercial Relations Between the United States and Peru from 1883 to 1918" (Ph.D. diss., University of Minnesota, 1969), 135ff.

Chapter 7. Argentina

1. *FRUS* (1866), 2:320. For an Argentine view of the war see Ramon J. Carcano, *Guerra del Paraguay*, 3 vols. (Buenos Aires: Domingo Viau., 1941).

2. For a fuller discussion see Carlos F. Díaz Alejandro, *Essays on the Economic History*

of the Argentine Republic (New Haven: Yale University Press, 1970); Laura Randall, *An Economic History of Argentina in the Twentieth Century* (New York: Columbia University Press, 1978); Aldo Ferrer, *The Argentine Economy* (Berkeley: University of California Press, 1967).

3. The literature on U.S. expansion is vast. For a variety of perspectives see Milton Plesur, *America's Outward Thrust: Approaches to Foreign Affairs, 1865–1890* (DeKalb: Northern Illinois University Press, 1971); LaFeber, *The New Empire;* Foster Rhea Dulles, *Prelude to World Power: American Diplomatic History, 1860–1900* (New York: Macmillan, 1965); Ernest R. May, *American Imperialism: A Speculative Essay* (New York: Atheneum, 1968).

4. LaFeber, *The New Empire,* 15–25.

5. May, *American Imperialism.*

6. David F. Healy, *The United States in Cuba, 1898–1902* (Madison: University of Wisconsin Press, 1963), 247.

7. May, *American Imperialism.*

8. S. R. Williamson, Jr., *Politics of Grand Strategy* (Cambridge, Mass.: Harvard University Press, 1968).

9. Quoted in Thomas F. McGann, *Argentina: The United States and the Inter-American System* (Cambridge, Mass.: Harvard University Press, 1957), 128.

10. The best discussion of the conference and of the entire period from the Argentine perspective is McGann, *Argentina,* passim. For another view, see Russell H. Bastert, "A New Approach to the Origins of Blaine's Pan American Policy," *Hispanic American Historical Review* 39 (August 1959): 374–412, and "Diplomatic Reversal: Frelinghuysen's Opposition to Blaine's Pan-American Policy in 1882," *Mississippi Valley Historical Review* 51 (March 1965): 615–32.

11. Saénz Peña to Saldías, 21 August 1908, Gobierno Nacional, Buenos Aires, Argentina, Archivo Saldías, File 3-6-10.

12. Studies by the Ministry of Agriculture include Carlos D. Girola, *Investigación agrícola de la República Argentina* (Buenos Aires: Imprenta Nacional, 1904); Emilio Lahitte, *Informes y estudios de la dirección de economía rural y estadística,* 3 vols. (Buenos Aires, 1916). More recent studies include Guillermo Flichmann, *La renta dal suelo* (Buenos Aires: Siglo XXI, 1975); Joseph Tulchin and Ramón Castillo, "Developpement capitaliste et structures sociales des regions en Argentine (1880–1930)," *Annales* 6 (1986); Joseph Tulchin, "Labour and Capital in Rural Argentina, 1880–1914," in *The Political Economy of Argentina, 1880–1914,* edited by G. DiTella and D. C. M. Platt (London: Macmillan, 1986).

13. James R. Scobie, *Argentina* (New York: Oxford University Press, 1964), 123. On the social question see J. L. Romero, *A History of Argentine Political Thought* (Stanford: Stanford University Press, 1963); Carl Solberg, *Immigration and Nationalism* (Austin: University of Texas Press, 1970).

14. Cited in McGann, *Argentina* 119.

15. Cited in ibid., 61.

16. Cited in ibid., 61.

17. For a discussion of the concept of progress in Argentina, see R. Cortés Conde, *El progreso argentino, 1880–1914* (Buenos Aires: Sudamericana, 1979); N. R. Botana, *El orden conservador* (Buenos Aires: Sudamericana, 1977).

18. Cited in McGann, *Argentina,* 197.

19. *La Prensa,* 5 August 1914, 5; Saénz Peña to de la Plaza, 20 November 1908, Gobierno Nacional, Archivo Saénz Peña, File 22-21-15.

20. Cited in McGann, *Argentina,* 119.

21. *La Prensa,* 18 December 1895, cited in McGann, *Argentina,* 184; Hebe M. García de Bargero, "Repercusión en la república argentina de la controversia entre estados unidos y gran bretaña, acerca de la frontera entre venezuela y la guayana," *Jornadas de Historia y Lit-*

eratura Argentina y Norteamericana 5 (1970); Ricardo Caillet-Bois and Ernesto Annecou, "La política argentina y el conflicto hispanonorteamericano en 1898," *Jornadas de Historia y Literatura Argentina y Norteamericana* 3 (1968).

22. Carlos Escudé refers to this posture as *principismo* and considers it to have had a negative effect on Argentine foreign policy for the past century. See his *La Argentina? Paria Internacional?* (Buenos Aires: Belgrano, 1984).

23. Cited in McGann, *Argentina*, 311.

24. Ambassador Reginald Tower's No. 10, 2 January 1910, Public Records Office, London, Foreign Office File 368/378. This makes a great deal of British political abnegation, although he chronicles case after case of diplomatic intervention on behalf of private interests. While his argument most certainly is overstated, the point remains that the British never attempted to build a structure of control analogous to their areas of influence in Africa and Asia. They operated through informal empire, with influence exerted through the leverage of the marketplace and the diffuse pressure exerted by the importance of trade and investments. In this case, the Foreign Office felt Tower overreacted to the Argentine government's decision to award the battleship contract to a U.S. firm.

25. Pillado to O'Brien, 28 January 1910, Gobierno Nacional, Archivo de la Plaza, File 4-6-1.

26. Richard Oliver, *La vida cotidiana* (Buenos Aires: Sudamericana, 1969), 15.

27. Carlos Escudé argues that Canada, Australia, Switzerland, and other nations participate effectively in international affairs without the trappings of power. The difference is that they do not delude themselves concerning their influence or power. The problem, says Escudé, resides in the unrealistic goals set by Argentine leaders and the illusory effects of their reliance upon *principismo*. Personal communication to the author, 25 July 1988.

28. Robert N. Burr, *By Reason or Force* (Berkeley: University of California Press, 1965); Burr, "The Balance of Power in Nineteenth-Century Latin America," *Hispanic American Historical Review* 34 (August 1955): 314–43. Burr suggests that Argentina focused on a regional power struggle because it was too weak to participate in a global balance of power, and that the same was true for Chile and Brazil. At the same time, the European powers were prevented from dominating South America politically. Thus, South American nations were in a position to assume roles in relation to one another that they could not play with any hope of success on a larger world stage. Although this is probably a realistic analysis of the limited potential of the South American states, there is no evidence that the Argentine leaders consciously adopted policies that were designed as adaptations to their power level or their geographical area or the patterns of thinking and action adopted by European powers on a world stage.

29. Zeballos to Saénz Peña, 27 June 1908, Gobierno Nacional, Archivo Saénz Peña, File 22-2-14. This presents Zeballos's view of the events. A different view is M. A. Carcano, *Saénz Peña*, 224–25. Support for the mission is in Saénz Valiente, chief of naval operations, to Saénz Peña, 11 August 1910, Juan P. Gomez to Saénz Peña, 12 August 1910, Gobierno Nacional, Archivo Saénz Peña, File 22-2-18.

30. Roberto Etchepareborda, *Historia de las relaciones internacionales Argentinas* (Buenos Aires: Editorial Pleamer, 1978), 118. The late Roberto Etchepareborda had privileged access to the Zeballos papers and at his death was in the middle of a significant study of the statesman's life and times. The published collection of essays cited here represents the first fruits of his research, which included a comprehensive review of documents relating to Argentine foreign relations in the German, Italian, and U.S. archives. As is often the case in studies in which the author immerses himself in the life of an individual, Etchepareborda overstates Zeballos's influence on Argentine policy, but he demonstrates beyond the slightest doubt that the generation of which Zeballos was an integral part was fully cognizant of

the ideas of European and U.S. writers concerning international affairs and that they understood those ideas and their implications for national policy.

31. Public Records Office, FO 371/1295, File 971, Tower, 9 December 1911.

Chapter 8. Chile

1. Quoted in Ernesto de la Cruz and Guillermo Feliu Cruz, *Epistolario de Don Diego Portales, 1811–1837,* 3 vols. (Santiago: Imprenta de Dirección de Prisones, 1936–37), 1:76–77.

2. Sergio Sepulved, *El trigo chileno en el mercado mundial* (Santiago: Universitaria de Chile, 1959), 41–46.

3. Carl A. Ross, Jr., "Chile and Its Relations with the United States during the Ministry of Thomas Henry Nelson, 1861–1866" (Ph.D. diss., University of Georgia, 1966), 21.

4. Reginald Horsman, *Race and Manifest Destiny* (Cambridge, Mass.: Harvard University Press, 1981), 280.

5. Benjamín Vicuña Mackenna, *Páginas de mi diario durante tres años de viaje, 1853–1854–1855,* 2 vols. (Santiago: Imprenta de la Libertad, 1936), 1:254.

6. Carlos Lopez, *Chilenos in California: A Study of the 1850, 1852, and 1860 Census* (San Francisco: R and E Research Associates, 1973), xviii. For various reasons, Lopez believes that the correct figure should be at least 16,000. Mario Barros Van Buren indicates that the Chilean government paid for the passage of some 8,000 Chileans and that an additional 2,000 paid their own way. See his *Historia diplomática de Chile, 1541–1938* (Barcelona: Ediciones Ariel, 1970), 194.

7. Quoted in Carolyn Ann H. Richards, "Chilean Attitudes Toward the United States, 1860–1867" (Ph.D. diss., Stanford University, 1970), 41, 198.

8. Ross, "Chile and Its Relations," 22.

9. Starkweather to March, Santiago, 29 May 1855, in "Despatches from United States Ministers to Chile, 1823–1906" (hereafter known as Despatches/Chile).

10. Bigler to Cass, 30 April 1860, 17 December 1860, Despatches/Chile; Henry C. Evans, Jr., *Chile and Its Relations with the United States* (Durham: Duke University Press 1927), 73.

11. Quoted in Hernán Ramírez Necochea, *Historia del imperialismo en Chile* (Santiago: Austral, 1970), 82.

12. Burr, *By Reason or Force,* 84; "Circular del Ministerio de Relaciones Exteriores de Chile a los Gobiernos Sud-Americans y a algunos de Europa," *Correspondencia de Don Antonio Varas: Cuestiones americanas* (Santiago: Editorial Universitaria, 1929), 131–32.

13. *El Mercurio* (Valparaíso), 13 February 1856.

14. Francisco Bilbao, *Obras completas,* 2 vols. (Santiago: El Correo, 1897), 1:168, 171.

15. Richards, "Chilean Attitudes," 68, 70.

16. Daniel J. Hunter [Benjamín Vicuña Mackenna], *Chili, the United States, and Spain* (New York: S. Hallet, 1866), 61.

17. Quoted in Stephen D. Brown, "The Power of Influence in United States–Chilean Relations" (Ph.D. diss., University of Wisconsin, 1983), 135.

18. Ibid., 142.

19. For a description of the conflict see William F. Sater, *Chile and the War of the Pacific* (Lincoln: University of Nebraska Press, 1986).

20. Quoted in James W. Pierce, *Life of James G. Blaine* (Baltimore, 1893), 440–41; Richard C. Winchester, "James G. Blaine and the Ideology of American Expansionism" (Ph.D. diss., University of Rochester, 1966), 74, 83.

21. Pletcher, *The Awkward Years,* 42.

22. *La Patria* (Valparaíso), 20 and 27 January 1883, 30 June 1883; *Los Tiempos* (Santiago), 1 February 1883. For additional material on this topic see William F. Sater, *Chile and*

the United States: Empires in Conflict (Athens: University of Georgia Press, 1990), 31–50; Herbert Millington, *American Diplomacy and the War of the Pacific* (New York: Columbia University Press, 1948).

23. Quoted in Brown, "Power of Influence," 283, 286; U.S. Congress, House, House Report no. 653, 47th congress, 1st session, 8 March 1882, vii.

24. Quoted in Pletcher, *The Awkward Years*, 79.

25. Albert G. Browne, "The Growing Power of the Republic of Chile," *Journal of the American Geographical Society of New York* 16 (July 1884): 62–64.

26. William E. Curtis, "The South American Yankee," *Harper's Magazine* 75 (1887), 564.

27. *Congressional Record*, 47th congress, 2nd session, 20 January 1883, 1404; *Congressional Record*, 47th congress, 1st session, 28 June 1882, 5474; quoted in Joyce S. Goldberg, *The Baltimore Affair* (Lincoln: University of Nebraska Press, 1986), 116.

28. Quoted in Francisco A. Encina, *La presidencia de Balmaceda*, 2 vols. (Santiago: Nascimento, 1952), 1:336.

29. J. Douglas Porteos, "The Annexation of Eastern [*sic*] Island: Geopolitics and Environmental Perception," *North-South* 6, no. 11 (1981): 79.

30. Wicks, "Dress Rehearsal," 582–83.

31. Rodrigo Fuenzalida Bade, *Marines ilustres y recuerdos del pasado* (Santiago, 1985), 111–12; Wicks, "Dress Rehearsal," 594, 596–97, 603.

32. "We Cannot Fight the Chilean Navy," *Army and Navy Journal*, 1 August 1885.

33. As quoted in Emilio Meneses, "Coping with Decline: Chilean Foreign Policy During the Twentieth Century, 1902–1972" (Ph.D. diss., Oxford, Balliol College, 1988); Kennedy to Rosebery, Santiago, 4 August 1893, Public Records Office, FO 16/286; *La Ley* (Santiago), 10 December 1902; *El Mercurio*, 12 November 1903; Ferenc Fischer, "La expansión indirecta de la ciencia militar alemana en América Latina del Sur: La cooperación militar entre Alemania y Chile y las misiones militares germanófilas chilenas en los países latinoamericanos, 1885–1914," in *Tordesillas y sus consecuencias: La política de las grandes potencias europeas respecto a América Latina, 1491–1899* (Frankfurt am Main, 1995), 259.

34. Robert Seager II, *Alfred Thayer Mahan: The Man and His Letters* (Annapolis: Naval Institute Press, 1977), 147.

35. Egan to Blaine, 4 December 1891, Despatches/Chile; quoted in Goldberg, *The Baltimore Affair*, 56.

36. Egan to Blaine, 30 January 1892, Despatches/Chile.

37. Goldberg, *The Baltimore Affair*, 107.

38. *Nation*, 18 May 1893.

39. *Harper's Weekly*, 30 January 1892, 110.

40. Ventura Blanco Viel, quoted in Oscar Espinosa Moraga, *La postguerra del Pacifico y la Puna de Atacama* (Santiago: Andres Bello, 1958), 287.

41. Barros Van Buren, *Historia diplomática*, 492.

42. Porter to Gresham, 8 August 1893, Egan to Gresham, 10, 17, 19, and 27 April 1893; McGreery to Foster, 3 January 1893, Despatches/Chile.

43. *La Nueva República* (Santiago), 24 December 1895; *El Ferrocarril*, 28 December 1895, quoted in Frederick Pike, *Chile and the United States, 1880–1962* (Notre Dame: University of Notre Dame Press, 1963), 137.

44. Quoted in Ramírez Necochea, *Historia del imperialismo*, 182.

45. Wilson to Sherman, 23 December 1895, 26 April 1898, Despatches/Chile.

46. Wilson to Sherman, 11 March, 11 April, 25 June, 9 July, 1856, Despatches/Chile.

47. Francisco Valdés, *La situación económica y financiera de Chile* (Valparaíso: Trautmann, 1894), 136; Pike, *Chile and the United States*, 99–100; Frederick Nunn, *Yesterday's Sol-*

diers (Lincoln: University of Nebraska Press, 1983), 47; Eyzaguirre, *Chile durante el Gobierno de Errazuriz, Echavrren,* 2nd ed. (Santiago: Impresa Romani, 1957), 227.

48. Barros Van Buren, *Historia diplomática,* 500.

49. Wilson to Hay, 9 August 1899, Despatches/Chile; quoted in Pike, *Chile and the United States,* 124; *El Ferrocarril,* 6 July 1899; *La Tarde* (Santiago), 5 July 1899; *La Ley* (Santiago), 6 July 1899.

50. Hutchinson to Hay, 15 November 1902, Despatches/Chile; *La Libertad Electoral* (Santiago), 31 July 1901; *El Ferrocarril,* 10 December 1902; *La Ley* (Santiago), 10 December 1902; *La Libertad Electoral,* 31 July 1901; *La Ley,* 10 December 1902.

51. Wilson to Hay, 26 January 1903, Despatches/Chile.

52. *El Mercurio,* 14 December 1904.

53. Wilson to Hay, 19 June 1903, Despatches/Chile; *El Ferrocarril,* 10 June 1903; *El Chileno* (Santiago), 11 June 1903, 4 July 1903; *El Mercurio,* 4 July 1903; *El Ferrocarril,* 4 July 1903.

54. *El Ferrocarril,* 14 March 1903, 19 November 1903; *El Diario Ilustrado* (Santiago), 21 November 1903.

55. *Las Ultimas Noticias* (Santiago), quoted in *El Mercurio,* 11 November 1903.

56. Wilson to Hay, 21 and 22 November 1903, 7 March 1904, Despatches/Chile.

57. Wilson to Hay, 26 January 1903, Despatches/Chile.

58. Roberts to Bayard, 8 July 1885, Despatches/Chile.

59. Eyzaguirre, *Chile durante el Gobierno,* 372.

60. Ibid., 337–38.

61. Ames to Hay, 11 January 1905, Despatches/Chile.

62. *El Mercurio,* 13 August 1905, 28 September 1905, 7 October 1905.

63. Macchiavello Varas, *El problema de la industria de cobre y sus provecciones económicos y sociales* (Santiago: University of Chile, 1923), 106–8; Clark W. Reynolds, "Development Problems of an Export Economy: The Case of Chile and Copper," in *Essays on the Chilean Economy* (Homewood, Ill.: Irwin, 1965), 221.

64. Wilson to Hay, 22 November 1900, Ames to Root, 12 August 1905, 22 September 1905, Despatches/Chile.

65. Sotomayor to Walker, 16 January 1904, Despatches/Chile; quoted in Meneses, "Coping with Decline," 83.

Chapter 9. Brazil

1. There is no scholarly study dealing specifically with U.S.-Brazilian relations during the period from 1850 to 1903. The principal work on the subject is Joseph Smith, *Unequal Giants: Diplomatic Relations Between the United States and Brazil, 1889–1930* (Pittsburgh: University of Pittsburgh Press, 1991). Diplomatic events at the beginning of the twentieth century are examined in E. Bradford Burns, *The Unwritten Alliance: Rio Branco and Brazilian-American Relations* (New York: Columbia University Press, 1966). An excellent diplomatic study by a Brazilian author is Clodoaldo Bueno, *A república e sua política exterior (1889 a 1902)* (São Paulo: Editora UNESP, 1995). The importance of economic factors is highlighted in Victor C. Valla, *A penetração norteamericano na economia brasileira 1898–1928* (Rio de Janeiro: Livro Técnico, 1978), and Moniz Bandeira, *Presença dos Estados Unidos no Brasil (dois séculos de história)* (Rio de Janeiro: Editora Civilizaçao Brasileira, 1973). For the influence of European powers see Richard Graham, *Britain and the Onset of Modernization in Brazil, 1850–1914* (Cambridge: Cambridge University Press, 1968).

2. Webb to Seward, 24 January 1867, *FRUS* (1860), 2:251.

3. Daniel P. Kidder and James C. Fletcher, *Brazil and Brazilians Portrayed in Historical and Descriptive Sketches* (Philadelphia: Childs and Peterson, 1857), 21.

4. Ibid., 611–12.

5. See Nicia Vilela Luz, *A amazônia para os negros americanos* (Rio de Janeiro: Editora Saga, 1968), 169.

6. Matthew Fontaine Maury, *The Amazon and the Atlantic Slopes of South America* (Washington, D.C.: Frank Taylor, 1853), 5.

7. Professor and Mrs. Louis Agassiz, *A Journey in Brazil* (Boston: Ticknor and Fields, 1868), 496.

8. Thomas Ewbank, *Life in Brazil* (New York: Harper, 1856).

9. Agassiz, *Journey in Brazil*, 93.

10. William E. Curtis, *The Capitals of Spanish America* (1888; reprint, New York: Praeger, 1969), 661.

11. Bayard to Jarvis, 19 February 1888, *FRUS* (1888), 57.

12. Kidder and Fletcher, *Brazil*, 195.

13. John Codman, *Ten Months in Brazil* (Boston: Lee and Shepard, 1867), 41, 51.

14. Maury, *Amazon*, 45.

15. Partridge to Fish, 24 March 1873, *FRUS* (1866), 2:96.

16. Maury, *Amazon*, 5, 62.

17. Kidder and Fletcher, *Brazil*, 579.

18. Webb to Seward, 7 August 1866, Despatches/Chile.

19. Webb to Seward, 7 August 1866, *FRUS* (1866), 2:320; Seward to Webb, 17 June 1867, *FRUS* (1867), 2:255.

20. *Congressional Record,* 45th congress, 3rd session, ser. 2131, 28 February 1879.

21. Earl Richard Downes, "The Seeds of Influence: Brazil's 'Essentially Agricultural' Old Republic and the United States, 1910–1930" (Ph.D. diss., University of Texas, 1986), 99.

22. Christopher C. Andrews, *Brazil: Its Condition and Prospects* (New York: Appleton, 1891), 103.

23. MacDonnell to Iddesleigh, 16 December 1886, Public Records Office, Chile, FO 13/621.

24. White to Evarts, 27 February 1879, *FRUS* (1879), 133.

25. Trail to Bayard (no. 72), 21 January 1886, Despatches/Brazil.

26. See Carlos Süssekind de Mendonça, *Salvador de Mendonça: Democrata do imperio e da república* (Rio de Janeiro: Instituto Nacional do Livro, 1960), 126–27.

27. Armstrong to Bayard, 28 November 1888, Despatches/Brazil.

28. Blaine to Osborn, 1 December 1881, Despatches Instructions/Brazil; Pereira da Costa to Augusto da Silva, 12 April 1889, Pereira da Costa to Diana, 8 August 1889, Missoes Diplomáticas Brasileiras, Oficios, File 233/4/9, Arquivo Histórico do Itamaraty, Rio de Janeiro (hereafter referred to as AHI).

29. Adams to Blaine (no. 20), 19 November 1889, Despatches/Brazil.

30. *Congressional Record,* 51st congress, 1st session, 20 December 1889, 315.

31. For the debate of 20 December 1889, see *Congressional Record,* 51st congress, 1st session, 313–24.

32. *New York Sun,* 20 December 1889.

33. *New York Times,* 24 December 1889.

34. Ibid., 20 December 1889.

35. Wyndham to Salisbury, 24 February 1890, Public Records Office, FO 13/666.

36. *Rio News,* 10 February 1890.

37. Wyndham to Salisbury, 26 February 1890, Public Records Office, FO 13/666.

38. *New York Daily Tribune,* 25 June 1890; *New York Times,* 24 June 1890.

39. John W. Foster, *Diplomatic Memoirs,* 2 vols. (Boston: Houghton Mifflin, 1909), 2:7.

40. John W. Foster, "Loss of Revenue," undated memorandum, John W. Foster Papers, Library of Congress.

41. Conger to Blaine, 26 February 1891, 6 March 1891, 2 April 1891, Despatches/Brazil.

42. *Rio News,* 10 February 1891.

43. Adee to Conger, 23 May 1891, Despatches Instructions/Brazil.

44. Salvador de Mendonça to Foster, undated memorandum enclosed in Salvador de Mendonça to Chermont, 19 June 1891, AHI 233/4/10.

45. Ibid.

46. Conger to Blaine, 13 November 1891, Despatches/Brazil.

47. Conger to Blaine, 15 August 1892, Despatches/Brazil.

48. Wyndham to Salisbury, 6 May 1892, Public Records Office, FO 13/695.

49. *Rio News,* 5 July 1892.

50. Gresham to Salvador de Mendonça, 26 October 1894, *FRUS* (1894), 82.

51. Andrews, *Brazil,* xiv.

52. Pauncefote to Salisbury, 10 July 1891, Public Records Office, FO 5/2120.

53. Gresham to Thompson, 1 November 1893, Despatches Instructions/Brazil.

54. *Rio News,* 14 September 1893.

55. Thompson to Gresham, 22 and 24 October 1893, Despatches Brazil; Gresham to Thompson, 25 October 1893, Despatches Instructions/Brazil.

56. Thompson to Gresham, 3 October 1893, 13 December 1893, Despatches/Brazil.

57. Gresham to Thompson, 9 and 10 January 1894, Despatches Instructions/Brazil.

58. Gresham to Thompson, 30 January 1894, Despatches Instructions/Brazil.

59. Gresham to Bayard, 21 January 1894, Walter Q. Gresham Papers, Library of Congress.

60. *New York Times,* 21 January 1890.

61. Picking to Herbert, 14 October 1893, Records of the Department of the Navy, National Archives, Record Group 45.

62. U.S. Congress, House, "Report of the Secretary of the Navy," House Document No. 1, 53rd congress, 3rd session (1894), 23.

63. Wyndham to Rosebery, 2 and 5 February 1894, Public Records Office, FO 13/724.

64. U.S. Congress, House, House Document No. 377, 54th congress, 1st session (12 October 1895), part 1, 92.

65. Gresham to Salvador de Mendonça, 29 August 1894, enclosed in Salvador de Mendonça to Carlos de Carvalho, 7 February 1895, AHI 233/4/11.

66. *South American Journal* [London], 29 September 1894.

67. Hay to Dawson, 16 November 1901, Despatches Instructions/Brazil.

68. Hay to Bryan (no. 115), 4 March 1899, Despatches Instructions/Brazil.

69. Salvador de Mendonça to Cerqueira (no. 5), 3 April 1897, Salvador de Mendonça to Curtis, 6 April 1897, AHI 234/4/12.

70. Phipps to Salisbury, 13 August 1899, Public Records Office, FO 13/786.

71. Sherman to Conger, 16 November 1897, Despatches Instructions/Brazil.

72. Dawson to Hay (no. 390), 19 December 1901, Despatches/Brazil.

73. Assis Brasil to Olinto de Magalhães, 2 June 1899, AHI 233/4/12.

74. Hay to Bryan, 2 October 1900, Despatches Instructions/Brazil.

75. Bryan to Olinto de Magalhães, 21 September 1900, AHI 280/2/6.

76. Coleman to Root, memorandum, 3 January 1906, Despatches/Brazil.

77. Hay to Assis Brasil, 29 May 1899, Assis Brasil to Hay, 10 June 1899, *FRUS* (1899), 119.

78. Seeger to Hay, 20 January 1903, Despatches/Brazil.

79. George Chamberlain, "A Letter from Brazil," *Atlantic Monthly* 90 (1902), 831.

80. Memorandum by Bryan, 19 July 1902, AHI 280/2/6.
81. Seeger to Hay, 20 January 1903, Despatches/Brazil.
82. Enclosures in Assis Brasil to Rio Branco, 19 February 1903, AHI 234/1/2.
83. Hay to Bryan, 15 December 1902, Despatches Instructions/Brazil.
84. Thompson to Hay, 12 May 1904, 15 January 1905, Despatches/Brazil.
85. Hay to Thompson, 13 June 1904, Despatches Instructions/Brazil.
86. Bryan to Hay, 17 April 1902, 18 November 1902, Despatches/Brazil.
87. Thomas L. Thompson, "Brazil: Its Commerce and Resources," *Forum* 25 (1898): 49.
88. Thompson to Gresham, 15 April 1895, Despatches/Brazil.

Chapter 10. Paraguay and Uruguay

1. H. G. Warren, *Paraguay: An Informal History* (Norman: University of Oklahoma Press, 1949), 147.

2. E. Bradford Burns, *Latin America: A Concise Interpretive History* (Englewood Cliffs, N.J.: Prentice-Hall, 1982), 44; Hubert Herring, *A History of Latin America from the Beginnings to the Present* (New York: Knopf, 1967), 713.

3. Robert Jones Shafer, *A History of Latin America* (Lexington: D. C. Heath, 1978), 116; James L. Busey, *Latin American Political Guide* (Manitou Springs, Colo.: Juniper Editions, 1991), 79.

4. George Pendle, *Uruguay* (London: Oxford University Press, 1963), 24.

5. Martha Edwards Correa, "The Rise of Fructuoso Rivera" (Ph.D. diss., University of New Mexico, 1983), 285.

6. Buchanan to Hopkins, 10 June 1845, Manning, *Diplomatic Correspondence*, 10:30–32; Harold F. Peterson, "Edward A. Hopkins, A Pioneer Promoter in Paraguay," *Hispanic American Historical Review* 22 (May 1942): 248.

7. Charles A. Washburn, *The History of Paraguay, with Notes of Personal Observations and Reminiscences of Diplomacy under Difficulties*, 2 vols. (Boston: Lee and Shepard, 1871), 2:353–54; Harris Gaylord Warren, "The Hopkins Claim Against Paraguay and the Case of the Missing Jewels," *Inter-American Economic Affairs* 22 (Summer 1968): 25.

8. Peterson, "Edward A. Hopkins," 248; Buchanan to Hopkins, 30 March 1846, Manning, *Diplomatic Correspondence*, 10:33.

9. Clare V. McKanna, "The *Water Witch* Incident," *American Neptune* 31 (1971): 8; Robert Conrad Hersch, "American Interest in the War of the Triple Alliance" (Ph.D. diss., New York University, 1974), 50.

10. McKanna, "The *Water Witch* Incident," 9–10; John Hoyt Williams, "The Wake of the *Water Witch*," *United States Naval Institute Proceedings* 3 (January–April 1985): 15; Hersch, "American Interest," 64. Built in 1845, the *Water Witch* was considered a warship although it had only three cannons instead of the normal five.

11. Hopkins to Buchanan, 27 December 1853, Manning, *Diplomatic Correspondence*, 10:113.

12. Page to Marcy, 20 October 1853, Manning, *Diplomatic Correspondence*, 10:111–12.

13. Hopkins to Marcy, 22 August 1853, Manning, *Diplomatic Correspondence*, 10:123–30; *El Semanario*, 7 November 1853; Hersch, "American Interest," 65; McKanna, "The *Water Witch* Incident," 11; Williams, "The Wake," 15; Washburn, *The History of Paraguay*, 2:356; Peterson, "Edward A. Hopkins," 256.

14. José Falcón to Hopkins, 5 August 1854, Falcón to Marcy, 9 August 1854, "Notes from the Paraguayan Legation in the United States to the Department of State," National Archives, Record Group 59 (hereafter referred to as Paraguay/Notes); Washburn, *The History of Paraguay*, 2:368.

15. Falcón to Hopkins, 9 August 1854, Paraguay/Notes; Hopkins to Marcy, 25 August 1864, Manning, *Diplomatic Correspondence*, 10:123.

16. Hopkins to Marcy, 2 and 25 September 1854, Manning, *Diplomatic Correspondence*, 10:137; Williams, "The Wake," 15.

17. Falcón to Marcy, 4 February 1855, 3 October 1854, Wenceslao Robles to Carlos Antonio López, 1 February 1855, Paraguay/Notes; Page to Falcón, 16 October 1854, Page to Marcy, 17 October 1854, Falcón to Page, 25 October 1854, Page to Marcy, 5 November 1854, Manning, *Diplomatic Correspondence* 10:142; *El Semanario*, 21 September 1854, 4. On 28 February 1853 the United States, along with England, France, and Sardinia, recognized the independence of Paraguay. On 4 March 1853 the same countries signed treaties of friendship, commerce, and navigation with Paraguay. Paraguay ratified the treaty eight days later, but because the U.S. representative John S. Pendleton had used different names to refer to the United States, the Senate amended the treaty; Lopez found the amendments objectionable, thus the need for a new ratification. See Warren, "The Hopkins Claim," 27; Williams, "The Wake," 15–17; McKanna, "The *Water Witch*," 14.

18. James A. Peden to Marcy, 6 and 20 April 1855, Louis Bamberger to Marcy, 1 December 1855, Fitzpatrick to Nicolás Vázquez, 18 November 1856, Vázquez to Fitzpatrick, 26 November 1856, Bowlin to Lewis Cass, 16 January 1859, Bowlin to Cass, 17 February 1859, Manning, *Diplomatic Correspondence*, 10:160–61, 174–75, 198; Hersch, "American Interest," 67, 73, 168; McKanna, "The *Water Witch*," 14–18; Peterson, "Edward A. Hopkins," 258.

19. Bowlin to Cass, 31 January 1855, Manning, *Diplomatic Correspondence*, 10:210–11.

20. Charles Ames Washburn to William Henry Seward, 19 November 1861, in "Despatches from United States Ministers to Paraguay and Uruguay," National Archives, Record Group 95 (hereafter referred to as Despatches/Paraguay, Uruguay); Warren, "The Hopkins Claim," 29; Hersch, "American Interest," 78–80.

20. Washburn to Seward, 20 February 1862, Despatches/Paraguay, Uruguay.

21. Washburn to Seward, 2 November 1862, Despatches/ Paraguay, Uruguay.

22. Washburn to Seward, 28 September 1862, Despatches/Paraguay, Uruguay.

23. Washburn to Seward, 6 October 1863, Despatches/Paraguay, Uruguay; Francisco Solano López was the eldest son of Carlos Antonio López. In 1845 he became a general in the Paraguayan army and was later sent to Europe to purchase modern weapons for the army. While in Paris, the five-foot-six-inch Solano López pledged himself to become the Napoleon of South America. Charles J. Kolinski, *Independence or Death: The Story of the Paraguayan War* (Gainesville: University of Florida Press, 1965), 9; Pelham Horton Box, *The Origins of the Paraguayan War* (New York: Russell and Russell, 1967), 185.

24. Washburn to Seward, 6 October 1862, 20 May 1863, Despatches/Paraguay, Uruguay; John Hoyt Williams, *The Rise and Fall of the Paraguayan Republic, 1800–1850* (Austin: University of Texas Press, 1979), 24–25.

25. Washburn to Seward, 3 November 1862, Despatches/Paraguay, Uruguay.

26. Hersch, "American Interest," 82.

27. Washburn to Seward, 3 November 1863, 4 March 1864, Despatches/Paraguay, Uruguay.

28. Washburn to Seward, 28 November 1864, 13 December 1864, 10 January 1865, Despatches/Paraguay, Uruguay; Seward to Washburn, 2 January 1865, Instructions/Paraguay, Uruguay; Hersch, "American Interest," 85–86; Kolinski, *Independence*, 74–75; Charles E. Akers, *A History of South America, 1854–1904* (New York: Dutton, 1904), 131–32; Gilbert Phelps, *Tragedy of Paraguay* (New York: St. Martin's, 1975), 83.

29. Phelps, *Tragedy*, 96–97; Akers, *A History*, 139; Kolinski, *Independence*, 97–98; Phelps, *Tragedy*, 133.

30. Seward to Washburn, 15 December 1866, Despatches Instructions/Paraguay, Uruguay.

31. Washburn to Seward, 17 January 1868, September 21, 1868, McMahon to Seward, 11

December 1868, 31 January 1869, Benítez to Fish, 28 June 1869, 4 August 1869, Despatches/Paraguay, Uruguay; Warren, *Paraguay,* 238; Washburn, *The History of Paraguay,* 2:436, 447, 460; Hersch, "American Interest," 207–10. The Bliss-Masterman controversy, fueled by Washburn's vitriolic comments against López, Davis, and McMahon, prompted the U.S. House of Representatives to pass the Bliss-Masterman Resolution, which appointed a subcommittee to conduct hearings. The Grant administration, however, was too preoccupied with the problem of Reconstruction to press the issue.

32. Hersch, "American Interest," 343.

33. Kolinski, *Independence,* 186–187; Warren, *Paraguay,* 32; Herring, *A History,* 714; Hersch, "American Interest," 548.

34. Stevens to Fish, 8 September 1870, Despatches/Paraguay, Uruguay.

35. Stevens to Fish, 2 August 1871, Despatches/Paraguay, Uruguay.

36. Stevens to Fish, 2 September 1872, Caldwell to Fish, 16 March 1876, Bacon to José Decoud, 18 and 27 February 1866, Bacon to Bayard, 5 May 1882, 7 October 1886, 19 October 1887, 30 November 1888, Hopkins to Bacon, 19 and 22 October 1887, Despatches/Paraguay, Uruguay; Gordon Ireland, *Boundaries, Possessions, and Conflicts in South America* (New York: Octagon Books, 1971), 32; Warren, "The Hopkins Claim," 32–39.

37. William R. Finch to John Sherman, 18 March 1898, 17, 23, and 27 April 1898, Finch to Day, 13 and 26 May 1898, 2, 12, and 14 June 1898, 25 August 1898, Despatches/Paraguay, Uruguay.

38. Bowlin to Cass, 20 December 1858, Despatches/Paraguay, Uruguay; William Spence Robertson, *Hispanic-American Relations with the United States* (New York: Oxford University Press, 1923), 40, 205.

39. Frank J. Merli and Theodore A. Wilson, eds., *Makers of American Diplomacy: From Benjamin Franklin to Henry Kissinger* (New York: Scribners, 1974), 244.

40. Stevens to Rodríguez, 5 July 1870, Stevens to Fish, 16 July 1870, Despatches/Paraguay, Uruguay.

41. Simon Hanson, *Utopia in Uruguay: Chapters in Economic History* (Westport, Conn.: Hyperion, 1979), 4.

42. Caldwell to Fish, 16 April 1875, Despatches/Paraguay, Uruguay.

43. Merli and Wilson, *Makers of American Diplomacy,* 258.

44. Bacon to Bayard, 27 August 1886, 25 May 1887, 15 September 1887, 12 March 1888, Despatches/Paraguay, Uruguay; Juan José Arteaga y María Luisa Coolighan, *Historia del Uruguay desde los orígenes hasta nuestros días* (Montevideo: Talleres Gráficos Barreiro y Ramos, 1992), 407; Peterson, "Edward A. Hopkins," 248.

45. Bacon to Bayard, 20 February 1886, 6 and 9 March 1886, 27 August 1886.

46. Chaplin to Bayard, 24 February 1886.

47. Bacon to Bayard, 20 and 25 May 1887, 20 May 1886, 21 December 1888.

48. Bacon to Bayard, 27 January 1886, 27 July 1886; Doris Brandenberg McLaughlin, "From Battle to Battle: Uruguay in the Late Nineteenth Century" (Ph.D. diss., University of Texas, 1977), 307–8; Russell Fitzgibbon, *Uruguay: Portrait of a Democracy* (New York: Russell and Russell, 1966), 126.

49. Peter Winn, "British Informal Empire in Uruguay," *Past and Present* 73 (1976): 111–12.

50. Stuart to Gresham, 14 and 25 January 1895, Stuart to Olney, 15 November 1895, 13 January 1897, Despatches/Paraguay, Uruguay.

51. Finch to Sherman, 16 March 1898, Despatches/Paraguay, Uruguay.

52. Finch to Hay, 10 November 1899, 19 March 1901, 11 December 1901, Finch to Sherman, 3 March 1898, Despatches/Paraguay, Uruguay; Roger M. Haigh, *The Role of José Artigas in the Independence of Uruguay* (Gainesville: University of Florida Press, 1958, 18; Akers, *A History,* 230.

53. Finch to Hay, 10 December 1901, Despatches/Paraguay, Uruguay.
54. Finch to Hay, 12 August 1899, Despatches/Paraguay, Uruguay.
55. Finch to Hay, 3 February and 2 March 1901, Despatches/Paraguay, Uruguay.
56. Finch to Hay, 19 March 1901, Despatches/Paraguay, Uruguay.
57. Finch to Hay, 4 April 1901, Despatches/Paraguay, Uruguay.
58. Winn, "British Informal Empire," 113.

SELECT BIBLIOGRAPHY

Agassiz, Louis. *A Journey in Brazil.* Boston: Ticknor and Fields, 1868.

Alvarado, Lisandro. *Historia de la revolución federal en Venezuela.* Caracas: Ministerio de Educación, 1956.

Andrews, Christopher C. *Brazil: Its Condition and Prospects.* New York: Appleton, 1891.

Bargero, Hebe M. García de. *Repercusión en la república argentina entra estados unidos y gran bretaña, acerca de la frontera entre venezuela y la guayana.* Córdoba: Jornadas de Historia y Literatura Argentina y Norte Americana, 1970.

Barros Van Buren, Mario. *Historia diplomática de Chile, 1541–1938.* Barcelona: Ediciones Ariel, 1970.

Basadre, Jorge. *Historia de la república de Perú, 1822–1833.* 11 vols. 7th edition. Lima: Editorial Universitaria, 1983.

Bastert, Russell H. "A New Approach to the Origins of Blaine's Pan American Policy." *Hispanic American Historical Review* 39 (August 1959): 375–412.

Beilharz, Edwin A., and Carlos U. López. *We Were 49ers!: Chilean Accounts of the California Gold Rush.* Pasadena: Ward Ritchie Press, 1976.

Bemis, Samuel Flagg. *The Latin American Policy of the United States: An Historical Interpretation.* New York: Harcourt, Brace, 1943.

Blumberg, Arnold. *The Diplomacy of the Mexican Empire, 1863–1867.* Philadelphia: American Philosophical Society, 1971.

Brown, Charles H. *Agents of Manifest Destiny: The Lives and Times of the Filibusters.* Chapel Hill: University of North Carolina Press, 1980.

Burns, E. Bradford. *The Unwritten Alliance: Rio Branco and Brazilian-America Relations.* New York: Columbia University Press, 1966.

Burr, Robert N. "The Balance of Power in 19th Century South America." *Hispanic American Historical Review* 1 (February 1955): 37–60.

Caldwell, Robert G. *The López Expedition to Cuba: 1848–1851.* Princeton: Princeton University Press, 1915.

Campbell, Charles S. *The Transformation of American Foreign Relations, 1865–1900.* New York: Harper and Row, 1976.

Carcano, Ramon J. *Guerra del Paraguay.* 3 vols. Buenos Aires: Domingo Viau., 1941.

Carr, Albert Z. *The World of William Walker.* New York: Harper and Row, 1963.

Castañeda, Tiburcio P. *La explosión del Maine y la guerra de los Estados Unidos contra España.* Havana: Libreria e imprenta "La Moderna poesia," 1925.

Cavelier, Germán. *La política internacional de Colombia.* 2 vols. 2nd ed. Bogotá: Editorial Iqueima, 1959.

Clayton, Lawrence A. *Grace: W. R. Grace and Co., The Formative Years, 1850–1930*. Ottawa, Ill.: Jameson Books, 1985.

Codman, John. *Ten Months in Brazil*. Boston: Lee and Shepard, 1867.

Coerver, Don M. *The Porfirian Interregnum: The Presidency of Manuel González of Mexico, 1880–1884*. Fort Worth: Texas Christian University Press, 1979.

Collin, Richard. *Theodore Roosevelt's Caribbean: The Panama Canal, the Monroe Doctrine, and the Latin American Context*. Baton Rouge: Louisiana State University Press, 1990.

Cosio Villegas, Daniel. *The United States versus Porfirio Díaz*. Translated by Nettie Lee Benson. Lincoln: University of Nebraska Press, 1963.

Dabbs, Jack Autrey. *The French Army in Mexico, 1861–1867*. The Hague: Mouton, 1963.

DiTella, Guido, and D. C. M. Platt. *The Political Economy of Argentina, 1880–1914*. London: Macmillan, 1986.

Dozier, Craig L. *Nicaragua's Mosquito Shore: The Years of British and American Presence*. Tuscaloosa: University of Alabama Press, 1985.

Etchepareborda, Roberto. *Historia de las relaciones internacionales Argentinas*. Buenos Aires: Editorial Pleamer, 1978.

Ferrer, Aldo. *The Argentine Economy*. Berkeley: University of California Press, 1967.

Fifer, J. Valerie. *United States Perceptions of Latin America, 1850–1930: A "New West" South of Capricorn?* Manchester: Manchester University Press, 1991.

Fillol, Robert. *Social Factors in Economic Development: The Argentine Case*. Cambridge: Massachusetts Institute of Technology Press, 1961.

Findling, John E. "The United States and Zelaya: A Study in the Diplomacy of Expediency." Ph.D. diss., University of Texas at Austin, 1971.

Folkman, David I., Jr. "Westward via Nicaragua: The United States and the Nicaraguan Route, 1826–1869." Ph.D. diss., University of Utah, 1966.

Foner, Philip S. *The Spanish-Cuban-American War and the Birth of American Imperialism, 1895–1902*. 2 vols. New York: Monthly Review Press, 1972.

Frankel, Benjamín A. *Venezuela y los Estados Unidos, 1810–1888*. Caracas: Ediciones de la Fundación John Boulton, 1977.

Froncek, Mary Z. "Diplomatic Relations Between the United States and Costa Rica, 1823–1882." Ph.D. diss., Fordham University, 1959.

Garber, Paul N. *The Gadsden Treaty*. Philadelphia: University of Pennsylvania Press, 1923.

García Valdés, Pedro. *La idea de la anexión de Cuba a los Estados Unidos*. Pinar del Río: La Habana, Imprenta "El Siglo XX.," A. Muniz y hno., 1925.

Gilmore, Robert L. *Caudillism and Militarism in Venezuela, 1810–1910*. Athens: Ohio University Press, 1964.

Goldberg, Joyce S. *The Baltimore Affair*. Lincoln: University of Nebraska Press, 1986.

González Guinán, Francisco. *Historia contemporánea de Venezuela*. 12 vols. Caracas: Ediciones de la Presidencia de la República, 1954.

Gootenberg, Paul. *Between Silver and Guano: Commercial Policy and the State in Post Independence Peru*. Princeton: Princeton University Press, 1991.

Graham, Richard. *Britain and the Onset of Modernization in Brazil, 1850–1914.* Cambridge: Cambridge University Press, 1968.

Gregg, Robert D. *The Influence of Border Troubles on Relations Between the United States and Mexico, 1876–1910.* Baltimore: Johns Hopkins University Press, 1937.

Hanna, Alfred Jackson, and Kathryn Abbey Hanna. *Napoleon III and Mexico.* Chapel Hill: University of North Carolina Press, 1971.

Harris, William Lane. *Las reclamaciónes de la Isla de Aves: Un estudio de las técnicas de las reclamaciónes.* Caracas: Universidad Central de Venezuela, 1968.

Healy, David F. *The United States in Cuba, 1898–1902.* Madison: University of Wisconsin Press, 1963.

Herrán, Tomás. *La crisis de Panamá: Cartas de Tomás Herrán, 1900–1904.* Edited by Thomas J. Dodd. Bogotá: Banco de la República, 1985.

Hill, Lawrence F. *Diplomatic Relations Between the United States and Brazil.* Durham: Duke University Press, 1932.

Hood, Miriam. *Diplomacia con cañones, 1895–1905.* Caracas: Universidad Católica Andres Bello, 1978.

James, Marquis. *Merchant Adventurer: The Story of W. R. Grace.* Wilmington, Del.: Scholarly Resources, 1993.

Jones, Wilbur D. *The American Problem in British Diplomacy, 1841–1861.* Athens: University of Georgia Press, 1974.

Kidder, Daniel P., and James C. Fletcher. *Brazil and the Brazilians Portrayed in Historical and Descriptive Sketches.* Philadelphia: Childs and Peterson, 1857.

Knapp, Frank Averill, Jr. *The Life of Sebastian Lerdo de Tejada, 1823–1889.* Austin: University of Texas Press, 1951.

Kortge, Dean. "The Central American Policy of Lord Palmerston." Ph.D. diss., University of Kansas, 1973.

Lael, Richard L. *Arrogant Diplomacy: U.S. Policy toward Columbia, 1903–1922.* Wilmington, Del.: Scholarly Resources, 1987.

LaFeber, Walter. *The New Empire: An Interpretation of American Expansion, 1860–1898.* Ithaca: Cornell University Press, 1963.

Langley, Lester D. *The Cuban Policy of the United States.* New York: Wiley, 1968.

Lemaitre, Eduardo. *La bolsa o la vida: Cuatro agresiones imperialistas contra Colombia.* Bogotá: Banco de Colombia, 1974.

Leonard, Thomas M. *Central America and the United States: The Search for Stability.* Athens: University of Georgia Press, 1991.

Manning, William R., ed. *Diplomatic Correspondence of the United States: Inter-American Affairs, 1831–1860.* 12 vols. Washington, D.C.: Carnegie Endowment for International Peace, 1932–39.

Manthorne, Katherine Emma. *Tropical Renaissance: North American Artists Exploring Latin America, 1839–1879.* Washington, D.C.: Smithsonian Institution Press, 1989.

Martínez, Oscar J. *Troublesome Border.* Tucson: University of Arizona Press, 1988.

Maury, Matthew Fontaine. *The Amazon and the Atlantic Slopes of South America.* Washington, D.C.: Frank Taylor, 1853.

May, Robert E. *The Southern Dream of a Caribbean Empire, 1854–1861*. Baton Rouge: Louisiana State University Press, 1973.

Mazarr, Michael J. *Semper Fidel: America and Cuba, 1776–1988*. Baltimore: Nautical and Aviation Publishing Co. of America, 1988.

McCullough, David. *The Path Between the Seas: The Creation of the Panama Canal, 1876–1914*. New York: Simon and Schuster, 1977.

McGann, Thomas F. "Argentina at the First Pan American Conference." *Inter-American Economic Affairs* 1 (1947): 21–53.

Miller, Robert Ryal. *Arms Across the Border: United States Aid to Juárez During the French Intervention in Mexico*. Philadelphia: American Philosophical Society, 1973.

Millington, Herbert. *American Diplomacy and the War of the Pacific*. New York: Columbia University Press, 1948.

Minor, Dwight C. *The Fight for the Panama Route*. New York: Columbia University Press, 1940.

Monaham, Jay. *Chile, Peru, and the Gold Rush of 1849*. Berkeley: University of California Press, 1973.

Nicaragua Canal Construction Co. *The Inter-Oceanic Canal of Nicaragua*. New York: Nicaragua Canal Construction Co., 1891.

Nolan, L. C. "The Diplomatic and Commercial Relations of the U.S. and Peru." Ph.D. diss., Duke University, 1935.

Núñez, Enrique Bernardo. *Tres momentos en la controversia de limites de Guayana*. Caracas: Imprenta Nacional, 1962.

Olliff, Donathon C. *Reforma Mexico and the United States: A Search for Alternatives to Annexation, 1854–1861*. Tuscaloosa: University of Alabama Press, 1981.

Osorio Jiménez, Marco A. *La Guayana Esequiba*. Caracas: Academia Nacional de la Historia, 1984.

Owsley, Frank Lawrence. *King Cotton Diplomacy: Foreign Relations of the Confederate States of America*. 2nd edition. Chicago: University of Chicago Press, 1959.

Page, A. Nayland. "United States Diplomacy in the Tacna-Arica Dispute, 1884–1929." Ph.D. diss., University of Oklahoma, 1958.

Parks, E. Taylor. *Colombia and the United States, 1765–1934*. Durham: Duke University Press, 1935.

Pérez, Louis A., Jr. *Cuba and the United States: Ties of Singular Intimacy*. Athens: University of Georgia Press, 1990.

——. *Cuba Between Empires, 1878–1902*. Pittsburgh: University of Pittsburgh Press, 1983.

Peterson, Dale William. "The Diplomatic and Commercial Relations Between the United States and Peru from 1883 to 1918." Ph.D. diss., University of Minnesota, 1969.

Pike, Frederick B. *Chile and the United States, 1880–1962: The Emergence of Chile's Social Crisis and the Challenge to United States Diplomacy*. Notre Dame: University of Notre Dame Press, 1963.

——. *The United States and the Andean Republics: Peru, Bolivia, and Ecuador*. Cambridge, Mass.: Harvard University Press, 1977.

——. *The United States and Latin America: Myths and Stereotypes of Civilization and Nature*. Austin: University of Texas Press, 1992.

Plesur, Milton. *America's Outward Thrust: Approaches to Foreign Affairs, 1865–1890*. DeKalb: Northern Illinois University Press, 1971.

Polanco Alcántara, Tomás. *Guzmán Blanco (Tragedia en seis partes y un Epílogo)*. Caracas: Grijalbo, 1992.

Portell Vilá, Herminio. *Historia de Cuba en sus relaciones con los Estados Unidos y España*. 4 vols. Havana: La Habana, J. Montero, 1938–41.

Portell Vilá, Herminio. *Narcisco López y su época*. 3 vols. Havana: La Habana Cultural, 1930–58.

Ramierez M., José. *José de Marcoleta, padre de las diplomacia Nicaraguense*. Managua: Imprenta Nacional, 1975.

Randall, Stephen J. *Colombia and the United States: Hegemony and Independence*. Athens: University of Georgia Press, 1992.

Rivas, Raimundo. *Historia diplomática de Colombia: 1810–1934*. Bogotá: Imprenta Nacional, 1961.

Rodríguez, José Ignacio. *Estudio histórico sobre el origen, desenvolvimiento y manifestaciones prácticas de la idea de la anexión de las Isla de Cuba los Estados Unidos de América*. Havana: Habana Imprenta La Propaganda Literaria, 1900.

Rodríguez, Mario. *A Palmerstonian Diplomat in Central America: Frederick A. Chatfield, Esq*. Tucson: University of Arizona Press, 1964.

Roig de Leuchsenring, Emilio. *Cuba no debe su independencia a los Estados Unidos*. 3rd edition. Havana: Ediciones La Tertulia, 1949.

——. *Cuba y los Estados Unidos, 1805–1898*. Havana: Sociedad Cubana de Estudios Historicas e Internationales, 1949.

Rojas, Armando. *Historia de las relaciones diplomáticas entre Venezuela y los Estados Unidos*, vol. 1: *1810–1899*. Caracas: Ediciones de la Presidencia de la Repúbilca, 1979.

Rolle, Andrew F. *The Lost Cause: The Confederate Exodus to Mexico*. Norman: University of Oklahoma Press, 1965.

Ross, Marvin C., ed. *George Gatlin: Episodes from Life Among the Indians and Last Rambles*. Norman: University of Oklahoma Press, 1959.

Santovenia, Emeterio S. *El Presidente Polk y Cuba*. Havana: La Habana Imprenta "El Siglo XX.," A. Muniz y hno., 1936.

Sater, William F. *Chile and the United States: Empires in Conflict*. Athens: University of Georgia Press, 1990.

Schmitt, Karl M. *Mexico and the United States, 1821–1973: Conflict and Coexistence*. New York: Wiley, 1974.

Scholes, Walter V. *Mexican Politics during the Juárez Regime, 1855–1872*. Columbia: University of Missouri Press, 1969.

Schoonover, Thomas D. *Dollars over Dominion: The Triumph of Liberalism in Mexican–United States Relations, 1861–1867*. Baton Rouge: Louisiana State University Press, 1978.

——. "Imperialism in Central America: United States Competition with Britain, Germany, and France in Middle America, 1820s–1920s." In *Eagle Against Empire:*

American Opposition to European Imperialism, edited by Rhodri Jefferys-Jones. Aix-en-Provence, France: Université de Provence, 1983.

——. *The United States in Central America, 1860–1911: Episodes of Social Imperialism and the Imperial Rivalry in the World System.* Durham: Duke University Press, 1991.

Shurbutt, T. Ray, ed. *United States–Latin American Relations, 1800–1850: The Formative Generations.* Tuscaloosa: University of Alabama Press, 1991.

Skaggs, James M. *The Great Guano Rush: Entrepreneurs and American Overseas Expansion.* New York: St. Martin's Press, 1994.

Smith, Joseph. *Illusions of Conflict: Anglo-American Diplomacy Toward Latin America, 1865–1896.* Pittsburgh: University of Pittsburgh Press, 1979.

Sparks, Dade. "Central America and Its Relations with the United States, 1860–1893." Ph.D. dissertation, Duke University, 1934.

St. John, Ronald Bruce. *The Foreign Policy of Peru.* Boulder and London: Lynne Reinner, 1992.

Stewart, Watt. *Henry Meiggs: Yankee Pizarro.* Durham: Duke University Press, 1946.

——. *Keith of Costa Rica: A Biographic Study of Minor Cooper Keith.* Albuquerque: University of New Mexico Press, 1974.

Süssekind de Mendonça, Carlos. *Salvador de Mendonça: Democrata do imperio e da république.* Rio de Janeiro: Instituto Nacional do Livro, 1960.

Tansill, Charles Callan. *The Foreign Policy of Thomas F. Bayard.* New York: Fordham University Press, 1940.

Werlich, David. *Admiral of the Amazon: John Randolph Tucker, His Confederate Colleagues, and Peru.* Charlottesville: University Press of Virginia, 1990.

Williams, Mary W. *Anglo-American Isthmian Diplomacy, 1815–1915.* Washington, D.C.: American Historical Association, 1916.

——. *Dom Pedro the Magnanimous: Second Emperor of Brazil.* Chapel Hill: University of North Carolina Press, 1937.

Wolff, William George. "The Diplomatic Career of William L. Scruggs: United States Minister to Colombia and Venezuela, and Legal Adviser to Venezuela, 1872–1912." Ph.D. diss., Southern Illinois University, 1974.

Yoacham, Cristian Guerrero. "La misión de Vicuña Mackenna a los Estados Unidos, 1865–1867." *Atenea* 454 (July–December 1986): 239–75.

Zorrilla, Luis G. *Historia de las relaciones entre México y los Estados Unidos de America, 1800–1958.* 2 vols. Mexico City: Editorial Porrua, 1965–66.

CONTRIBUTORS

Lawrence A. Clayton received a Ph.D. from Tulane University. He has taught history at the University of Alabama since 1972. He also served as a Fulbright lecturer in Costa Rica and Peru. A specialist in the Andean region, Clayton wrote several books and articles on subjects as diverse as *The Shipyards of Colonial Guayaquil* to *Grace: W. R. Grace and Co., The Formative Years, 1850–1930*. He is currently completing a Latin American history textbook with Michael Conniff for Harcourt Brace and a study of U.S. relations with Peru for the University of Georgia Press.

Don M. Coerver, professor of Latin American and Business History at Texas Christian University, received his Ph.D. from Tulane University and is the author or coauthor of six books relating to the history of Mexico and U.S.-Mexican relations. His articles have appeared in *Historia Mexicana, The Americas, Inter-American Economic Affairs, Journal of the West,* and *Journal of Church and State,* among others. He is contributing editor of the Modern Mexico section of the *Handbook of Latin American Studies* and is a consultant to the Hispanic Division of the Library of Congress.

Helen Delpar received her doctorate from Columbia University and is Professor of History at the University of Alabama. In addition to several articles and edited works, her publications include *Red Against Blue: The Liberal Party in Columbian Politics, 1863–1899* and *"The Enormous Vogue of Things Mexican": Cultural Relations Between the United States and Mexico, 1920–1935.*

José B. Fernández is Professor of History and Director of the Latin American and Iberian Studies Program at the University of Central Florida. Fernández obtained his Ph.D. from Florida State University and received a Senior Fulbright Lecturing Award to Argentina. A specialist in Spanish Colonial Letters, Fernández is the author of fourteen books and numerous journal articles.

William L. Harris, Professor Emeritus of History at The Citadel, received his Ph.D. from the University of Florida. A corresponding member of the Venezuelan National Academy of History, he received several prestigious grants for research and study in Venezuela and elsewhere in the western hemisphere and in major European archives. He is the author of *Las Reclamaciónes de la Isla de Aves* and *La Diplomacia de José María Rojas*.

Thomas M. Leonard is Distinguished Professor and Director of the International Studies Program at the University of North Florida. He has served as a Fulbright Lecturer in Argentina and Mexico. In addition to having written articles in several professional journals and chapters in other books, he has published eight books, the most recent being *A Guide to Central American Collections in the United States*, *Central America and the United States*, and *Panama, The Canal, and the United States*. His *Castro and the Cuban Revolution* will be published by Greenwood Press.

Louis A. Pérez, Jr., completed his Ph.D. at the University of New Mexico. He is currently J. Carlysle Sitterson Professor of History at the University of North Carolina-Chapel Hill. His principle research interests include nineteenth- and twentieth-century Cuban and U.S. relations with the Caribbean. Among his several publications are: *Cuba: Between Reform and Revolution, Lands of the Mountain: Survival Banditry and Peasant Protest in Cuba, 1878–1918, Cuba and the United States: Ties of Singular Intimacy,* and most recently *Slavery, Sugar and Colonial Society: Travel Accounts of Cuba, 1801–1899*.

William F. Sater is a Professor of History at California State University-Long Beach. In addition to having published numerous articles in professional journals in the United States and abroad, Sater serves as a consultant to the Rand Corporation and is a contributor to the *Handbook of Latin American Studies*. Among his books are *Chile and the War of the Pacific* and *Chile and the United States: Empires in Conflict*. He is also coauthor with Simon Collier of *A History of Chile*, published by Cambridge University Press.

Joseph Smith received his Ph.D. from the University of London and is Reader in American Diplomatic History at the University of Exeter, England. He has been a Visiting Professor of History at the College of William and Mary and the University of Colorado at Denver. He is the author of several books on diplomatic history, including *Illusions of Conflict: Anglo-American Diplomacy toward Latin America, 1865–1896, Unequal Giants: Diplomatic Relations between the United States and Brazil, 1889–1930,* and *The Spanish-American War: Conflict in the Caribbean and the Pacific, 1895–1902*.

After earning his Ph.D. from Harvard, **Joseph S. Tulchin** held several teaching assignments including posts at Yale University, the Naval War College, the University of Buenos Aires, El Colegio de Mexico, and the University of North Carolina-Chapel Hill before becoming Director of the Latin American Program at the Woodrow Wilson Center for International Scholars. A contributor to numerous journals, Tulchin has written several books including *Latin American Nations in World Poli-*

tics, Argentina and the United States: A Conflicted Relationship, and *Consolidation of Democracy in Latin America.*

Jennifer M. Zimnoch recently earned her master's degree in Latin American Studies at the University of Central Florida. She is a recent Phi Kappa Phi Fellowship recipient, and her research focus is Uruguay and Southern Cone relations.

INDEX